WRITE SOURCE
2000
A Guide to WRITING,
THINKING, and LEARNING

Written and Compiled by
**Patrick Sebranek, Dave Kemper,
and Verne Meyer**

Illustrated by
Chris Krenzke

WRITE SOURCE®

GREAT SOURCE EDUCATION GROUP
a Houghton Mifflin Company
Wilmington, Massachusetts

Acknowledgements

We're grateful to many people who helped bring **Write Source 2000** to life. First, we must thank all the teachers from across the country who contributed ideas and student writing models.

Janice Hollow   Marlyn Payne   Judith Ruhana

Abbie Laskey   Arlene Pinkus   Marilynn Toler

Cheryl McKay   Samantha Polek   Elma Torres

Lucretia Pannozzo   Linda Rief

Also, thanks to consultant Vicki Spandel from **Write Traits** for her contributions in the areas of revising and assessment.

In addition, we want to thank our Write Source/Great Source team for all their help: Laura Bachman, Diane Barnhart, Colleen Belmont, Jeani Berndt, Sandra Easton, Carol Elsholz, Sherry Gordon, Lori Hintz, Lois Krenzke, Ellen Leitheusser, Shiere Melin, Tina Miller, Linda Neiman, Candyce Norvell, Sue Paro, Randy Rehberg, Julie Sebranek, Lester Smith, Richard Spencer, Randy VanderMey, John Van Rys, and Sandy Wagner.

Printed in the United States of America

International Standard Book Number: 0-669-46773-1 (hardcover)
      7 8 9 10 -HWK- 02 01 00

International Standard Book Number: 0-669-46774-X (softcover)
      6 7 8 9 10 -HWK- 02 01 00

Using the Handbook

The *Write Source 2000* handbook is loaded with concise, useful information—guidelines, samples, and strategies—to help you with all of your writing. If that's not enough, you can also refer to our Web site for more information about writing and publishing. The address is **thewritesource.com**.

Write Source 2000 will help you with other learning skills, too—study-reading, test taking, note taking, speaking, Internet searches, and more. In addition, the "Student Almanac" in the back of the handbook contains tables, lists, maps, and charts covering everything from science to history. In other words, *Write Source 2000* can serve as your personal writing and learning guide in all of your classes.

Your handbook guide . . .

With practice, you will be able to find information in the handbook quickly and easily using the guides explained below:

The **Table of Contents** (starting on the next page) lists the five major sections in the handbook and the chapters found in each section. Use the table of contents when you're looking for a general topic.

The **Index** in the back of the handbook (starting on page 528) lists all of the specific topics discussed in *Write Source 2000*. Use the index when you are looking for a specific piece of information.

The **Color Coding** used for the "Proofreader's Guide" (the pages are yellow) makes this important section easy to find. These pages contain rules for spelling, grammar, punctuation, capitalization, and so on.

The **Special Page References** throughout the book tell you where to turn in the handbook for more information about a particular topic. Example:

(See page 457.)

Note: If at first you're not sure how to find something in the handbook, ask your teacher for help.

Table of Contents

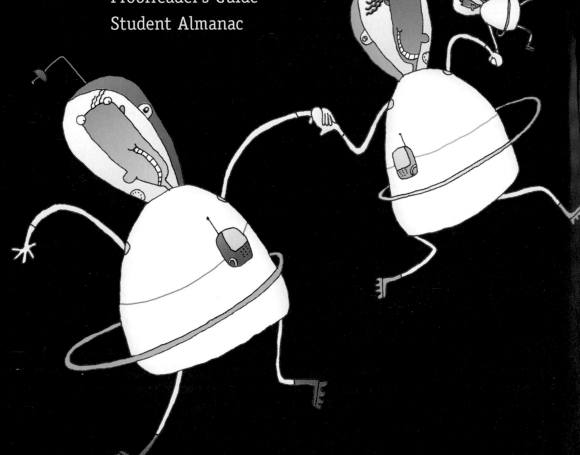

The Process of Writing

The Forms of Writing

The Tools of Learning

Proofreader's Guide

Student Almanac

Why Write?

For all the right reasons . . .

For one thing, writing makes you a better thinker because it helps you explore and analyze new experiences. For another thing, it makes you a better learner by leading to improved understanding of what you are taught in class. And finally, the writing you do now will make you a better writer next month, next semester, next year, forever.

"Writing is the ultimate learning tool for all students of all ages in all subjects."

In all the right ways . . .

Write to Explore Your Personal Thoughts

Writing in a personal journal helps you learn important things about yourself and become more comfortable with the writing process.

Write to Better Understand New Ideas

Writing in a classroom journal or learning log helps you make sense of what you are learning and remember things better.

Write to Show Learning

Compiling reports, answering essay-test questions, and writing summaries show teachers what you have learned. These types of writing help both you and your teachers measure your understanding of new ideas and concepts.

Write to Share

Writing stories, personal essays, and poems to share with your classmates brings out the best in you as a writer because you are writing for an interested audience.

Approach all of your writing as a special opportunity to learn and to grow, and you will soon appreciate its value both in and out of school. So what should you do? Just start writing . . . for all the right reasons!

Learning About the Writing Process

Understanding Writing

Technology makes things happen quickly. If you want to be entertained, you turn on the TV. If you need to talk to a friend, you pick up a phone. And if you have to do some quick research, you surf the Net. Technology puts the world at your fingertips. It provides seemingly instant action.

Of course, technology can make writing happen more quickly as well. It's much quicker to keyboard (once you become skilled at it) than it is to work with pen and paper. But when it comes to writing, speed alone doesn't count for a whole lot. What really counts is your ability to develop a piece of writing into an effective finished product, whether on a computer or with pen and paper. There is nothing "instant" about good writing.

WHAT'S AHEAD

This chapter provides tips for building good writing habits. It also contains key background information about the writing process—the series of steps that you should follow to produce your best writing.

- ○ Building Good Writing Habits
- ○ Reviewing the Writing Process
- ○ The Writing Process in Action
- ○ Thinking Aloud About the Process

Building Good Writing Habits

To become a good writer, you should think and act like one. The tips that follow will help you develop the "proper" writing habits.

Become a regular reader. ■ All of the pros read a lot. Reading helps them see how effective stories and essays are put together; it gives them a foundation to build on for their own work. Reading will help you in the same way. Read anything and everything—books, magazines, newspapers, newsletters, fliers . . . even the backs of cereal boxes.

> "Read everything. Read! You'll absorb it. Then write."
> —William Faulkner

Write every day, preferably at a set time. ■ Write early in the morning, late at night, or sometime in between. Just get into a regular writing routine, and stick to it. You probably set aside time to practice your musical instrument or an athletic skill. Do the same with your writing.

Write about subjects that truly interest you. ■ Doing otherwise makes about as much sense as going out for softball when track is really your first love. Writing is hard enough. It becomes pure torture if you don't have strong feelings about your subject.

Write as well as you can . . . by your own standards. ■ This tip comes from William Zinsser, an authority on writing. He knows from experience that writers set high standards for themselves. You should, too. Zinsser also says, "Quality is its own reward." You will feel good about your writing if it reflects your best efforts.

Try different forms of writing. ■ Stories, letters, essays, reports, and poems—they all have something special to teach you about writing.

Become a student of writing. ■ Learn to recognize the traits of good writing, such as clear organization and effective word choice. (See pages 19-24.) Build your writing vocabulary. Learn, for example, the difference between *abstract* and *concrete,* between *description* and *narration.* And approach writing as a process in which you develop your thoughts about a subject. (See the next page.)

Reviewing the Writing Process

When experienced writers put their fingers to the keyboard, they know that their writing will go through a series of steps, or stages, before it develops into a quality finished piece. That is why writing is called a process. The steps in the writing process are described below.

Prewriting   At the start of a project, writers explore possible subjects before selecting one to develop. Then they collect details about their subjects and plan how to use these details in their writing.

Writing   Writers then complete a first draft using their plan as a general guide. This draft is a writer's first look at an emerging writing idea. (A writer may find it necessary to write more than one early draft if his or her thoughts about the subject are still forming.)

Revising   After reviewing the first draft, writers change any parts that are not clear or complete. They may ask a writing peer to review the draft as well.

Editing   Writers then check their revised writing for style and accuracy before preparing a neat final copy of their work. The final copy is then proofread for errors before publication.

Publishing   This is the final step in the writing process. Publishing is to a writer what an exhibit is to an artist—an opportunity to share his or her work with others.

POINTS TO REMEMBER . . .

Experience shapes writing. A writer's experience becomes part of what he or she knows, thinks, and has to say. Writing is the process of exploring these thoughts and experiences on paper.

Writers seldom move neatly through the process. For example, after completing a first draft, a writer may decide to collect more details before going any further.

Writers work differently. Some writers do a lot of their early work in their heads, while others put everything on paper. Still other writers need to talk about their work throughout the process, and so on.

The Writing Process in Action

Each writing project presents different challenges. For one project, you may have trouble selecting a subject or discovering an interesting way to write about it. For another project, you may find that writing an effective beginning or ending is your main challenge.

The next two pages show the writing process in action. Use this information to help you meet all of your writing challenges.

Prewriting ----[Choosing a Subject]

1. Search for possible subjects to write about. If you need help, refer to the selecting strategies listed in this handbook. (See pages 45-52.)

2. Select a specific subject that genuinely interests you and meets the requirements of the assignment.

[Gathering Details]

1. Learn as much as you can about a subject before you write. If you need help, refer to the collecting strategies listed in this handbook. (See pages 53-58.)

2. Think of an interesting or special part of your subject to write about. This is your focus. (See page 59.)

3. Decide which details you may want to include in your writing. Also decide on the best way to organize and present these details to support your focus. (See page 60 for help.)

Writing ----[Writing the First Draft]

1. Complete the first draft of your writing. Concentrate on developing your ideas. (And don't worry about making mistakes.)

2. Use your collecting and planning as a general guide. Also feel free to add new ideas as you go along.

3. Keep going until you come to a logical stopping point. Your writing should include a beginning, a middle, and an ending.

Revising ----[Improving Your Writing]

1. Read and review your first draft (but only after setting it aside for awhile). Also have at least one other person review your work.
2. Decide which parts need to be revised or changed. Your revision should answer any questions readers may have about your subject. Your revision should also address the traits or qualities of good writing. (See pages 19-24.)
3. Improve your writing by rewriting, reordering, adding, or cutting different parts. Focus on the content and quality of your ideas, not on surface issues (spelling, mechanics, usage, etc.).
4. Pay special attention to the beginning and ending parts of your writing. They should accurately introduce and reflect the focus of your writing.

Editing ----[Checking for Style and Accuracy]

1. Check your revised writing for style and for accuracy.
2. Reread your paragraphs and sentences, making sure that they are clear and smooth reading. Also make sure that you have expressed your ideas using specific and colorful words. (See page 135 for help.)
3. Next, review your writing for punctuation, mechanics, spelling, and grammar errors. (See pages 386-457 for help.) Also ask a reliable editor to check your writing for errors.
4. Prepare a neat final copy of your writing. Proofread this copy for errors as well.

Publishing

1. Share your finished work with your writing peers, teacher, friends, and family members.
2. Decide if you are going to include the writing in your portfolio. (See pages 31-36 for help.)
3. Consider submitting your work to your school or local newspaper or to an appropriate magazine.

Thinking Aloud About the Process

The students quoted below have some good advice to share with you about different aspects of the writing process. Keep all of these ideas in mind when you develop your own writing.

"Never stop jotting things down that you see, hear, smell, etc. These things make great ideas or topics for freewriting and writing projects."

—Joe Strekall

"Explore different ideas, and then pick one subject that you really like and care about."

—Whitney Michener

"Include many details in your writing. Details let you show the readers instead of telling them something."

—Ra'Shelle Chapa

"It is very important to be organized and to make things clear."

—Kathryn Beasley

"I love first drafts. I just write and write. But I've learned that no matter how good I think my first draft is, it can always be better."

—Emma Tobin

"Revising is very important. It allows you to change things to make your piece of writing come to life."

—Markelle Gray

"When I write a piece, I show it to my friends and family and listen to the feedback they give me. Then I make changes."

—Ben Disesa

"Don't change something you really like just to fit what someone else likes."

—Bailey O'Keefe

One Writer's Process

The writing process is really all about effort. If you put in the time, and do the necessary prewriting, drafting, and revising, you will almost always be pleased with the final results of your writing. But don't just take our word for it. Listen to what these two young writers have to say about their experiences.

Dan Jenkins understands that writing multiple drafts is important: "I know that it takes a lot of time and many drafts to get a piece of writing to satisfy yourself and your readers." Olivia Nold knows that personal satisfaction comes from hard work: "I keep working on a piece of writing until it makes me feel fulfilled."

WHAT'S AHEAD

This chapter shows you how student writer Brian Krygsman used the writing process to develop one of his writing assignments. As you will see, he worked hard to produce an effective piece of writing.

- Prewriting: Choosing and Gathering
- Writing: Writing the First Draft
- Revising: Improving Your Writing
- Editing: Checking for Style and Accuracy
- Publishing

Prewriting ----[Choosing a Subject]

Brian Krygsman had been studying the Middle Ages in social studies class. As a final project, he was given this assignment:

> **Write an essay about one part of medieval life that interests you. Remember to limit your subject. For example, "training for knighthood" will work as a subject, while "medieval knights" is too broad.**

Brainstorming for Ideas ■ To begin his subject search, Brian thought of three general areas about medieval life that interested him: daily life, castles, and war. He then wrote down these two headings and made a brief list of his first thoughts about each one:

Daily Life
  Men worked in fields, women
      at home
  Rich = good life, partying,
      hunting, banquets
  Poor = bad life, dirty, hard
      work, cold, bad food, etc.

Castles
  Walls / moats for protection,
      built on hills, cliff by
      water
  Took a long time to build
  Primitive compared to
      modern construction

Clustering ■ Brian decided to focus his subject search on castles. To generate some possible writing ideas, he completed a cluster. (See page 48.)

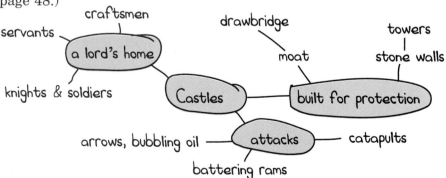

Focusing on a Limited Subject ■ After reviewing his cluster, Brian knew that he wanted to write about the construction of castles and, more specifically, how they were built for protection against attacks.

Prewriting ----[Gathering Details]

Collecting Personal Thoughts ■ To gather details about his subject, Brian started by writing freely about castles, recording his thoughts and ideas as they came to mind. Here is part of that freewriting:

> Castles were built for function, not looks. But they were pretty impressive constructions. It must have been a pain to build one, especially when they were built on cliffs or on islands. Just think about carrying loads of huge stones without any trucks or anything, just wheels and horses.

Carrying Out Additional Research ■ To get more information about castles, Brian interviewed a social studies teacher and consulted two books. Here is a portion of the writer's notes from his interview:

> Interview with Mr. Dolman   Feb. 8/99
> * Castle builders were smart—took care of all the little details
>   - picked spot that enemies couldn't reach easily, where defenders could see far from towers
>   - one defense after the other, from the moat to the keep
> * Enemies used both bloody attack and trickery
>   - catapults, wooden tower-ladders, tunneling under walls
>   - siege: tried to starve people in castle, but castle storeroom could last two years!

Planning the First Draft ■ To get ready for his first draft, Brian wrote this working thesis (focus) statement to guide his writing: *Castles were created because the lords of the land needed protection.* He also listed three main ideas he wanted to cover in his essay:

> 1. Why castles were built
> 2. What they were like
> 3. How they were attacked and defended

After doing a lot of prewriting work, Brian's head was full of information. He wrote his first draft freely, using his planning and notes as a general guide. His goal was to get the ideas on paper, and he did not worry about saying everything exactly right.

Castles Were Safe Houses

Life in the Middle Ages was hard!
Rich people owned the land and poor people
farmed it and gave most of the food to
there landlords. Lords wood often try to
take each others land and wealth and that's
why castles came into the picture. A lord's
castle offered the best protection.

The thesis statement introduces the writer's subject.

First of all, the lord looked for a good
location to build his home--a place that was
hard to get to and had a clear view.
Sometimes they were built on islands.
Sometimes on hills or cliffs. A safe location
forced enemys to work really hard to get

near the castle and prevented sneak attacks.

Secondly, the castle needed to be built out of a strong substance. The earliest castles had been maid of wood. Then tha lords started using stone to build their castles. it was hard work, but worth it.

The third thing that made a castle safe was its design. Often the castle had a ring of water around the castle to keep attackers away. A drawbridge that could be razed was the only way across the moat. There was a heavy iorn gate called a port-sumthing that slammed down tight to stop enemys from getting inside the castle walls. . . .

Transitional
words
indicate
new ideas.

Revising ----[Improving Your Writing]

Brian took a break after finishing his first draft. When he went back and read it over, he made some comments in the margin. Then he made his revisions.

Brian's Comments

Castles Were Safe Houses

~~Life in the Middle Ages was hard!~~

First part is off the subject.

~~Rich people owned the land and poor people~~

~~farmed it and gave most of the food to~~
In the Middle Ages, powerful lords
~~there landlords.~~ ⋀ ~~Lords~~ wood often try to

take each others land and wealth and that's

Get to the point about castles.

why castles came into the picture. A lord's
because of its location, building material, and design.
castle offered the best protection⋀

First of all, the lord looked for a good

location to build his home--a place that was

hard to get to and had a clear view.
                    castles
Sometimes ~~they~~ were built on islands.

Add an example.

For example, Harlech Castle of wales was built
                    on a cliff by the ocean.
Sometimes on hills or cliffs.⋀A safe location

forced enemys to work really hard to get

near the castle and prevented sneak

attacks.

Secondly, the castle needed to be built

Clarify these ideas.

out of a strong substance. The earliest
, but many were burned down by attackers.
castles had been maid of wood. Then the

lords started using stone to build their
                  stone castles were very safe.
castles. it was hard work, but worth it.

The third thing that made a castle

Be more specific.

safe was its design. Often the castle had a
                        it called a moat.
ring of water around the castle to keep

attackers away. A drawbridge that could be
                                    , and there
razed was the only way across the moat.

Check notes about name of gate.

There was a heavy iorn gate called a
        portcullis
port-sumthing that slammed down tight to

stop enemys from getting inside the castle

walls. . . .

After the last revision, Brian was ready to check his work for word choice and accuracy. This page shows the types of corrections he made to get his paper ready for publishing.

Castles Were Safe Houses

In the Middle Ages, powerful lords ~~wood~~ would often try to take each other's land and wealth∧and that's why castles came into the picture. A lord's castle offered the best protection because of its location, building material, and design.

First of all, the lord looked for a good location to build his home--a place that was hard to get to and had a clear view. ~~Sometimes~~ Castles were built on islands. ~~Sometimes~~ on hills∧or∧cliffs. For example, Harlech Castle of Wales was built on a cliff by the ocean. A safe location forced ~~enemys~~ enemies

Usage and punctuation errors are corrected.

A sentence fragment is fixed.

to work really hard to get near the castle and prevented sneak attacks.

Secondly, the castle needed to be built out of a strong ~~substance~~ material. The earliest castles had been ~~maid~~ made of wood, but many were burned down by attackers. Then the lords started using stone to build their castles. It was hard work, but stone castles were very safe.

The third thing that made a castle safe was its design. Often the castle had a ring of water around it called a moat. A drawbridge was the only way across the moat, and there was a heavy ~~iofn~~ iron gate called a portcullis that slammed down tight to stop ~~enemys~~ enemies from getting inside the castle walls. . . .

A word is changed, and a usage error is corrected.

A capital letter is added.

Spelling errors are corrected.

Publishing

Brian produced a neat final copy of his essay to share with his classmates and teachers. He made sure that this copy was as clean and correct as he could make it. (See pages 27-29 for designing tips for final copies.) Here is a portion of Brian's first page.

Brian Krygsman
Ms. Bach
History
April 16, 1999

Castles Were Safe Houses

In the Middle Ages, powerful lords would often try to take each other's land and wealth, and that's why castles came into the picture. A lord's castle offered the best protection because of its location, building material, and design.

POINTS TO REMEMBER . . .

Do the necessary prewriting. Brian learned a lot about his subject before he started writing. It also helped that he was truly interested in his subject. Thorough prewriting makes the rest of the writing process go more smoothly.

Write with confidence. After thorough prewriting and preparation, Brian was able to write his first draft freely and easily. Writing can be a real struggle if you haven't learned enough about your subject.

Expect to make many changes. Brian wasn't satisfied with making just a few changes. He wanted to make all of his ideas as clear and complete as possible. *Remember:* No writer, not even your favorite author, ever gets it right the first time.

Traits of Effective Writing

Coaches know what it takes to build a successful basketball team: strong rebounders, tough defenders, and good shooters. So, too, with experienced writers. They know what it takes to develop effective pieces of writing: good ideas, clear organization, effective word choice, and so on. Learning about these traits of good writing—and putting them into practice—will help you become a better writer yourself.

Make no mistake about it. Writers are not born with a special writing gene or blessed by the writing fairy. Although some seem to come by the ability to write more easily than others, most writers must study and practice their writing skills often. Basketball players—even the Michael Jordan's of the world—must continually develop their skills; the same goes for writers. All good writers are "students of their game," always ready to learn something new.

WHAT'S AHEAD

The next page in this chapter summarizes six important traits of effective writing. The remaining pages give writing samples that show these traits in action. Think of this chapter as your guide to good writing.

- Quick Guide
- The Traits in Action
- Checklist for Good Writing

QUICK GUIDE

The traits listed below identify the main features you find in the best essays, reports, stories, and articles. If you write with these traits in mind, you—and your readers—will surely be pleased with the results.

- **STIMULATING IDEAS:** Effective writing presents interesting and valuable information about a specific subject. It has a clear message or purpose. The ideas are thoroughly developed and hold the reader's attention.

- **LOGICAL ORGANIZATION:** In terms of basic structure, good writing has a clearly developed beginning, middle, and ending. Within the text, each main point is developed with examples, explanations, definitions, specific details, and so on.

- **ENGAGING VOICE:** In the best writing, you can hear the writer's voice—his or her special way of expressing ideas and emotions. Voice gives writing personality; it shows that the writer sincerely cares about his or her subject and audience.

- **ORIGINAL WORD CHOICE:** Simply put, good writing contains good words. Nouns and verbs are specific; modifiers are colorful; and the overall level of language helps communicate a particular message or tone.

- **SMOOTH-READING SENTENCES:** Effective writing flows smoothly and clearly from one sentence to the next. But it isn't, by any means, predictable. Sentences will vary in length, and they won't all begin in the same way. Sentence smoothness, or fluency, gives writing rhythm, which helps make it enjoyable to read.

- **CORRECT, ACCURATE COPY:** Good writing follows the basic standards of punctuation, mechanics, usage, and spelling. It is edited with care to ensure that the work is accurate and easy to follow.

The Traits in Action

On the next three pages, a writing sample is provided for each of the six traits. These samples show you effective writing in action.

Stimulating Ideas

The following passage comes from *Bareback!* by Jerry Ellis. In one short paragraph, this writer presents a lot of interesting information about an outdoor cooking experience.

The lid on my small pot begins to rattle as the smoky flames do their good deeds. Up till now I have used a plastic spoon to eat the meals I cooked. Now, however, as the rice simmers, I sit by the fire to carve a spoon from a piece of cottonwood. It is softer than pine and the type of wood that many Indian tribes used to carve their toys and totems. I carve the head of a crow in the handle of the spoon. I see nothing wrong with eating with a bird in my hand.

At first, Ellis helps readers visualize his simple campfire meal: ". . . my small pot begins to rattle as the smoky flames do their good deeds." He then describes the eating utensil he is making and, in the process, shares some of his knowledge of Native American history.

Logical Organization

In this passage from *The Headmaster*, writer John McPhee develops a main point about Frank Boyden, the headmaster of Deerfield (Massachusetts) Academy. Each new idea adds another level of detail, helping readers understand Boyden's style of leadership.

His art as a disciplinarian often enables him to prevent things before they happen. He listens to the noise level in a group of boys, and watches the degree of restlessness; he can read these things as if they were a printed page. This is one reason he believes in meetings that involve the entire school. "You must have your boys together as a unit at least once a day, just as you have your family together once a day."

The main point of this passage is Boyden's "art as a disciplinarian." McPhee gives important examples ("He listens to the noise level . . .") to develop this point. Added detail ("This is one reason he believes . . .") and a quotation make the idea clearer.

Engaging Voice

In *Move On*, writer Linda Ellerbee shares many of the adventures in her life. In the passage below, she describes how she lost her best childhood friend, who had decided that watching television was more fun than playing with Ellerbee.

The August I was eight years old, a television ate my best friend. My very first very best friend. I took it personally. What if I never found a second? Lord only knew how long it might be before I met another little girl as qualified as Lucy, whose house was right across the street from mine and, no, I did not mind that Lucy was so much younger, because she was not like most people who lived near you when they were barely seven.

"Write visually, write clearly, and make every word count."
—Gloria D. Miklowitz

See how Ellerbee's writing brings to life her thoughts and feelings as a young girl—as someone with a great deal of imagination and personality ("a television ate my best friend"). Her voice is so appealing that it immediately grabs the reader's attention.

Original Word Choice

In the following passage from *Mapping the Farm*, writer John Hildebrand describes a fall ride on a family farm. As you will see, he chooses the best words to capture the experience.

I swung the stock gate open and jumped into the pickup, and then we were bouncing down the lane through the old orchard and into the lower pasture. The two-track road narrowed to a single cow path before disappearing altogether among milkweed and Canadian thistle. Ed gunned the Jeep to climb the grassy slope that marks the farm's northern border, and for a brief moment I felt airborne . . .

Note how Hildebrand uses specific verbs—"swung," "jumped," "bouncing," "narrowed," and so on. Also note the effective adjectives that help readers visualize the scene: "*old* orchard," "*lower* pasture," "*two-track* road," "*single* cow path," and so on.

Smooth-Reading Sentences

In *Wild Mind,* writer Natalie Goldberg shares many interesting thoughts about being a writer. In the passage below, she discusses the importance of reading your writing aloud. As you will see, she pays careful attention to the length and shape of her sentences.

It is important to read aloud what you write. . . . I cannot say why, but the simple act of reading it aloud allows you to let go of it. Do not forget this. Believe me, it helps. At first it is a very scary thing to do. Your voice shakes, your heart pounds, your breath gets tight. In one class we jokingly called it the breathing disease. But no one has ever died of it, so don't worry.

 See how Goldberg varies the sentence beginnings in this passage. No two sentences start in the same way. Also note the varied sentence length—the longest sentence contains 19 words, and the shortest ones contain 4. The overall style of her sentences helps make this passage interesting for readers.

Correct, Accurate Copy

In the following passage from *Old Friends,* writer Tracy Kidder describes a scene in a nursing home in which an older man attempts to raise himself up from a chair. As you will see, Kidder uses punctuation to control the flow of his ideas.

Lou stood up. Beside him, Joe inched himself to the edge of his low metal chair, planted his cane, and started to rise. Many days had passed since he had gone to M&M's [Music & Motion] or ridden the bike, because of his blister. Joe's arm trembled. He rose a little, and then settled back. He tried again. His arm shook as it tried to push him up.

 See how the well-placed periods and commas draw the reader's attention to each and every detail. Correct punctuation establishes an appropriately slow, careful pace in the passage.

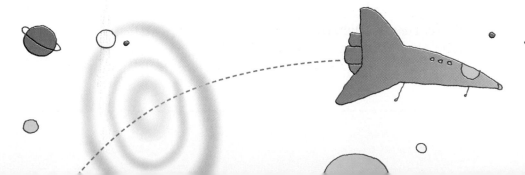

Checklist for Good Writing

How can you tell if something you read (or write) displays the traits of good writing? It should meet the following standards:

✔ Stimulating Ideas

The writing . . .

_____ presents interesting and valuable information.

_____ has a clear message or purpose.

_____ holds the reader's attention.

✔ Logical Organization

_____ includes a clear beginning, middle, and ending.

_____ contains specific details to support main ideas.

✔ Engaging Voice

_____ speaks in a pleasing and sincere way.

_____ shows that the writer really cares about the subject.

✔ Original Word Choice

_____ contains specific and colorful words.

_____ presents an appropriate level of language.

✔ Smooth-Reading Sentences

_____ flows smoothly from sentence to sentence.

_____ displays varied sentence beginnings and lengths.

✔ Correct, Accurate Copy

_____ follows the basic rules of grammar, spelling, and punctuation.

Writing with a Computer

What are the tools of the writer's trade? Notebooks, a good supply of favorite pens and pencils, file folders, a few reference books such as your handbook, and a personal computer—all of these might be used during a writing project. For many writers, however, the most important tool is the computer.

Those of you who have used a computer for writing already understand its value. Once you know how to use it, the computer can save you a lot of time. It also makes it easy to work with your writing, allowing you to rearrange information and add new ideas. And it helps you produce clear, readable copy to share with your readers.

WHAT'S AHEAD

Writers who are just getting into computers will find this chapter especially helpful. (Experienced "users" will learn some things as well.) It includes, among other things, a basic guide for writing with a computer and a special section on graphic design.

- Understanding the Basics
- Designing Your Writing
- Effective Design in Action
- Using a Word-Processing Program

Understanding the Basics

Like pen and paper, the computer is a medium for writing—you must still supply the words. The computer simply captures them more quickly and efficiently. The following observations will help you use your computer as efficiently as possible, whether you are already using computers or just beginning to.

- Until you become "keyboard fluent," you may want to use pen and paper for your freewriting and drafting to ensure a free flow of ideas. Keep practicing until you master keyboarding. Then you will be able to make full use of the computer as a writing tool.

- Word-processing programs turn computers into high-tech writing machines that allow you to enter, delete, add, and move information. Most programs also allow you to check for spelling and grammar errors. But no spelling or grammar checker is foolproof. You must still check for errors after using these editing features.

Misspelled or missing words are easier to spot on paper than on a screen, so make sure to do your final editing and proofreading on a printed copy.

- Word-processing programs have many design and format options to help you create interesting and effective page layouts. Don't get carried away with these options and overuse them. You may clutter up your pages. (See pages 27-29 for more information.)

- Work from a written copy of your composition until you get used to word processing. Remember, too, that it's always a good idea to save your work at regular intervals.

- Staring at a monitor can cause eyestrain. If your eyes begin to ache, save your text, turn off your machine, and come back to your work at a later time.

Note: You should adjust the contrast and brightness on your monitor and check the lighting in the room to reduce glare.

- Writing with a computer involves a whole different vocabulary—*bugs, bytes, bombs, menus.* Learning the language of computers will help you become a better computer user. (See pages 486-490.)

Designing Your Writing

The test of good page design is that it makes your writing clear and easy to follow. Remember to focus on content first and then follow these tips for creating clean, attractive essays, reports, and research papers. (Also see pages 28-29.)

TYPOGRAPHY

- **Use an easy-to-read serif font for the main text.** (*Serif* type, like this type, has tails at the tops and bottoms of the letters.) For most types of writing, use a 10- or 12-point type size.
- **Make titles and headings short and to the point.** Follow the rules for capitalizing titles and headings. (See 407.3.)
- **Consider using a sans serif font for the title and headings.** (Sans serif type, like this, does not have tails.) Use larger type, perhaps 18-point, for your title and 14-point type for any headings. (Use boldface for headings if they seem to get lost on the page.) By varying the size and style of your type, you help the readers follow your writing. Avoid elaborate typefaces that are hard to read.

SPACING AND MARGINS

- **Maintain a one-inch margin around each page** (top, bottom, left, and right).
- **Hit the tab key to indent** the first line of each paragraph. This key should be set at five spaces.
- **Leave only one space after a period** to make your writing easier to read.
- **Avoid placing headings, hyphenated words, and new paragraphs** at the bottom of a page. Also avoid *widows* (single words at the bottom of a page) and *orphans* (single words at the top of a page).

GRAPHIC DEVICES

- **Create bulleted lists.** Most programs allow you to do this. (See page 29.) Be selective; you don't want too many lists in your writing.
- **Include charts or other graphics.** These can add visual appeal. Graphics should not be so small that they get lost on the page, nor so large that they overpower the page. (You can also put graphics on separate pages.)

Effective Design in Action

The following two pages from a sample student research paper show effective design features.

Kendall McGinn
Mr. Gilding
Social Studies
Feb. 20, 1999

The title is 18-point sans serif type.

The Return of the Buffalo

At one point in the early twentieth century, it seemed that the American buffalo would continue to exist only in pictures or on the buffalo nickel. Its population of 100 million in 1700 had been reduced to 1,000 by 1889. In recent years, that number has increased to nearly 200,000 (Hodgson 71). The buffalo, once endangered, has returned.

Before the Europeans came to North America, the native people of the North American plains and the buffalo were one *Pte Oyate,* or Buffalo Nation. The big bull *tantanka* was life itself. These Native Americans followed the herds and used the buffalo for food, clothing, shelter, religious ceremonies, and medicine. A Lakota leader summed up this unity between human and animal: "When the Creator made the buffalo, he put power in them. When you eat the meat, that power goes into you, heals the body and spirit" (qtd. in Hodgson 69).

The main text is 10-point serif type.

Open Season on Buffalo

The heading is 14-point sans serif.

During the expansion of the United States, a cultural clash occurred, and the Europeans practically destroyed the buffalo. By the year 1800, it was reported that there were about 30 million buffalo left in the United States.

McGinn 5

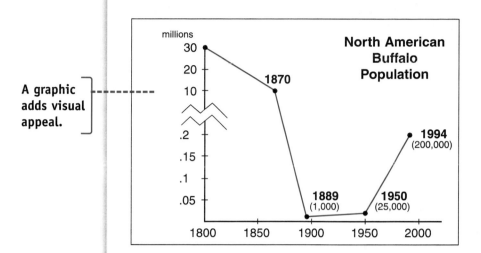

A graphic adds visual appeal.

The buffalo is "returning" to North America in ever-increasing numbers. Cable Network News owner Ted Turner and his actress wife, Jane Fonda, raise almost 10,000 buffalo on their Montana and New Mexico ranches. "I guess I've gone buffalo batty," Turner says. Both he and his wife support the raising of buffalo as an excellent source of low-fat meat and as a way to help save this once endangered species (Hodgson 75).

Buffalo ranchers are, in fact, learning that raising buffalo has many benefits. Raising buffalo is more cost-effective and more environmentally safe than raising cattle. Here are four main benefits:

A bulleted list is used.

- Buffalo don't overeat.
- Their sharp hooves loosen hard soil.
- Buffalo improve grass products.
- They adapt to any climate.

Buffalo living in Florida seem just as happy as those living in Alaska. In Hawaii, they even survived Hurricane Iniki in 1992. Hawaiian rancher Bill Mowry recalls how the buffalo "loved every minute of it."

Using a Word-Processing Program

When using a word-processing program on your computer, all of the important features are right at your fingertips. All you have to do is use the different commands and symbols that appear on the monitor. The following example shows you the types of features found on most programs.

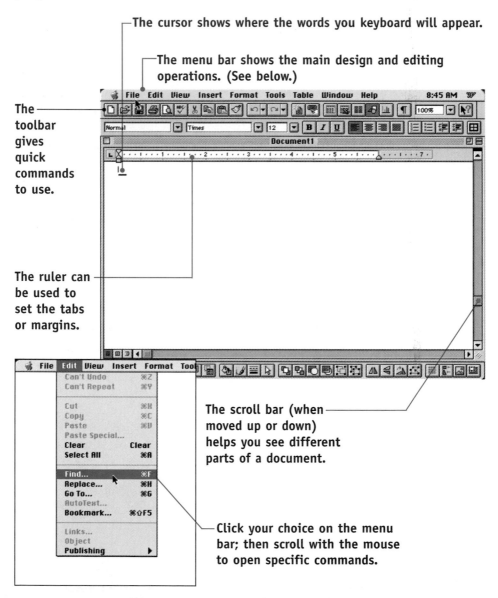

The cursor shows where the words you keyboard will appear.

The menu bar shows the main design and editing operations. (See below.)

The toolbar gives quick commands to use.

The ruler can be used to set the tabs or margins.

The scroll bar (when moved up or down) helps you see different parts of a document.

Click your choice on the menu bar; then scroll with the mouse to open specific commands.

Developing a Portfolio

Someone looking at one of your weakest stories or reports will not get a clear picture of you as a writer. It would be like looking at a photo of you when you were having a bad hair day. "That's me all right," you might say, "but you're certainly not seeing me at my best."

We get a better picture of how someone writes by looking at several different samples of his or her work—a collection of writing— created at different times. Such a collection is often called a *writing portfolio,* and it is extremely useful for giving a clear, complete picture of you as a writer.

WHAT'S AHEAD

This chapter will help you better understand how to develop a writing portfolio. It includes helpful background information, guidelines, and explanations as well as sample portfolio reflections by different student and professional writers.

- Understanding Portfolios
- Two Classroom Portfolios
- Creating a Portfolio
- Planning Ideas
- Example Portfolio Reflections

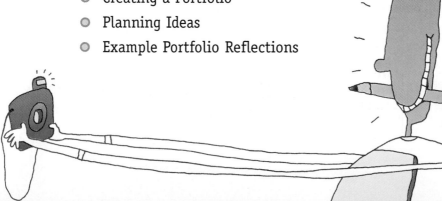

Understanding Portfolios

What Is a Portfolio?

Writer Barry Lane jokes that a portfolio is the old box in the cupboard or attic stuffed with anything and everything your mother or grandmother thought was important to keep. If he were serious, then the best way to create a writing portfolio would be to save every piece of writing you ever wrote and stuff it all into one big box. By the time you were in eighth grade, the box would be overflowing!

Actually, you cannot create a top-notch portfolio without being very picky. Imagine yourself making a mini-version of a photo album by picking six to ten of your favorite snapshots and putting them into a smaller collection. That is exactly how a portfolio is made.

Why Keep a Portfolio?

Many professional people, including writers, artists, and designers, compile portfolios to showcase their talents. A portfolio, in a way, speaks for the person. It says, "This is who I am; this is what I can do." A portfolio also helps potential employers and clients evaluate an individual's talents.

In many schools, students are asked to compile writing portfolios. Portfolios help students . . .

"A writing portfolio is a carefully chosen collection of work telling the story of one person's journey as a writer."

- ⊙ **preserve** important thoughts, feelings, and experiences,
- ⊙ **show** their growth as writers,
- ⊙ **display** important pieces of work,
- ⊙ **showcase** the whole range of their writing skills, and
- ⊙ **reflect** upon their own process of becoming writers.

You can also keep a personal portfolio, containing writing that is special to you. You might divide it according to the different types of writing you like to do on your own: poems, stories, plays, songs, and so on.

Two Classroom Portfolios

In most cases, you will create either a showcase portfolio or a growth portfolio. You and your teacher will probably decide together which type of portfolio to create.

A Showcase Portfolio

A showcase portfolio shows the range of things you can do as a writer. For example, it might include different kinds of writing: a story, a poem, an expository essay, a persuasive essay. It might also include samples that show off specific skills: revising/editing/research/organizational skills, and so on. A showcase portfolio is usually presented for evaluation at the end of a grading period. As its name implies, it is meant to show you at your best.

A Growth Portfolio

A growth portfolio notes the ways in which you are changing and growing as a writer. In a growth portfolio, examples of similar types of writing are collected regularly—say, once a month—over a long period of time. Anyone who looks at the portfolio (including you!) will be able to see how your skills are developing. You may check your growth in . . .

- writing beginnings and endings,
- supporting a thesis effectively,
- creating a believable character,
- using colorful language,
- writing dialogue,
- and so on.

Creating a Portfolio

A showcase portfolio may contain the following parts, but always check with your teacher for specific requirements. (A growth portfolio will not include as many parts.)

- A **table of contents** listing the information included in your portfolio
- A **brief reflective essay or letter** detailing the story behind your portfolio (*how you compiled it, how you feel about it, what it means to you,* etc.)
- A **number of finished pieces** representing some of your best writing (Your teacher may require that you include all of your planning, drafting, and revising for one or more of these pieces.)
- A **cover sheet** attached to each piece of writing, discussing the reason for its selection, the amount of work that went into it, and so on
- **Evaluation sheets or checklists** charting, among other things, the basic skills you have mastered as well as the skills you still need to work on

Portfolio Tips

1. Keep track of all of your writing, including planning notes and drafts. When you need to put together your portfolio, you'll have all the pieces to choose from.

2. Make sure that you understand the specific requirements for the type of portfolio you are putting together.

3. Work with an expandable or pocket-type folder to avoid dog-eared and ripped pages.

4. Establish a schedule for working on your portfolio. You can't put together an effective portfolio on the night before it's due.

5. Take pride in your portfolio. Make it a positive reflection of you.

Compiling a portfolio makes the writing process much more real and meaningful for you. You will, after all, be judged on the writing *you* decide to include in your portfolio.

Planning Ideas

Putting together an effective portfolio takes time and effort. The following planning ideas should help.

1 COLLECT

Don't make quick decisions about which pieces to include in your portfolio. Instead, as you write things, date them and tuck them into your general writing folder until you are ready to review them. Then make your choices.

Special Note: Never, ever lose any of the drafts for a piece of writing that you may want to include in your portfolio.

2 SELECT

When your general writing folder contains at least three to five finished pieces, it's probably time to choose something for your portfolio. Get out everything you have written and lay it out in front of you. Skim through each piece. Try to recall the feeling you had as you wrote each paper. Which one was the *hardest?* The most *satisfying?*

3 REFLECT

A collection of writing doesn't become a portfolio until you have taken a careful look at your choices, reflecting on the various pieces and answering questions like these:

- Why did I choose this piece for my portfolio?
- What does it tell me about myself as a writer?
- What would I do differently in another similar piece?
- What have I learned that will make me a better writer?

4 PROJECT

Use what you've learned about your writing to set goals for yourself. Keep your goals focused and write them down: *I will use my natural voice more. I will write stronger beginnings. I will learn to use semicolons.* That way, it's easier to know when you've achieved them!

Example Portfolio Reflections

When you reflect upon your work, you come to an understanding of your progress as a writer. Your personal reflections also help readers appreciate the contents of your portfolio. The following reflections will show you some of the things writers think and write about.

Student Reflections

"In my portfolio, you'll find the work I think represents my best efforts in my eighth grade year. I have included expository, informative, and creative pieces, and you will see, if you read them carefully, how my voice and word choice have gotten stronger in each type of writing."

—Sherry Jamison

"I have learned to put more detail in my writing. If you read the first piece in my portfolio, you will see it is very general and boring. It doesn't say all that much. But I left it in because when you compare it to the last story in my portfolio, you go Wow, this is so, so much better."

—Tom Millser

Professional Reflections

"Sometimes books seem to happen in strange ways, come from strange places. This book happened sitting on the back of a dead horse in the woods of northern Minnesota with soft snow falling and ice and dogs and winter all around, in the quiet sigh of an old man's life."

—Gary Paulsen
Clabbered Dirt, Sweet Grass (Foreword)

" 'Finn MacCool, the Irish Giant, was the only giant in all of Ireland.' This was the first sentence in my first book. I think I wrote that story because I love giants . . . and I love Ireland."

—Eve Bunting
Once Upon a Time

Publishing Your Writing

Student writer Katie Jean Larsen gives this advice about writing: "Make sure YOU like it, because that's what matters." Katie is absolutely right. You are your most important audience. After all, your writing contains your very own thoughts and feelings, so it should always meet with your personal approval, whether you are writing a poem, an essay, or a business letter. You should also be your most *demanding* audience. Every piece of writing that you complete should reflect your best efforts.

Your writing is ready for publication once it says exactly what you want it to say from start to finish. Sharing a personal narrative with your classmates is a form of publishing—so is selecting an essay for your portfolio or presenting some poems at a writing conference.

WHAT'S AHEAD

This chapter will help you with all of your publishing needs, from getting your writing ready for publication to deciding where to publish it. (You will also find help in "Writing with a Computer" on pages 25-30.)

- Getting Your Writing Ready
- Publishing Ideas
- Sending Your Writing Out
- Places to Publish
- Publishing On-Line
- Making Your Own Web Site

Getting Your Writing Ready

Publishing is the final step in the writing process, offering that "other audience"—all of your readers—a chance to enjoy your writing. The following checklist will help as you prepare your writing for that final step.

Work with your writing until you feel good about it from start to finish. If any part (*ideas, organization, voice,* etc.) still needs work, then your writing isn't ready to publish.

Ask for input and advice during the writing process. Your writing should answer any questions your readers may have about the ideas you share. Confusing parts must be made clear.

Save all drafts for each writing project so you can keep track of the changes you have made. In addition, if you are preparing a portfolio, you may be required to attach early drafts to finished pieces. (See pages 31-36.)

Check for style and correctness before sharing your writing. Have at least one trusted editor (a classmate or family member) check your work, too. (See pages 83 and 92 for help.)

Present your finished piece clearly and neatly. Use pen (blue or black ink) and one side of the paper if you are writing by hand. If you are using a computer, avoid fancy, hard-to-read typefaces (fonts) and odd margins. (See pages 27-29.)

Know your options. There are many different ways to publish your work depending on the type of writing you are doing. (See the next page.)

Follow the necessary publication guidelines. Your teacher may want assignments presented in a certain way—so too with any writing you send to newspapers, magazines, and writing contests. (See pages 40-41.)

> "I wrote *The Outsiders* when I was 16 years old. It was the third book I'd written, but the first one I tried to get published."
> —S. E. Hinton

Publishing Ideas

Publishing covers a lot of territory as you will see in the ideas listed below. Some of these ideas are easy to carry out, like sharing your writing with your classmates. Others are more adventurous and take some time and effort, such as entering a writing contest. Try a number of these publishing ideas during the school year. All of them will help you grow as a writer.

Performing

Sharing with Classmates
Reading to Other Audiences
Recording for a Class Project
Videotaping for Distant Audiences
Performing on Stage

In School

School Newspaper
Literary Magazine
Classroom Collection
School Handbook
Writing Portfolio
(See pages 31-36.)

Posting

Classroom Bulletin Boards
School or Public Library
Hallway Display Cases
Business Windows
Clinic Waiting Rooms

Self-Publishing

Family Newsletter
Greeting Cards
Binding Your Writing
On-Line Publishing
(See pages 42-43.)

Sending It Out

Local Newspapers
Church Publications
Young Writers' Conferences
Magazines and Contests
(See pages 40-41.)

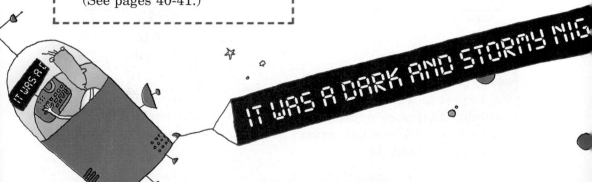

IT WAS A DARK AND STORMY NIG

Sending Your Writing Out

The questions and answers listed below will help you submit your writing to publishers.

Q What types of writing can I submit?

A There are markets for all types of writing. For example, newspapers are interested in essays and articles. With magazines, it all depends. Some magazines publish fiction, nonfiction, and poetry; others focus on nonfiction only.

Q Where should I send my writing?

A Your chances of getting published are best if you stick close to home, so first consider local publications. If you're interested in submitting something to a national publication, turn to the *Writer's Market* (Cincinnati, Writer's Digest Books) for ideas. It includes one section devoted to teen and young adult publications. If your school library doesn't have this resource, your city library will. (Also see pages 41-42.)

Q How should I submit my work?

A Most publications expect you to include these things:

a brief cover letter identifying the title and the form of your writing (*story, essay, article,* etc.), the word count, and so on;

a neat copy of your work with your name on each page; and

a SASE (*self-addressed stamped envelope*) large enough for your writing so it can be returned after it has been read.

Check the masthead in the publication for more specific guidelines. (The masthead is the small print on one of the opening pages that lists key people, addresses, subscription rates, etc.)

Q What should I expect?

A Expect to wait a long time for a reply. Also be prepared for the possibility that your writing will not be accepted for publication. It's best to think of the whole process as a learning experience; just keep writing and submitting.

Places to Publish

Here are a few writing contests to enter and some magazines that accept student submissions. (Refer to the *Writer's Market*—found in most libraries—for more places to publish.)

Writing Contests

The Acorn (Grades 3-6,7-8)
FORMS: Prose—300 words or less
SEND TO: 1530 7th Street
       Rock Island, IL 61201

National Council of Teachers of English (NCTE) Promising Young Writers Program (Grade 8)
FORMS: Samples of best writing plus one impromptu theme on a topic selected by NCTE
SEND TO: Promising Writers Program
       NCTE
       1111 Kenyon Road
       Urbana, IL 61801-1096

Read Writing Contests (Grades 6-12)
FORMS: Short stories/personal essays
SEND TO: *Read* Writing and Art Awards
       Weekly Reader Corporation
       200 First Stamford Place
       P.O. Box 120023
       Stamford, CT 06912-0023

Scholastic Writing Awards (Grades 7-9)
FORMS: Short story, essay, dramatic script, poetry, humor, science fiction, fantasy, writing portfolio
SEND TO: The Scholastic Art and
       Writing Awards
       555 Broadway
       New York, NY 10012

Magazines

Creative Kids (Students, ages 8-14)
FORMS: Fiction, poetry, plays, songs, editorials (No school assignments)
SEND TO: P.O. Box 8813
       Waco, TX 70714-0010

Kids Byline: A Magazine for Kids by Kids (Grades 2-12)
FORMS: Fiction, nonfiction, poetry
SEND TO: P.O. Box 1838
       Frederick, MD 21702

Merlyn's Pen (Grades 6-12)
FORMS: Fiction, poetry, essays, reviews
SEND TO: P.O. Box 910
       E. Greenwich, RI 02818-0910

Stone Soup (Students, ages 8-13)
FORMS: Fiction, personal narratives, literary essays, book reviews, poetry
SEND TO: P.O. Box 83
       Santa Cruz, CA 95063

Writing! (Grades 6-12)
FORMS: Fiction, essays, book reviews, poetry
SEND TO: 900 Skokie Boulevard
       Suite 200
       Northbrook, IL 60062-4028

Note: Always check with the contest or publication and with your teacher about guidelines for submitting your writing. Include a self-addressed stamped envelope (SASE) with any inquiry.

Publishing On-Line

The Internet is another avenue for getting your writing out to an audience. There are on-line magazines, writing contests, and other special publishing sites that accept submissions from young people. And, if you're really adventurous, you can even create your own site. (See page 43.) The questions and answers below will help you get your writing on the Internet.

Q Where do I start my search?

A Begin by checking with your teachers to see if your school or school district has its own Internet site where students can post their work. If not, suggest that one be started.

And don't forget to ask your teachers about Web sites they might be familiar with. They often have a knack for discovering writing contests and places that accept student submissions.

Q How do I actually search for these sites?

A Use a search engine to find places to publish. (See pages 270 and 271 for help using a search engine.) Be prepared, though, to spend some time exploring; there are many pages and links.

Before beginning your search, take a moment to explore the search engine's home page. Many search engines offer their own kids' links. Also, because search engines have a lot of traffic, your work has a good chance of being seen by many people there.

Q Where else can I go for help?

A You can check your Internet provider's home page to see if it lists a kids' site where you can post your work. If not, send your provider an e-mail message asking if they know of such a site.

Q Does the Write Source have a Web site?

A Yes, you can visit our Web site at **thewritesource.com**. We list many places where students can publish on the Net.

Making Your Own Web Site

It is possible to make your own Web site. If your family has an Internet account, check with your provider to find out how to get started. If you are using a school account, ask your teacher for help. Then start designing your site. Use the questions and answers below as a basic starting point.

Q. How do I plan my site?

A Think about how many pages you want on your Web site. Should you put everything on one page, or would you like to have a number of pages (perhaps a home page, a page of poetry, a page of favorite links, etc.)? Check out other student sites for ideas.

Then plan your pages by sketching them out. Note how the pages will be linked by marking the hot spots on your sketches.

Q. How do I make the pages?

A Start each page as a file using a word processor. Many new word-processing programs let you save a file as a Web page. If yours doesn't, you will have to add HTML codes to format the text and make links to graphics and other pages. Your teacher may be able to explain how to do this. Otherwise, you can find instructions about HTML on the Net.

Q. How do I know whether my pages work?

A You should always test your pages. Using your browser, open your first page. Then follow the links to make sure they work correctly and that all the pages look right.

Q. How do I get my pages on the Net?

A You must upload your finished pages to your Internet provider's computer. Ask your provider how to do this. Your provider will also tell you how you can access the pages later in case you want to make changes. After the upload, visit your site to make sure it still works.

Q. How do I let people know about my site?

A Once your site is up and working, e-mail your friends and tell them to visit it! Ask your provider to advertise it on their home page. Your provider can also tell you how to advertise your site to the rest of the Net.

Using the Writing Process

Prewriting:
Choosing a Subject

The writing process begins long before you actually put your fingers to the keyboard (or pen to paper). As a matter of fact, the process begins the day you think your first thought . . . and just keeps going on from there. Each of life's experiences becomes part of what you know, what you think, and what you have to say. You automatically tap into these experiences for ideas whenever you write.

Of course, your first conscious step into the writing process occurs when you decide to write or when you are given a specific assignment. This first step is called **prewriting**—the all-important time in which you think about and plan a writing project. If you give the proper attention to prewriting, you've laid a solid foundation for the drafting that follows.

WHAT'S AHEAD

The next page offers you a quick guide to prewriting. The rest of the chapter includes strategies that will help you gather ideas and select writing subjects. (The following chapter includes prewriting strategies that will help you collect and organize details once you've selected your subject.)

- Quick Guide
- Creating a Writing "SourceBank"
- Selecting a Writing Subject
- Starting Points for Writing
- Additional Strategies

QUICK GUIDE

Prewriting

● **PURPOSE:** Prewriting is the first step in the writing process, and it involves selecting and developing a subject for writing. It deals with all of the thinking, brainstorming, talking, and collecting you do before you write.

Special Note: You may also do some prewriting-type activities later in the writing process. For example, once you start revising a first draft, you may decide to gather some additional information about your subject.

● **STARTING POINT:** During prewriting, you carry out the following activities:

- selecting a specific subject for writing,
- gathering information about it,
- focusing on a specific part of the subject for writing, and
- planning how to use all of the supporting information.

When you select a subject, make sure that it meets the requirements of the assignment and also interests you.

● **FORM:** Prewriting can be carried out in many different ways. You may start a subject search with a list or a cluster. This may prompt you to write freely about some item from your list. After you gather your initial thoughts about it, you may do some additional research and note taking. And, finally, you may decide to use a graphic organizer to put everything together.

● **THE BIG PICTURE:** When prewriting, pay special attention to two traits of good writing: ideas and organization.

Ideas: Collect as much information as you can. The more you know about your subject, the easier it will be to write about it. (See pages 53-58.)

Organization: Decide on the best arrangement of the facts and details you have collected. There has to be a master plan that holds all of the information together. (See page 60.)

Creating a Writing "SourceBank"

To writers, discovering what's going on in the world around them is very important. They save every nugget of experience they can, knowing they may use it in their writing some day.

To think and act like a writer, you should develop your own "SourceBank" of writing ideas. The strategies and guidelines that follow will help you get started.

Finding Writing Ideas

Be alert for writing ideas you find unexpectedly as you read, ride the bus, visit friends, shop, goof around, and so on. Different "scenes" may bring to mind a number of writing subjects.

Writers often carry small pocket notebooks to capture images and ideas they happen upon. They also write regularly about their daily experiences in their journals. You should do the same.

Getting Involved

Get involved in your community. Visit museums, churches, parks, libraries, manufacturing plants, businesses, and so on. As you expand the scope of your world, you will naturally build a supply of potential writing ideas.

Searching and Surfing

Prowl around your library for writing ideas. Also surf the Internet since it contains all kinds of interesting information and ideas. (See pages 266-271.)

Maintaining a Writing Folder

As you work on your writing in school, especially if you are in a writing group, you will constantly come up against new ideas during your discussions. Reserve part of your folder to write these ideas down.

Reading like a Writer

Reserve part of your writing folder for interesting ideas that you find as you read—an interesting name, a surprising turn in a story, a well-phrased sentence, and so on.

Selecting a Writing Subject

A distinguished writer once said, "There are few experiences quite so satisfactory as getting a good writing idea. You're pleased with it, and feel good about it." Many writing assignments are related to a general subject area you are studying. Let's say, for example, you were asked to write a report about current health and medicine as part of a science unit. Your job would be to select a specific part of that subject to write about:

> **General Subject Area:** Current Health and Medicine
> **Specific Writing Subject:** Laser Eye Surgery

The following strategies will help you select effective, specific subjects that you can feel good about.

Journal Writing ■ Write on a regular basis in a personal journal, exploring your experiences and thoughts. Review your entries on occasion and underline ideas that you would like to further explore in writing assignments.

Clustering ■ Begin a cluster with a nucleus word. Select a general term or idea that is related to your writing assignment. Then cluster related words around it, as in the model below.

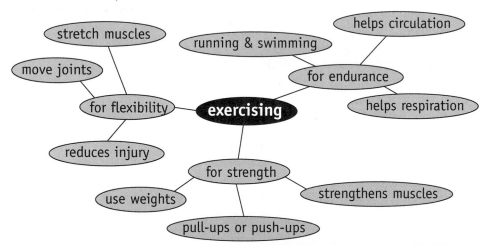

Note: After 3 or 4 minutes of clustering, you will probably be ready to write. Scan your cluster for a word or idea that interests you and write nonstop for about 5-8 minutes. A few writing subjects will probably begin to develop.

Listing ■ Freely list ideas as they come to mind when you think about your assignment. Keep your list going as long as you can. When you are finished, look for words in your list that you feel would make good writing subjects.

Freewriting ■ Write nonstop for 5-10 minutes to discover possible writing ideas. Begin writing with a particular idea in mind (one related to your writing assignment). Underline ideas that might serve as specific subjects for your assignment.

Sentence Completion ■ Complete an open-ended sentence in as many ways as you can. Try to word your sentence so that it leads you to a subject you can use for a particular writing assignment.

I wonder how . . .	I hope our school . . .	Television is . . .
Too many people . . .	I just learned . . .	Cars can be . . .
The good thing about . . .	One place I enjoy . . .	Grades are . . .

Try alternating responses with a friend or classmate and work from each other's ideas. Keep the ideas flowing as long as you can.

Review the Essentials of Life Checklist ■ The words listed below name the categories or groups of things that we need in order to live a full life. The checklist provides an endless variety of subject possibilities. Consider the first category, *clothing*. You could write about . . .

- the wardrobe of a friend or a family member,
- your all-time favorite piece of clothing, or
- clothing as a statement (the "we are what we wear" idea).

clothing	machines	rules/laws
housing	intelligence	tools/utensils
food	history/records	heat/fuel
communication	agriculture	natural resources
exercise	land/property	personality/identity
education	work/occupation	recreation/hobby
family	community	trade/money
friends	science	literature/books
purpose/goals	plants/vegetation	health/medicine
love	freedom/rights	art/music
senses	energy	faith/religion

Starting Points for Writing

The writing prompts listed below and the sample subjects and forms listed on the next page provide plenty of starting points for writing assignments.

Writing Prompts

Every day is full of experiences that make you think. You do things that you feel good about. You hear things that make you mad. You wonder how different things work. You're reminded of a past experience. These common everyday thoughts make excellent prompts for writing.

■ **Best and Worst**

My worst day
My craziest experience on the Web
An unforgettable dream
The hardest thing I've ever done
My best hour
The worst thing to wait for
My best kitchen creation

■ **As My World Turns**

My secret snacks
A day in the life of my pet
Last time I was at the mall, I . . .
When I played the rebel
Wheezing and sneezing
Joining the global village
When I'm in charge

■ **Deep in Thought**

List words that define you as a friend.
   (Write about one of these words.)
What car are you like and why?
List the duties of a good citizen.
   (Write about one or more duties.)

■ **Inside Education**

My best class ever
Here's the next episode of
   "As the School Swings."
Dear Chalkboard,
On-line discoveries
I memorized every word.
A classmate I once worshipped

■ **It could only happen to me!**

It sounds crazy but . . .
Putting my foot in my mouth
Guess what I just heard?
Creepy, crawly things
Whatever happened to my . . .
I got so mad when . . .
E-mail adventure

■ **What If . . . ?**

Where do I draw the line?
What should everyone know?
Here is my wish list.
Why do people like to go fast?
What if I never forgot?

■ **Quotable Quotations**

"There are only so many feelings you can capture on a keyboard."
"My interest is in the future."
"Democracy means 'I am as good as you are, and you are as good as I am.' "
"He that seeks trouble always finds it."

Sample Subjects

You come across many people, places, experiences, and things—all of which are potential subjects for writing. We've listed a number of possible subjects below, so you'll get the idea.

- **Describing**
  People: teacher, relative, classmate, coach, neighbor, bus driver, someone you spend time with, someone you wish you were like, newsgroup acquaintance
  Places: hangout, garage, classroom, rooftop, locker room, zoo, hallway, corner, barn, bayou, lake, river, cupboard, yard
  Things: billboard, poster, video game, cordless phone, key, bus, book, boat, drawing, model, doll, junk drawer, ladder, locket

- **Narrating**
  stage fright, just last week, a big mistake, a reunion, a dance, getting hurt, flirting, learning to _____, all wet, getting caught, cleaning up, being a friend

- **Explaining**
  How to . . . eat popcorn, make a taco, improve your memory, care for a pet, entertain a child, impress your teacher, earn extra money, get in shape
  The causes of . . . acid rain, acne, hiccups, tornadoes, shinsplints, dropouts, rust, computer viruses
  Kinds of . . . crowds, friends, commercials, dreams, pain, neighbors, clouds, stereos, heroes, chores, homework, traffic jams
  Definition of . . . class, a good time, a conservative, "soul," grandmother, loyalty, alternative music, adolescence, advice, empathy, surfing

- **Persuading**
  dieting, homework, testing, smoking in public places, shoplifting, air bags, teen centers, something that needs improving, something that deserves support, something that's unfair, something that everyone should see

Writing Forms

Have you ever written and designed a children's storybook, your own book of riddles, your own Web site? Just thinking about all of the forms of writing available to you might "prompt" you to write.

- **Personal Writing**—journals, logs, diaries, freewriting, friendly letters, e-mail, clustering, listing, autobiographical essays and narratives, brainstorming

- **Creative Writing**—poems, myths, plays, stories, anecdotes, sketches, essays, jokes, parodies

- **Subject Writing**—reports, reviews, business letters, memos, research papers, essays, news stories, interviews, instructions, manuals

- **Persuasive Writing**—editorials, letters, research papers, advertisements, essays, slogans, pamphlets, petitions, commercials

Additional Strategies

Don't limit yourself to pen and paper when collecting and selecting possible writing ideas. You might have fun trying one or two of the following strategies.

TAKING PICTURES

Photo albums of important experiences can be a terrific resource of writing ideas. Make sure to label the photographs. This way you can keep track of when, where, why, and how things happened. (You can also keep a videotape library of your experiences.)

TAPE-RECORDING

Tape-record conversations with special people in your life, such as grandparents and other older relatives. These recordings may trigger many ideas for biographies and reports.

ILLUSTRATING

Take inventory of the highs and lows in your life—either in a life map or some other artistic representation. Here is a sample life map by student writer (and artist) Celia Gomez.

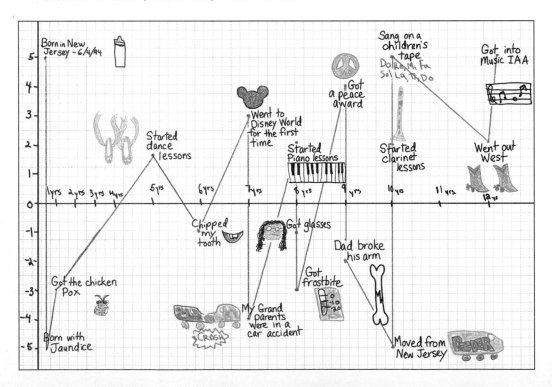

Gathering Details

Student writer Brandy Holladay feels that a story called "The Accident" is her best piece of writing. She explains, "It [the accident] really happened to me; therefore, I knew exactly what to say." Brandy's experience illustrates the following point: When you write about a personal experience, most of the details will already be clear in your mind. You will know exactly what to say.

For other writing projects, you may know only a little about your subject and will need to do some gathering. Gathering refers to the collecting and planning you do during prewriting. First, you collect details about your subject. Then, you plan how you will use these details in your writing. Gathering is especially important when you are developing research papers, reports, essays, and so on.

WHAT'S AHEAD

The first part of this chapter provides strategies and graphic organizers for gathering details. The second part will help you with your planning and organizing.

- Using Gathering Strategies
- Using Graphic Organizers
- Using Collection Sheets
- A Closer Look at Gathering
- Planning Your Writing

Using Gathering Strategies

How much collecting should you do? If you know plenty about a particular subject, you may simply collect your own thoughts about it in a freewriting. Then again, if you need more information about your subject, you may attempt two or three different collecting strategies. A variety of such strategies are listed on these two pages. Read through the entire list before you choose which ones to use.

① GATHERING YOUR THOUGHTS

Freewriting ■ Write freely for at least 5-10 minutes, exploring your subject from a number of different angles.

Listing ■ Jot down things that you already know about your subject, and the questions you have about it. Keep your list going as long as you can.

Clustering ■ Create a cluster with your specific subject as the nucleus word. (See page 48.)

Analyzing ■ Think carefully about a subject by answering the following types of questions:

- What parts does my subject have? (*Break it down.*)
- What do I see, hear, or feel when I think about it? (*Describe it.*)
- What is it similar to? What is it different from? (*Compare it.*)
- What are its strengths and weaknesses? (*Evaluate it.*)
- What can I do with it? How can I use it? (*Apply it.*)

5 W's of Writing ■ Answer the 5 W's—*Who? What? Where? When?* and *Why?*—to identify basic information about your subject. Add *How?* to the list for even better coverage.

HELPFUL HINT

Try this strategy: Keep asking the question *Why?* about your subject until you run completely out of answers. Then sum up what you've learned.

Offbeat Questions ■ Think creatively about a subject by creating and answering offbeat questions. Examples follow.

Writing About a Person
- What type of clothing is this person like?
- What type of weather is he or she like?

Writing About an Important Issue
- What sport would your viewpoint participate in?
- What food does your viewpoint resemble?

Writing to Explain a Process
- What television show is the process like?
- Where in a hardware store would this process feel most at home?

Debating ■ Develop a debate between two people in which your subject is explored. (You could be one of the debaters.)

 RESEARCHING

Reading ■ Refer to nonfiction books, magazines, pamphlets, newspapers, and so on, for information about your subject.

Viewing and Listening ■ Watch relevant television programs and videos or listen to tapes about your subject.

Surfing ■ Explore the Internet for information about your writing ideas. (See pages 265-272.)

Experiencing ■ Visit or watch your subject in action to learn about it. If your subject involves an activity, participate in it.

 TALKING TO OTHERS

Interviewing ■ Interview an expert about your subject. Meet the expert in person, communicate by phone, or send questions to be answered in writing. (See page 170 for more on interviewing.)

Discussing ■ Talk with your classmates, teachers, or other people to see what they know about your subject. Take notes to help you remember the important things they say.

Using Graphic Organizers

Graphic organizers help you gather and organize details for writing. Clustering is one method (see page 48), and this page lists other useful organizers.

LINE DIAGRAM ------------------

To collect and organize details for expository essays (See page 110.)

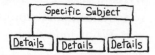

5 W'S CHART ------------------

To collect the *who? what? when? where?* and *why?* details for news stories, narratives, and so on. (See page 170.)

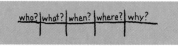

VENN DIAGRAM ----------------

To collect details for a comparison of two subjects (See page 313.)

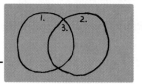

CYCLE DIAGRAM ------------------

To collect details for science-related writing, such as "how flowering plants reproduce" (See page 319.)

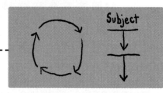

SENSORY CHART -------------

To collect details for descriptions and observation reports (See page 211.)

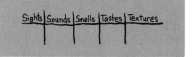

CAUSE/EFFECT --------------------
ORGANIZER

To collect details for cause/effect essays, such as "the causes and effects of security guards in school" (See page 317.)

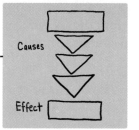

TIME LINE --------------------------

To collect details chronologically for essays and reports (See page 315.)

Using Collection Sheets

Collection sheets work well for gathering and organizing ideas for reports that require a lot of research. The sample below may work for you, but you can also design your own collection sheet.

Gathering Grid

Gathering grids are useful for recording and organizing facts and details you learn and for information you gather from various sources. The questions down the side, which you compose yourself, will guide your learning about the subject.

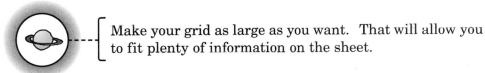

Make your grid as large as you want. That will allow you to fit plenty of information on the sheet.

SAMPLE Gathering Grid

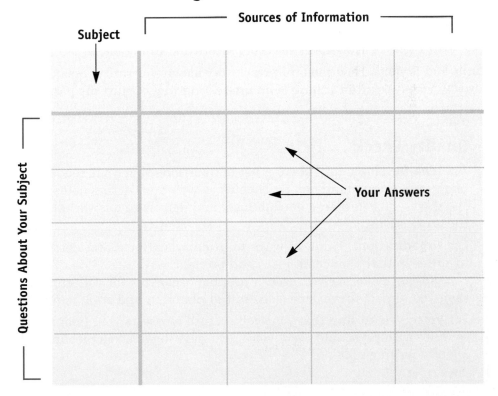

A Closer Look at Gathering

Let's say you've thought about your subject, collected some interesting details about it, and discussed it with your classmates and teacher. What should you do next? You may be ready to plan and write your first draft, or you may want to consider how well you really match up with your subject before you go any further.

Taking Inventory of Your Thoughts

Use the questions that follow to help you assess your feelings about your subject. After you do this, it should be easier to either move ahead with your writing, or reconsider your subject if necessary.

Situation: Does my subject meet the assignment requirements?
Am I writing to explain, describe, persuade, or share?

Self: How do I feel about the subject?
Is it worth spending additional time on?

Subject: How much do I know about this subject?
Is there additional information available?

Audience: How much do my readers know about this subject?
How can I get them interested in my ideas?

Form and Style: How should I present my ideas—narrative, essay, etc.?
Can I think of an interesting way to start my paper?

Quality Check . . .

For Idea Development: Make a list of questions that your readers might ask about your subject. Then review your collecting notes to see if you have gathered enough facts and details to answer all of these questions.

For Organization: Think of ways to group your facts and details together so that your main ideas will be clear.
Special Note: If you used a graphic organizer for collecting, then you already have done some initial planning and organizing.

For Voice: Make sure that your subject still interests you. In order to write with personality and voice, you must have strong feelings about a writing idea.

Planning Your Writing

Gathering details helps you learn about your subject. Planning how to use the details helps you get ready to write. The steps that follow will guide your planning.

- Review the details you have collected.
- Think of an interesting focus (way to write about your subject). (See below.)
- Organize the details in the most effective way to support or develop your focus. (See the next page.)

Focusing Your Efforts

Sooner or later, you need to identify a specific way to write about your subject. This is called your focus. A focus helps you gain control of your subject, and it helps you organize your ideas for writing.

A focus statement is similar to a topic sentence, which is the controlling idea of a paragraph. It is also similar to a thesis statement, which is the controlling idea of an essay.

Finding a Focus

To choose a focus, decide what it is about your subject that you want to emphasize. Your focus should express a specific part of your subject, or a special feeling about it.

SAMPLES:

Writing Assignment: Essay about current medicine
Specific Subject: Laser eye surgery
Focus Statement: Laser eye surgery will greatly improve eye care.

Writing Assignment: Report on health and fitness
Specific Subject: Three main types of exercises
Focus Statement: An effective conditioning program requires three main types of exercises.

Your writing will go on and on, and be hard to follow, if you try to say too many things about your subject. That is why it is so important to establish a specific focus for your essays, reports, and reviews.

Organizing the Details

All good writers—even the most creative ones—make some decisions about the organization of their writing before they attempt a first draft. Good writing has a design. It moves clearly and smoothly from one main idea to the next. It leads readers somewhere.

You can organize the details of your writing in a list, a cluster, or a brief outline. (See page 119 for help with outlining.) Use your focus statement as the starting point for your planning at this stage. You will want to arrange your details so that they support your focus statement in the most effective way.

METHODS OF ORGANIZATION

The list below identifies different ways to organize details in your writing. (See page 106 for a chart of transition or linking words that can be used with many of these methods of organization.)

- **Chronological (Time) Order** You can arrange details in the order in which they happened (*first, second, then, next, later,* etc.).

  Autobiographical and biographical essays are almost always organized chronologically, as are science and history reports.

- **Order of Location (Spatial)** You can arrange details in the order in which they are located (*above, below, beneath,* etc.).

  Descriptions, observation reports, and certain explanations (such as giving directions) are organized spatially.

- **Order of Importance** You can arrange details from the most important to the least—or from the least important to the most.

  Persuasive essays, news stories, and most expository essays are organized by order of importance.

- **Cause and Effect** You can begin with a general statement giving the cause of a problem and then add a number of specific effects.

  Essays that explore or analyze problems (often based on current events) are organized in this way.

 Note: The **problem and solution** method is closely related to the cause and effect method of organization. You state a problem and explore possible solutions.

- **Comparison** You can develop two or more subjects by showing how they are alike and how they are different.

Writing the First Draft

When you write a first draft, you connect all of your thoughts about your subject. Always try to write as much of your first draft as possible in the first sitting, while all of your gathering is still fresh in your mind. Refer to your plan (if you have one), but keep an open mind. New and improved ideas may pop into your head as you write. Write until you come to a logical stopping point.

Remember that your first draft is your first look at a developing writing idea. (It will almost always go through many changes before it is ready to publish.) Author Donald Murray calls this writing a "discovery draft" because there is no way to know for sure how it will all turn out, even if you have done a lot of planning. The element of surprise inherent in drafting stimulates experienced writers and draws them back to the writing process time and time again. Let it do the same for you.

WHAT'S AHEAD

The next page provides a quick guide to writing a first draft. The rest of the chapter includes drafting tips, guidelines, and examples to help you develop different parts of your writing.

- ◎ Quick Guide
- ◎ Writing an Opening Paragraph
- ◎ Developing the Middle Part
- ◎ Bringing Your Writing to a Close

QUICK GUIDE

Drafting

PURPOSE: Writing a first draft shows you how well you match up with your subject and sets in motion the actual development of your writing (additional drafts and revisions).

STARTING POINT: You're ready to write a first draft, once you . . .

- know enough about your subject,
- establish a focus for your writing, and
- organize your supporting ideas.

Some writers pay special attention to the specific wording in their opening paragraph before they launch full throttle into their first draft. Once the beginning part is set, they find it much easier to complete the rest of their writing. Other writers are more interested in getting all of their thoughts on paper right away.

FORM: First drafts should be freely written, without being too concerned about neatness and correctness (just make sure everything is legible).

Write on every other line, and use only one side of the paper when drafting with pen and paper. Double-space when using a computer. (This will make revising much easier.)

THE BIG PICTURE: When writing a first draft, give special attention to these traits of good writing: ideas, organization, and voice.

Ideas: Connect all of the important ideas that you collected, and include new ideas as they come to mind.

Organization: Use your planning as a guide when you write. Remember to include a beginning, a middle, and an ending in your writing. (See pages 63-66.)

Voice: Speak honestly and naturally so the real you comes through in your writing.

Writing an Opening Paragraph

If you are writing a personal narrative, an essay, a report, or a research paper, you need to plan an opening or a lead paragraph. Your opening should introduce your subject, gain your reader's attention, and identify the specific focus, or thesis, of your writing. There are many different ways to begin an opening paragraph. You might . . .

- share some interesting or important details,
- ask the readers a question,
- begin with an informative quotation,
- start with some thoughtful dialogue, or
- simply identify the main points you wish to cover.

By all means try to make your opening interesting and entertaining; but, more importantly, make sure it reflects your true feelings. If you don't like how your first attempt sounds, try again.

SAMPLE Opening Paragraph

The following opening paragraph comes from student writer Seema Setia's essay about her grandfather in Delhi, India. Note how effectively Seema uses interesting details to lead readers into the essay. Also note the sincere, honest voice she establishes. (The focus statement is underlined.)

Interesting details

He has shown me the love and beauty of nature ever since I was born. He gives me his huge bedroom while he sleeps in the smallest room in the house. He doesn't take me to movies, or to big, fancy restaurants. Instead, he tells me stories and shows me new flowers that he has planted. He is always available to answer my questions with his immense knowledge. He is my grandfather, someone who has always done the small things to please me.

—*from* Lessons Learned with Love

Developing the Middle Part

Types of Support

The middle part of your draft should support or explain the focus of your writing. *Remember:* The focus, or thesis, is the special part of the subject you have decided to write about. Use the planning and organizing you've done as a general guide. Here is a list of different ways to support your writing idea:

Explain ■ Support your writing focus with facts and examples.

Define ■ Tell what the key words or subject means.

Describe ■ Share specific, sensory details about the subject.

Argue ■ Use logic and evidence to prove something is true.

Illustrate ■ Tell a story or share an experience to clarify an idea.

Reflect ■ Think carefully about the importance of something.

Analyze ■ Examine the parts to better understand the whole.

Compare ■ Use examples to show how two things are alike.

In most pieces of writing, you will use several of these methods to develop your focus. For example, if you are writing about an important event, you might *describe* the event, *illustrate* it with a story, and so on.

Levels of Detail

Usually, each *main* supporting idea is developed in a separate paragraph. A well-written supporting paragraph may contain three different levels of detail:

LEVEL 1: Controlling (topic) sentences name and control the topic: **Nana knew everything about gardening.**

LEVEL 2: Clarifying sentences support the main point and help make the topic clearer: **When I was little, Nana showed me how to plant an orange seed and tend it once it started growing.**

LEVEL 3: Completing sentences add specific details to complete the point: **To this day, the orange tree from that seed still bears fruit.**

 Note: In a longer paragraph, you may have two or three level-2 sentences, each followed by one or two level-3 sentences.

SAMPLE Middle Paragraphs

In the paragraphs that follow, the writer uses different methods of supporting each main point. Also note the various levels of detail used in each paragraph. In the first paragraph shared here, Seema Setia tells a story to illustrate a main idea about her subject.

Illustrating a point with a story

> Nana [the grandfather] often entertained me the most, right around his home. I remember the day I saw Nana placing two wooden bowls on the ledge of the veranda. One of the bowls was filled with water and the other one was filled with bread crumbs. He took a few steps back, next to me, watching the bowls intently. Suddenly, I saw a small, chestnut-colored thing quietly hop behind a plant along the wall. Then, it quickly flew toward the bowls. Soon, there were many sparrows, all going toward the food that awaited them.

In the next paragaph, the writer reflects on the importance of this story about her grandfather.

Reflecting upon a story

> It was such a simple moment. And it seems now, while putting it on paper, that it wasn't the most wonderful and exciting experience. But if you could have felt my Nana's happiness while watching the birds, as a baby feels when he or she first learns to walk, his joy would have spread over you as it did me. . . .

Later in the essay, Seema supports the main point of a paragraph by sharing descriptive details.

Sharing descriptive details

> There were many simple and memorable moments, but my favorite activity to do with Nana, even today, is to listen to him read stories. He would read from a book of fables called Panchatantra. They're Indian tales with a moral for each story. Nana would sit in a wooden chair on the veranda, wearing his somber beige and ginger-brown shirt, or some other dull-colored clothing, complete with his boring, faded, ashen-gray shawl. But these tales are fun. . . .

Bringing Your Writing to a Close

A closing paragraph or idea may not be needed if your writing comes to an effective conclusion after the last main point is made. However, when a closing is needed, it should do one or more of these things:

- Answer any questions left unanswered in the middle paragraphs.
- Summarize the main points.
- Emphasize the special importance of one of the main points.
- Restate the focus or the primary message.
- Say something that will keep readers thinking about the subject.

SAMPLE Closing Paragraph

In this sample closing, Seema Setia restates the focus of her essay. In addition, the final thought extends the author's feelings beyond the context of the essay. Her feelings for her grandfather "will only grow greater in the years to come."

Restating the focus

> I dislike his bleak wardrobe, and sometimes I dislike his perspective about different situations, but I still love him. He is Nana, one of my favorite people. And even though I might someday outgrow listening to his stories or doing small things with him, my love and respect for my Nana will only grow greater in the years to come.

Special Drafting Tips

If you have trouble . . .

- **getting started,** try "telling your story" as if you were surrounded by a group of friends, and go from there.
- **staying with your writing,** time yourself. Write in short bursts (3 minutes) and see what happens.
- **ending your writing,** wait awhile. An effective closing may come to mind later on while you revise your work.

Revising
Your Writing

What if a batter stepped up to the plate knowing he had to get a hit on the very first swing? What a lot of pressure that would be! Fortunately, batters get more than one swing, and more than one time at bat. Sooner or later, they usually connect.

Luckily, as a writer, you do not need to get a hit on the very first try, either. You can make as many changes as necessary until your writing says exactly what you want it to say. Most professional writers will tell you that the process of making changes, or revising, is the most exciting, challenging, and important part of writing.

WHAT'S AHEAD

This chapter will help you revise your early drafts. The next page helps you understand what the revising process is all about. After that, you'll find many different guidelines, tips, and strategies to help you make effective changes in the content of your writing.

- Quick Guide
- Five Keys to Good Revision
- A Link to the Traits
- Revising in Action
- Revising Checklist

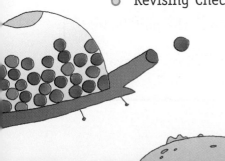

QUICK GUIDE

Revising

PURPOSE: Revising helps you turn your early drafts into more complete pieces of writing. It deals with the big changes you make to improve the ideas in your writing.

Special Note: Don't get sidetracked by surface errors (spelling, punctuation, and grammar) when you're revising. You can deal with them later on in the process.

STARTING POINT: You're ready to revise, once you . . .

■ complete your first draft (or an additional early draft),
■ set it aside for a day or two, and then
■ review your writing for its meaning.

To get started, look first at the big picture. Decide if there is a focus or main idea that holds your writing together. Then look at specific chunks of information. Add, reorder, cut, and rewrite different parts as needed. Each sentence or paragraph should support your focus.

FORM: If you're working on a computer, make your revisions on a printed copy of your draft. Then enter the changes on the computer. Make sure to save the original copy so you have a record of the revisions you've made.

If you're writing with pen and paper, work in the same way. Make your revisions on the first draft. Then recopy your work, incorporating all of your changes. Save the original draft for your records.

THE BIG PICTURE: When revising, pay special attention to the following traits of good writing: ideas, organization, and voice.

Ideas: Check the information in your first draft to make sure that it supports your main idea.

Organization: Make sure that the beginning, the middle, and the ending parts are easy to follow.

Voice: Consider the way you have stated your ideas. Have you used an appropriate tone?

Five Keys to Good Revision

❶ Take a break.

A break can help you see your writing more clearly and completely. So unless you're working on a deadline, step away from your writing for awhile before you make any changes. You will find it much easier to see what works—and what doesn't.

❷ Keep your purpose in mind.

Why are you writing? To tell a story? To give information? To explain how to do something? To get your readers to agree with you? Different kinds of writing require different kinds of language, different voices, and different patterns of organization. When your purpose is set, it is much easier to know what changes are needed in your writing.

❸ Picture your audience.

Who are your readers? People your own age? Adults? Young children? How much do they already know about your subject? What do they need to know? Try to imagine the top questions they may have about your subject. Then ask yourself whether your writing answers these questions. In addition, does your writing grab your readers' attention right away, and does it hold their attention throughout?

❹ Read your work aloud.

Always read what you have written aloud—to yourself or to an audience. Learn to think like a reader: Does this make sense? Is this the right voice for my purpose and audience? Does it begin and end effectively?

Put a star (*) next to parts of your draft that you like. It's good for the spirit because these parts may not need any changes. Then put a check (✔) next to the parts that need work. This is where you will focus your attention.

❺ Share your draft.

Have at least one other person read and react to your writing. A reader's advice can be invaluable. (See pages 75-78 for help.)

A Link to the Traits

Revising for Ideas

When the ideas are unclear in a piece of writing, it's usually for one or both of these reasons:

1. You started writing before you knew enough about the subject.

2. You had no focus in mind, which results in rambling writing.

Have enough information.

Writing without enough information is like trying to drive a car that is just about out of gas. You won't get far. Know your topic inside and out so you can include plenty of details.

General, vague sentence:

Sharks are interesting creatures.

Specific, appealing sentences:

Sharks cannot blink their eyes, and they shed no tears. Their favorite food is crabs; it is said they dislike the taste of humans.

Get focused.

All of your sentences and details should be focused around one main idea. Everything should work together to form a unified whole.

Unfocused writing:

Gus had always wanted to be a police officer. Of course, other careers might have interested him, too, especially since he was a star athlete.

Focused writing:

Gus had always wanted to be a police officer. He wanted people to look at him and think, "There's Gus, the person who keeps our neighborhood safe."

When writing teachers say "Be specific," they often mean "Move in"—add some up close details. So instead of writing "Juan was nice," you might write "Juan was the kind of friend who would share with me his favorite treat—frosted brownies—during lunch."

Revising for Organization

You can have the best information, but if you just throw it together, there's a good chance that your reader won't be able to follow it. Think of yourself as a guide, walking someone through the maze of your writing. An organized guide would help a reader know what to look for, what is most important, where to go next, and so on.

Check your opening.

A good opening hooks your readers and makes them want to read on. Gary Paulsen's book *Foxman* begins, "That first summer I was fifteen   the summer when the judge sent me to my uncle Harold's farm up in northern Minnesota on the edge of the woods that went north forever." Right away we have a question: *Why* was he sent to his uncle's farm? (See page 63 for ideas for openings.)

Follow a pattern.

Author Stephen Kramer organizes his book *Avalanche* around a series of questions. Each question becomes a section of his book: *Where do avalanches happen? What kinds of avalanches are there? What causes them? What should you do if you are caught in an avalanche?* Question-answer, question-answer. It's a simple pattern, but it works. (See page 60 for other ideas.)

Get rid of filler.

Filler is any information you do not need. It bogs down your writing. Cut all information that does not . . .

- develop your focus,
- make your main points clearer,
- support your argument, or
- advance the action of your story.

Check your ending.

At the end of his biography, *Boy,* Roald Dahl invites readers to look ahead to his next story: "But all that is another story . . . and if all goes well, I may have a shot at telling it one of these days." You, too, should leave your reader with something to think about—a scene, a comment, a question, a story left untold. (See page 66 for more ideas.)

Revising for Voice

Remember that voice, the special way you state your ideas, is your personal imprint on your stories, essays, and reports.

Match voice to purpose.

A conversational, "from-the-heart" sort of voice may be just right for a story. E. B. White puts this kind of voice into his book *Charlotte's Web.* Charlotte, a spider, talks to Wilbur in words that make us feel as if we know her: "I am not entirely happy about my diet of flies and bugs, but it's the way I'm made." On the other hand, a professional, "right-to-the-point" sort of voice would better carry the message in a letter of complaint.

Enjoy your topic.

Writer Steven Caney, author of *The Invention Book,* has a good time explaining to readers that the first athletic "shoes" were nothing more than a kind of gum that oozed from the bark of trees, smeared on bare feet. His fascination with this fact is contagious. Make sure that your writing oozes with your own energy and fascination.

Write to your best listener.

Writing to one special person, such as a trusted friend, brings out your voice as nothing else can. Write with so much enthusiasm that it will be *impossible* for this person to put your paper down.

Take a risk.

Voice is partly about letting go—taking a risk. To ensure that your writing has voice . . .

- say what you really think,
- let your own feelings show in your writing,
- write as if you were having a conversation, and
- keep your enthusiasm for your topic strong.

Once you've improved the ideas, organization, and voice, you should have a strong paper that is clear, easy to follow, and interesting to read. (See the chapter "Editing and Proofreading" for additional ways to improve your writing.)

Revising in Action

Note the changes made in this sample to improve the quality of the ideas, organization, and voice. (See pages 14-15 for another example.)

An interesting detail is added.

A paragraph is reordered.

More personal feeling (voice) is added.

An unnecessary detail is cut.

Ever since movies like <u>Jaws</u>, sharks have gotten a bad reputation. There are more than 300 kinds of sharks from the 19-inch cookie-cutter shark to the 50-foot whale shark. But only about 25 kinds of sharks have ever attacked people. Of the 100 attacks reported each year, few of them are ever fatal.

Sharks are very beneficial to people. Sharks clean the seas of garbage and feed on sick and weak fish. They are also harvested for their luxurious hides for clothing and their flesh for eating.

The great white shark, as seen in <u>Jaws</u>, has attacked people, but then the great white shark will attack just about anything. However, sharks are mostly scavengers and eat dead fish and garbage. Cans, jars, hats, tires, and even license plates have been found in the stomachs of great white sharks. Whatever gets dumped off a boat may end up inside of one of these sharks.

~~Their favorite food is really crab.~~

[Revising Checklist]

Use this checklist as a guide when you revise a first draft. *Remember:* Wait until all of your ideas are clear and complete before you spend time trying to edit your writing.

✔ **Does my writing focus on an interesting part of my subject or on a certain feeling I have about it?** (See page 59.)

✔ **Does the information in my writing follow a clear method of organization?** (See page 60.)

✔ **Do I need to add any information?**

_____ Do I need to add details to make my beginning clearer or more interesting?

_____ Do I need to add ideas to support my subject?

_____ Do I need to make my closing more effective?

✔ **Do I need to cut any information?**

_____ Do any of my details not belong?

_____ Do I repeat myself in any parts?

_____ Do I say too much about a certain idea?

✔ **Do I need to rewrite any parts?**

_____ Do some ideas sound unclear?

_____ Do I need to reword any explanations?

✔ **Do I need to reorder any parts?**

_____ Do any ideas or details seem out of place?

_____ Does the most important point come near the beginning or near the end? (Either is a good choice.)

Group Advising

Sharing a piece of writing with your peers can be a nerve-racking experience. Even professional writers like Mem Fox sometimes get nervous when reading their own work aloud to others:

"In those sessions in which each of us reads our writing to the class, we shake with nerves, knowing that our naked talent is about to be exposed for all to hear."

The truth is, though, writers need an audience. They need someone to respond to their writing, letting them know what makes sense, what expresses genuine thoughts and feelings, and what is unclear. This chapter is all about sharing your writing and making the best possible use of the responses you get from your fellow writers.

WHAT'S AHEAD

During group advising, you play one of two roles. Sometimes you are the writer-reader, the person sharing his or her writing. At other times you are the listener-responder, the person reacting to someone else's work. On the pages that follow, you will find useful tips for performing each of these roles, as well as suggestions for making helpful responses.

- Group Advising Guidelines
- Making Helpful Responses
- Student Response Sheet

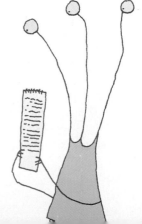

Group Advising Guidelines

Some of you might belong to writing groups, so you already know the value of writers sharing their work. If you don't, start by working in small teams of two or three classmates. The following guidelines will help you get started.

Role of the Writer-Reader

1. Come prepared with a meaningful piece of writing. (Make a copy for each group member if this is part of normal group procedure.)
2. Introduce your writing. But don't say too much.
3. Read your copy out loud.
4. Listen carefully and take brief notes as the group reacts to your writing. Answer all of their questions. Don't be defensive about your writing, since this will stop some members from commenting honestly about your work.
5. If you have some special concerns or problems, share these with your fellow writers.

Role of the Listener-Responder

1. Listen carefully as the writer reads. Take notes if you need to. Some groups just listen and then do a freewriting after the reading. Other groups use a response sheet as a guide when they react to a piece of writing. (See the response sheet on page 78.)
2. Don't be afraid to share your feelings about a piece of writing.
3. Keep your comments positive and constructive. (See page 77.)
4. Ask questions of the author: "Why? How? What do you mean when you say . . . ?" Also answer questions the author might have for you.
5. Listen to others' comments and add to them.

Seek the help of your writing group throughout the writing process. It is especially helpful to get advice early, after a first or second draft.

Making Helpful Responses

Make Focused Comments

The most useful responses are focused and specific. They give a writer information he or she can use to improve the writing. Here are some examples:

- Your opening makes me want to know more about your science teacher.
- It isn't quite clear to me why the tigers are endangered.
- That phrase "snaking into the room" stuck in my mind. I could really picture that.
- I love the way you kept the ending a total surprise.

Ask Good Questions

The best questions are those that cannot be answered with a simple *yes* or *no*. Instead, they really get a writer thinking and talking about his or her work.

- I heard the word "special" a lot. What was it that actually made your trip so special?
- What is the strongest point you want to make in this paper?
- If you had to describe your main character in three words, what would they be?

A feel-good comment like "Great paper!" may make a writer feel good, but it doesn't give any clear direction for revision. Be sure that you give the writer information she or he can use.

Respond Tactfully

How do you get ideas across without hurting someone's feelings?

- Leave writing decisions to the writer. Your job is to share your responses. It is up to the writer to decide what to do with that information.
- Begin your comments with "I," not "You" or "Your paper." Comments that begin with "You" or "Your paper" often sound like criticisms, even when they are not meant that way.

Student Response Sheet

A response sheet, such as the one below, can be used to make comments about a piece of writing in progress.

Response Sheet

I noticed . . .

I wondered . . .

Strong words, phrases, images in the writing:

Questions to be answered:

Editing and Proofreading

You're heading out the door for a special occasion. You stop to take one last look in the mirror. Oops! Your shirt is hanging out on one side, or your hair is sticking up in back. These are simple things to fix; but suppose you hadn't taken a final look? You might not have noticed these little details, but other people certainly would have.

When you edit and proofread, you get your revised writing ready for publishing. More specifically, when you edit, you make sure your words and sentences are clear and correct. When you proofread, you check the final copy of your writing for errors. Once you complete this step in the process, your writing should sound, and look, its best.

WHAT'S AHEAD

This chapter provides tips and guidelines that will help you edit your writing, including suggestions for checking word choice and sentence smoothness. Also included is an editing and proofreading checklist.

- Quick Guide
- Checking for Sentence Smoothness
- Checking for Word Choice
- Editing and Proofreading Checklist

QUICK GUIDE

Editing and Proofreading

PURPOSE: Editing and proofreading helps turn your revised writing into a clear, stylistic, and accurate copy. It deals with the line-by-line changes you make to improve the smoothness, readability, and accuracy of your work.

STARTING POINT: You're ready to edit and proofread, once you . . .

■ make the major changes in the content of your writing,

■ recopy your revised writing, and

■ set your work aside for a day or two (if time permits).

To get started, focus on the style of your writing, checking for the smoothness and clarity of each sentence and the effectiveness of the word choice. Next, turn your attention to the accuracy of your writing, focusing on one type of error at a time.

FORM: If you're working on a computer, do your editing on a printed copy of your revised writing. Then enter the changes on the computer. Save the edited copy so you have a record of the changes you've made.

If you're working with pen and paper, do your editing on a fresh copy of your revised writing. Then recopy your work again, and save the edited copy for your records.

THE BIG PICTURE: When editing and proofreading, pay special attention to the following three traits of effective writing: smoothness, word choice, and correct, accurate copy.

Sentence Smoothness: Make sure that your sentences lead readers smoothly from one point to the next.

Word Choice: Change any troublesome or overused words to improve the overall quality of your writing.

Correct, Accurate Copy: Carefully check your writing for grammar, spelling, and punctuation errors.

Checking for Sentence Smoothness

When you edit your writing for sentence fluency, check for the following types of problems:

- Too many short, choppy sentences
- Fragments, run-ons, or rambling sentences
- Too many sentences with the same beginning words
- Too many sentences of the same length

Evaluating Your Sentence Editing

You should be able to say these things about your writing after checking your sentences for style and correctness:

- Every sentence in my paper is important.
- Someone else could read my work aloud and like the sound of it.
- I've combined short, choppy sentences into longer ones.
- I use connecting words and phrases—*later, on the other hand,* etc.—to show how ideas relate to one another.
- Most of my sentences begin in different ways.
- I use a variety of sentence lengths. (See below.)

Testing Your Sentences

Use the following strategy to test your sentences for variety, length, and verb choice.

1. In one column on a piece of paper, list the opening words in each of your sentences. (Then decide if you need to vary some of your sentence beginnings.)

2. In another column, identify the number of words in each sentence. (Then decide if you need to change the length of some of your sentences.)

3. In a third column, list the verbs in each sentence. (Then decide if you need to replace any overused verbs—*is, are, see, look,* etc.—with more vivid ones.)

Checking for Word Choice

When you check for word choice, watch out for problems like these: (Also see pages 135-136 for help.)

- Redundancy—using several words that say the same thing (*add additional* lines)

- Repetition—using the same words over and over

- Words used incorrectly (*their* instead of *they're* or *there*)

- Too many vague words such as *nice, special,* or *neat*

- Too many verbs like *is, are, was,* and *were* instead of strong, lively verbs

- Too many adjectives and adverbs (It was a *sunny, warm, balmy, pleasant* day with the *hot, blazing* sun shining *glowingly* on the *dry, dusty, brown* pavement.)

- Technical words left unexplained

 Read your copy out loud when you check for word choice. Also check your writing once by starting right in the middle of your text. Otherwise, you might miss some of the errors in the second half of your paper.

Evaluating Your Editing for Word Choice

After checking for word choice, you should be able to say these things about your writing:

- I know the meaning of every word in my paper.

- I define any technical terms clearly for my reader.

- For the most part, I use vivid verbs: *lunge, tweak, cringe, squeeze, pout, peek,* and so on.

- I double-checked for repetition and substituted synonyms for key words whenever possible.

- I use specific words and phrases instead of general modifiers (*nice, happy*).

- I include some colorful adjectives and adverbs without sounding wordy or flowery.

Editing and Proofreading Checklist

✔ Sentence Structure

_____ Did I write clear and complete sentences?

_____ Did I add style to my sentences? (See pages 130-131.)

✔ Word Choice and Usage

_____ Did I use specific nouns and verbs and colorful adjectives? (See pages 135-136.)

_____ Did I use the correct word (*to, too,* or *two*)? (See pages 419-433.)

✔ Punctuation

_____ Does each sentence have end punctuation?

_____ Did I use commas and apostrophes correctly?

_____ Did I punctuate dialogue correctly?

✔ Capitalization

_____ Did I start all of my sentences with capital letters?

_____ Did I capitalize the names of people and places?

✔ Grammar

_____ Did I use the correct form of verbs? (See pages 446-450.)

_____ Do all the subjects and verbs agree in number? (See pages 88-89.)

✔ Spelling

_____ Did I check for spelling errors (including ones the spell checker could have missed)? (See pages 411-418.)

Basic Elements of Writing

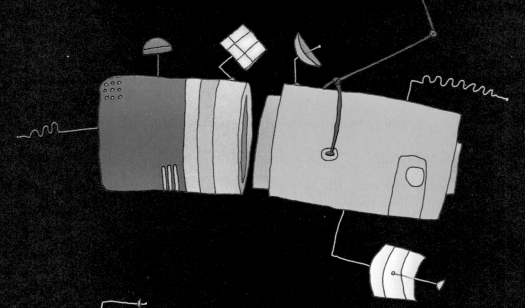

Composing Sentences

The *physical* part of writing has undergone many changes throughout the ages. Among other things, writers have used quill pens, ballpoint pens, pencil stubs, manual typewriters, electric typewriters, and personal computers. The *mental* part of writing, however, has not changed. Writers today, as in the past, still express their thoughts in sentences. As one writer has said, "Writers think sentences."

To become a good writer, you need to learn as much as you can about sentences. You need to read plenty of other writers' sentences, you need to practice writing your own, and you need to acquire a working knowledge of sentence basics.

WHAT'S AHEAD

This chapter covers all of the common sentence errors—from sentence fragments to misplaced modifiers. Turn here for help whenever you have questions about the correctness or clarity of the sentences in your writing. (Also see pages 434-438 for more information.)

- ○ Write Complete Sentences
- ○ Write Agreeable Sentences
- ○ Write Clear, Concise Sentences
- ○ Checklist for Sentence Clarity

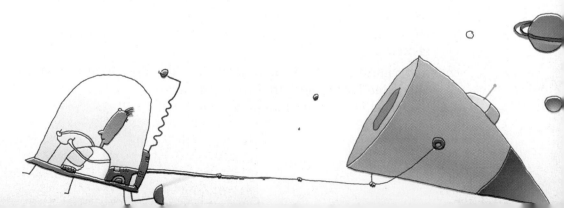

Write Complete Sentences

Use only complete sentences in your writing. A complete sentence contains a subject and verb and expresses a complete thought. Sentence fragments, comma splices, and run-on sentences are errors that you should avoid. Avoid rambling sentences, too.

SENTENCE FRAGMENT

A *sentence fragment* may look and sound like a sentence, but it isn't. Instead, it is a group of words that is missing either a subject or a verb or doesn't express a complete thought.

- *Sentence fragment:* **Thinks bugs are fascinating.**
  (The subject is missing.)

  Complete sentence: **My little sister thinks bugs are fascinating.**
  (A subject has been added.)

- *Sentence fragment:* **Not my mom's favorite things.**
  (The subject and verb are missing.)

  Complete sentence: **However, they are not my mom's favorite things.**
  (A subject and a verb have been added.)

- *Sentence fragment:* **Jars of live bugs, dead bugs, squirming and still.**
  (The thought is incomplete.)

  Complete sentence: **Jars of live bugs, dead bugs, squirming and still, often show up on our kitchen table.**
  (The sentence is now a complete thought.)

COMMA SPLICE

A *comma splice* is an error made when you connect two simple sentences with a comma instead of a semicolon or end punctuation.

- *Comma splice:* **Reva thought about her favorite school classes, she listed lunch, gym, free time, and art.**
  (A comma is used incorrectly to connect, or splice, the two sentences.)

  Corrected sentences: **Reva thought about her favorite school classes. She listed lunch, gym, free time, and art.**
  (A period is used in place of the comma.)

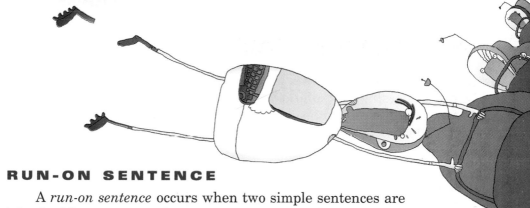

RUN-ON SENTENCE

A *run-on sentence* occurs when two simple sentences are joined without punctuation or a connecting word.

- *Run-on sentence:* **I thought the ride would never end my eyes were crossed and my fingers were numb.** (Punctuation is needed.)

  Corrected sentences: **I thought the ride would never end. My eyes were crossed, and my fingers were numb.** (Punctuation has been added.)

RAMBLING SENTENCE

A *rambling sentence* occurs when you connect too many ideas with the word *and.*

- *Rambling sentence:* **We learned that in 1914, two years after the *Titanic* sank, the International Ice Patrol was formed and their job was to report icebergs and the United States gave this vital job to the U.S. Coast Guard.** (Too many *and*'s are used.)

  Corrected sentences: **We learned that in 1914, two years after the *Titanic* sank, the International Ice Patrol was formed. Their job was to report icebergs. The United States gave this vital job to the U.S. Coast Guard.** (Unnecessary *and*'s are omitted and three sentences are formed.)

WORDY SENTENCE

A *wordy sentence* occurs when you repeat words (or their synonyms) unnecessarily.

- *Wordy sentence:* **When Ray got up out of bed at 7 a.m. in the morning, he felt like he had the flu and was not feeling well, so he decided to go back to bed to take a rest.**

  Corrected sentence: **When Ray got up at 7 a.m., he felt like he had the flu so he decided to go back to bed.**

Write Agreeable Sentences

The subjects and verbs in your sentences must agree in *number*. If you use a singular subject, use a singular verb. (John *likes* pizza.) If you use a plural subject, use a plural verb. (We *like* pizza.) Be especially careful of agreement mistakes in the following types of sentences.

COMPOUND SUBJECTS

Compound subjects connected by *and* need a plural verb.

Alicia and Todd love amusement parks.

In sentences with compound subjects connected by *or* or *nor,* the verb must agree with the subject that is nearer the verb.

Neither Todd nor his friend likes the Ferris wheel.
(Use a singular verb because the subject nearer the verb—*friend*—is singular.)

Neither Alicia nor her friends ride the bumper cars.
(Use a plural verb because the subject nearer the verb—*friends*—is plural.)

UNUSUAL WORD ORDER

When the subject is separated from the verb by words or phrases, you must check carefully to see that the subject agrees with the verb.

Damien, as well as Brian and Paco, works on the truck farm.
(*Damien*, not *Brian* and *Paco,* is the subject, so the singular verb *works* is used to agree with the subject.)

When the subject comes after the verb in a sentence, you must check carefully to see that the "true" subject agrees with the verb.

Out in that field are the two new tractors that my uncle bought.
(The plural subject *tractors* agrees with the plural verb *are.*)

Behind those machine sheds is the garage.
(The singular subject *garage* agrees with the singular verb *is.*)

Has Lea seen the new kittens yet?
(The singular subject *Lea* agrees with the singular helping verb *has.*)

INDEFINITE PRONOUNS

In sentences with a singular indefinite pronoun as the subject, use a singular verb. (Use a singular verb with these indefinite pronouns: *each, either, neither, one, everyone, everybody, everything, someone, somebody, anybody, anything, nobody,* and *another.*)

Each of the kittens has white paws.

Some indefinite pronouns (*all, any, most, none, some*) can be either singular or plural.

Most of my uncle's fields are planted by the end of May.
> (Use a plural verb when the noun in the prepositional phrase that follows the indefinite pronoun is plural. In the example sentence, the noun *fields* is plural.)

Most of my uncle's field is under water.
> (Use a singular verb if the noun in the prepositional phrase is singular. In the example sentence, the noun *field* is singular.)

COLLECTIVE NOUNS

When a collective noun is the subject of a sentence, it can be either singular or plural. (A collective noun names a group or unit: *faculty, committee, team, congress, species, crowd, army, pair.*)

The committee is developing a stricter dress code.
> (The collective noun *committee* is singular because it refers to the committee as one group. As a result, the singular verb *is* is required.)

The night crew are asked to take separate lunch breaks.
> (The collective noun *crew* is plural because it refers to the crew as individuals. As a result, the plural helping verb *are* is required.)

 There is additional information on indefinite pronouns, compound subjects, collective nouns, and agreement of subjects and verbs in the "Proofreader's Guide." See pages 386-457 or consult the index.

Write Clear, Concise Sentences

Use sentences that are clear and to the point (concise). Confusing or wordy sentences will make your writing assignments difficult to read. Refer to the guidelines that follow.

PROBLEMS WITH PRONOUNS

Avoid sentences in which a pronoun does not agree with its *antecedent*. An antecedent is the word the pronoun refers to.

- *Agreement problem:* **Everyone on the team must perform at their peak.**
- *Corrected sentence:* **Everyone on the team must perform at his or her peak.**
  (A pronoun must agree in number—singular or plural—with its antecedent. *Everyone* is singular, as are *his or her*.)

Avoid sentences with a confusing pronoun reference.

- *Confusing pronoun reference:* **When he opened the freezer to take out the fish, it made a startling hissing sound.**
- *Corrected sentence:* **The freezer made a startling hissing sound when he opened it to take out the fish.**
  (It is unclear in the first sentence which noun—*freezer* or *fish*—the pronoun *it* refers to. Rewording has clarified this.)

Avoid sentences that include a pronoun shift.

- *Pronoun shift:* **If parents need childcare services during the assembly, you should contact the school office.**
- *Corrected sentence:* **If parents need childcare services during the assembly, they should contact the school office.**
  (Since *parents* is a third-person subject, *they*—a third-person pronoun—correctly replaces the second-person pronoun *you*. See 442.4-442.5 for more about second- and third-person pronouns.)

Avoid sentences in which a pronoun is used immediately after the subject—the result is usually a double subject.

- *Double subject:* **Best friends they are always there for you.**
- *Corrected sentence:* **Best friends are always there for you.**

MISPLACED MODIFIERS

Make sure that your modifiers, especially the descriptive phrases you use, are located as close as possible to the words they modify. Otherwise the sentence can become very confusing.

■ *Misplaced phrase:* **After putting on the virtual-reality headgear, a giant anaconda dropped in front of my face and scared me silly!** (*After . . . headgear* appears to modify *a giant anaconda.*)

Corrected sentence: **After putting on the virtual-reality headgear, I was scared silly by a giant anaconda that dropped in front of my face!** (Now the phrase *after . . . headgear* correctly modifies *I.*)

NONSTANDARD LANGUAGE

Avoid sentences that include a double negative.

■ *Double negative:* **Never let no one convince you that you're small.**

Corrected sentence: **Never let anyone convince you that you're small.** (*No* was changed to *any* because the word *never* is a negative word. Do not include two negative words in the same phrase unless you understand how these words change its meaning.)

Do not use *hardly, barely,* or *scarcely* with a negative word; the result is a double negative.

> **I don't hardly know what to do.**
> **I don't know what to do.**

■ *Incorrect substitution:* **I would of enjoyed biology class more without the dissecting part.**

Corrected sentence: **I would have enjoyed biology class more without the dissecting part.** (Avoid sentences that incorrectly use *of* for *have.*)

Checklist for Sentence Clarity

✔ **Are my sentences complete?**

_____ Are there any **fragments** (incomplete thoughts) to correct?

_____ Are there any **comma splices, run-ons,** or **rambling sentences** to change?

✔ **Do my subjects and verbs agree in number (singular or plural)?**

_____ Are there any **compound subjects** connected with _and, or,_ or _nor?_

_____ Are **indefinite pronouns** (_each, all,_ etc.) or **collective nouns** (_team, crowd,_ etc.) used as subjects?

_____ Is there any **unusual word order?**

✔ **Are my sentences clear and concise?**

_____ Are there **problems** with pronoun-antecedent agreement? Confusing pronoun reference? Or pronoun shift?

_____ Are there any **misplaced modifiers?**

_____ Are there any examples of **nonstandard language?**

✔ **In a longer piece, do my sentences fit these descriptions?**

_____ My sentences begin in different ways.

_____ My sentences are smooth reading.

_____ My sentences vary in length.

_____ My sentences sound natural, almost as if I were talking.

_____ Items in my sentences are parallel (worded similarly), as in "Commit yourselves _to reading, to writing, to learning._"

Combining Sentences

Sentence combining is the act of making one smoother, more detailed sentence out of two or more short, choppy sentences. For instance, take a look at the following sentences:

In the movie, the giant reptile wagged its tail.
The tail knocked over the skyscraper.
The tail was thick and scaly.
The reptile's name was Godzilla.

Sound a little choppy? Here are two ways to combine these shorter sentences into one.

In the movie, the giant reptile named Godzilla wagged its thick, scaly tail and knocked over the skyscraper!

In the movie, the giant reptile named Godzilla knocked over the skyscraper by wagging its thick, scaly tail!

WHAT'S AHEAD

The guidelines in this chapter will show you how to combine choppy sentences into smooth-reading sentences, one of the traits of good writing. Learning this skill will help you write with more style, which in turn will make your essays and reports more enjoyable to read.

- Combining with Key Words
- Combining with Phrases
- Combining with Longer Sentences

Combining with Key Words

USE A KEY WORD

Ideas from shorter sentences can be combined by moving *a key word* from one sentence to the other sentence.

- *Shorter sentences:* **The boy waited in line. The boy was little.**
  Combined sentence using an adjective: **The little boy waited in line.**

- *Shorter sentences:* **The figure skaters twirled over the frozen pond. They were moving fast.**
  Combined sentence using a compound adjective: **The fast-moving figure skaters twirled over the frozen pond.**

- *Shorter sentences:* **A child sped down the slope on an inner tube. The child was squealing.**
  Combined sentence using a participle: **A squealing child sped down the slope on an inner tube.**

- *Shorter sentences:* **Our group is going skiing on Wildcat Mountain. We are going soon.**
  Combined sentence using an adverb: **Our group is going skiing on Wildcat Mountain soon.**

USE A SERIES OF WORDS OR PHRASES

Ideas from shorter sentences can be combined into one sentence using *a series* of words or phrases.

- *Shorter sentences:* **The room is quiet. The room is dark. It is cool.**
  Combined sentence: **The room is quiet, dark, and cool.** (A series of three words was used to combine the three sentences into one.)

All of the words or phrases you use in a series should be *parallel*—stated in the same way. (All should be nouns or *ing* words or the same in some other way.) Otherwise, your sentences will sound awkward and unbalanced.

- *Awkward series:* **Hawks help farmers by preying on mice, rats, and by killing and eating pocket gophers.**
  Corrected sentence: **Hawks help farmers by preying on mice, rats, and pocket gophers.** (The three items are now parallel.)

Combining with Phrases

USE PHRASES

Ideas from shorter sentences can be combined into one sentence using *prepositional, appositive, infinitive,* and *participial phrases.*

- *Shorter sentences:* **Dolly is a sheep that was cloned. She was cloned from a six-year-old ewe.**

  Combined sentence using a prepositional phrase: **Dolly is a sheep that was cloned from a six-year-old ewe.**

- *Shorter sentences:* **Recently, Dolly gave birth to a lamb. The lamb is a little female named Bonnie.**

  Combined sentence using an appositive phrase: **Recently, Dolly gave birth to a lamb, a little female named Bonnie.**

- *Shorter sentences:* **The red wolves yipped, barked, and howled. They were communicating with the distant pack.**

  Combined sentence using an infinitive phrase: **The red wolves yipped, barked, and howled to communicate with the distant pack.**

- *Shorter sentences:* **Snaggle Tooth looked determined to escape. He circled the inside perimeter of the enclosure.**

  Combined sentence using a participial phrase: **Snaggle Tooth, circling the inside perimeter of the enclosure, looked determined to escape.**

USE COMPOUND SUBJECTS AND VERBS

Ideas from shorter sentences can be combined using compound subjects and compound verbs (predicates). A compound subject includes two or more subjects in one sentence. A compound verb includes two or more verbs in one sentence.

- *Shorter sentences:* **Ron loves playing soccer. Mark loves playing soccer.**

  Combined sentence using a compound subject: **Ron and Mark love playing soccer.**

- *Shorter sentences:* **Mrs. Dziekan made apple pies. She sold them at the PTA bake sale.**

  Combined sentence using a compound verb: **Mrs. Dziekan made apple pies and sold them at the PTA bake sale.**

Combining with Longer Sentences

USE COMPOUND SENTENCES

Ideas from shorter sentences can be combined into a compound sentence. A compound sentence is made up of two simple sentences that are equal in importance. The coordinating conjunctions *and, but, or, nor, for, yet,* and *so* are used to connect the two simple sentences. Place a comma before the conjunction in a compound sentence.

- *Shorter sentences:* **The mother grizzly bear and her cub look sweet. Going any closer to them would be dangerous.**

  Combined into a compound sentence: **The mother grizzly bear and her cub look sweet, but going any closer to them would be dangerous.**

USE COMPLEX SENTENCES

Ideas from shorter sentences can be combined into a complex sentence. A complex sentence is made up of two clauses that are not equal in importance. The more important idea should be included in an independent clause and can stand alone as a single sentence. The less important idea should be included in a dependent clause and cannot stand alone.

The two clauses in a complex sentence can be connected with subordinate conjunctions. *After, although, as, because, before, if, since, when, where, while, until,* and *unless* are common subordinate conjunctions. The two clauses can also be connected with the relative pronouns *who, whose, which,* and *that.*

- *Shorter sentences:* **Mrs. Lopez returned to work. School lunches taste good again.**

  Combined into a complex sentence: **Because Mrs. Lopez returned to work, school lunches taste good again.**

  (A complex sentence was formed by using the subordinate conjunction *because.*)

- *Shorter sentences:* **Our puppy took one sniff and lunged at the platter of hot dogs. He loves people food.**

  Combined into a complex sentence: **Our puppy, who loves people food, took one sniff and lunged at the platter of hot dogs.**

  (A complex sentence was formed by using the relative pronoun *who.*)

Building Paragraphs

For many student writers, the key to writing well is being able to select a good subject and then stick to it until it's been supported with plenty of details. This is especially true of writing that is done for assignments. One thing that can help you gain control of your writing is learning to write good paragraphs.

A paragraph focuses on one specific topic that can be developed in the form of a description, a narrative (story), an explanation, or an opinion. The form will depend upon your subject and the kinds of details you are able to gather and use in your paragraph. Whatever form it takes, your paragraph must contain enough information— enough supporting details—to give readers a clear and interesting picture of the topic.

WHAT'S AHEAD

This chapter will help you with all of your paragraph writing. It covers everything from the different types of paragraphs to the various transitions, or linking words, that you can use to connect your ideas.

- ○ The Parts of a Paragraph
- ○ Types of Paragraphs
- ○ Writing Guidelines
- ○ Details in Paragraphs
- ○ Transitions or Linking Words

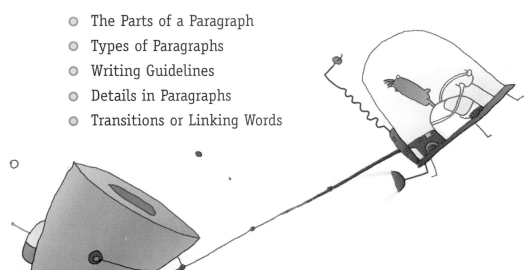

The Parts of a Paragraph

Most paragraphs begin with a **topic sentence,** identifying the subject of the writing. The sentences in the **body** of the paragraph develop or explain the subject, while the **closing sentence** brings the paragraph to a logical stopping point.

 Note: The first line in a paragraph is indented.

Adventure Sports

Topic Sentence

Many outdoor enthusiasts are looking for more adventure in their sports. Why else would a sane person jump out of an airplane, do some acrobatic tricks on a skyboard, and then parachute to the ground? Other airborne adventure sports include skydiving and hang gliding. By water, people navigate the same rivers and shoot the same rapids that early

Body

Native Americans, fur traders, and explorers did. They travel by canoe, kayak, or raft. On land, adventurers backpack and camp in the wilderness, in areas where they might meet bear, moose, and mountain lions. After climbing mountains, they ski, snowboard, or even bike down to the bottom. Today, there seems to be an adventure sport for

Closing Sentence

just about everyone, with more being invented all the time.

A Closer Look at the Parts

The Topic Sentence

The **topic sentence** tells your reader what the paragraph is about. It also helps you keep your writing under control. Here is a formula for writing good topic sentences:

Formula:

An interesting subject
+ your specific feeling about it

= a good topic sentence.

Topic sentence. **Many outdoor enthusiasts** *(interesting subject)* **are looking for more adventure in their sports.** *(specific feeling)*

Note: A sentence like *Many outdoor enthusiasts are out there* would not make a good topic sentence. It contains an interesting subject (**outdoor enthusiasts**), but it does not express a specific feeling about it.

The Body

The **body** is the main part of the paragraph. This is where you give readers all of the information they need to understand the subject. The sentences in the body should contain details that make the subject both interesting and clear.

Organize your sentences in the best order. There are three main ways to do this: *chronological (time) order, order of location,* and *order of importance.* (See page 60.)

The Closing Sentence

The **closing** or **clincher sentence** comes after all the details have been included in the body of the paragraph. This sentence should try to do two things: remind readers of the subject and keep them thinking about it.

Closing Sentence: **Today, there seems to be an adventure sport for just about everyone, with more being invented all the time.**

Types of Paragraphs

You can write four types of paragraphs: *descriptive, narrative, expository,* and *persuasive.* Each one requires a different kind of thinking and planning.

SAMPLE Descriptive Paragraph

In a **descriptive paragraph**, you give a clear, detailed picture of one person, place, thing, or event.

Rainbow Rock

Topic Sentence

Rainbow Rock, a huge man-made wall, helps people learn rock-climbing techniques. Rainbow Rock rises 30 feet above the ground, and it is filled with purple, green, and red markings, noting different climbing paths. Each path contains a variety of footholds, outcroppings, and overhangs.

Body

The purple path offers a cool climbing experience that just about anybody can do. The green path is a little more advanced and ends with a very tricky overhang right at the top. The challenging red path contains tiny toeholds that are only about one inch in diameter. It almost takes a mountain goat to maneuver on this one. If someone missteps and falls, a harness catches the climber, leaving him or her swinging in midair. Rainbow Rock is just an

Closing Sentence

artificial training ground, but it does test a rock climber's balance, strength, and courage.

SAMPLE Narrative Paragraph

In a **narrative paragraph,** you "tell the story" of a memorable event or an important experience. The details in this paragraph should answer the 5 W's (*who? what? when? where?* and *why?*) about the event or experience.

Wilderness Camping

Topic Sentence

Camping in the wilderness can be a real adventure, especially if you have a close encounter with a bear. One night while camping, my mom, dad, and younger sister were sound asleep in the tent, but I was wide-awake. Suddenly I heard these slurping, snorting noises coming from our campsite. I crept to the door and peered out cautiously. By the light of the moon, I saw a big brown bear munching on a bag of our

Body

marshmallows. I wanted to shout a warning, but I was so scared that I couldn't get out one sound. As I crawled across the tent to wake my dad, I must have bumped my sister. She sat up and screamed. Her scream startled me, and I yelled, "It's a bear!" Our shouts must have scared the bear because when we opened the tent, there was no bear and no marshmallows. My family said I was

Closing Sentence

dreaming, but they can't explain how that bag of marshmallows disappeared.

SAMPLE Expository Paragraph

In an **expository paragraph,** you give information. You can explain a subject, give directions, or show how to do something.

Snowboarding

Topic Sentence
Snowboarding is one of the most popular and exciting winter sports in America. While people have been skiing and ice-skating for centuries, snowboarding has only been around for about 30 years. In 1992, there were 1.2 million snowboarders. Now, there are almost four million "shredders" hitting the slopes every year. Snowboarding has become so popular it is now an Olympic sport.

Body
Because so many kids saw snowboarding on TV during the Olympics, they became excited about it and took it up. Almost half of all snowboarders are between the ages of 7 and 17. Many adult skiers have started snowboarding, too. Most snowboarders like it because they can control the board with just their feet instead of using two skis and two poles. This gives them more freedom and maneuverability. They can also do more tricks when snowboarding than they could ever do on skis.

Closing Sentence
Snowboarding has taken the winter sports scene by storm, and may soon surpass skiing in popularity.

SAMPLE Persuasive Paragraph

In a **persuasive paragraph,** you give your opinion (or strong feeling) about a subject. You also try to convince readers that this opinion is worthy of their consideration.

High Ropes Course

Topic Sentence   The high ropes course is waiting to help you and your friends build confidence and group cooperation. It's also lots of fun. Many courses, indoor and outdoor, are available in camps, clubs, and schools across America. You may think that climbing the high ropes is dangerous, but it isn't. Safety ropes and harnesses are carefully managed by course experts and members of your group to give you lots of support. When **Body** you attempt to cross a suspended log or move by rope across an expanse that seems scary, you'll receive encouragement from your teammates. You'll also feel great when you can encourage someone else to succeed. Even if you cannot complete the course, you'll feel supported and know the accomplishment of having faced the challenge. Why not get a group **Closing Sentence** together this summer and grow into a team on a high ropes course?

Writing Guidelines

Before you begin your writing, make sure you understand all of the requirements for the assignment. Then follow the steps listed below.

Prewriting ----[Choosing a Subject]

Your teacher may give you a general subject area to write about. You will then have to select a specific subject for the assignment. (If you have trouble finding a suitable topic, see pages 48-49.)

[Gathering Details]

- Collect ideas and details about your subject.
- Write a topic sentence that states what your paragraph is going to be about. (See page 99 for help.)
- Plan the rest of your paragraph. Which details will you include? (See page 59.) How will you organize them? (See page 60.)

Writing ----[Writing the First Draft]

- Start your paragraph with the topic sentence. Make sure this statement accurately reflects your feelings about the subject.
- Follow with sentences that support your topic. Use your planning as a general guide.
- Close with a sentence that reminds readers about the topic.

Revising ----[Improving Your Writing]

- Add information if you need to say more about your topic.
- Rewrite sentences that are not easy to understand.

Editing ----[Checking for Style and Accuracy]

- Check the revised version of your writing for capitalization, punctuation, and spelling errors.
- Write a neat final copy of your paragraph to share.

Details in Paragraphs

Details are an important part of any paragraph. They are the facts and examples that support or prove your topic sentence. Some of the information you use may be *personal* details—things you know or remember from your own experience. However, you will often go to other sources—books, magazines, or experts—for the facts you need.

Details from Other Sources

Here are some tips for collecting details from other sources:

1. **Ask someone you know.** Parents, neighbors, and teachers may know a lot about your topic.

2. **Talk to an expert.** Ask an expert about your subject by making a phone call, sending a letter, or visiting in person.

3. **Write or call for information.** If you think a museum, a business, or a government office has information you need, send for it. You may also be able to visit these places and gather facts for yourself.

4. **Gather details** from books, magazines, the Internet, and so on.

Personal Details

DETAILS FROM YOUR SENSES

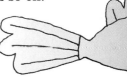

These details are things that you see, hear, smell, taste, and touch. (Sensory details are especially important in descriptive paragraphs.)

Rainbow Rock rises 30 feet above the ground, and it is filled with purple, green, and red markings, noting different climbing paths.

DETAILS FROM YOUR MEMORY

These details are things you remember from past experiences. (Memory details are especially important in narrative paragraphs.)

I crept to the door and peered out cautiously.

DETAILS FROM YOUR IMAGINATION

These details are things you wonder about, hope for, or wish. (They are often used in narrative and descriptive writing.)

I wondered what the bear would eat next!

Transitions

Words that can be used to **show location**:

above	behind	by	near	throughout
across	below	down	off	to the right
against	beneath	in back of	onto	under
along	beside	in front of	on top of	
among	between	inside	outside	
around	beyond	into	over	

Words that can be used to **show time**:

while	first	meanwhile	soon	then
after	second	today	later	next
at	third	tomorrow	afterward	as soon as
before	now	next week	about	when
during	until	yesterday	finally	suddenly

Words that can be used to **compare two things**:

likewise	as	while	in the same way
like	also	similarly	

Words that can be used to **contrast things** (show differences):

but	still	although	on the other hand
however	yet	otherwise	even though

Words that can be used to **emphasize a point**:

again	truly	especially	for this reason
to repeat	in fact	to emphasize	

Words that can be used to **conclude or summarize**:

finally	as a result	to sum up	in conclusion
lastly	therefore	all in all	because

Words that can be used to **add information**:

again	another	for instance	for example
also	and	moreover	additionally
as well	besides	along with	other
next	finally	in addition	

Words that can be used to **clarify**:

that is	for instance	in other words

Writing Expository Essays

When you *explain* or *inform* in a longer piece of writing, you're developing an expository essay. An effective expository essay begins with your complete understanding of a subject, and it ends with a written piece that shows your ability to share this knowledge clearly with your readers. What happens in between is all of the planning, drafting, and revising you do to produce your essay.

Writing essays in school helps you to think clearly and carefully about important subjects. (Your teachers like it when you think clearly.) Professional writers develop essays, too, for a number of different reasons. For example, journalists often write essays in newspapers and magazines, informing readers about important current topics.

WHAT'S AHEAD

This chapter contains a model and guidelines for developing an expository essay. It also includes special guidelines for writing two-part essays and suggestions for "personalizing" your informational essays.

- Sample Expository Essay
- Writing Guidelines
- Developing Two-Part Essays
- Personalizing Your Essays

Sample Expository Essay

Justin Monson wrote this essay in response to the following assignment: *What four new faces would you add to Mount Rushmore?*

To develop this essay, he had to gather information about each of his choices. As you read this sample, notice how the three parts of the essay—the beginning, the middle, and the ending—work together.

BEGINNING
General comments lead up to the focus, or thesis, (yellow highlight) of the essay.

MIDDLE
Each middle paragraph develops one of the writer's specific choices.

Mount Rushmore's Famous Faces

Four faces and 70 years ago, Mount Rushmore became part of South Dakota's history. This monument honors George Washington, Thomas Jefferson, Theodore Roosevelt, and Abraham Lincoln, all great American presidents who have earned their place in history. But what if we decided to add four new faces to this monument? Whom should we select? My four choices are people who have contributed something special to others here and around the world.

My first choice is Martin Luther King, Jr., who was a leader in the civil rights movement as well as a great speaker. His demands for a peaceful revolution for blacks in America resulted in his winning the 1964 Nobel Peace Prize. Unfortunately, he also became the target of racial violence, which resulted in his assassination at the young age of 39. Under his leadership, the civil rights movement gained wide support. In honor of his efforts, King became one of the few Americans whose birthday is observed as a holiday.

The next choice is Helen Keller, who overcame severe physical handicaps and inspired many others with disabilities. When Keller was about two years old, she was stricken with a serious illness that left her deaf and blind. A teacher named Anne Sullivan moved in with Helen's family and taught Keller to read and to communicate. During her lifetime, Keller became a very influential author and lecturer in this country and abroad. After World War II, she even visited wounded veterans in the United States and Europe, encouraging the handicapped soldiers to lead a full life.

MIDDLE
Important details about each choice are provided.

Neil Armstrong, the most famous person in our space program, would also be honored on the monument. He made his first spaceflight in 1966 aboard *Gemini 8* along with David Scott. They performed the first successful docking of two space vehicles. Then in 1969, Armstrong accomplished his greatest feat in space. He and fellow astronaut Edwin E. Aldrin, Jr., landed the *Apollo 11 Lunar Module* on the moon. Armstrong was the first person to set foot on the moon's surface, and his unforgettable words at that moment will echo forever: "That's one small step for a man, one giant leap for mankind."

Albert Einstein is my final choice for the monument, even though he didn't become a United States citizen until later in his life. Einstein was one of the greatest scientists of all time. When he was only 26, he expressed his theory of relativity: $E=mc^2$. This theory is the basis for atomic energy, and it was said that only 12 people in the world could understand what the theory is all about. He also made several inventions possible, including sound motion pictures and television. In addition, Einstein showed great concern for oppressed people throughout the world.

ENDING
The ending summarizes the main points and leaves readers with something to think about.

Famous presidents certainly deserve to be honored on Mount Rushmore, but so do people from other walks of life, including my four choices. Martin Luther King, Jr., fought for civil rights and equality, and Helen Keller helped disabled people lead better lives. Neil Armstrong led us to the moon, and Albert Einstein had one of the greatest scientific minds of all time. Who knows? Seventy years from now South Dakota's famous historical monument may, indeed, have four new faces for people to enjoy and celebrate.

Writing Guidelines

----[Choosing a Subject]

In most cases, your teacher will provide a general subject area or a writing prompt to get you started in your subject search. (If not, see pages 48-51 for ideas.) Your job is to select a specific subject, or focus, for your writing.

> **General Subject Area**
> _____
> **Writing Prompt**

Specific Writing Subject

Consider a number of possible subjects before you select one. The best idea may be just around the next corner in your thinking. *Remember:* Select a subject that truly interests you and that you know something about (or are able to research).

[Gathering Details]

Start gathering information by listing all of your ideas about the specific subject. After reviewing this list, collect additional information as necessary. (See pages 53-58 for ideas for gathering details.)

Using a Graphic Organizer: The line diagram below is one type of graphic organizer that will help you organize the ideas you collect.

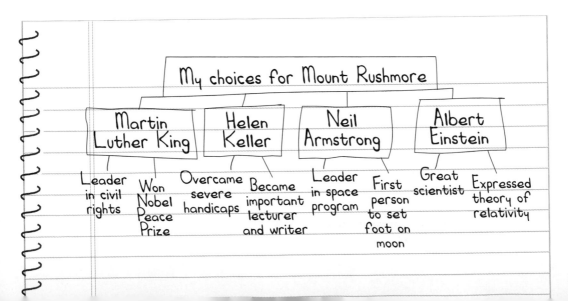

Writing ----[Writing the First Draft]

When you write an expository essay, remember that each part must be developed with special care and attention. (See pages 108-109 for a model.)

BEGINNING In the opening paragraph, start with general comments about your subject that draw readers into the essay. Then state the specific part of the subject (your focus, or thesis statement) that your writing will cover. (See page 59 for more information about focus statements.)

MIDDLE In the body of the essay, include information that supports your focus statement. Present this information in the best possible order; develop one main point per paragraph.

ENDING In the closing, you may want to restate the subject, summarize the main supporting points, and/or leave readers with a clear idea of the essay's importance.

Revising ----[Improving Your Writing]

Review the first draft of your essay using the checklist below as a guide. Then make the necessary changes.

- ■ Does the opening paragraph introduce the subject in an interesting way and state the *specific* focus of the essay?
- ■ Does all of the information in the middle paragraphs support the subject? Is enough information included?
- ■ Are the ideas organized in the best way?
- ■ Does the closing paragraph bring the essay to an effective close?
- ■ Does the writing sound like you really care about the subject?

Editing ----[Checking for Style and Accuracy]

Check your revised writing first for style, making sure that all of your sentences read smoothly and clearly and that you have used the best words to express your ideas. Then pay attention to accuracy by checking for spelling, grammar, punctuation, and capitalization errors. Make a neat final copy to share.

Developing Two-Part Essays

The most challenging essays require two different types of thinking about a subject. There's the *problem and solution* essay, the *comparison and contrast* essay, and so on. The guidelines that follow will help you develop effective two-part essays.

- **Collect** your own thoughts and any additional information about your subject. Use one of the graphic organizers on the next page to keep track of your collecting.

- **Create** a *starter sentence* for your essay after you have gathered enough facts and details.

    Example: *Severe budget cuts in our school district (Part 1) have led to overcrowded classrooms (Part 2).*

- **List** ideas or write freely about each part of your starter sentence. Keep the ideas flowing for 5 minutes or more.

- **Review** your writing and note any ideas that you would like to explore further or use in your essay.

- **Develop** your essay by connecting your thoughts about each part of your starter sentence.

- **Review** and revise your draft after setting it aside for a day or two.

Starter Sentences

If you can't think of a starter sentence for your two-part essay, complete one of the patterns below.

For *problem and solution* essays:
    . . . has resulted in . . .
    . . . has led to . . .

For *cause and effect* essays:
    Because of . . . we now . . .
    When . . . happened, I (we, they) . . .

For *comparison and contrast* essays:
    _____ and _____ are both . . . , but they differ in . . .
    While _____ and _____ have . . . in common, they also . . .

For *before and after* essays:
    Once I (we, they, it) . . . , but now . . .
    I (we, they, it) . . . until . . .

Using Graphic Organizers

Here are four graphic organizers for planning two-part essays. (See page 56 for others that may help you.)

Problem/Solution

Problem:

Causes of the Problem
.
.
.
.
.

Possible Solutions
.
.
.
.
.

Cause/Effect

Subject: _____

Causes	Effects
(Because of...)	(... these conditions resulted)

Comparison/Contrast

Features of Subject A	Features of Subject B

Circle the similarities and underline the differences. (Also see page 313.)

Before/After

Subject: _____

Before
After

Personalizing Your Essays

In *Writing with Power,* Peter Elbow suggests different ways to add spark to your expository essays—and to have some fun in the process.

- **Pretend** that you are the first person who has ever thought in a certain way about your subject, and write freely about your discoveries. Some fresh ideas are bound to develop.

- **Approach** the subject of your writing as if it were dangerous, scandalous, or controversial, and argue against it.

- **Become** the person whose ideas you are reading or writing about. Get inside of his or her mind, and write as if you were that person.

- **Ask** yourself, "What am I trying to say in this part?" And then answer the question. Pick up on anything that sounds better than the way you initially expressed yourself and work it into your essay.

- **Explore** your subject from a number of different angles. (See pages 54-55 for ideas.)

- **Get** into your writing. Clench your fist when the words aren't coming the way you want them to. Clap your hands when you hit on the right way to say something. Fidget or squirm when you really think you're onto something.

> Personalizing your essays will add spark, energy, and interest to your writing.

- **Bend** the rules (if you have your teacher's okay). If you don't feel like starting with a typical opening paragraph, open in a way that feels right to you—perhaps with a personal story that got you interested in your subject in the first place.

- **Include** a personal story in the middle of your essay, even though it may not have been part of your original planning. Taking a detour or a side trip is a sign that you are making your writing part of your own thinking, which is good.

- **Create** some offbeat questions about your subject and develop some creative answers. (See page 55 for help.)

Writing Persuasive Essays

You've heard about the food pyramid, classifying foods according to their health benefits. The higher you go, the richer the foods become. (Yes, ice cream is way up there.) Now suppose that someone were to create a writing pyramid, classifying the different forms of writing according to their level of difficulty. The higher you would go, the **more** challenging the writing would become. The subject of this chapter— the persuasive essay—would be way up there, near the top.

What makes persuasive writing so challenging? For one thing, it requires a lot of careful thinking and planning. You must learn as **much** as you can about your subject and, in the process, form an opinion about it that you can develop and support. (*Persuading* means arguing for or against something.) Then you must connect all of your thoughts in an essay that sounds reasonable, reliable, and convincing to your readers.

WHAT'S AHEAD

This chapter will help you write effective persuasive essays. It includes a student sample, writing guidelines, and tips for thinking through an argument. At the end of the chapter is a special section that will help you collect details for different types of essay subjects.

- Sample Persuasive Essay
- Writing Guidelines
- Thinking Through an Argument
- Gathering Ideas for Essays

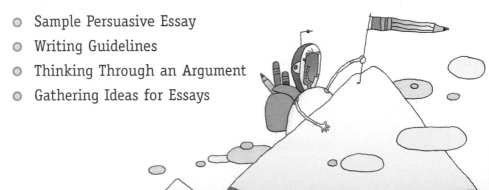

Sample Persuasive Essay

In this persuasive essay, student writer Sally Dickerson offers her opinion concerning our dependency on the automobile. She develops three main points to support her opinion.

BEGINNING
Opening comments lead up to the focus, or thesis, (yellow highlight) of the essay.

MIDDLE
The writer admits, or concedes, that the auto has value.

The American Dream?

It destroys its surroundings and causes many problems. It is a major cause of pollution. And it is extremely dangerous. You would think that something as destructive as this would not be tolerated in our society. You would think that people would have the common sense not to let something like this happen. Ironically, Americans and many others around the world have become addicted to this thing. It is the automobile. Something that was once the American Dream has now become the American Nightmare, and people are sitting back in their cars watching it happen.

There's no doubt that the automobile is an important part of modern life. It is our main means of transportation, making many things in our lives much easier. But too many of us have become too dependent on the car. It may be hard to believe, but a new car is put on the road every second. As a result of this growth, 50 percent of all North American cities are now made up of roads. More cars and more roads mean more congestion, and less natural beauty around us.

Our need for the automobile has made it one of the leading sources of air pollution. The average car gives off more than five tons of carbon dioxide every year, which is the number one cause of global warming. As many developing countries use more and more cars, global warming will rapidly increase. The emissions from

She follows with facts and details that support her thesis.

cars also contribute to the problems of acid rain and urban smog. With the way things are going, the automobile may directly contribute to the destruction of our world unless some action is taken in the near future.

While the pollution problem is bad enough, cars are also the leading cause of death and serious injury. Globally, auto accidents kill 265,000 people each year and injure another 10 million. And, as we have more and more cars on the road, the potential for serious auto accidents increases. In this country, two new developments are contributing to the dangers of car travel: the popularity of sport utility vehicles and the increasing reports of road rage. Sport utility vehicles are so big that they make the highways more dangerous for people driving smaller cars. Reports of road rage have risen 51 percent since 1990, and each time a driver becomes angry and reckless on the highways, a serious accident is in the making.

ENDING
The writer restates her opinion and asks for the reader's support.

The automobile has become an important and valued part of modern life. Because we are so attracted to the automobile, we too easily overlook its dangers. Unfortunately, the longer we ignore them, the harder it will become to change anything. As a result, we must rethink our feelings about the automobile. Once we do this, we might be able to make car use less harmful to the environment, and less dangerous to our lives.

Writing Guidelines

----[Choosing a Subject]

In a persuasive essay, it is important to choose a subject that you have strong feelings about. (Your goal, after all, is to get readers to accept your opinion about it.) Your teacher may provide writing ideas for you to choose from. If not, review the list of persuasive topics in your handbook. (See page 51.)

Your subject should be specific, timely, and debatable (meaning that people have differing opinions about it). This brief chart shows the difference between subjects for an expository essay and those for a persuasive essay.

Subjects for an Expository Essay	Subjects for a Persuasive Essay
How automobiles pollute	The automobile has become the American Nightmare.
How year-round school works	Year-round schooling offers the best opportunities for students.

[Gathering Details]

Gather your own thoughts (*freewrite, list, cluster,* etc.) about a specific subject. Then collect additional information as needed.

Form an opinion statement about some part of your subject. (This statement will be the thesis or focus of your essay.) Then list main points in support of your opinion. (You may also want to list one or two arguments against your opinion.) Here are the main points in the sample essay:

Opinion: The automobile has become the American Nightmare.

Main Supporting Points: 1. A major source of congestion
2. A leading source of air pollution
3. A leading cause of death and injury

Then organize your information for writing, using an outline or other graphic organizer. (See pages 110 and 113 for examples.)

Using an Outline

An **outline** is an organized list of the information you will use for the main part of your essay or report. (Do not outline your opening and closing paragraphs.) In an outline, list details from general to specific. And remember, if you have a I, you must have at least a II. If you have an A, you must have at least a B, and so on.

Topic Outline

A topic outline lists the main ideas to be covered in your writing. These ideas are stated in words and phrases rather than in sentences. This makes the topic outline useful for short essays.

Subject: The automobile has become the American Nightmare.
- I. Main means of transportation
  - A. Creates dependency
  - B. Causes congestion and too many roads
- II. Leading source of air pollution
  - A. Gives off huge amounts of carbon dioxide
  - B. Contributes to acid rain and smog problems
- III. Leading cause of death and injury
  - A. Kills 265,000 and injures millions annually
  - B. Adds danger with two new developments
    - 1. Large sport utility vehicles
    - 2. Road rage

Sentence Outline

A sentence outline organizes ideas using complete thoughts, which means you can include more information and details. Sentence outlines are used most often for longer reports and research papers.

Subject: The automobile has become the American Nightmare.
- I. Cars are the main means of transportation.
  - A. But too many of us have become too dependent on the car.
  - B. More cars and more roads mean more congestion.
- II. Our need for the automobile has made it a leading source of air pollution.
  - A. The average car gives off more than five tons of carbon dioxide every year.
  - B. The emissions from cars also contribute to the problems of acid rain and smog.
- III. Auto accidents are the leading cause of death and serious injury.
  - A. Accidents kill 265,000 each year and injure another 10 million individuals.
  - B. Two developments are contributing to the dangers of car travel.
    - 1. Large sport utility vehicles make highways more dangerous for people in smaller cars.
    - 2. Incidents of road rage, angry and reckless driving, have risen.

Writing ----[Writing the First Draft]

BEGINNING The opening paragraph should introduce your subject, give any necessary background information, and state your opinion.

> Pay special attention to the opening comments in your essay. They must be interesting enough to grab your reader's attention. (See page 63 for ideas.)

MIDDLE Each main point should be developed in a separate paragraph. Use your outline or other organizer as a guide. In a persuasive essay, the strongest argument is usually presented first or last.

ENDING The closing paragraph may do any combination of these three things: (1) restate your opinion, (2) summarize the main points in your argument, and (3) leave readers with a final thought about your subject. (Sometimes this final thought is a call to action, asking for the readers to get involved.)

Revising ----[Improving Your Writing]

Review your first draft using the following checklist as a guide.

- Does the opening paragraph give the necessary background information and state the opinion?
- Do the main points in the body, or middle part, support the opinion?
- Are the main points developed with enough details, and are they organized in the best way?
- Does the closing paragraph tie everything together and help readers understand the importance of the subject?
- Does the writing sound like I really care about my subject?

Make the necessary changes or improvements in your essay. (Also see pages 67-74 for more revising ideas.)

Editing ----[Checking for Style and Accuracy]

Check your revised writing first for sentence style and word choice and then for errors in spelling, grammar, and punctuation. Also have one other person check your writing for errors. Then make a neat final copy to share.

Thinking Through an Argument

The next two pages will help you state and support opinions, as well as make concessions for any arguments against your opinions.

STATING AN Opinion

Opinion statements fall into three main categories: statements of fact, statements of value, and statements of policy.

Statements of fact claim that something is true or not true.

> **Contrary to popular belief, most hunters are friends of the environment.**

Statements of value claim that something has or does not have worth.

> **The automobile has turned into the American Nightmare.**

Statements of policy claim that something should or should not be done.

> **The Appleton School Board should implement year-round schooling.**

USING Qualifiers

Qualifiers are terms that make an opinion more flexible and easier to support. Note the difference between the two claims below:

> **Contrary to popular belief, hunters are friends of the environment.**

> **Contrary to popular belief, most hunters are friends of the environment.**

"Most" qualifies the above opinion, changing it from an all-or-nothing claim. Here are some useful qualifiers:

almost	usually	maybe	probably
often	some	most	in most cases

ADDING Support

Your opinion needs evidence for support. The more types of convincing evidence you offer, the stronger your argument will be. Here are some types of evidence.

Prediction	More cars and more roads will mean more congestion.
Statistics	Our high school has room for 1,702 students, but last year 1,860 registered.
Observation	In Garfield Park, young men play soccer around the clock.
Expert Testimony	According to Emma Hernandez, the director of the Riverside Missions Shelter, most homeless people are unemployed males.
Comparison	In the past, fishing was a way of putting food on the table, almost a matter of survival. Today, for most individuals who fish, it is a sport, a hobby, or a form of relaxation.

MAKING Concessions

When you make a concession, you identify other valid opinions about your subject. Making a concession often makes your overall argument more convincing.

Here are some expressions for making a concession:

even though	**I agree that**	**I cannot argue with**
while it is true that	**admittedly**	**granted**

Gathering Ideas for Essays

On the next five pages, you will find tips that will help you collect details when you write about people, places, objects, events, and so on.

Writing About a   PERSON

When writing about a person, choose someone you know well—or would like to know well. That makes it easier to share interesting details about this person. It's important to include many details so readers can picture your subject in their minds. But it's also important to say nothing that will hurt your subject's feelings. The following guidelines will help you collect details for your writing:

Observe ▪ Watch the person you plan to write about. Take special note of any details that make this person different from others.

Investigate ▪ Plan to talk with your subject. Write down a few questions to ask. Then listen closely to the answers. You will probably think of more questions while you talk.

Classify ▪ Think about the type of person you are writing about (student, teacher, friend, relative). What are your subject's best traits?

Remember ▪ Recall stories that reveal important things about your subject.

Compare ▪ What other person, place, or thing could your subject be compared to? Is he or she like a sports hero, a roaring lion, a quiet pond, or a personal computer?

Question ▪ Ask other people about this person.

Evaluate ▪ Ask yourself why this person is important to you.

Describe ▪ List your subject's important physical characteristics, mannerisms, and personality traits. Notice the way he or she smiles, talks, sits, moves, and so on.

Writing About a PLACE

When writing about a place, think of somewhere you have been, or somewhere you have learned about. Your writing should help readers know why this place is important to you. The following guidelines will help you collect ideas for your writing:

Observe ■ Study the place you plan to write about. Use photos, postcards, or videos if you can't go there yourself. Jot down details that make this place different from others.

Record ■ Write down important details about your subject. Think about the sights, sounds, smells, and colors related to this place.

Question ■ Ask yourself, "If this place could talk, what would it tell me?" Also talk to other people who know about this place. Ask questions about its past, present, and future.

Classify ■ Consider the type of place you are describing. Is it a public place like a park or a theater? Is it a private place like a room in your home?

Remember ■ Think of a story about this place. It could involve something that happened to you, or it could be a story you heard or read about.

Compare ■ Compare your subject to other places. What other place is it most like? A little bit like? Not at all like?

Analyze ■ What is the outstanding feature of this place? What is its worst feature? When is the best time to go there?

Evaluate ■ Why is this place important to you? How would you feel if this place were no longer there?

When you write about a place, don't try to say every-thing you know about it. Instead, focus on a few main ideas, and present them clearly and colorfully.

Writing About an   OBJECT

When writing about an object, tell your readers why it is special to you. An object is anything you can see or feel, like a poster or a piece of jewelry. An object by itself may not be very interesting; but if you connect it to people and their feelings about it, the object may very well take on special interest. Use the following guidelines to collect ideas:

Observe ■ Think about these questions as you study your object: How is the object used? Who uses it? How does it work? What does it look like?

Record ■ Write down details about its color, size, and shape. Describe the most important parts and how they fit together.

Research ■ Learn about the object. Try to find out when it was first made and used. Ask other people about it.

Define ■ What class or category does this object fit into? (See "Writing a Definition" below.)

Remember ■ Recall interesting stories about this object.

Compare ■ Think of similar objects you could compare your subject to. Also consider surprising comparisons. What type of person is the object like? What flavor of ice cream is it like?

Analyze ■ Consider the object's strengths and weaknesses. What changes would you make in it if you could?

Evaluate ■ Why is this object important? Would you or anyone else miss this object if it suddenly disappeared?

Writing a   DEFINITION

Put the term you are defining (computer) into a class or category of similar objects or ideas (electronic machines). Then list special characteristics that make this object different from others in the same group (stores and arranges information).

Term—A computer . . .

Class—is an electronic machine . . .

Characteristic—that stores and arranges information.

Writing About an EVENT

When writing about an event, try to make it come alive for your readers by sharing plenty of details; but don't try to say everything. Focus on the important ideas or on one interesting part. The following guidelines will help you collect ideas for your writing:

Observe ■ Study the event carefully. What are the sights, sounds, tastes, and smells of this event? (Listen to what people around you are saying. If you are able, notice what is going on before and after the event.)

Remember ■ If you are writing about something that happened to you, list or cluster ideas related to this event. (See page 48.)

List ■ Answer the who? what? when? where? why? and how? questions for the event.

Investigate ■ If possible, read about the event. Ask other people what they know about it. Get their impressions, disappointments, surprises, and so on.

Identify ■ What type of event is this? Is it a public event like a city festival, or a private event like a family gathering?

Compare ■ Consider how this event is like (or different from) other events.

Evaluate ■ Decide why the event is important to you. Does it have an interesting background? Did it prove something to you? Has it changed you? Did it affect anyone else?

Recommend ■ What would you have changed to make this event more noteworthy or memorable?

Writing an EXPLANATION

When writing an explanation, you are trying to make something easier to understand. You may be asked to explain how to do or make something. You may need to explain how something works, or how to get from one place to another. The following guidelines will help you collect ideas:

Observe ■ If possible, observe or try out your subject. Pay close attention to the steps and details that will help you write your explanation.

Research ■ If necessary, read and learn about your subject. Find out what makes it different or important.

Ask ■ Talk to people who already understand or know about your subject. Ask them questions about anything you don't understand.

Describe ■ List the steps or parts that your readers need in order to follow your explanation. Include all of the important details—size, shape, colors, sounds, and smells.

Compare ■ Compare your subject to something that might be more familiar to readers. (Baking bread is like playing basketball. You need to follow certain rules, and timing is important.)

Analyze ■ What is the most important part or step? What happens if you leave a part out or skip a step?

Evaluate ■ Why is your subject important? How might it help your readers?

After you write your first draft, share it with a friend. Ask if your explanation makes sense. Does any step or part need to be clearer? Use linking words like *first, second, next,* and *then* to help your readers move from step to step. (See page 106 for a complete list of linking words.)

The Art of Writing

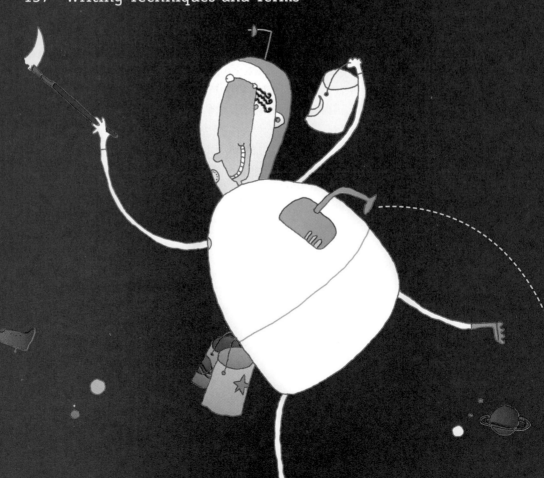

Writing with Style

Your personal style is the way you present yourself to the world, from your hairstyle to the things you like to do, from your taste in jeans to your favorite expressions. Your style helps establish your place in the world. It may be your style to blend in, to be part of the crowd, while the next person may want to stand out. Either way is okay; that's style.

Your writing style says something about you, too, but not in the same way as your hairstyle and clothes do. This style presents your inward thoughts, feelings, and beliefs. And you'll be glad to know that, for the most part, it will develop naturally as you continue to write. There are, however, a few things that you can do right now to help improve your writing style—as you will see in the pages ahead.

WHAT'S AHEAD

The first part of this chapter explains how your personal writing style can best develop. The pages after that talk about writing stylistic sentences, using colorful words, and much more.

- Developing a Sense of Style
- Studying Sentences with Style
- Modeling the Masters
- Writing Naturally
- Using Strong, Colorful Words

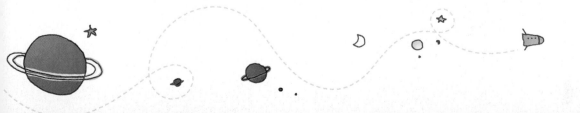

Developing a Sense of Style

Here's how your style—your special way of saying something—can best develop:

Write clearly. ■ This is one of the most important principles of style. It is also one of the hardest to follow.

Strive for simplicity. ■ Essayist E. B. White advises writers to "approach style by way of simplicity, plainness, orderliness, and sincerity." That's good advice from a writer who oozes with style.

Know when to cut. ■ And as writer Kurt Vonnegut says, "Have the guts to do it." Give the axe to sentences that don't support your main point and any words or phrases that don't strengthen your sentences.

Acquire a writer's sixth sense. ■ Know when your writing needs work. Watch for groups of sentences that sound too much alike and individual sentences that hang limp like wet wash.

Be specific. ■ Writing without specific details is like baking bread without yeast. One of the most important ingredients is missing. But be careful not to overdo the detail. Your writing may sound forced.

Write with specific nouns and verbs. ■ Specific nouns (*Godzilla*) and verbs (*lunged*) give your writing energy. Writing with general nouns (*creature*) and weak verbs (*is, are, was, were*) forces you to use a lot of modifiers.

Write active, forward-moving sentences. ■ Make it clear in your sentences that your subject is actually doing something.

> Out of Style:
> **A surplus of calories is necessary for growth in children.**
> (This thought is wordy and slow moving.)
>
> In Style:
> **Children need plenty of calories for growth.**
> (This revised sentence is much more direct and active.)

HELPFUL HINT

Place subjects and verbs close to each other. This will help make your sentences active, forward moving, and easy to follow.

Studying Sentences with Style

Professional writers usually work rather unscientifically. They go with what feels right in the heat of writing. Of course, when they revise, they pay special attention to sentences that don't work for them—often rewriting them many times until the sentences do.

Generally, your favorite authors write in a relaxed, somewhat *informal style*. This style is characterized by sentences of different types and lengths.

Special Types of Sentences

The four special types of sentences listed below add a lot of style to writing. Look for these types when you read, and practice writing your own versions.

A **loose sentence** expresses the main idea near the beginning (in the regular print below) and adds explanatory details as needed.

> **"Wil nodded to himself and slipped away,** *softly as a mouse, toward the back of the house where tourists were never taken."*
>
> —from "A Room Full of Leaves," Joan Aiken

A **balanced sentence** includes two or more parts equal in structure, which means that the parts are *parallel*. (The parallel parts are underlined in the example below.)

> **"He goes out onto his baseball field, spins around second base, and looks back at the academy."**
>
> —from *The Headmaster*, John McPhee

A **periodic sentence** holds back the most important idea until the end (in regular print below).

> **"*There, hidden in a maze of axles, wheels and springs,* it was difficult for policemen or trainmen to find him."**
>
> —from "Hoboing," William Z. Foster

A **cumulative sentence** adds life to the main clause (in regular print) by including modifiers before it, after it, or in the middle of it.

> **"*All that winter in the new house,* Raymond sat around talking about becoming a big-time farmer,** *raising lots of kids, making plenty of money, and being his own man."*
>
> —from *Coming of Age in Mississippi*, Anne Moody

Modeling the Masters

You can learn a lot about writing by studying the sentences and passages of some of your favorite authors. When you come across sentences that you really like, practice writing sentences of your own that follow the author's pattern of writing. This process is sometimes called **modeling.** Listed below are basic guidelines you can use for modeling.

Guidelines for Modeling

- Find a sentence or short passage you would like to use as a model.
- Copy it in your writing notebook or on a separate piece of paper.
- Think of a subject for your practice writing.
- Follow the pattern of the sentence or passage as you write about your own subject. (You do not have to follow the pattern exactly.)
- Build each sentence one small part at a time. (Don't try to work too quickly.)
- Review your work and change any parts that seem confusing or unclear.
- Save your writing. Share it with your classmates.
- Find other sentences or passages to use as models. Keep practicing, just as you would practice your basketball or music skills.

"Take care of the sense and the sounds will take care of themselves."
—Lewis Carroll

Modeling Samples

MODELING SENTENCES

Here is a smooth-reading sentence from the novel *A Solitary Blue* by Cynthia Voight.   This is an example of a loose sentence with the main idea, in regular type, expressed at the beginning.

> **"Jeff couldn't see the musician clearly,** *just a figure on a chair on the stage, holding what looked like a misshapen guitar.***"**

Here is a student's sentence modeled after Voight's:

> **"Larisa couldn't identify the person immediately,** *just a shadow in the dark alley behind the store, carrying what appeared to be a heavy box.***"**

MODELING SHORT PASSAGES

Here is a passage from the novel *The Talking Earth* by Jean Craighead George.   (The four sentences in this passage vary in terms of length and word order.)

> **"Billie Wind eased out of the dugout, testing the depth of the mire. It was only a few inches deep. Beneath the black residue from the swamp was firm sand. She walked swiftly, not even turning around to bid her dugout good-bye."**

Here is a student's passage modeled after George's:

> **"Julisa rushed into the cafeteria, looking for her best friends. They were in line only 10 yards away. In front of these girls were many other hungry classmates. Julisa moved quickly, not even looking at the other students around her."**

Additional Modeling Ideas

- Explain what your favorite authors do to give their writing its special style (use different types of sentences, include specific details, keep things very clear, etc.).
- Rewrite a section of one of your stories to resemble the style of one of your favorite authors.
- Exchange favorite sentences with your classmates. Use your classmates' sentences for additional modeling practice.
- Search through your own writing for sentences you really like. Then see how many ways you can rewrite them.

Writing Naturally

Writing naturally might not sound like a difficult thing to do, but, for many of us, it is. For some reason, we switch to another personality when we write—the personality of someone who uses vague words and boring sentences. Before any of us can write well, we must be able to speak in an honest, sincere, and natural style.

Improving Your Style of Writing

Those students whose writing is most appreciated no doubt write in a natural style. Something in their writing moves you and makes you say, "Hey, I like that." That "something" is the ability of the writer to make his or her voice come through in a piece of writing. Voice is a writer's special way of saying something on paper and is a trait of good writing. Here are some things you can do to allow your voice to come through your writing.

- **Write** regularly in a personal journal. (See pages 145-148.)
- **Correspond** regularly with friends and relatives. "Talk" in these letters as if your reader were in the room with you.
- **Choose** writing subjects that genuinely interest you. It's difficult to sound natural when you're bored with your subject.
- **Begin** writing assignments by freely recording your thoughts about your subject. Work some of these ideas into your actual writing, and it will start to sound more natural and interesting.
- **Pay** careful attention to the advice of your peers in group-advising sessions. They will help you identify the parts of your writing that show your voice, and the parts that still need to be "personalized."

"Voice is the imprint of ourselves in our writing. Take the voice away . . . and there's no writing, just words following words."
—Donald Graves

Using Strong, Colorful Words

Your writing style will greatly improve if you choose words that fit the purpose of your writing. The best words are the ones that effectively contribute to the overall meaning, feeling, and sound in a piece of writing. Pay special attention to the nouns, verbs, and modifiers (*adjectives* and *adverbs*) that you use. These are the words that make your writing come alive. The guidelines given below will help you use strong, colorful words in all of your writing.

CHOOSE SPECIFIC NOUNS

Some nouns are general (*car, house, animal*) and give the reader only a fuzzy picture. Other nouns are specific (*minivan, cabin, skunk*) and give the reader a much clearer, more detailed picture. In the chart that follows, the first words written under each category are very general nouns. The second set of words are nouns that are more specific. Finally, each of the words at the bottom of the chart is a very specific noun. These last nouns are the type that can make your writing clear and colorful.

person	place	thing	idea
woman	monument	food	government
writer	national monument	snack food	one-person government
Lois Lowry	Statue of Liberty	popcorn	monarchy

CHOOSE VIVID VERBS

Use vivid, action-packed verbs to make your writing lively and interesting. For example, the vivid verbs *surveyed, glared, observed, spied,* and *inspected* all say more than an overused, ordinary verb such as *looked*. The statement "Ms. Lang *glared* at the disruptive students" is much more descriptive than "Ms. Lang *looked* at the disruptive students."

 Avoid using the "be" verbs (*is, are, was, were*) too often. Many times a better verb can be made from another word in the same sentence.

A "be" verb: Rosa is a persuasive speaker in debates.

A stronger verb: Rosa speaks persuasively in debates.

CHOOSE EFFECTIVE MODIFIERS

Use specific, colorful **adjectives** to describe the nouns in your writing. Strong adjectives make the nouns you choose even more interesting and clear to the reader. For example, you may tell your readers that Beau is a farm dog; however, telling them that he is a *bossy* but *hardworking* farm dog says so much more.

 Avoid adjectives that are used so frequently that they carry little meaning.

Overused adjectives: *neat, big, pretty, small, cute, fun, bad, nice, good, dumb, great,* and *funny.*

Use **adverbs** when you think they can help describe the action in a sentence. For example, the adverb "barely" clarifies the action in the following sentence: "We *barely* squeezed through the subway door before it slid shut."

 Don't use two words—a verb and an adverb—when a single vivid verb would be better.

Verb and adverb: Joan sat quickly on the whoopee cushion.

A single vivid verb: Joan plopped on the whoopee cushion.

CHOOSE WORDS WITH FEELING

The words you include in your writing should not only be specific and colorful, but they should also have the right feeling or **connotation.** Let's say you are writing about a particular dream. If this dream happens to scare you every time you think about it, you can't simply call it a dream. Nor can you call it a fantasy or a vision or an omen. Those words don't have the right connotation. You're talking about a *nightmare.* That's the word with the right feeling.

 Don't settle for just any old word—find the word with the right meaning and feeling.

Use a thesaurus: The thesaurus lists synonyms, words with the same meaning. Pick the word that best fits the meaning, feeling, and sound of your writing assignment. (See page 325 for help.)

 You can also use a number of special writing techniques from time to time to make your writing engaging, clear, and creative. (See pages 138-140 for definitions and examples.)

Writing Techniques and Terms

As you gain more experience as a writer, you should begin to build your writer's vocabulary. For example, you should, in time, know what it means to write with *sensory details*. You should also know the difference between *exposition* and *persuasion,* between *sarcasm* and *simile,* between *puns* and *personification,* and so on.

You'll find this chapter very helpful because it explains all of the important techniques and terms associated with writing—including the seven italicized above. It's important that you understand these expressions because your teachers will use them in writing assignments, and your writing peers will use them in group-advising sessions.

WHAT'S AHEAD

Think of the following pages as your glossary to the vocabulary of writing. A listing of special writing techniques and general writing terms is included.

- o Writing Techniques
- o Writing Terms

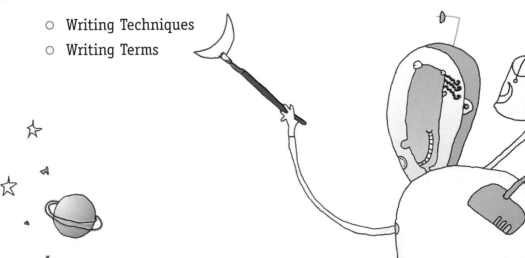

Writing Techniques

Writers use different **techniques** or methods to add interest and details to their stories and reports. Look over the following writing techniques and then experiment with some of them in your own writing. (Also see pages 202-205 for poetic devices and techniques.)

Allusion ■ A reference to a well-known person, place, thing, or event that the writer assumes the reader will be familiar with.

> **Hector rushed in like Superman and rescued the cat from the burning building.**

Analogy ■ A comparison of similar objects. An analogy suggests that since the objects are alike in some ways, they will probably be alike in other ways.

> **Pets are like plants. If you give them lots of care and attention, they grow strong and healthy. If you neglect them, they become weak and sickly.**

Anecdote ■ A brief story used to illustrate or make a point.

> **Abe Lincoln walked two miles to return several pennies he had overcharged a customer.** (This anecdote shows Lincoln's honesty.)

Antithesis ■ Antithesis means "exact opposite." In writing, it usually means using opposite ideas in the same thought or sentence.

> **We decided to have the bear for supper before he "had" us.**

Colloquialism ■ A common word or phrase that is used when people talk to one another. Colloquialisms are usually not used in a formal speech or in most assigned writing.

> **"How's it goin'?" and "What's happenin'?" are colloquialisms for "How are you?"**

Exaggeration ■ An overstatement or a stretching of the truth to emphasize a point. (See *hyperbole* and *overstatement*.)

> **My shoes are killing me.**

Flashback ■ A technique in which a writer interrupts a story to go back and explain an earlier event.

Foreshadowing ■ Hints or clues that a writer uses to suggest what will happen next in a story.

Hyperbole ■ An extreme exaggeration or overstatement that a writer uses for emphasis. (See *exaggeration* and *overstatement*.)

My brother exploded when he saw the damage to his car.

Idiom ■ Words used in a special way that may be different from their literal meaning.

Rush-hour traffic moves at a snail's pace. (This idiom means "very slowly.")

Irony ■ A technique that uses a word or phrase to mean the exact opposite of its normal meaning.

Danielle smiles and laughs all of the time, so we call her Grumpy.

Juxtaposition ■ Putting two ideas, words, or pictures together to create a new, often ironic meaning. (An *ironic statement* uses words to mean the opposite of their usual meaning.)

Oh, the joys of winter blizzards!

Loaded words ■ Words that make people feel for or against something. Persuasive writing, such as advertising, often uses loaded words.

This new product is <u>very affordable</u> and <u>easy to use.</u>

Drinking and driving is a <u>deadly combination.</u>

(The underlined words are loaded words.)

Local color ■ The use of details that are common in a certain place (a *local* area). A story taking place on a seacoast would probably contain details about the water and the life and people near it.

Metaphor ■ A figure of speech that compares two things without using the word *like* or *as*.

The cup of hot tea was the best medicine for my cold.

Overstatement ■ An exaggeration or a stretching of the truth. (See *exaggeration* and *hyperbole*.)

We screamed until our eyes bugged out.

Oxymoron ■ A technique in which two words with opposite meanings are put together for a special effect.

jumbo shrimp, old news, small fortune, bittersweet

Paradox ■ A statement that is true even though it seems to be saying two opposite things.

The more free time you have, the less you get done.

Parallelism ■ Repeating similar grammatical structures (words, phrases, or sentences) to give writing rhythm.

> **The doctor took her temperature, checked her heartbeat, and tested her reflexes.**

Personification ■ A figure of speech in which a nonhuman thing (an idea, object, or animal) is given human characteristics.

> **The low clouds bumped into the mountains.**

Pun ■ A phrase that uses words in a way that gives them a funny effect. The words used in a pun often sound the same but have different meanings.

> **That story about rabbits is a real hare raiser.** (*Hare,* another word for rabbit, is used instead of *hair.* A *hair-raiser* is a scary story.)

Sarcasm ■ The use of praise to make fun of or "put down" someone or something. The praise is not sincere and is actually intended to mean the opposite thing.

> **"That was a graceful move!" he said, as I tripped over the rug.**

Sensory details ■ Specific details that are usually perceived through the senses. Sensory details help readers to see, feel, smell, taste, and/or hear what is being described.

> **As Derrick spoke, his teeth chattered and his breath made little clouds in the icy cold air.**

Simile ■ A figure of speech that compares two things using the word *like* or *as.*

> **The dog danced around like loose litter in the wind.**
> **The ice was smooth as glass before the skaters entered the rink.**

Slang ■ Informal words or phrases used by particular groups of people when they talk to each other.

> **chill out   hang loose   totally awesome**

Symbol ■ A concrete or real object used to represent an idea. *Example:* A *bird,* because it can fly, has often been used as a *symbol for freedom.*

Synecdoche ■ The use of part of something to represent the whole.

> **"All hands on deck!"** (*Hands* is being used to represent the whole person.)

Understatement ■ The opposite of *exaggeration.* By using very calm language, an author can bring special attention to an object or idea.

> **These hot red peppers may make your mouth tingle a bit.**

Writing Terms

Below you will find a glossary of words used to describe different parts of the writing process. This glossary also includes terms that explain special ways of stating an idea.

Argumentation: Writing or speaking that uses reasoning, debate, and logic to make a point. (See pages 121-122.)

Arrangement: The order in which details are placed or organized in a piece of writing.

Audience: Those people who read or hear what you have written.

Balance: Arranging words and phrases in a similar way to give them equal importance. (Also see *parallelism* on page 140.)

Beginning: The opening part in a piece of writing. In a paragraph, the beginning is the first (topic) sentence. In an essay or a report, the beginning is the first paragraph, including the thesis statement.

Body: The sentences or paragraphs between the beginning and ending that develop the main idea(s) of the writing.

Brainstorming: Collecting ideas by thinking freely and openly about all the possibilities; used most often with groups. (*See illustration.*)

Central idea: The main point or purpose of a piece of writing, often stated in a thesis statement or topic sentence.

Cliche: An overused word or phrase that is no longer a good, effective way of saying something—as in "bright as the sun" or "fresh as a daisy."

Clincher sentence: The sentence (usually located last) that summarizes the point being made in a paragraph.

Closing: The summary or final part in a piece of writing. In a paragraph, the closing is the last sentence. In an essay or a report, the closing is the final paragraph.

Coherence: Putting your ideas together in such a way that the reader can easily follow from one point to the next.

Composition: Writing in which ideas are combined into one, unified piece.

Description: Writing that paints a colorful picture of a person, a place, a thing, or an idea using vivid details.

Details: The words used to describe a person, persuade an audience, explain a process, or in some way support the main idea; to be effective, details should be vivid, colorful, and appealing. (See pages 135-136.)

Diction: A writer's choice of words: slang, colloquial, formal, and so on.

Emphasis: Giving great importance to a particular idea in a piece of writing by placing it in a special position, by repeating a key word or phrase, or by simply writing more about one idea than the others.

Essay: A piece of factual writing in which ideas on a single topic are presented, explained, argued, or described in an interesting way.

Exposition: Writing that explains.

Extended definition: Writing that goes beyond a simple definition of a term. It can cover several paragraphs and include personal definitions and experiences, similes, metaphors, quotations, and so on.

Figurative language: Writing that uses *hyperbole, metaphor, personification,* or *simile* to enhance and clarify meaning. (See pages 139-140.)

Fluency: The ability to express yourself freely and naturally.

Focus: The specific part of a subject written about in an essay, a paragraph, or a report.

Form: The way a piece of writing is organized or structured.

Freewriting: Writing openly and freely on any topic; focused freewriting is writing openly on a specific topic.

Generalization: An idea or statement that emphasizes the general characteristics rather than the specific details of a subject.

Grammar: The study of the structure of language; the rules and guidelines that you follow to write and speak acceptably.

Issue: A topic that people have varying, definite feelings about.

Jargon: The technical language of a particular group (musicians, journalists). Computer jargon: *download, interface, RAM, footprint, peripheral, write-protect,* and so on.

Journal: A daily record of thoughts, impressions, and autobiographical information. A journal can be a source of ideas for writing.

Limiting the subject: Narrowing the subject to a specific topic suitable for a writing or speaking assignment.

General Subject		Specific Topic
swimming →	different strokes →	mastering the butterfly

Literal: The actual or dictionary meaning of a word. Language that means exactly what it appears to mean.

Logic: The use of reasons, facts, and examples to support a point. (See pages 291-296.)

Modifiers: Words, phrases, or clauses that describe a subject.

Narration: Writing that tells a story or recounts an event.

Objective: Writing that gives factual information without adding feelings or opinions.

Personal narrative: Personal writing that covers an event in the writer's life. It may contain personal comments and ideas as well as a description of an event.

Persuasion: Writing that is meant to change the way the reader thinks.

Plagiarism: Copying someone else's writing or ideas and then using them as if they were your own.

Point of view: The position or angle from which a story is told. (See page 344.)

Process: A method of doing something that involves steps or stages. The writing process involves prewriting, writing the first draft, revising, and editing and proofreading.

Prose: Writing or speaking in the usual sentence form. Prose becomes poetry when it takes on rhyme and rhythm.

Purpose: The specific reason a person has for writing; the goal of writing.

Revision: Changing a piece of writing to improve the ideas.

Satire: Using sarcasm, irony, or humor to make fun of people's habits or ideas. Satire is often used to raise questions about a current event or political decision. (See *irony* and *sarcasm* on pages 139 and 140.)

Spontaneous: Writing or speaking off the top of your head with no planning.

Structure: The way writing is organized; much like *form*. When authors have something to say, they must fit their words into a form or pattern in order to get their point across.

Style: *How* authors write (their choice and arrangement of words).

Subjective: Thinking or writing that includes personal feelings, attitudes, and opinions.

Summary: Writing that presents only the most important ideas in something you have read.

Supporting details: The details used in writing to prove or explain or describe a topic (examples, anecdotes, facts, etc.).

Syntax: The way words are put together in a sentence.

Theme: The central or main idea in a piece of writing.

Thesis statement: A statement that gives the main idea or focus of an essay.

Tone: The writer's attitude toward his or her subject. A writer's tone can be serious, sarcastic, objective, and so on.

Topic: The specific subject of a piece of writing.

Topic sentence: The sentence that contains the main idea of a paragraph.

Transitions: Words or phrases that connect or tie ideas together. (See page 106.)

Trite: Overused expressions or ideas like cliches. *Examples:* true blue, red as a beet, flat as a pancake.

Unity: A sense of oneness in writing in which all sentences work together to develop the main idea.

Universal: A topic or an idea that applies to everyone.

Usage: The way in which people use language, usually either standard (formal and informal) or nonstandard. Standard language is required for most of your writing assignments. (See page 340.)

Voice: A writer's distinctive, personal tone.

Personal Writing

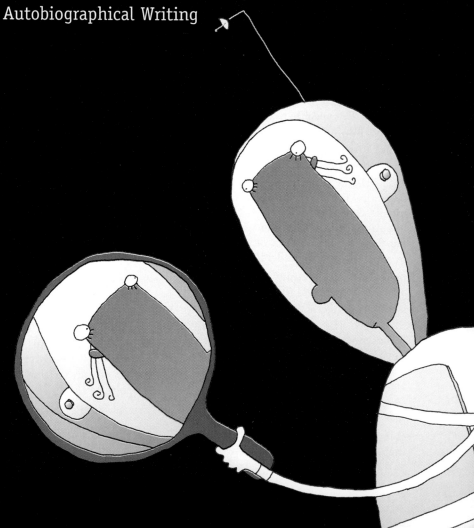

Journal Writing

Journal writing can benefit you in a number of ways. Four of the most important ways are listed below. After reading the list and then doing some journal writing, you will discover the enjoyment and benefits it offers.

Writing to Understand ■ You can write about everything that happens to you (both good and bad). In this way, journal writing helps you think about your daily experiences.

Writing to Practice ■ Writing is like many other skills. In order to improve, you need to practice. Writing regularly in a journal is one of the best ways to develop fluency.

Writing to Learn ■ Writing in a journal about the subjects you are studying can help you become a better learner.

Writing to Create ■ If you like to write poems and stories, you can try out new ideas in a journal, with no one looking over your shoulder.

WHAT'S AHEAD

This chapter will help you learn more about journal writing, including how to get started and how to make discoveries as you write. You'll also find information about different types of journals.

- Getting Started
- A Closer Look at Journal Writing
- Sample Journal Entry
- Types of Journals

Getting Started

A personal journal is your own special place to write. And it can be whatever you want it to be—a place to practice writing, a place to explore your experiences, and so on. To get started, follow these steps:

1 **Collect the proper tools.** All you really need is a notebook and a supply of your favorite pens or pencils. And there's always a computer . . . that is, if you know how to keyboard. Now might be a good time to learn.

2 **Choose a regular time to write.** It could be early in the morning, late at night, or sometime in between. Also find a comfortable place to write, a place that is quiet enough for you to concentrate.

3 **Write often.** Try to write for at least 5 to 10 minutes at a time. Write as freely as you can. Just make sure that all your entries are clearly legible.

If you regularly write for the same amount of time—let's say 10 minutes—count the number of words you produce. That number will probably increase over time—which means you are gaining fluency as a writer.

4 **Write about things that are important to you.** Here are some topics to get you started:

- interesting things you see and hear
- personal thoughts and feelings
- daily happenings
- important events
- books you've read
- ideas for stories and poems
- subjects you are studying

5 **Keep track of your writing.** Date your journal entries, and save them. Read through your journal from time to time. Underline ideas that you would like to write more about in the future. Also make comments in the margins. Here are two sample comments: "I could write a whole story based on this idea" or "I want to write more about . . . "

A Closer Look at Journal Writing

Journal writing works best when you reflect upon your experiences and feelings. Reflecting means really thinking about something and learning from it. Asking questions and wondering are two ways to reflect in your writing.

Ask questions ■ As you write, ask yourself questions. *"What was fun or interesting about this experience?"* *"How do I feel about it now?"* Or ask yourself *"Why does this matter to me?"* and try to discover some answers.

Wonder ■ Think about what you have learned from an experience. Compare it to other experiences you've had. Let yourself wonder what you could have done differently, or predict what the experience will mean to you in the future.

Sample Journal Entry

Here is a journal sample written by Christina Sung. Notice how she reflects on learning in a group.

Sept. 14

Today, I went to my cello teacher's house for a special group lesson. We do this once a month. Besides me, there was Darlene and Nicky, my cello friends. We practice together and learn from each other. This helps us get better and better. We also play in duets and trios sometimes.

At about 12:00 our cello teacher bought us lunch and played games with us. (Sometimes our cello teacher acts like a kid.) After that we played a duet. I played the piano, and Darlene played the cello. Then we played in a trio. I played the piano, Darlene played the cello, and Nicky played the flute. The teacher said we were good!

Then we had an open lesson, and we learned some new finger movements. Sometimes I'm a little bit embarrassed in an open lesson because everyone hears about my mistakes. We all made lots of mistakes today, so I felt okay.

Today was a very, very busy day, but we really had fun. We all went home feeling good about our music and with stacks of cello homework!

Types of Journals

If you enjoy keeping a personal journal, you may want to keep other types of journals as well.

Diary

A diary is very closely related to a personal journal. It usually contains a writer's record of daily events, experiences, and observations, with some reflection on personal relationships and concerns. A diary often contains more specific and exact details than a regular journal.

Dialogue Journal

In a dialogue journal, two individuals (a teacher and student, two friends, a parent and child, etc.) carry on a written conversation. A dialogue journal can help the writers get to know each other better, work through a problem, or share a common interest.

Learning Log

A learning log (classroom journal) gives students the opportunity to explore concepts, facts, and ideas covered in a specific class. Learning logs are very helpful in math and science classes, especially when the material is difficult or challenging. (See pages 366-368.)

Reader Response Journal

A response journal is a kind of learning log. In it students write about their feelings and reactions to some of the books they are reading.

Specialized Journal

When writers write about specific events or experiences, they are writing in a specialized journal. They may want to explore their thoughts and feelings while at summer camp, while participating in a team sport, while involved in a school production, or while working on a group project.

Travel Log

In a travel log, writers simply explore their thoughts and feelings while vacationing or traveling. It's a way to preserve memories . . . and a way to make use of time while waiting in lines and stations!

Writing Friendly Letters

We all enjoy receiving letters and cards from friends and relatives, especially from those special people who have moved or live far away. Letters from friends can make friendships stronger or renew old friendships. Letters from relatives can draw extended families close. So go ahead and give the people in your life a reason to write to you— send them a letter. Here are some special benefits of friendly letters:

- You don't have to worry about due dates. Write letters and send them as you wish.
- You can enjoy waiting for and receiving letters in return.
- When you receive a letter, you can save it and read it again and again.

WHAT'S AHEAD

This chapter covers what you need to know about writing friendly letters, including the basic parts of the letter and a model showing proper form.

- ○ Parts of a Friendly Letter
- ○ Sample Friendly Letter
- ○ Writing Guidelines

Parts of a Friendly Letter

There are five basic parts in a friendly letter: the heading, the salutation, the body, the closing, and the signature.

1 Heading

The heading includes your address and the date. Write the heading in the upper right-hand corner, about an inch from the top of the page.

2 Salutation

The salutation is a way of saying hello to the person you are writing to. It usually begins with the word *Dear* and is followed by the person's name. Place a comma after the person's name. Write the salutation at the left-hand margin, two lines below the heading.

3 Body

The body of the letter contains the thoughts and ideas you want to share. Begin writing on the second line after the salutation. Keep the paragraphs short for easy reading.

4 Closing

The closing is a way of saying good-bye. Write your closing two lines below the body of the letter. Capitalize only the first word and follow the closing with a comma. Here are some closings to choose from:

Love,   Sincerely,   Your friend,   Respectfully,   Regards,

5 Signature

The signature is the final part of a friendly letter. Write it beneath the closing. Your first name is usually enough, unless the person you are writing to doesn't know you very well.

6 P.S.

A postscript is an afterthought that you write at the end of a letter. The letters *P.S.* stand for the Latin words *post* (meaning "after") and *script* (meaning "write").

 Note: See pages 254-255 for help if you are writing a letter or friendly note via e-mail.

Sample Friendly Letter

1 100 Maple Road
Roslyn, New York 11576
November 12, 2000

2 Dear Benny,

While you were having your vacation day last Friday, I had to go to school. I even had to take a big test in social studies. I guess Eastwood Middle School doesn't believe in days off. You're so lucky. I sure wish my school was more like yours.

How's your football team doing? My soccer team was undefeated this season. We won all nine of our games, including the big one against Great Neck. I scored a goal—kind of. I kicked the ball real close to the goal, and the other team accidently knocked it in!

3 The funniest mistake happened on my sister Ilene's birthday. All of her friends came to our house to surprise her when she got home from school. Usually, Ilene and I get home at the same time, but that day I got home before her. When I opened the door, everybody yelled, "Surprise!" When they realized it was me, they were the ones who were surprised.

How have you been doing in school? My classes are much harder than last year, but I'm still doing pretty well. Spanish and social studies are my favorite subjects this year. Spanish is interesting and pretty easy for me. *Mi profesora, Sra. Morales, es muy amable.* Social studies is a lot of fun because Mr. Erin tells lots of jokes.

I decided that since we're such good friends, we could write letters to each other. Actually, I had to write a friendly letter for English class, so I wrote to you.

4   Your friend,

5   *Nathan*

6 P.S. I hope you'll write back. This could be fun!

Writing Guidelines

Prewriting ----[Choosing a Subject]

Make a list of the main ideas you want to include in your letter. Gather all the details you will need to make these ideas clear and interesting. If this letter is a response to one you have received, be sure to answer any questions. Include some of the following:

■ Describe some things that are going on in your life.

■ Share a good joke or story.

■ Include a photograph or a newspaper article.

Writing ----[Writing the First Draft]

Write your first draft freely and naturally. Write as though you were face-to-face with your friend or relative, sharing experiences, stories, and information with that person.

Revising ----[Improving Your Writing]

You want your letter to be easy to read, so check your first draft.

■ Be sure your sentences read smoothly.

■ Make certain your paragraphs are fairly short and that each one develops a single idea.

■ Include enough details to make your ideas clear, interesting, and fun to read.

Editing ----[Checking for Style and Accuracy]

Check your letter for spelling, capitalization, punctuation, and usage errors. (This handbook and a friend can help.) Check the form of your letter, too.

Write your final letter neatly by hand, or enter it on your word processor. Center your letter on the page and keep the margins as equal as possible. Use at least a one-inch margin on all sides. Finally, address the envelope neatly, add the correct postage, and mail your letter. (See pages 246-247.)

Autobiographical Writing

The words "Let me tell you a story" contain a kind of magic. Consider all of the family stories you've heard and enjoyed throughout the years. And just think of all the personal stories you and your friends share. It's easy and natural to share experiences. It's how you make sense out of your lives, how you confirm that you are part of this world: "Hey, listen to me, I've got a story to tell."

But what makes a good story? Well, a good story unfolds with enough snap and crackle to hold a listener's (or a reader's) interest from start to finish. It builds in excitement or suspense, one detail after another, until something big happens near the end. And it always has some point to make when it is over. A good story leaves everyone satisfied, looking forward to the next time someone says, "Let me tell you a story."

WHAT'S AHEAD

This chapter contains a sample and guidelines for developing a personal narrative, which is another term for an autobiographical story. It also includes tips for making your narratives come alive, plus a sample phase autobiography, which is a special type of autobiographical writing.

- Sample Personal Narrative
- Writing Guidelines
- Making Your Narrative Work
- Sample Phase Autobiography

Sample Personal Narrative

In the following sample, Jodi Klion shares a brief experience that started out as plain fun, but ended up to be much more.

Splash Mountain

BEGINNING
The writer starts right in the middle of the action.

This was it. There was no turning back. As the well-greased wheels pulled slowly up the track, my grip on the steel bar across my lap tightened. I heard shrill screams of excitement from the people in the front row. The train groaned to a halt, halfway up the hill, just far enough for me to see the water rushing down like a powerful natural waterfall.

My father glanced over at me from my right. He was wearing his favorite Mickey Mouse shirt, the one on which Mickey is golfing. His smile matched Mickey's. "Ready?"

MIDDLE
Dialogue helps make the story seem real.

"Even if I wasn't," I answered humorously, "do I have a choice now?"

"Don't forget to smile for the camera when we hit the drop," my father said, reminding me of the Disney tradition of photographing the screaming riders.

My thoughts were interrupted as the train jerked forward, racing us against the wind. It seemed to be only a few seconds. Then, SPLASH! The water at the bottom of the drop covered us like a blanket. When we had finally caught our breath, my father and I exclaimed together, "That was great! Let's go again!" We laughed, and it was then that I felt it. Sitting in drenched clothes, at 7:30 p.m., on a Disney World ride, with trees swaying in the breeze, I felt the strong bond between my father and me. I'm sure he felt it, too, as we climbed out of the train.

ENDING
The writer notes the importance of the event.

As we walked to see how our pictures had turned out, Dad put his arm around me. We laughed at our facial expressions in the pictures, and I knew my father and I had done something special.

Writing Guidelines

Prewriting ----[**Choosing a Subject**]

Any event that you find hard to forget is a good subject for a personal narrative. This event doesn't have to be big and important (a trip to China). In fact, something much smaller in scale (the first dinner you made) may make a far better story.

Think of events that took place within a fairly short period of time. Judi Klion's story about Splash Mountain is based on an experience that probably lasted 5 to 10 minutes.

[**Gathering Details**]

The experience you choose to write about may be very clear in your mind. If this is the case, you may not need to do much collecting. A simple, quick listing of the basic facts may be enough. Just jot down things as they happened. (See the "Sample Quick List" below.) Or you may want to use a 5 W's chart to collect this information. (See page 170.)

SAMPLE Quick List

~~We drove to Disney World.~~
We bought tickets.
We got on the Splash Mt. ride.
We felt nervous.
The ride started up!
I could hear people screaming.
(I felt so close to my dad.)
In a second, it was over.
↱ ~~Later, we ate hamburgers.~~

Once you finish your list, review all of the details you've included, using the following points as a general guide:

- Get rid of any information that is not that important.
- Move things around if they're not in the right order.
- Add important details you forgot.
- Use your list to begin your rough draft.

Writing ----[Writing the First Draft]

In any good personal narrative, three elements are key.

1. The people (*Who was involved in the event?*)
2. The setting (*Where and when did the story occur?*)
3. The action (*What exciting or important thing happened?*)

BEGINNING In the beginning, introduce the people involved and describe the setting. Use specific details to make readers feel as if they were right in the middle of the action.

> **This was it. There was no turning back. As the well-greased wheels pulled slowly up the track . . .**

MIDDLE Next, describe the action. Good storytellers never tell everything. Instead, they focus a lot of attention on capturing the main thing that happened. For Jodi Klion, it was surviving Splash Mountain.

ENDING The ending should bring your story to a close, either by showing what you learned from the experience, or by sharing how you (and anyone else) felt after it was over.

Revising ----[Improving Your Writing]

Use this checklist as a general guide when you revise your first draft. (Also see page 157 for more ideas.)

- Does the opening part effectively set the scene?
- Do I express genuine feelings in the narrative?
- Do I capture the important sights and sounds related to the experience?
- Is every detail in the story necessary?
- Does my narrative build in excitement and make a point in the end?
- Does my natural voice come through? Does the story reveal the true me to my readers?

Editing ----[Checking for Style and Accuracy]

Once your revision is complete, check the style of your writing by carefully reviewing the smoothness of your sentences and the effectiveness of your word choice. Then edit your writing for spelling, grammar, and punctuation errors.

Making Your Narrative Work

Knowing Where to Begin

Jodi Klion's story jumps right into the thick of the action: In the opening scene, she and her dad are already on the ride, waiting to plummet down the waterfall. Think how tedious it would be if she had begun with getting up in the morning, brushing her teeth, putting on her socks . . . yawn. Who would want to read all that? Figure out the most important thing that happens in your story, and begin right before that.

Being Selective

Like any good storyteller, Jodi didn't waste time telling us a lot of things that really didn't matter. As novelist Elmore Leonard says, "I try to leave out the parts that people skip." Do that. Leave out anything that's boring or unimportant to your story.

Here are some things Jodi *didn't tell* us:

- What she had for breakfast the day of the ride
- How tall her dad is
- How much the ride tickets cost
- What color clothes they were wearing
- How many other people were on the ride

Ending It

Begin your narrative right before the most important moment in your story, and end shortly after that. This is what Jodi did. Her organization looks like this:

Beginning At the start of the big ride. She and her dad are nervous!

The Most Important Moment The ride! They survive it, have a good laugh, and feel closer.

Ending As they go to check their pictures, they realize they did something special together.

Jodi's ending works because she didn't go on too long. She didn't tell about their ride home, stopping for burgers, or going to a movie the next day. She knew when her story was over. She knew when to quit.

Sample Phase Autobiography

A **phase autobiography** is a special type of autobiographical writing that focuses on an extended period of time, or phase, in the writer's life. In the following sample, Erin Winston Dolan writes about her first year in school.

Kindergarten

BEGINNING
The writer introduces the subject in a clear, creative way.

Kindergarten was, I have to admit, a chaotic year for me. At first, I loved the idea of going to school like my older sister. I was finally turning into the big girl I had always wanted to be. But that was before I realized I would be there all alone—without my mother.

I remember the first day. I clung to my mother's leg, holding on with all my strength. When we went inside, I pulled away for less than a second and looked around. I saw what looked like hundreds of other kids just like me, not wanting to be there, but curious enough not to be screaming for their mothers. That's when I turned back to my mother—only she wasn't there!

MIDDLE
Specific details help readers visualize the action.

I started screaming, and out of nowhere my mom scooped me up, and oh, the embarrassment. Everyone was looking at me. Mom quietly explained that she would pick me up later, and we would go out for lunch. "NOOOO!" I whimpered, making sure no one heard me. I wanted to crawl into one of the cubbies. Well, that was Day 1. . . .

Every day at school I would yell at an annoying girl named Jane. Then I would talk to my new friend, Nancy. Nancy, of course, was a bit older than I—in fact, she was my teacher. She had a sense of humor, and like any good teacher and mother, she knew how to make all things better.

She showed her skill the day my older sister Shannon let me take her sacred stuffed dog to school for show-and-tell. My sister loved that dog. So the morning I took it in, she explained that if anything happened to the dog, she would never speak to me again.

Now, I went to a Waldorf School for kindergarten. For show-and-tell, we would form a circle on the floor. Then the teachers would turn out all the lights, and light candles around the room. Everyone had to be quiet while each "teller" told about his or her object.

MIDDLE

A personal tone, or voice, helps readers feel comfortable with the writer.

When Jane finally finished telling about her pinky pig slippers, she plunked down next to me. Unfortunately, she landed right on part of the blanket draped over the table behind us, bringing five blazing candles down with her. Neither of us was hurt, but I watched in horror as a splotch of burnt fur spread over my sister's stuffed dog. I immediately melted like the candle wax and started crying. Through my tears, I saw Nancy carefully snipping out the waxy and burnt fur. "We can fix this," she kept saying, but I knew the world had ended.

Luckily or unluckily—depending on how you look at it—it was Friday. I didn't have to go to school for two whole days. No Jane. But, I would be with the sister who might want to kill me.

All the way home I sat watching my sister hugging her "puppy wuppy." She never noticed the burnt part. Nancy had saved the day. There was not a mark, not a trace. Aaaaah, if only that had been the end of the story. But no—I have always been the kind of kid who thinks honesty is the best policy.

"It was an accident!" I blurted out. "I didn't mean to do it! Jane pulled the candles down, and they burned your dog!"

ENDING

The ending effectively captures the young girls' emotions and feelings.

"How could you?" my sister said, hugging her puppy. "Show me where he's burned, the poor darling." We both looked, but neither one of us could find the spot. Nancy had done her work too well.

"I still don't forgive you," my sister announced—and to this day, I don't think she has.

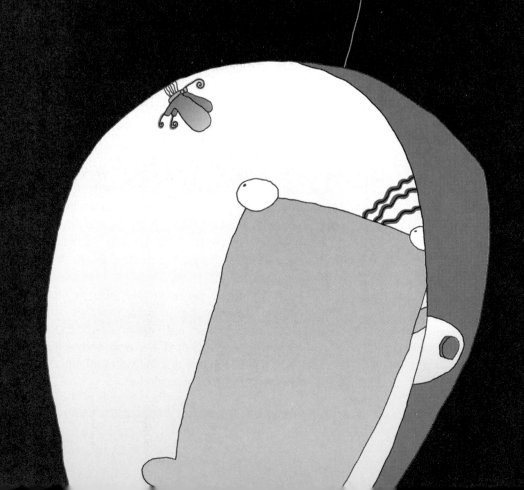

Subject Writing

Biographical Writing

In a biography, you write about a person you find interesting (besides yourself). This person could be someone you admire, someone who has done something you find fascinating, or someone you are simply curious about. Just make sure that you have access to plenty of information about your subject.

The word "biography" comes from two Greek words meaning "life writing." It's your goal as a biographer to share a story from your subject's life in an informative and appealing manner. As you develop your writing, you will discover an interesting world beyond yourself, which may, in turn, help you understand your own world a little better.

WHAT'S AHEAD

This chapter contains a sample biographical story along with step-by-step writing guidelines. It also includes tips for telling a good story and a sample phase biography.

- ○ Sample Biographical Story
- ○ Writing Guidelines
- ○ Special Planning and Writing Tips
- ○ Sample Phase Biography

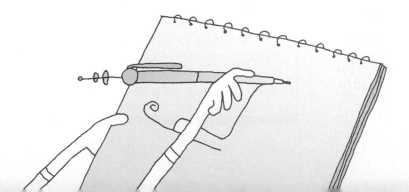

Sample Biographical Story

Meridel Thomson wrote a story about a person she admires. To gather information, Meridel used her own observations. She also interviewed her subject and included some of her subject's thoughts.

A Hero of Many Colors

BEGINNING
The opening lines grab the reader's attention.

Margaret "Peggy" Helen Lipshutz's wrinkled hand flew across the poster paper, producing bold, beautiful strokes of color while folk music floated through the air. I will never forget the first time I saw Peggy draw, slowly working her magic on all who watched. At the age of 80, she continues to inspire and bring joy to many people through art. This alone makes her a hero in my eyes, but she is also an incredibly active woman who fulfilled her childhood dream.

MIDDLE
Important details highlight the artist's life.

Peggy had wanted to be an artist since she was seven growing up in London. She was inspired by the colorful posters in the Underground (subway) that featured many different artistic styles. She pursued her dream and went on to Hornsby Art School in London and the Pratt Art Institute in New York, after moving to America when she was nineteen.

In 1948, Peggy met folksinger Vivian Walsch. They "performed" together, Walsch supplying the music and Peggy, the art. She now performs her chalk artistry several times each week accompanied by live music and also does oil paintings in her studio.

Her art is displayed in galleries around the world. My personal favorite, and hers, is called "Release." It is a picture of a man who is playing a cello that slowly transforms into an alligator.

ENDING
The closing examines one of the subject's beliefs.

Peggy believes that "all people should be free and live well." Her philosophy has grown out of her art and her strong beliefs in peace and freedom. If more people were like Peggy, and they expressed their beliefs in their work, the world would have more heroes.

Writing Guidelines

Finding a subject for a biography should be easy. You should be able to think of many people to write about. Here are three ways to search for a subject:

1. Think of a person you know better than anyone else does.

2. Think of a person who has had a big influence in your life.

3. Think of an interesting person you have heard about in one of your classes or from a friend or family member.

Make sure to select a subject that truly interests you and would probably interest your readers, too.

[Gathering Details]

Gathering the best details for your writing may or may not be easy for you. It all depends on the subject you choose to write about. Here is a chart that can help you collect details. (Also see "Planning Tips" on page 165.)

KNOWLEDGE LEVEL	EXAMPLES	SOURCE OF INFORMATION
Well-known subject	mother, brother	Search your memory for ideas. Talk with your subject.
Somewhat-known subject	teacher, grandparent	Search your memory. Watch and take notes. Interview your subject.
Little-known subject	veterinarian, judge	Interview your subject. Watch and take notes. Read any related information.
Famous person	historical figure, author, athlete	Read magazines, library books, encyclopedias. Listen to radio/TV interviews. Surf the Net.

Writing ----[Writing the First Draft]

Use the following guidelines to develop your first draft. (Also see "Writing Tips" on page 165.)

- Review the details you have collected to find the ones that interest you the most.
- Make the most interesting details the focus of your writing; think of the best way to share these details.
- Pay special attention to the beginning. It should grab your reader's attention and state the focus of your writing.
- In the middle part, include specific details that help tell your story. These details should answer the 5W's (*who? what? where? when?* and *why?*).

Revising ----[Improving Your Writing]

Here's a reminder of what to keep and what to cut when you are ready to revise your first draft:

KEEP (or Add)	CUT (or Rewrite)
Sentences and paragraphs that are interesting, important, or entertaining	Ideas that are unclear or uninteresting
Sentences that relate to your main point or focus	Sentences that include "extra ideas" not related to your main point
Sentences that add supporting examples and details	Sentences that are confusing or lack specific details

Check your sentences and paragraphs to make sure they follow one another in the best order. If they don't, rearrange them.

Editing ----[Checking for Style and Accuracy]

Also check your revised writing for spelling, punctuation, usage, and capitalization errors. (Have somebody else check it, too.) Then write a neat final copy of your writing to share.

Special Planning and Writing Tips

The tips that follow give additional information about planning and writing a biographical story. Use these tips in combination with the regular guidelines on the previous two pages.

Planning Tips

- Check several sources if your subject is a famous person. Different sources may present different facts and details. If you find conflicting data, go with the source that you think is most reliable.

- Double-check the information you record. Make sure all of your facts and details are accurate. Any small error may make your readers question the rest of your story.

- Do some background research before you interview anyone. If you sound knowledgeable, your subject will enjoy talking to you.

- Take notes and/or use a cassette recorder for interviews. Otherwise, you'll miss some important details. (See page 170.)

Writing Tips

- Make a personal connection with your subject. This will help answer an important question for readers: *Why did you choose this subject?*

  I will never forget the first time I saw Peggy draw, slowly working her magic on all who watched.

- Add physical (sensory) details in your writing to make your subject come alive for readers.

  Margaret "Peggy" Helen Lipshutz's wrinkled hand flew across the poster paper, producing bold, beautiful strokes of color while folk music floated through the air.

- Include your subject's personal thoughts and feelings. These ideas will make your story seem more authentic and real for readers.

  Peggy believes that "all people should be free and live well." Her philosophy has grown out of her art and her strong beliefs in peace and freedom.

- Work in background information to give readers the full story.

  Peggy had wanted to be an artist since she was seven growing up in London.

Sample Phase Biography

A **phase biography** focuses on an important time, or phase, in a person's life. It briefly describes the person, captures the time, and relates how it affected the subject. In this phase biography, Tracey Yelen tells how her grandfather was affected by the Holocaust.

My Grandpa's Story

BEGINNING
The opening paragraph sets the scene.

In 1939 when my grandfather, Abraham Yelen, was 20 years old, he was drafted into the Polish Army. Abe didn't mind that much because he knew that he had to go. He packed his bags, kissed his family good-bye, and left. Little did he know what pain and suffering would follow.

Two weeks after World War II started, he was captured by the Germans and was sent to a P.O.W. (Prisoner of War) camp in Germany. When Abe was released in 1940, he went back to his hometown to see his family, and on the way, he discovered that the Jews were going to be killed. His parents knew that their family was too big to hide anywhere, so they decided to stay in Poland. Abe went back to Russia, but he was captured by the Russians on the border. Because he was in Russia illegally, he was sent to Siberia to do hard labor.

MIDDLE
The history of this time is provided.

After the Germans invaded Russia in 1941, Abe was released early to join a Polish Army unit that was going to fight the Germans in Africa. On the way to Libya, his unit passed through Palestine (Israel), where he stayed and met Sarah Weinberg, my grandma. Abraham didn't know what happened to his family, but he feared for their lives because he knew the Jews were being killed.

After the war ended in 1945, Abe slowly found a few survivors from Chenstekova, his hometown, who were coming to live in Israel. He found out that all of his family members were killed by the German Nazis in different concentration camps.

ENDING
The closing lines bring us to the present.

As I listened to my grandpa's story, I felt like I was going to cry. My grandpa is a loving man, and the Holocaust is still a part of his life, but he doesn't let that affect the way he treats people or acts around them.

Writing News Stories

When a civil war in Somalia leaves 100,000 people homeless, that's big news. And when a group of junior-high students raises more than $2,000 to help feed the homeless in Salt Lake City, Utah, that's news, too. Granted, a local fund-raiser may not have national importance, but it is an inspiring story that deserves to be told in a school or a local newspaper.

Writing an effective news story requires good reporting skills. First, you need to find a subject (like a very successful fund-raiser) that readers should know about. Then you need to gather your facts by making visits, asking questions, carrying out background research, and so on. Most of a reporter's work is done *before* he or she gets the story on paper. The actual writing isn't hard if you've done your homework.

WHAT'S AHEAD

The first part of this chapter will help you write a basic news story. The second part contains a sampler of other types of "stories" often found in newspapers.

- ○ Sample News Story
- ○ Writing Guidelines
- ○ Newswriting Sampler

Sample News Story

In the following news story, Rachel Tate and Amy Thompson report on a schoolwide service project that raised funds for the homeless.

Exceeding Expectations

BEGINNING

The reporters begin with a quotation.

"We knew our school would want to help feed the homeless, but we were so happy when we were able to raise enough money to help four charities. Oly Jr. [Olympus Junior High School] is a great school with tons of caring individuals," said Ms. Kelley, the adviser for a schoolwide service project for providing Thanksgiving dinner for homeless people. She also teaches a Peer Leadership Team class (the PLT class). Their goal was to provide 200 Thanksgiving dinners for individuals at a cost of $1.83 each.

MIDDLE

The main part of the story contains all of the important details.

In two months, the PLT students collected $2,100 in their school and throughout the community, far exceeding their expectations. Five hundred dollars was given to the Salt Lake Mission to feed about 250 homeless people. Six hundred dollars went to Utahns Against Hunger. Five hundred dollars was contributed to the Angel Tree, and the last five hundred will be used to make Christmas more joyful for a family in our school.

During Christmas many people donate to the homeless, but the PLT has ongoing projects. Each student in the class has to do one to two hours of service a week. Some visit the elderly, while others help neighbors shovel snow and rake leaves. Some help in various agencies like the Heart Association, and the Food Bank, and some help elementary students with reading and math two days a week.

ENDING

Additional information completes the story.

The PLT class was begun by a Learn and Serve grant to help students learn through service and technology. This grant has been very good for the Salt Lake community and for many students at Oly Junior High who are learning their lessons well.

Writing Guidelines

Prewriting ----[Choosing a Subject]

To choose a subject for a news story you'll need to know what's happening in your school and community and decide whether it's news or not. If everybody knows about the monthly food drive at your school, that may not be news. But if somebody vandalizes the food pantry, that's definitely news. Here are some tips that will help you decide whether something is news or not. (Also see "Finding News Stories" below.)

- **Timeliness** News stories must focus on current subjects. People aren't interested in old news. They want to know what has just happened.
- **Importance** What difference does your story make? What group of people is it important to? Who is affected by it? Why would people *want* to know about it? Why do people *need* to know about it?
- **Local Angle** News about national or international homelessness is important, but your story about homelessness needs to bring in local people, problems, and solutions.
- **Human Interest** People like to read about individuals who have worked hard, overcome great odds, won awards, and so on. These types of stories touch the readers' emotions.

Finding News Stories

The headlines below show the difference between subjects that are newsworthy, and those that are not.

News: Not News:

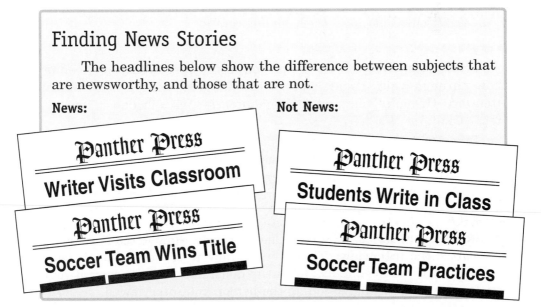

Panther Press
Writer Visits Classroom

Panther Press
Students Write in Class

Panther Press
Soccer Team Wins Title

Panther Press
Soccer Team Practices

Prewriting ----[**Gathering Details**]

To make sure you have the basic information to write your story, create a 5 W's chart. The one below was created for the news story on page 168.

5 W's Chart				
who?	what?	when?	where?	why?
students at Oly Jr.	collected $2,100 for four agencies	current school year	in school and community	to help people in need

Interviewing Tips

One of the most important ways to gather information for news stories is to interview people. Use these tips as a general guide when you conduct interviews.

BEFORE . . .

Be prepared. Set up a time for an in-person or telephone interview. Write out the questions that you want to ask. Check to see that your questions are open-ended rather than yes/no questions. Put a star next to the questions that you *must* have answers to.

DURING . . .

Listen attentively. Look the person in the eye. Nod your head or show through your facial expression that you are paying careful attention. (If you're doing a telephone interview, give feedback, such as "Yes," "Okay," or "I see.")

Take notes. Take notes of any details, especially things that involve dollar amounts, dates, names of people, and so on. Ask how to spell names. Remember to thank the person you've interviewed. Also, ask ahead of time for permission if you want to tape-record your interview.

AFTER . . .

Review your notes. The best time to review your notes is immediately after the interview. Then you'll know if you covered all your questions or if you need to ask follow-up questions. Send a copy of your article, along with a thank-you, to the person you interviewed.

Writing -----[**Writing the First Draft**]

Lead: Spend extra time writing your beginning paragraph. It must grab the reader's attention and summarize the main points in your story. The lead usually answers who did what?; what happened?; or a similar question.

Body: Next, write the body of your news story, using your planning notes as a basic guide. This part must "fill in" all of the important facts and details that readers need to know about the subject. The further you get into the story, the less important the information should become. (Then nothing essential will be lost if an editor has to cut the last part of your story to make it fit in the newspaper.)

 Note: Sentences in news stories are typically short, and paragraphs generally do not include more than three or four sentences.

Try to include quotations in your story, but always check your notes to make sure that you quote individuals accurately. If someone says that working with the students was a "delight," but rolls her eyes in a way that makes you know it was not a delight, it would be wrong to quote her as saying how "pleasant" the students were.

Revising -----[**Improving Your Writing**]

Ask yourself the following questions when you review your work:
- Does the lead hook my readers into the story?
- Have I missed any details, or am I unsure of any facts?
- Could I write a headline for this story? (If you can't, your story may need a clearer focus.)
  Revise your story as needed. (See page 24 for additional help.)

Editing -----[**Checking for Style and Accuracy**]

Check for both grammatical and factual errors. Accuracy is important in every form of writing, but especially when you are writing for the public. Double-check every fact and the spelling of every name.

 Note: At a school newspaper, you will have an editor or an adviser check your story before it is printed. But in the end, *you* are responsible for the accuracy of your story.

Newswriting Sampler

The first part of this chapter focuses on the basic news story. The next three pages will show you other ways to present information in newspapers.

Editorials: An editorial expresses the writer's opinion or position on a timely news story or event. Read the following editorial by student writer Elizabeth Nagem Kuhn.

Foreign-Born Need Not Apply

BEGINNING
The writer begins with a simple story about fairness.

Children who say that they want to be doctors or movie stars when they grow up are seldom told they can't. But if a child wants to be president of the United States, he or she may need to be told, "Sorry, you can't."

MIDDLE
She quotes U.S. law and develops her position.

The United States Constitution, Article II, Section I, states that "no person except a natural-born citizen shall be eligible to the office of president." Is a person unfit to be president just because he or she was not born here? If you came to the U.S. when you were five, would someone who was born here have special citizenship skills that you would not have?

Everyone except Native Americans has roots in another country. Many foreign-born citizens hold high positions in the government and businesses of this country. For example, two people who might have made good presidents because of their experiences as secretaries of state are Henry Kissinger and Madeleine Albright. Under our current laws, however, neither could become president because neither is a U.S. citizen by birth.

ENDING
The writer concludes with a strong statement of opinion.

The children of today should grow up knowing that no doors are closed to them because of where they were born. The Constitution needs to be amended. It is time that the presidency be open to the best qualified of *all* the nation's citizens.

Editorial Cartoons: An editorial cartoon expresses an opinion using a dominant visual image combined with a few words. Study the following examples to see how it is done.

This simple picture by Tashi Peling shows the classic "ups and downs" of the stock market.

Ryan Mock's cartoon captures a timely sports-related issue.

LeeAnne Gomes personifies the population problem in her cartoon.

Feature Articles: A feature article is meant to entertain and to inform. It often covers an interesting angle related to a straight news story. In this feature article, student writer Aaron Kaplan describes the life and adventures of one very special veterinarian.

Cat Doctor of a Million Tales

BEGINNING

The writer introduces his unusual subject.

Louis J. Camuti is an 80-year-old New York veterinarian who specializes in treating cats. He treats all kinds of cats: fat cats, skinny cats, and even cats that bite. But before he can treat his patients, he has to find them. What he has learned to do is go from room to room examining every nook and cranny. When he has narrowed his search to one room, he closes the door behind him until he finally finds the patient. One time he found his patient inside the mattress!

MIDDLE

He gives examples from his subject's life. He adds a funny quotation.

Since Camuti makes house calls, he has seen many weird things. One of his strangest patients actually liked it when his master vacuumed him as if he were a rug. The only difference was that this rug purred. Camuti has examined as many as 27 cats in one house. Once he was asked to make a house call in Italy, but he solved the problem over the phone.

Another time he got a call from a lady who said there was something terribly wrong with her cat. When Camuti went inside the home, he found a cat who stared at him but couldn't run because the cat was just too fat! Camuti looked in the trash and found lots, and I mean lots, of cans of dog food. Then he went up to the butler and said, "Admit it, you committed the crime of feeding a cat dog food." The butler confessed and said, "All I wanted was to have the heaviest cat in the world. The heaviest cat is 33 pounds, while this one is only 28 pounds. I was so close."

ENDING

The closing sentences refer back to the beginning.

Dr. Camuti enjoys having been a vet for 50 years and never plans on quitting. He enjoys treating all his patients and meeting all their interesting owners.

Writing About Literature

Writing a review is one way that you can express your thoughts and feelings about a piece of literature. In a review, you first form an opinion about a novel, play, or short story, and then support it with examples and details from the reading. Ideas for reviews usually come from the main elements of literature—*plot, characterization, setting,* and *theme*. (See pages 343-344.)

Base the ideas in your review on a careful reading of the text. (You will need to reread the specific parts that you plan to use in your writing.) Present the results of your work in a carefully planned paragraph or essay. Your goal is to share something important you have learned through your reading and exploring. Think of a review as your unique interpretation of a piece of literature.

WHAT'S AHEAD

The main part of the chapter lists ideas for reviews, followed by writing guidelines and a sample book review. The last two pages show other ways to respond to literature—writing in a journal, writing a poem, and writing a letter to an author.

- Finding an Idea
- Writing Guidelines
- Sample Book Review
- Other Responses to Literature

E. A. Poe

Finding an Idea

This list of ideas for reviews is arranged according to the four main elements of literature: *plot, characterization, setting,* and *theme.* If you choose from these ideas and enhance them, you will be on your way to writing a well-developed book review.

Plot — The action of the story

- How is suspense built into the story? (Consider the important events leading up to the climax.)
- The climax (the most important event) changes the story in an effective way . . . in a believable way . . . in an unbelievable way.
- The ending is surprising . . . predictable . . . unbelievable.
- Are there any twists or reversals in the plot? (What do they add to the story?)

Characterization — The people or animals in a story

- The main character changes from _____ to _____ by the end of the story.
- Certain forces or circumstances—people, setting, events, or ideas—make the main character or characters act as they do.
- _____ is the main character's outstanding personality trait.
- I can identify with the main character when . . .
- What if the main character had (or hadn't) . . .

Setting — The time and place of the story

- The setting helps make the story exciting.
- The setting has an important effect on the main character.
- The setting (in a historical novel) has increased my knowledge of a certain time in history.
- The setting (in a science-fiction novel) creates a new and exciting world.

Theme — The author's statement or lesson about life

- Ambition . . . courage . . . jealousy . . . greed . . . happiness . . . peer pressure . . . is clearly a theme in (title of book).
- This book showed me what it is like to be . . .
- The moral "Don't judge a book by its cover," "Haste makes waste," "Hard work pays off," . . . is developed in (title of book).

Writing Guidelines

Prewriting ----[Choosing a Subject]

Choose one of the ideas listed on the previous page to develop in your review. If you are writing a longer review, you may want to choose more than one idea to develop. (Also feel free to change any of the ideas to meet your specific needs.)

Talk about possible writing ideas with your teacher or a classmate. (Keep in mind that a review is a type of persuasive writing in which your subject is an opinion that you must support.)

[Gathering Details]

Use a basic collection sheet to plan your review. State your subject on the first line. Then list ideas and examples from the book that you will use to develop your subject. (The sample below lists ideas for the model review on page 179.)

SAMPLE Collection Sheet

Subject: Jonas, the main character in The Giver, is quite satisfied with his world until he meets the Giver, and then everything changes.

Main Points

- The Elders in Jonas's world make all the decisions.
- When he turns 12, Jonas gets chosen as the Receiver of Memory, and the Giver is his teacher.
- The Giver teaches Jonas about choices.
- Jonas has to choose between a "safe" world and a risky world.

Writing ----[Writing the First Draft]

BEGINNING Pay special attention to the opening paragraph of your review. It should gain your reader's attention, name the title and author of your reading, and state the subject of your review.

Notice how the opening lines that follow effectively draw readers into the sample review. (See page 179.)

> **Imagine a "safe" world with no muggings, stealing, or war. Would you like to move there? What if this place didn't let you make your own choices? Would you still want to go?**

MIDDLE Then develop the main part of your writing using your collection sheet to help you add ideas.

ENDING In the closing paragraph, tie up any loose ends, summarize your main points, and/or help readers understand the significance of your opinion or main point.

Revising ----[Improving Your Writing]

Ask yourself these questions as you review and revise your first draft. (Also see page 24 for help.)

- ■ Does the opening name the title and author of my reading—as well as the subject of my review?
- ■ Does the information in the middle support or explain the subject?
- ■ Does my review include examples or ideas from the reading?
- ■ Are my ideas arranged in the best order?

Editing ----[Checking for Style and Accuracy]

Check your revised writing for style and for spelling, grammar, punctuation, and capitalization errors. Have someone else check your work as well. Then write a final copy to share.

 Note: Titles of novels, plays, and other longer pieces of literature should be underlined or in italics. Titles of short stories and individual poems should be enclosed in quotation marks.

Sample Book Review

In his review of Lois Lowry's *The Giver*, Jamell Baker focuses on an important change in the main character's life.

BEGINNING
The opening lines set the scene for the rest of the review.

MIDDLE
Specific examples from the novel support the focus.

ENDING
The reviewer suggests the outcome, but doesn't give it away.

Better Safe Than Sorry?

Imagine a "safe" world with no muggings, stealing, or war. Would you like to move there? What if this place didn't let you make your own choices? Would you still want to go? This is the world where Jonas lives, the main character in Lois Lowry's science-fiction novel The Giver. He is quite satisfied with his world until he meets the Giver, and then everything changes.

Jonas's world is an eerie place where the Elders control everything. When a boy wants to get married, the elders choose his wife. When a girl needs new clothes, the Elders give her a uniform. When a family needs food, the elders choose the items. Worst of all, when someone turns 12, the Elders assign the person a job—for life! Now that's spooky.

Jonas is pretty happy in this world. Then, when he turns 12, the Elders make him the next Receiver of Memory. His job is to remember lessons from the past when people made their own choices. The Giver is Jonas's teacher. He shows Jonas people in the past making bad choices that led to fighting and hate. But he also shows people making good choices that led to fun with friends, family parties, and love.

Jonas has to choose between his safe, controlled world or a riskier world in which he must live with his own choices. The Giver informs Jonas that the only "safe" people in the Elders' world are the ones they think are useful. "Useless" people are usually killed. In the end, Jonas can choose which world to live in because the Giver taught him what living is really all about.

Other Responses to Literature

There are many different ways to respond thoughtfully to literature, including the sample responses on the following two pages.

Responding in a Journal

This journal entry is a response to *Huckleberry Finn* by Mark Twain. The writer explains the connection between the book and his own life.

The writing sounds as if it were part of a conversation with a friend.

> Huck takes a great risk when he decides to help Jim escape. But to turn him in goes against some very basic beliefs that he can't really explain. (I guess this is what makes Huck such a likeable character—his natural goodness and "uncivilized" way of living.) I think there is a little bit of Huck Finn, the risk taker, in me. Take my choice of friends. I know that my parents may not approve of all of my friends. (No names will be mentioned.) But they don't see and know my friends like I do. . . .

Responding with a Poem

This poem is a personal response to the main character in *The True Confessions of Charlotte Doyle* by Avi.

The poem captures the main character's feelings.

> **Desolate Charlotte**
> by Danielle Hansche
>
> The cool wind slapped my saddened face
> As I stood on the deck feeling out of place.
>
> Frightened and alone with no one to turn to,
> I was wondering just what I should do.
>
> The sailors were working, leaving me alone.
> Oh, how I wished I was with my family at home.
>
> A great emptiness was eating inside of me
> As I watched the rough, rolling waves of the sea.
>
> I doubted myself and wondered if I would survive.
> Would I ever reach America alive!

Responding with a Letter

In the following letter to author Lois Duncan, Whitney Michener shares her thoughts about Ms. Duncan's style of writing.

9 Marigold Lane
Durham, NH 03824
March 25, 2000

Dear Lois Duncan,

I'm doing an author study of your works. So far, I've read Killing Mr. Griffin, Locked in Time, and The Twisted Window. My favorite was Killing Mr. Griffin. I found it to be very suspenseful, and I really like that in books. I have now just started reading They Never Came Home, and I hope it's as great as the others!

I like your writing a lot. I've been keeping a list of things I learned from your writing. One technique that I noticed was the way you end a chapter with a sentence that makes the reader want to keep going. A sentence from Locked in Time stands out in my mind: "The shocking word that flashed through my mind was death." Sound familiar?

Another technique I noticed is your use of very clear descriptions of places. I see that you tend to write about places near your home in Albuquerque. When I read your books, I feel like I could go out my front door and walk right into the scene you have described.

I do have one question for you, and I'll be interested to hear your response. Sometimes when I'm writing, I have trouble taking the story to where I want it to go. Sometimes I know the beginning and ending for a story, but I have trouble writing the material in between. What do you do when you get stuck? Do you have any tips for me?

Thanks so much for writing all your books. I can't wait for your next book to come out!

Sincerely,

Whitney Michener

Whitney Michener

Creative Writing

Writing Stories

Each one of you is a born storyteller—especially when it comes to sharing true stories with your friends. You probably enjoy inventing stories, too, but it may not be as easy for you as it once was. Why? Your imaginations might not be what they once were; they've gone south on you, so to speak. It's no fault of your own. You're simply at a point in your life when you're much more focused on real-life experiences.

The best way to feel more comfortable with the process of inventing is simple: Sit down and start writing stories. Write simple stories, crazy stories, stories modeled after the ones you read now and the ones you read when you were younger. Acquire a feel for inventing, and recapture that rich imagination you had as a young child.

WHAT'S AHEAD

This chapter contains all of the information you need to write effective stories. It includes everything from an explanation of the essential parts of a story to an effective student model, from step-by-step writing guidelines to a sampler of different story types.

- How Stories Develop
- Sample Story
- Writing Guidelines
- A Short-Story Sampler

How Stories Develop

Writing a story is like cooking food. First you gather the primary ingredients and prepare them according to a basic recipe. As you go along, you season your story with "spices" such as effective dialogue, colorful descriptions, and thoughtful explanations.

The Plot

The plot is the main ingredient in any story. It refers to all of the action—the events that move a story along from start to finish. A plot has five basic parts: *exposition, rising action, climax, falling action,* and *resolution.* The plot line that follows shows how these parts all work together.

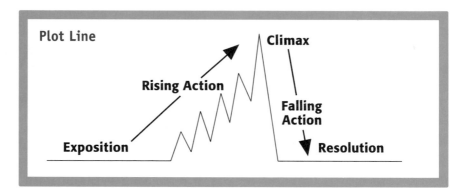

A Closer Look at the Parts . . .

EXPOSITION

The exposition is the beginning part of a story in which the characters, setting, and conflict are usually introduced. There is at least one main character in all stories and, almost always, one or more supporting or secondary characters. The setting is where the story takes place, and the conflict is the main problem that really gets the action under way.

> **Tracy Jones is a 13-year-old girl who lives in Houston, Texas. She is having trouble seeing things at a distance, but she doesn't want to wear glasses. She is afraid that people will make fun of her, especially at school.**

RISING ACTION

In the rising action, the main character tries to solve his or her problem. The main character should be involved in at least two or three important actions because of the problem. This builds suspense into the story.

First Action: Tracy goes to a movie with her mother, who asks why she squints to see the screen. Tracy says that she is just thinking hard about the film.

Second Action: Later, her parents learn that she has trouble seeing the board in class. Tracy says the classroom lights are too bright.

Third Action: Her parents insist that Tracy see an eye doctor. That night, Tracy dreams she is in class wearing big magnifying lenses.

CLIMAX

The climax is the most exciting or important part in a story. At this point, the main character comes face-to-face with his or her problem. (All of the action leads up to the climax.) This part is sometimes called the turning point.

The eye doctor says Tracy does need glasses. When they arrive a few days later, she dreads wearing them to school. While she is teased by a few kids, her close friends actually like her new look.

FALLING ACTION

In this part, the main character learns to deal with life "after the climax." Perhaps, he or she makes a new discovery about life or comes to understand things a little better.

Tracy learns that one of her friends has had glasses for weeks but was too shy to wear them. The two girls joke about starting a "spectacles" club. She also discovers that no one really pays much attention to her glasses when she wears them in class.

RESOLUTION

The resolution brings a story to a natural, surprising, or thought-provoking conclusion. (The falling action and the resolution often are very closely related.)

Tracy asks if she and her mom could go to another movie, and she promises to wear her glasses.

Sample Story

Read and enjoy this sample story by Jessica Houdek. It contains engaging characters, suspenseful action, and a clever twist at the end.

The Magic Coin

**Exposition
The main
character
introduces
herself.**

My parents think I'm the biggest con artist. Well, I'm really not. I just do minor things to get money from my younger sister because she is so gullible. Like a few months ago, when she bought a "magic" coin from a friend.

"Karen, you are so stupid! There is no such thing as a magic coin," I said to my sister.

"There is so! Sarah said it really works!" she protested.

"Then why did she sell it to you?"

"Her mom wouldn't let her keep it. It's against their religion or something." She led me upstairs to my parents' room, where my mom was elevating her sprained ankle.

"Mom. Karen bought some stupid magic coin," I told her.

"I know," she said. "She told me about it when she got home. Look, she fixed my foot." Mom got up and started jumping around.

**Rising
Action
Dialogue
effectively
moves the
story along.**

My eyes popped out of my head. Then I got suspicious. "Yeah, well how do I know you didn't plan this?"

Just then my dad came into the room. "Where's my checkbook?"

"Check your jacket," Karen piped up.

"No, I already looked there."

Karen sat for a few minutes and said, "My coin tells me it's between the seats of your car."

My dad left the room and returned a few minutes later with his checkbook in hand. "Wow! That's amazing. That coin must be magic!"

"It is, but Jessica doesn't believe me. Look, it cured Mom's foot," said Karen.

"You're right! How do you feel, honey?"

"I feel better, thanks to Karen's magic coin."

**Each new
interaction
adds
suspense.**

I said, "Well, if it is magic, let me borrow it. I have to give a speech tomorrow, and you know how nervous I can get."

"No, you can't borrow it . . . but I'll sell it to you for ten dollars," said Karen.

"Fine. Let me get my bank." I returned with the money.

**Climax
The main
character is
"conned"
by her
family.**

"No refunds!" Karen warned. "I don't want the coin back if you ruin it." She took my ten dollars and walked off.

The next day at school my name was called first to give my speech. I went up front, with the magic coin clutched in my hand, and started speaking. But all my words got mixed up. I ended up getting a C- on my report. I felt betrayed.

I talked with my friend Michelle about it at lunch.

"I just don't get it. The coin worked fine for my sister."

Michelle started giggling.

"What's so funny?" I asked, glaring at her.

"Your family really got you this time," she said.

I nodded. "You're right. So you want to help me teach my parents and sister a lesson they won't forget?"

**Falling
Action
Jessica's
plan after
the climax
adds more
suspense.**

"Sure! What do I have to do?"

"Well . . ." I began, and told her the details of my plan.

At 3:30, Michelle rang the doorbell at my house. My mom answered the door.

"Michelle? My goodness! What happened to you?"

"Jessica sold me this magic coin and told me it works miracles. But when Betty came up to me in the hall and tried to grab my homework, I pushed her, and she beat me up! Now I want to get my money back from Jess."

"How much did she sell the coin for?" Mom questioned.

"Eighteen dollars. She asked for twenty, but all I had was eighteen."

"Well, here's the money, dear. I'm sorry about the coin and all. We were trying to teach Jessica a lesson about the downside of being a con artist," Mom explained.

"I understand. Well, I'd better get home for dinner. Bye Mrs. Vostrejs," said Michelle.

She raced around to meet me at the back of the house.

"It worked! Just like you planned. Here's the money."

"Thanks. You did a great job, Michelle. You should be an actress. Here's the half I promised you."

"No thanks. Keep it. I'd rather have the coin."

"You can have it. But why would you want that dumb old worthless thing anyway?"

**Resolution
The story
comes to a
surprising
close.**

"It's not worthless. I was looking through my rare coins book, and this one is worth about three hundred dollars."

Michelle laughed and walked off, leaving me with my mouth hanging open.

Writing Guidelines

Prewriting ----[Gathering Details]

Before you can write a story, you must identify two important story elements: (1) a main character and (2) a problem for this character to deal with.

Create a Character ■ To get ideas for your main character, think of people you know, have seen, or have read about. Your main character can be a living person, a historical figure, or someone you create in your imagination. (Remember not to embarrass anyone by making your character too much like that person.)

To get to know your main character, draw a picture of this person and write a brief character sketch in which you describe some of his or her main personality traits, beliefs, desires, and so on.

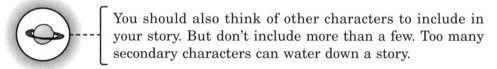 You should also think of other characters to include in your story. But don't include more than a few. Too many secondary characters can water down a story.

Form a Conflict ■ Your main character can be in conflict with another person (or persons), with him- or herself, with nature, with society, or with fate. (See page 343 for more information.) The character in the sample story is in conflict with her family members.

Make sure the problem is believable. You can't, for example, have your main character fight an entire army or travel around the world in search of a cure for a serious disease.

Other Elements to Consider . . .

Establish a Setting ■ Stick to one main location or setting; otherwise, your story may become difficult to control. Almost all of the action in the sample story takes place in the main character's home.

Think About the Action ■ What could your main character do about the problem? Try to list at least two or three of these actions. Also consider the climax or turning point in the story.

Consider an Ending ■ Decide how you want your story to end. Make sure that your ending is believable within the context of your story.

Prewriting ----[**Gathering Details**]

A story map can help you collect ideas for your story. Complete enough of the map so you have a good idea about the structure of your story. (The story map that follows lists the main parts in the sample story.)

Sample Story Map

Title: _The Magic Coin_

Main Character: _Jessica, a clever teenaged con artist_

Other Characters: _Karen, her sister_   _Father_

Mother   _Michelle, a friend_

Conflict: _Jessica has to deal with her family and their belief in a "magic" coin._

Setting: _Main character's house_

Rising Action:
  Event 1: _Karen buys a "magic" coin._

  Event 2: _The parents testify to its powers._

  Event 3: _Jessica is tricked into buying it._

Climax: _The coin fails Jessica in school._

Resolution: _Jessica is tricked again by her friend._

Writing ----[**Writing the First Draft**]

Use your story map as a general guide when you develop your first draft. (Also refer to pages 184-185 for help.)

Exposition ■ Grab your reader's attention by starting your story right in the middle of the action. As you develop this part, try to identify the main character, the setting, and the main problem. (See the beginning of the sample story, page 186, for an example.)

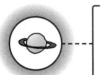

Choose one narrator—either a character within the story or someone outside of the story. The sample story is told from the main character's point of view. (See "Point of View," page 344, for more information.)

Rising Action and Climax ■ Let your characters' conversations (dialogue) and actions move the story along as much as possible. (See "Writing Dialogue" below.)

Falling Action and Resolution ■ In most stories, the action quickly comes to a close after the climax. What happens in this part should show how the main character has been affected by the climax.

Readers don't need (or necessarily want) a nice, neat, "everybody lived happily ever after" ending. But give them something—even if it's nothing more than a natural, smooth stopping point in the action.

Writing Dialogue

Refer to these guidelines when you develop dialogue in your short stories. (Also study the dialogue in the sample story, page 186.)

■ Write the dialogue as speakers actually speak. (People often interrupt each other.)

■ Focus on the speaker's beliefs or problem. (Generally one speaker's beliefs clash with another's.)

■ Keep the conversations moving along. (Characters don't have to say everything. Leave some things to the reader's imagination.)

■ Present the dialogue so it is easy to read. (Indent every time someone new speaks and identify the speaker if it isn't clear who is talking. See pages 399-400 for help with punctuation.)

Revising ----[Improving Your Writing]

Ask yourself the following questions when you review and revise your first draft. (Also see page 24.)

- Do the characters' words and actions make sense? (We wouldn't expect the neighborhood bully to talk like a college professor.)
- Is there a real or believable conflict that keeps the story going?
- Do all of the characters play an important role in the story? Are all of the conversations, explanations, and events important? (Make sure that your story moves along at a steady clip. You don't have to tell the reader everything.)
- Is the main character put to the test at the climax in the story? (The main character should undergo some change because of this event.)
- Does the story contain any holes? (Fill in any holes or gaps in the story line.)

Editing ----[Checking for Style and Accuracy]

When you edit your revised story, check first for the style of your writing. Do the sentences read smoothly? Have you paid special attention to word choice? (It always helps to read your story out loud.) Change any words, phrases, or ideas that cause you to stumble. Then edit for grammar, spelling, and punctuation errors.

TOPPING OFF YOUR WRITING

Here's how to top off your writing with a good title. Think of your title as fish bait: it should look juicy, it should dance slightly, and it should have a hook in it.

- To look juicy, a title must contain strong, colorful words (*The Black Stallion, Brave New World*).
- To dance, it must have rhythm (*The Old Man and the Sea*, not The Sea and the Old Man).
- And to hook your reader, it must grab the imagination (*Never Cry Wolf,* not Life Among the Wolves).

List a number of possible titles; then select the one that provides the best bait for your reader.

A Short-Story Sampler

Here are brief descriptions of popular short-story types. Use these as starting points for your own stories.

Mystery

Think of a crime, a list of suspects, a criminal, a star detective, and you're ready to write your first whodunit. Pay close attention to the mysteries on TV to see how screenwriters develop their stories, or try reading books by Agatha Christie, Richard Peck, Tony Hillerman, Norma Johnston, or M. E. Kerr.

Fantasy

Add some fantastic elements to real-world situations and create a fantasy. Think of some of your favorite childhood stories for ideas. Many of these stories contain fantastic elements (animals that talk and bathtubs that become pirate ships, etc.). Joan Aikens, Lloyd Alexander, and Alan Garner are fantasy writers you could try reading.

Science Fiction

Imagine a world 100 years after a nuclear war. Who would be living? What would life be like? What would the people know about life as it was before the war? This is science fiction—when life as we know it is dramatically altered in some way. Read "By the Waters of Babylon" by Stephen Vincent Benét for a great story along these lines.

Myth

All of us have a fascination with myths. They are wonderful stories that attempt to explain some natural phenomenon. Create your own myth, explaining why we cry, why early summer is tornado season, or, perhaps, why diamonds are so valued.

Fable

Write a brief story that makes a point, teaches, or advises. There are two basic ways you can go about doing this: Start with a moral and develop a story that leads up to it, or develop a story and decide afterward what it teaches or advises.

Writing Poetry

Of all the forms of creative writing, none is more loved, or more hated, than poetry. Some people love the unique way in which poetry allows them to share their thoughts and feelings. Others enjoy reading and listening to the rhymes, rhythms, and images of poetry. As for those who dislike poetry? Well, they probably haven't given it a good try lately—at least not as it is described in this chapter.

Actually, you've probably had more experience with poetry than you think. As an infant, you were rocked to sleep with cradle rhymes like "Rock-a-bye baby, in the treetop. . . ." Later, you chanted jump-rope jingles like "Hank and Frieda / sittin' in a tree / K-I-S-S-I-N-G." Today, you certainly have favorite song lyrics and advertising jingles. All of these examples are poetry of a sort.

WHAT'S AHEAD

This chapter begins by describing what poetry is all about. Next it explains how to read and write poetry. A three-part glossary of poetic terms and forms ends the chapter.

- What Is Poetry?
- Reading and Appreciating Poetry
- Writing Guidelines
- Traditional Techniques of Poetry
- Traditional Forms of Poetry
- Invented Forms of Poetry

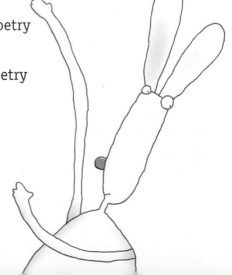

What Is Poetry?

The poet Marianne Moore defines poetry as "imaginary gardens with real toads in them." This definition may seem a strange way to explain something, but that's why it suits poetry so well. Other writing may be serious and factual, but good poetry is always creative and, at times, a bit playful. An effective poem takes us away to an "imaginary garden," yet it often springs from a real experience—one of the many "toads" hopping in and out of our daily lives.

What makes poetry different from prose (the regular writing you do)? Here are some of the differences that make poetry so special.

Poetry speaks to the senses.

Poets create word pictures that build an image in your mind. Notice how the following example appeals to your sense of sight:

> As night falls we head for bed,
> Great-Grandma in her velvet, royal blue nightgown,
> Her silver hair like a moon in a night sky,
> Her curlers, when the light hits them just right,
> Sparkling like stars.
>
> —Carrie Materi

Here are lines from poems that appeal to other senses:

> Noisy
> filled with laughter
> shrieking
> and quiet
> that is what cabin
> 8 sounds like.
>
> —Jaclyn Wohl

> A cup of hot chocolate,
> Steaming,
> Its warm breath kissing my face.
>
> —Jennifer Karakkal

Poetry speaks to the heart.

Poetry asks you to feel something (that's the heart part), not just think about it. You can tell how the poet feels about being alone in the following example:

> Silence is
> A friend in times of sorrow
> When all the amiable chatter in the world
> Brings no relief
>   —Jennifer Karakkal

Poetry looks different from prose.

Poems are written in lines and stanzas (groups of lines), and they usually leave a lot of white space on a page. Here is a four-line stanza from a poem about a roller coaster:

> Chugging slowly to the top
> Waiting for that long, long drop
> My stomach turns into a knot.
> I focus on the parking lot.
>   —Molly Jones

Poetry sounds different.

Poets pay special attention to sound in their work. Here are some of the techniques that make poems pleasing to the ear.

Repeat words: **I see water, I see sky, and I see sun.**

Rhyme words: **Ever go away? . . . Happy every day.**

Repeat vowel sounds: **Lonely old bones.**

Repeat consonant sounds: **Sparkling silver stars.**

Use words that sound like what they mean: **Eggs crack. Splat!**

Reading and Appreciating Poetry

If you know the rules and the strategies, watching a baseball game can be almost as much fun as playing baseball yourself. Real fans of the sport not only enjoy the game as it unfolds, but they also love to talk about the experience afterward.

The same is true of poetry. Once you know something about the rules and conventions, reading poetry can be extremely enjoyable. Of course, writing a poem or two of your own increases your appreciation, as does talking about favorite poems with other "fans." The following suggestions will help you get the most out of the poems you read.

APPLY YOUR KNOWLEDGE

As you read a poem, apply what you know about poetry in general.

- Ask yourself what pictures come to mind. What do you see and hear? How does the poem make you feel?
- Pay attention to the poem's structure. How does it look on the page? Does the poem have a unique shape?
- Pay attention to the words and the sounds in the poem. Is rhyme or repetition used? What other creative uses of language do you notice?
- Does the poem follow a definite pattern of rhythm, or does it seem to flow more naturally?

READ CAREFULLY

Use these tips as a general guide to reading poetry.

- Read the poem slowly and carefully. Enjoy each and every word.
- Read the poem several times. With each reading, you will notice new things about the poem, and you will enjoy it more.
- Read the poem aloud. Notice the way its words and phrases flow.
- Try to catch the general meaning of the poem during your first reading. Knowing the general meaning will help you understand the poem's more difficult parts.
- Share the poem with your friends and discuss it afterward. Their insights will help you enjoy the poem even more.

SAMPLE Poems

Read and enjoy the following two student poems. (Remember to follow the tips and strategies listed on the previous page.)

MATTHEW'S MEADOW

What pictures do you see as you read this poem? - - - - -

Ancient fruit trees sway back and forth,
Apple, pear, and plum.
Many are broken by time and wind.
Tall grass ripples from western gusts
And becomes an ocean before my eyes.

A hawk above scans the waves
for field mice.
Great, outstretched wings soar higher
in the morning sun.

He is a fisherman of the green sea.
This portrait, this picture, this space in time,
Dare I enter and break the spell?
Or must I leave it and just move on?

—Matthew Kratochvil

The Gift

Open it up,
But be careful.
Don't let any of the words escape,
But catch them like fireflies,
and keep them in the jar of your heart,
To be stored forever.

- - - - - What does this poem make you think of?

—Julia Kim

Writing Guidelines

Writing poetry is a lot of fun. It allows you to use language in special ways. It also lets you share an experience or a feeling in ways that will stir your reader's emotions.

Writing poetry is also work. Good poets write and rewrite their poems many times to get the most effect with the fewest words. The guidelines that follow will help you write a free-verse poem, a poem that does not require regular rhythm or rhyme.

Prewriting ----[Choosing a Subject]

Choose a subject you really care about.

- **Remember an important time or event in your life:** *a special trip, the first day at a new school, a special gathering you attended.*
- **Look at the world around you:** *the sparkle of summer sun on a pond, a stuffed animal, loose litter cluttering a yard.*
- **Describe something you like or dislike:** *a tasty food, a favorite sweater, a case of the flu, a muggy day.*
- **Think of a favorite person:** *a grandparent, a historical figure, a sports hero, your best friend.*

[Gathering Details]

Begin collecting ideas about your subject. Student writer Lauren Moran decided to write about a grassy lawn. Here is her initial cluster of ideas.

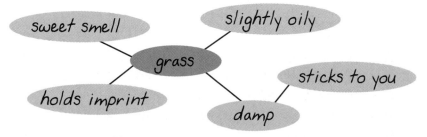

After you have collected enough details, look for a powerful idea or image (mental picture) to use as the main focus of your poem.

Writing -----[**Writing the First Draft**]

Don't worry about writing the perfect poem in your first draft; just write freely until you've said all that you need to say about your subject. And don't overlook the senses—the sights, sounds, and tastes, related to it.

One of the nice things about writing a free-verse poem is that it can take any form. Often the form will develop naturally as you write— perhaps a simple list of phrases will do the job. As long as it makes sense to you and the reader, your poem can look any way you like.

Lauren Moran wrote her first draft as one long sentence in list form. She decided to focus on one of the ideas in her cluster, that grass can stick to you.

GRASS POEM
Sweet-smelling grass
clippings cling to our hair,
and stick to our backs
as we rise, leaving
our own imprints
on the grass.

Revising -----[**Improving Your Writing**]

After you complete your first draft, carefully review your work. Also make sure to have at least one other person read and react to it. Use the following checklist as your reviewing guide:

- Are all of my ideas complete? Do they convey the feelings and meanings I want to convey?
- Did I use the best words and images to describe my subject?
- Do all of the words and phrases read effectively? (Think in terms of the meaning *and* the sound of the words.)
- Does the form of the poem add to its overall effect?
- Does my title add to the meaning of the poem?

Make the necessary changes in your poem after you review it.

Editing ----[**Checking for Style and Accuracy**]

Check your revised poem for capitalization, punctuation, spelling, and grammar errors. Ask someone else to check your work for errors as well. Then write a correct final copy of your poem. Proofread this copy before sharing it.

HELPFUL HINT

In a free-verse poem, you do not have to capitalize the first word in each line. The choice is yours. Use end punctuation marks or other punctuation as you would in regular prose. Or don't use punctuation at all if you don't feel it is necessary. (See the model below.)

SAMPLE Free-Verse Poem

Lauren Moran decided to write the final version of her poem in the shape of a blade of grass. (Or is it a sickle?) Notice that she changed some of the words and images she used in her first draft.

> **GRASS POEM**
>
> the grass
> smelling
> sweet
> slightly
> oily
> clung
> damp
> in our
> hair
> on our
> legs
> leaving
> imprints
> of our
> conversation
> on the lawn

Poems can be shared in many creative ways. For example, poetry and art complement each other extremely well. Poetry can also be performed. All you need is a bit of preparation and a willing audience.

Poetry and Art

Poster: Present your poem, together with an illustration or a drawing, on a piece of poster board.

Bookmark: Write your poem on a colorful piece of paper cut to bookmark size and shape. Decorate the bookmark in any way you wish.

Greeting Card: Create a greeting card. Write your poem on the outside and add a personal message inside. Or write your poem inside and illustrate the front of the card.

Poetry and Drama

Oral Reading: Reciting poetry aloud is an effective way to share its rhythm. Consider using background music for your performance. Be sure to practice your delivery until it is smooth and dramatic before you read to your audience.

Perform a Poem: It can be fun to perform a poem with different people reciting different sections. To get started, script the poem to show who should read the different lines. A sample script for "Matthew's Meadow" (page 197) is provided below.

SAMPLE Script

Line 1:	Three people (the trees) recite this line together.
Line 2:	The three "trees" divide this line. One says "Apple," the next says "pear," the last says "and plum."
Line 3:	One person (the narrator) recites this line.
Line 4:	One person (the grass) recites this line.
Line 5:	The narrator recites this line.
Lines 6-9:	One person (the hawk) recites these lines.
Line 10:	The "trees" recite this line together.
Lines 11-13:	The narrator recites these lines.

Traditional Techniques of Poetry

Most traditional poems follow exact patterns of rhyme and/or rhythm. Consider this famous traditional poem by Robert Frost:

STOPPING BY WOODS ON A SNOWY EVENING

Whose woods these are I think I know.	(a)
His house is in the village though;	(a)
He will not see me stopping here	(b)
To watch his woods fill up with snow.	(a)
My little horse must think it queer	(b)
To stop without a farmhouse near	(b)
Between the woods and frozen lake	(c)
The darkest evening of the year.	(b)
He gives his harness bells a shake	(c)
To ask if there is some mistake.	(c)
The only other sound's the sweep	(d)
Of easy wind and downy flake.	(c)
The woods are lovely, dark and deep	(d)
But I have promises to keep,	(d)
And miles to go before I sleep,	(d)
And miles to go before I sleep.	(d)

Rhyme and Meter

In most traditional poetry, the rhyme is organized in patterns called **rhyme schemes**. In the poem above, rhyming lines are labeled with the same letter. The rhyme scheme is *aaba / bbcb / ccdc / dddd*.

Meter is the rhythm or "pattern of accented (´) and unaccented (˘) syllables" in the lines of a poem. In the poem above, every other syllable is accented. (Whose woods these are I think I know.) This pattern of unaccented and accented syllables creates the poem's meter. (See "Foot" and "Verse" on page 203 for more information on meter.)

Other Poetry Techniques

Alliteration ■ The repeating of beginning consonant sounds.

  creamy and crunchy

Assonance ■ The repetition of vowel sounds, as in the following lines from "The Hayloft" by R. L. Stevenson.

  Till the shining scythes went far and wide
  And cut it down to dry.

Consonance ■ The repetition of consonant sounds anywhere within words, not just at the beginning.

> **The sailor sings of ropes and things**
> **In ships upon the seas.**

End Rhyme ■ The rhyming of words at the ends of lines of poetry, as in the following lines from "Aunt Jennifer's Tigers" by Adrienne Rich.

> **Aunt Jennifer's tigers prance across a screen,**
> **Bright topaz denizens of a world of green.**

Foot ■ One unit of meter. There are five basic feet:

Iambic: An unaccented syllable followed by an accented one (rĕ péat)
Anapestic: Two unaccented syllables before one accented (ĭn tĕr rúpt)
Trochaic: An accented syllable followed by an unaccented (old́ ĕr)
Dactylic: An accented syllable followed by two unaccented (ó pĕn ly̆)
Spondaic: Two accented syllables (heart́ breaḱ)

Internal Rhyme ■ The rhyming of words within one line of poetry, as in

> **Jack Sprat could eat no fat** (or) **Peter Peter pumpkin eater.**

Onomatopoeia ■ The use of a word whose sound makes you think of its meaning, as in **buzz, gunk, gushy, swish, zigzag, zing,** or **zip.**

Quatrain ■ A four-line stanza. Common rhyme schemes in quatrains are *aabb, aaba,* and *abab.* The Frost poem on the previous page is arranged in quatrains.

Repetition ■ The repeating of a word or phrase to add rhythm or to focus on an idea, as in the following lines from Poe's "The Raven."

> **While I nodded, nearly napping, suddenly there came a tapping,**
> **as of someone gently rapping, rapping at my chamber door—**

Stanza ■ A division in a poem named for the number of lines it contains. Below are the most common stanzas.

Couplet	two-line stanza	*Sestet*	six-line stanza
Triplet	three-line stanza	*Septet*	seven-line stanza
Quatrain	four-line stanza	*Octave*	eight-line stanza

Verse ■ A name for a line of poetry written in meter. Verse is named according to the number of "feet" per line. Here are eight types:

Monometer	one foot	*Pentameter*	five feet
Dimeter	two feet	*Hexameter*	six feet
Trimeter	three feet	*Heptameter*	seven feet
Tetrameter	four feet	*Octometer*	eight feet

Traditional Forms of Poetry

Poetry has been around for centuries, beginning with bards and messengers who used poems to pass along news, songs, and stories. Today, we find poetry in songs, on greeting cards, in reading anthologies, and so on. Here are some other traditional forms of poetry.

Ballad ■ A ballad is a poem that tells a story. Ballads are usually written in four-line stanzas called quatrains. Often, the first and third lines have four accented syllables; the second and fourth have three. (See "Quatrain" on page 203 for possible rhyme schemes.) Here is a quatrain from "The Enchanted Shirt" by John Hay.

> The King was sick. His cheek was red
> And his eye was clear and bright;
> He ate and drank with a kingly zest,
> And peacefully snored at night.

Blank Verse ■ Blank verse is unrhymed poetry with meter. The lines in blank verse are 10 syllables in length. Every other syllable, beginning with the second syllable, is accented. (*Note*: Not every line will have exactly 10 syllables.) Consider these first three lines from "Birches" by Robert Frost.

> When I see birches bend to left and right
> Across the lines of straighter darker trees,
> I like to think some boy's been swinging them.

Cinquain ■ Cinquain poems are five lines in length. There are syllable and word cinquain poems.

Syllable Cinquain

Line 1: Title	2 syllables
Line 2: Description of title	4 syllables
Line 3: Action about the title	6 syllables
Line 4: Feeling about the title	8 syllables
Line 5: Synonym for title	2 syllables

Word Cinquain

Line 1: Title	1 word
Line 2: Description of title	2 words
Line 3: Action about the title	3 words
Line 4: Feeling about the title	4 words
Line 5: Synonym for title	1 word

Couplet ■ A couplet is two lines of verse that usually rhyme and state one complete idea. (See "Stanza" on page 203.)

Elegy ■ An elegy is a poem that states a poet's sadness about the death of an important person. In the famous elegy "O Captain, My Captain," Walt Whitman writes about the death of Abraham Lincoln.

Epic ■ An epic is a long story poem that describes the adventures of a hero. "The Odyssey" by Homer is a famous epic about the Greek hero Odysseus.

Free Verse ■ Free verse is poetry that does not require meter (regular rhythm) or a rhyme scheme.

Haiku ■ Haiku is a type of Japanese poetry that presents a picture of nature. A haiku poem is three lines in length. The first line is five syllables; the second, seven; and the third, five.

> **Like a bad landscape**
> **with neither depth nor feeling;**
> **the world through one eye**
> —Derek Lam

Limerick ■ A limerick is a humorous verse of five lines. Lines one, two, and five rhyme, as do lines three and four. Lines one, two, and five have three stressed syllables; lines three and four have two.

> **There once was a panda named Lu,**   (a)
> **Who always ate crunchy bamboo.**   (a)
> **He ate all day long,**   (b)
> **Till he looked like King Kong.**   (b)
> **Now the zoo doesn't know what to do.**   (a)
> —Sarah Diot

Lyric ■ A lyric is a short poem that expresses personal feeling.

> **MY HEART LEAPS UP WHEN I BEHOLD** (first 5 lines)
>
> **My heart leaps up when I behold**
> **A rainbow in the sky;**
> **So was it when my life began;**
> **So is it now I am a man;**
> **So be it when I shall grow old.**
> —William Wordsworth

Ode ■ An ode is a long lyric that is deep in feeling and rich in poetic devices and imagery. "Ode to a Grecian Urn" is a famous ode by John Keats.

Sonnet ■ A sonnet is a fourteen-line poem that states a poet's personal feelings. The Shakespearean sonnet follows the *abab/cdcd/efef/gg* rhyme scheme. Each line in a sonnet is 10 syllables in length, and every other syllable is stressed, beginning with the second syllable.

Invented Forms of Poetry

Don't be afraid to try something new the next time you sit down to write a poem. The invented forms of poetry that follow will help you get started.

Alphabet Poetry ■ A form of poetry that states a creative or humorous idea using part of the alphabet.

> **Hot dogs on buns.**
> **I love them!**
> **Just drizzle with a little**
> **Ketchup, and they've**
> **Left for**
> **My tummy!**
> —Emily Trapp

Clerihew Poetry ■ A form of humorous or light verse created by Edmund Clerihew Bentley. A clerihew poem consists of two rhyming couplets. The name of some well-known person creates one of the rhymes.

> **Edmund Clerihew Bentley**
> **Brooded intently**
> **On many a foible**
> **He thus made enjoyable.**
> —Colin Burke

Concrete Poetry ■ A form of poetry in which the shape or design helps express the meaning or feeling of the poem.

> pEAKs VALLEYs LIFE!

Contrast Couplet ■ A couplet in which the first line includes two words that are opposites. The second line makes a comment about the first.

> **Some hours are too short, and some are too long.**
> **I wonder who it was that made the clocks all wrong.**
> —L. Winfred Smith

Definition Poetry ■ Poetry that defines a word or an idea creatively.

> **Temptation—**
> **the modern Pied Piper,**
> **calling, willing, drawing**
> **the soul resisting,**
> **the brain relenting.**
> —Kristin Mueller

List Poetry ■ A form of poetry that lists words or phrases.

> **ROOMS**
> There are rooms to start up in
> Rooms to start out in
> Rooms to start over in
> Rooms to lie in
> Rooms to lie about in
> Rooms to lay away in . . .
> —Ray Griffith

Name Poetry ■ A form of poetry in which the letters of a name are used to begin each line in the poem.

> Amazing
> Silly
> Happy
> Loud
> Even though she's only two, she can still say "I love
> You!"
> —Roman Leykin

Phrase Poetry ■ A form of poetry that states an idea with a list of phrases.

> Across the icy, frozen pond
> On a turn
> On a jump
> Into the air
> Down again
> For the win
> With a radiant smile.
> —Allison Bannerman

Terse Verse ■ A form of humorous verse made up of two words that rhyme and have the same number of syllables.

CLOCK POEM	WILTED FLOWER	TARDY VISITOR
Time	Floppy	Late
Rhyme	Poppy	Date

—Katheryn Smith

Title-down Poetry ■ A form of poetry in which the letters that spell the subject of the poem are used to begin each line.

Cuddled in my	Flits around my head.
Arms, purring as I	Lands on my nose. Makes me
Tickle its fur.	Yell!

—Candace Smith

Report Writing

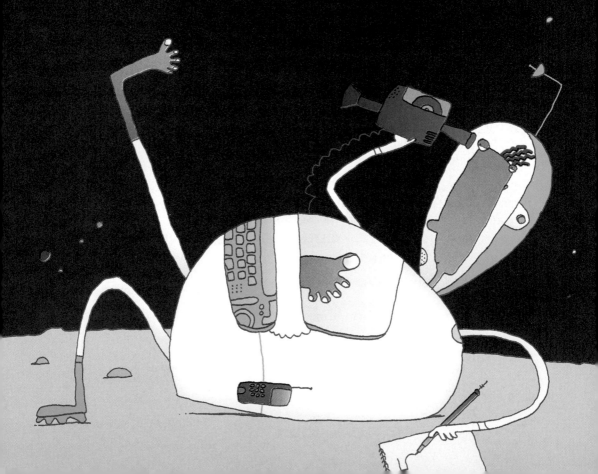

Writing
Observation Reports

"I pay a good deal of attention to matters of detail," said Sherlock Holmes. "Observation is second nature to me." To this famous fictional sleuth, observation and deduction were more important than knowing that the earth orbited the sun. Through skilled observation, Holmes could solve any mystery.

People in the real world often rely on the same keen sense of observation. For example, doctors thoroughly examine their patients before they make a diagnosis. Artists carefully study their subjects before they attempt any type of artistic expression. Investigative reporters diligently study the facts and details before they write their stories. In any meaningful endeavor, paying attention to "matters of detail" is extremely important.

WHAT'S AHEAD

This chapter contains a sample observation report, a form of writing that requires your best detecting skills. It also includes guidelines that apply to observation writing in general, and a sample science observation report.

- Sample Observation Report
- Writing Guidelines
- Sample Science Observation Report

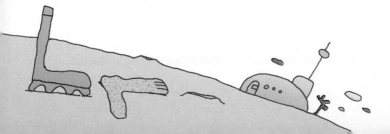

Sample Observation Report

Randy VanderMey's report describes what he observed in an airplane prior to takeoff. His observations include vivid details that appeal to all the senses. As you read this sample, you will see that he was saturated in different sights, sounds, and smells.

The writer uses the present tense ("are clicking") in his report.

The specific details display a keen sense of observation.

The writer makes a variety of sensory observations just prior to takeoff.

"Good Afternoon, Ladies and Gentlemen"

Safety belts are clicking all around with a sound like castanets. Up ahead all the middle seats are empty. One old man with a wide sunburned neck and gray curly hair wears a blue baseball cap with a red button at the peak. The blue visor has a red rim, green underneath. A woman comes on board, walks sideways down the center aisle. She has black hair, china-white skin, and bright red lips.

Suddenly a warm soft voice comes from overhead: "Good afternoon, ladies and gentlemen. I'd like to welcome you aboard United flight 596, nonstop to Toronto. We'll be under way in a few minutes."

In the background, behind his voice, I hear the sounds of the cockpit. I smell jet fuel and feel rumbles under the floor. The whole plane quivers. A woman's voice comes on: "Prepare doors."

A flight attendant up front is fanning herself with one of the safety cards we have in the seat pockets before us. A bell quietly goes "boing." Now there are about six kinds of whines all going at once. I feel hot; sweat-trickles under my shirt; the nozzle overhead blows hot, gasoliney air on my head. The flight attendant reads over the intercom about slides that will self-inflate and aisle lights that will go on. The plane begins to rock and rumble and roll backwards. The flight attendant tells us to sit back, relax, and enjoy our flight.

Writing Guidelines

Prewriting   ----[Choosing a Subject]

Choose a location that has interesting sights, sounds, and action. A cafeteria table during lunchtime or a bus or subway car would offer good possibilities. (See page 51 for ideas.)

[Gathering Details]

Make your observations by listing things in a notebook as you observe them. Or, fill in a graphic organizer like the one below by listing sights, sounds, smells, and so on, as you "observe" them.

Five Senses Organizer

Location				
Sights	Sounds	Smells	Tastes	Textures

Writing   ----[Writing the First Draft]

Share all of the details in the order that you listed them. In this way, your report will develop naturally from one sight or sound to another. (See page 210.) You may also choose to organize your observation around a main idea, just as you would in a descriptive paragraph. (See page 100.)

Revising   and   **Editing**

As you revise and edit your first draft, make sure that you have . . .
■ stated all of the important observations,
■ used the best descriptive words,
■ arranged your supporting details in the best order, and
■ checked your writing for punctuation, grammar, and spelling errors.

Sample Science Observation Report

In your science class, you may be asked to write an observation report on an experiment or a project. Jeffrey Mishler observed the sun for sunspots. Here is the summary report he prepared.

Sunspots

SCIENTIFIC PROBLEM (PURPOSE): How does the number of sunspots change over a given amount of time?

HYPOTHESIS: The number of sunspots will stay relatively the same over the six months I will observe them.

PROCEDURE: I covered one eyepiece on a pair of binoculars and made a filter for the other eyepiece. To do this, I cut a piece of black poster board into a 2-foot circle. In the center of the circle, I cut a hole just big enough for the open eyepiece and taped the filter in place. I positioned the binoculars so that the sun's rays would go through the eyepiece onto a drawing pad. On the paper, I traced the image of the sun and any sunspots. I repeated the process every sunny day.

OBSERVATIONS: On January 11, I saw a main sunspot group in the southeast. On January 21, there was a bulge in the sunspot region. On January 24, for the first time, the northeast was dotted with sunspots. The number of sunspots had slightly increased within these two weeks. On February 22, there was a huge area of sunspots on the northeast, one of the largest so far. On February 25, the large region I observed a few days ago was starting to decrease in size.

CONCLUSIONS: My hypothesis that the number of sunspots would stay the same was way off. I had not realized how quickly the number of sunspots would change, and I am not even halfway through the six-month project.

Writing Summaries

One of your challenges in school is to understand and learn from all the reading you do. You read so many textbooks, handouts, articles, reference books, and so on, that it can be hard to remember everything. Of course, there are strategies such as taking notes and using graphic organizers that will help you get more out of what you read.

Writing summaries is another good way to learn from your reading. A **summary** is a short piece of writing that restates the main idea of a reading selection. Writing summaries will help you find and understand the main ideas in what you read, and reviewing your summaries will help you prepare for tests.

WHAT'S AHEAD

In this chapter you will find guidelines for writing a summary, along with a sample summary. You will also learn about the paraphrase, another writing strategy that will lead to better understanding of reading selections.

- Writing Guidelines
- Sample Summary
- Paraphrasing

Writing Guidelines

Prewriting ----[Choosing a Subject]

Write a summary when you need to find and remember the main idea in a reading selection. State the main idea in words that are easy to understand and remember.

[Gathering Details]

- Read the selection at least twice. Pay special attention to titles and subheadings, words in italics or boldface, and the first sentence of each paragraph.
- Look up any new words. Then read the selection again.
- Ask yourself: *What is the most important idea in the reading? What idea are all the details connected to?*

Writing ----[Writing the First Draft]

Write a first sentence that states, in your own words, the main idea of the reading. Add only the important details that are needed to explain the main idea. Use your own words as much as possible.

Revising ----[Improving Your Writing]

Read the first draft of your summary and ask yourself:
- Have I clearly stated the main idea?
- Have I included all the important details needed to understand the main idea, and nothing extra?
- Is it clear how the details relate to the main idea?
- Are my sentences in the best order?
- Have I used my own words and writing style?

Editing ----[Checking for Style and Accuracy]

Check your summary for punctuation and capitalization errors. Then write a neat final copy.

Sample Summary

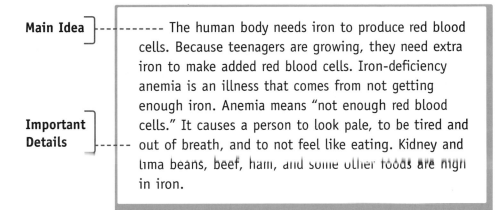

Main Idea - - - - - - - - - The human body needs iron to produce red blood cells. Because teenagers are growing, they need extra iron to make added red blood cells. Iron-deficiency anemia is an illness that comes from not getting enough iron. Anemia means "not enough red blood **Important** cells." It causes a person to look pale, to be tired and **Details** - - - - - - out of breath, and to not feel like eating. Kidney and lima beans, beef, ham, and some other foods are high in iron.

Original Reading Selection

Iron: A Necessary Nutrient

All human beings need the mineral iron in their diets, but teenagers need even more iron than adults. Iron is one of the ingredients the body uses to make red blood cells. Teenagers need additional iron because as they grow their bodies need to produce more blood, and that means more red blood cells, along with the other elements that comprise blood.

When a person doesn't get sufficient iron in his or her diet, a condition called iron-deficiency anemia results. Anemia is a medical term that means "not enough red blood cells." Anemia also can be caused by a shortage of vitamin B12, because it, too, is needed to make red blood cells. But iron-deficiency anemia is much more common than the anemia caused by B12 deficiency, which is called pernicious anemia.

The two kinds of anemia have the same symptoms: feeling fatigued much of the time; getting "out of breath" easily; a pale appearance; a fast, irregular heartbeat; and a lack of appetite. These symptoms may show up very soon when a person stops getting enough iron, because the body makes red blood cells every day.

Among the foods that deliver a healthy dose of iron are kidney beans and lima beans, beef, ham, turkey (dark meat), oysters and clams, sunflower seeds, and almonds.

Paraphrasing

A paraphrase is similar to a summary: Both are written using your own words and style, and both can help you understand and remember what you read. Here is the difference: A summary includes only the main idea of a reading selection; a paraphrase includes all the ideas in a reading selection. While a summary is much shorter than the reading selection, a paraphrase may be the same length or a little shorter.

Write a paraphrase when you want to . . .
- state something you've read in simpler words.
- rewrite what other people have written to support your ideas in a report or research paper.

To write a paraphrase . . .
- begin as if you were writing a summary.
- put all the ideas and details—not just the most important ones—into your own words. (You may also change the order in which you present the ideas.)

To revise a paraphrase, make sure that . . .
- you have included all the details.
- you have used your own words and style, not the author's.
- you have not changed the meaning of any ideas.

Paraphrase of "Iron: A Necessary Nutrient"

The human body needs iron to produce red blood cells. Since teenagers are growing, they need extra iron to make added red blood cells. Iron-deficiency anemia is an illness that comes from not getting enough iron. Anemia means "not enough red blood cells." It causes a person to look pale, to be tired and out of breath, to have an irregular heartbeat, and to not feel like eating. This can happen quickly, because the body needs iron daily to replace red blood cells.

Another kind of anemia, pernicious anemia, has the same symptoms but a different cause. Pernicious anemia comes from a lack of vitamin B12, another key nutrient in red-blood-cell production. It is rare compared to iron-deficiency anemia.

Kidney and lima beans, beef, ham, dark turkey meat, oysters, and clams are foods that are high in the iron that people need to be healthy.

Writing Personal Research Reports

Have you ever wondered about something? Maybe you've been curious about what it's like to work as a veterinarian or as a sailor on a cargo ship. Or maybe you've wondered how a music box works—or what people did for entertainment before television.

Did you ever go searching for answers? Maybe you've asked a veterinarian about his or her job, and what it took to get there. Or maybe you've taken apart a music box and put it back together. Or maybe talked with your grandmother about what things were like when she was a girl.

Did you ever write about what you discovered? That's what this chapter is about. Doing a "personal research report" is a fancy name for writing about something that made you curious enough to go searching for answers.

WHAT'S AHEAD

In this chapter, you'll learn how to write a personal research report. Included here are ways to identify questions you have, search for answers to your questions, and explain your discoveries to readers. You'll start by reading a sample report written by a student who found a role model in his personal search for answers.

- ○ Sample Personal Research Report
- ○ Writing Guidelines

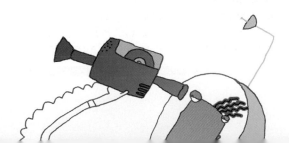

Sample Personal Research Report

In this report, student writer Luis Reyes explains how he discovered a role model and how that man has affected his life.

What I Learned from Roberto Clemente

BEGINNING

The writer explains a problem he had.

When I was 12 years old, I played for a baseball team called Puerto Rico. What a hard and unhappy season I had. I had practiced very hard, and at first I was hot. In my first five games, I hit 6 home runs and 14 RBI's (runs batted in). Everyone thought that we were going to be a championship team. But after the fifth game, I went into a terrible slump. In the next four games, I was 1 for 16. And we lost one game because I dropped an easy pop-up.

Benched for the Season

After that game, no one wanted to speak to me. The team was so mad that I got into a fight with one of my own teammates, who told me that I should go try out for Little League. Those words really hurt my feelings. And to make life worse, I was benched for the rest of the season.

I was angry. But in some ways, it was good that I got benched because I was too scared to go back out and play. I had lost all faith in myself. One day after I argued with our pitcher, my coach told me to sit down and relax. Then he started telling me that I reminded him of a baseball legend named Roberto Clemente.

MIDDLE

The writer reveals the question behind this report and where he looked for information.

"Who's Clemente?"

"Who is Roberto Clemente?" I asked.

My coach told me that he was the first Puerto Rican star in the major leagues. He told me that there was a time when, like Jackie Robinson, Clemente was hated because of his race. But Clemente did not give up. My coach told me that Roberto Clemente was a man of heart.

I went out to fish for more information about Roberto

Clemente. I went to the library and asked for old newspapers about his life and how he died.

The writer explains what he learned.

I learned that, starting in the 1950s, Clemente played
for the Pittsburgh Pirates for 15 seasons and helped lead
them to two World Series. He also played in nine All-Star
games and won the Most Valuable Player Award (MVP), 4
batting titles, and 10 consecutive Gold Gloves. Amazing!

On September 30, 1972, Clemente made his 3,000th
career hit. Only 10 other players before him had made as
many hits. But his achievements came to a sudden end.
On December 31, 1972, Clemente was killed in a plane crash
while taking supplies to earthquake victims in Nicaragua.

In 1973, Clemente became the first Puerto Rican player
to be admitted to the Baseball Hall of Fame. He got to the
Hall of Fame because he worked hard. My father told me
that Clemente was always the first player on the field to
practice. He said that when Clemente was down, he always
found a way to come back up.

He explains how this knowledge affected him.

Clemente Inspired Me

Learning about Roberto Clemente made me believe that
even when I want to give up, I have to have patience and
faith. It made me believe that I should and could still
achieve my dreams.

It gave me the strength to go outside with my friends
every other day and run around the bases an extra 10 times.
It gave me the willpower to throw the ball from left field to
home plate over and over. And it gave me the heart to stay
outside and hit fastballs that my neighborhood friends
would throw me.

**ENDING
The report has a convincing ending.**

Clemente is my role model. If I had never learned
about him, I would have given up long ago. It is because
of him that I try to play with faith, confidence, power, and
belief. That's why in 1998, I had a better season and won
my league's World Series MVP. Roberto Clemente made me
believe that it's not the way you begin that counts, it's the
way you finish. And my team and I finished number one.

Writing Guidelines

Sometimes work is fun. That's certainly true about personal research reports. You'll have to work to gather the information you need. And you'll have to work to write the report. But if you care about the subject, the work of researching and sharing will be fun.

Prewriting ----[Choosing a Subject]

The most important part of writing a personal research report is choosing something to write about. Here are three ideas for identifying a topic that interests you:

1. Make a list of things you're curious about.

2. Write a dozen "I wonder" questions. ("I wonder who was the first person to live in my town." "I wonder why some people are afraid of spiders.")

3. Talk with a friend about things that make you curious. Bounce ideas back and forth. (Don't forget to write down the best ones.)

[Gathering Details]

Every successful exploration begins with a plan. Here are a few suggestions for planning your research:

■ **Ask your friends and family** what they know. They might have some great information or know where you can find it.

■ **Check the library.** A reference librarian can be a resource. The *Readers' Guide* can direct you to current articles.

■ **Go to the source.** Write letters and make phone calls to experts on the subject. Ask if you can interview them in person.

■ **Plan your interview questions** ahead of time. People are more willing to talk if you have good questions.

■ **Take notes** or use a tape recorder. You don't want to forget an important detail when you're ready to write.

■ **Ask for recommendations.** Experts can introduce you to other sources of information: other people, special events, and literature.

■ **Use the Internet:** Pages 268-272 explain how to search the Net.

Prewriting ----[Gathering Details]

Here's one way to organize your initial research:

ORGANIZE WITH A GRID

To organize your thoughts, try using a grid like the one below. (The sample below shows how Luis Reyes planned for his report on pages 218-219.)

1 What I Knew	**2** What I Wanted to Know
I was miserable and needed help. Roberto Clemente was a Puerto Rican baseball player. (My coach told me about him.)	What was so special about Roberto Clemente? Why did my coach say I was like Clemente?
3 What I Found Out	**4** What I Learned
Clemente was an amazing ball-player and a great human being. Clemente overcame prejudice and other trouble to succeed.	Clemente became a role model for me. I can succeed if I have confidence and work hard.

Writing ----[Writing the First Draft]

1 **BEGINNING** This background information helps you introduce your topic. It may also help your readers identify with you.

2 **MIDDLE** Answering these questions should make your readers want to learn more, especially if you let your own excitement show.

3 **MIDDLE** This section of your report presents facts. Here you tell your readers what you discovered in your research.

4 **ENDING** The end of your report explains how your discoveries have affected you or influenced your attitude.

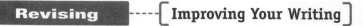

Revising ----[Improving Your Writing]

As you polish your writing, use the following checklist as a guide.

BEGINNING

- Have I clearly stated what my report is about?
- Have I explained how I became interested in the subject?
- Will my introduction make the reader curious?

MIDDLE

- Does the middle tell what I discovered from my search?
- Does it read like a story of how I carried out my search?
- Is the story interesting?
- Does the story flow naturally from one point to the next?
- Have I used dialogue and description well?

ENDING

- Does the ending reveal how my search has affected me?
- Does it answer all the questions from my introduction?
- Is the last paragraph strong?

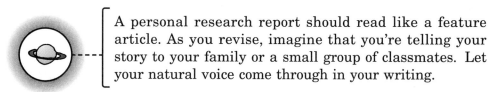

A personal research report should read like a feature article. As you revise, imagine that you're telling your story to your family or a small group of classmates. Let your natural voice come through in your writing.

Editing ----[Checking for Style and Accuracy]

Write a neat final draft in ink (or on your computer). Be sure to check your grammar, spelling, and punctuation for accuracy.

Consider presenting your personal research as a multimedia report. Use a video camera to capture live action, interviews, and on-location shots. You could share your discoveries in a talk-show interview format or as a documentary-style presentation.

Writing Research Papers

When you are asked to write a research paper, you must do two things. First, you must learn facts and details about a specific subject. You will do this by reading, observing, and asking questions. Second, you must share this information in a clear, organized paper.

A research paper may include ideas from books, magazines, newspapers, interviews, or the Internet. All ideas borrowed from different sources must be credited to the original writer or speaker. Most research papers are at least three pages in length and may include a title page, an outline, the actual essay, and a works-cited page (bibliography).

WHAT'S AHEAD

This section will help you develop a research paper from start to finish, from selecting a subject to producing a neat final copy to share.

- Writing Guidelines
- Adding a Works-Cited Page
- Adding a Title Page and Outline
- Sample Works-Cited Entries
- Sample Internet Entries
- Sample Research Paper

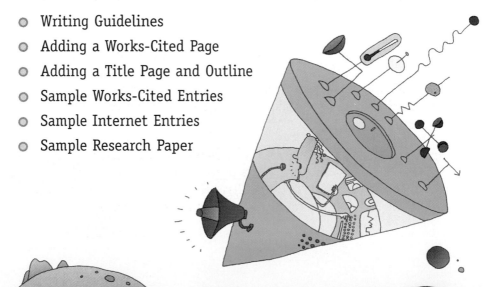

Writing Guidelines

Prewriting ----[Choosing a Subject]

Your teacher will probably give you the *general* subject for your research paper. It will be up to you to find a *specific* subject. You'll find it much easier to write a paper about a subject you are truly interested in.

Let's say you are assigned a research paper in your science class. The general subject is "modern-day pioneers." Your teacher has asked that you choose a group or a person who has made important discoveries or improvements in the field of science.

Begin by checking with your school library or by searching the Internet for information. As you scan and read this general material, keep looking for possible research topics. Keep in mind that whatever topic you choose, you must be able to find enough information to write a good paper.

Sample Subject Web

You may want to use a web or cluster to begin your subject search. Begin by writing the general subject in the center. Then write down all the related topics that come to mind.

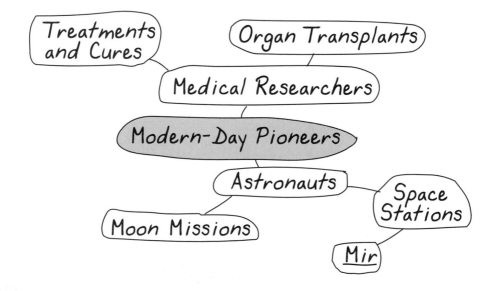

Prewriting ----[**Gathering Your Information**]

Once you have selected a topic, you need to begin gathering information. Suppose you pick the astronauts who have worked on the *Mir* space station as the topic of your paper. The next step is to find plenty of books, magazines, and other sources on that topic. Then you need to review these sources and take notes on the important facts and details you find. (See pages 261-281 for additional help.)

Ask questions: To help you organize your reading and note taking, write some basic questions about your subject that you would like to answer in your report. Put each of these questions at the top of a separate note card. (See the samples below.) Any time you find a fact that answers one of your questions, write it down on the appropriate card.

QUESTIONS

1. **Who** were the first astronauts on the Mir?
2. **What** was their mission?
3. **When** was Mir launched?
4. **Where** is the station located in space?
5. **Why** is it still in orbit?
6. **What** is life on the Mir space station like?
7. **What** problems has Mir had?
8. **How** were these problems overcome?

Sample Note Cards

What is life on the Mir space station like? ⑥

What problems has Mir had?   ⑦
- 1,500 problems, most small
- a fire in 1997
- a damaged solar panel
- many leaks and power failures
- outdated computers

"Space Jalopy," p. 96-99

Prewriting ----[Organizing Your Information]

Select a main point: Once you have finished your reading and note taking, you need to arrange and organize the information you have found. As you do this, try to narrow your subject down to a specific topic. For example, researching the *Mir* space station would have told you that life there is very difficult. This information could work as the main point for a report.

Arrange your cards: Keeping the main point of your report in mind, put the rest of your note cards in the best possible order.

[Outlining Your Information]

Write a rough outline: The final step in the organizational stage is writing an outline. Begin by listing the headings (questions) written on the top of your note cards in the same order that you have already arranged them. Leave enough space between the headings to list the important facts and details about each. If you are not required to include a formal outline with your report, this rough outline may be all you need.

Rewrite your outline: If you are required to do a final outline, rewrite your first draft into a clear sentence outline. The headings or questions are the main ideas and should follow Roman numerals (I., II., III., IV., etc.). The details under each main idea should follow capital letters (A., B., C., etc.).

Mir Flies on for the Next Generation

  I. The <u>Mir</u> space station has many problems.
    A. The space station is getting worn out.
    B. It has traveled over 1.8 billion miles.
    C. Its computer system is outdated.
    D. It has had numerous leaks and power failures.
 II. Life on the space station is hard.
    A. Cleanliness is a huge problem.
    B. Food is freeze-dried and not easy to digest.
    C. Air is very humid and smelly.
    D. Noise is constant.

Writing ----[Writing the First Draft]

At some point, during your planning and writing, you should see how well your writing matches up to your readers and what they need to know. Give them what's new, what's different, what's important. Ask yourself the questions that follow to get you started.

Questions to Consider

- Who am I writing for? Who are my readers? (You're probably writing for your teacher and classmates, but you may be involved in a special project in which your readers are younger children or, perhaps, a group of senior citizens.)
- What do they want to know? (No one is interested in reading the same old information.)
- What do they want to learn? (Readers want to learn something when they read a report. They also like to be entertained, so think about including a few surprises.)
- What do they need to know? (Your readers need to know anything that will help them understand and possibly react to the main point of your writing.)

Write your report: If you have a complete and well-organized outline, writing your paper should be no problem. Each main idea can serve as the topic sentence of a paragraph in your report. Then the details that support that main idea become the sentences for that paragraph. You are also free to add other facts that occur to you as you write your first draft.

Write an opening paragraph: This paragraph must state the main point of your paper and also say something interesting or catchy to get your reader's attention. You may write this paragraph before or after you develop the body of your paper. (See "Sample Research Paper" at the end of this unit for an example.)

Write a closing paragraph: If your paper does not come to a natural ending point, you may need to add a closing paragraph. This paragraph should summarize the main points made in the paper and end with a strong closing sentence—one that will make a lasting impression.

Revising ----[Improving Your Writing]

Revising a research paper, which is a complex piece of writing, naturally takes time. Use the following checklist as a guide.

Introduction ■ Your opening paragraph should introduce the topic and get the reader's attention.

Body Paragraphs ■ Each paragraph should be clear and contain a main idea and details about your topic. Your paragraphs should be arranged in the best possible order. (See "Organizing the Details" on page 60.)

Conclusion ■ Your closing paragraph should summarize the important points in your paper and leave your reader with a lasting impression.

Wording ■ Use your own words. Your writing should sound like it comes from you, a student writer. (Use quotation marks when you use someone else's words.)

Color ■ Use strong verbs and helpful comparisons. Add illustrations, charts, graphs, and other visual aids if they add interest and clarity.

Editing ----[Checking for Style and Accuracy]

Accuracy ■ Make sure your research paper is accurate. Include all necessary details and facts, but exclude any that cannot be proved, seem fuzzy, or are hard to believe.

Giving Credit ■ Give credit for an author's ideas or words if you are required to do so by your teacher. (Use "Giving Credit . . . ," page 229, as a guide.) If you are required to prepare a works-cited or bibliography page, follow the guidelines in this handbook. (See pages 230-232.)

Title Page and Outline ■ Prepare the title page and outline for your report if they are required. (Follow the guidelines on page 230.)

Final Copy ■ Write (in ink), type, or print out your final copy on unlined paper. Number your pages, along with your last name, in the upper right-hand corner starting with the first page of body copy. (See page 233.) Double-space the entire paper and leave a 1- to 1 1/2-inch margin on all sides.

A research paper should be as error-free as possible. Check carefully for spelling, usage, punctuation, and capitalization. Be especially careful to check all your works-cited entries for spacing and punctuation.

| Documenting | Giving Credit for Information |

If you are required to give credit to the authors whose ideas or words you have used in your paper, follow the guidelines set by your teacher. You may identify the authors on each page of your paper or in a list at the end.

Giving Credit in the Body

If your teacher asks you to give credit in the body of your research paper, you can do this by placing (in parentheses) the author's last name and the page number(s) on which you found the information. This reference is placed at the end of the last sentence or idea taken from that author. The sample reference below tells the reader that this information was originally written by the author Chien and was found on page 97. (For the author's full name and the title of the book, the reader can check the works-cited or bibliography page at the end of the paper.)

> **In February 1997, a fire shut down an oxygen generator. Then in June 1997, a spaceship carrying supplies to *Mir* crashed into a solar panel (Chien 97).**

Avoiding Plagiarism

Plagiarism is using another writer's ideas or words as if they were your own, without giving credit. When you write a research paper, be certain to avoid plagiarism. The following guidelines should help:

USING NEW INFORMATION

You should give credit in your paper (list an author and a page number) for the following kinds of information:

■ Information that is copied directly from another source.

■ Information that is written in your own words but contains key words or ideas taken from another source. (See page 216.)

USING COMMON KNOWLEDGE

It is not necessary to list an author and a page number for information that is considered common knowledge—knowledge already known by most people. When you are unsure whether your information is common knowledge, it is best to give the author credit.

Adding a Works-Cited Page

A works-cited page (also called a **bibliography**) lists in alphabetical order the books and materials you have used in your report. Follow your teacher's guidelines and those in this section. Double-space the information you include in your works-cited page. The second line of each entry should be indented 1/2 inch (5 typed spaces). Underline titles and other words that would be italicized in print. (See page 401.)

- Books—A typical listing for a book

  Author (last name first). Title of the book. City where book is

  published: Publisher, copyright date.

- Magazines—A typical listing for a magazine

  Author (last name first). "Title of the article." Title of the

  magazine day month year: page numbers.

Adding a Title Page and Outline

If you are required to prepare a title page, make sure you follow your teacher's guidelines. Usually, the following information is placed on the title page: *title of your report, your name, your teacher's name, the name of the course,* and *the date.* This information should be centered on a separate sheet of paper. (You may, however, be told to place this information on the top of the first page of your paper.)

If you are required to include an outline, make sure it meets the requirements of the assignment and follows your final research paper.

Sample Outline

Introductory Paragraph
    I. The struggles with Mir begin with the space station itself.
   II. The Mir astronauts have done the best they could with what they have.
  III. Life on Mir is unhealthy.
  IV. The living conditions are difficult.

Concluding Paragraph

Sample Works-Cited Entries

One Author

Gravett, Christopher. The World of the Medieval Knight. New York: Peter Bedrick Books, 1996.

Two or Three Authors

McKissack, Patricia C., and Fredrick McKissack, Jr. Black Diamond: The Story of the Negro Baseball Leagues. New York: Scholastic, 1994.

More Than Three Authors or Editors

Busbey, Arthur B., et al. Rocks and Fossils. San Francisco: Time-Life Books, 1996.

Single Work from an Anthology

Headlam, Dave. "Blues Transformations in the Music of Cream." Understanding Rock: Essays in Musical Analysis. Ed. John Covach. New York: Oxford University Press, 1997.

One Volume of a Multivolume Work

McMahon, Thomas, ed. Authors and Artists for Young Adults. Vol. 20. Detroit: Gale Research, 1997.

Encyclopedia Article

Barr, William. "Northwest Passage." World Book Encyclopedia. 1998 ed.

Signed Article in a Magazine

Safer, Barbara. "Secret Messages." Cricket Sept. 1998: 29-33.

Unsigned Article in a Magazine

"Deadly by Nature." World June 1998: 20-23.

Signed Newspaper Article

Salemy, Shirley. "Plan Will Aid Children." Des Moines Register 2 Sept. 1998, sec. M: 1.

Unsigned Editorial or Story

"Russia on the Verge." Editorial. New York Times 1 Sept. 1998, sec. A: 25.

Note: For an unsigned story, simply omit "Editorial."

Government Publication

United States. General Services Administration. Consumer Information Catalogue. Pueblo, CO: GPO, 1997.

Reference Book on CD-ROM

Grolier Multimedia Encyclopedia. CD-ROM. Danbury, CT: Grolier Interactive, 1998.

Signed Pamphlet

Grayson, George W. <u>The North American Free Trade Agreement</u>. New York: Foreign Policy
Association, Inc., 1993.

Filmstrip, Slide Program, Videocassette

<u>Island of the Giant Bears</u>. Videocassette. National Geographic, 1995. 59 min.

Television or Radio Program

"Crime and Punishment." <u>Nightline in Primetime</u>. ABC. WKOW, Madison, WI. 3 Sept. 1998.

Sample Internet Entries

Internet entries are more complicated than other sources and
require more attention to detail. See the sample entries below. (Also
check our Web site for additional entries at **thewritesource.com**.)

Items in an On-Line Entry

Author or editor. <E-mail address>. "Post title." <u>Book title</u>. Editor (if not listed earlier).
Printed version information (if any). <u>Site title</u> or description. Administrator. Version
number, volume, issue, etc. Post date, or last update. Listserv or forum name. Site
sponsor. Date accessed. <Electronic address>.

Article

Hoversten, Paul. "Life on <u>Mir</u>, or, roughing it on the 'frontier.'" <u>Florida Today: Space Online</u>.
20 Aug. 1997. 10 Sept. 1998 <http://www.flatoday.com/space/explore/stories/1997b/
082097c.htm>.

Book

Irving, Washington. <u>The Adventures of Captain Bonneville</u>. <u>UIarchive</u>. July 1988. Project
Gutenberg. 31 Aug. 1998 <ftp://uiarchive.cso.uiuc.edu/pub/etext/gutenberg/etext98/
taocb10.txt>.

E-mail

Write Source. <wsource@wi.net>. "Citing Internet sources." 4 Sept. 1998. E-mail to the
author. 8 Sept. 1998.

Web Site

<u>Camp Swift</u>. Kathy Kincheloe, Web manager. 31 Mar. 1998. Bastrop Middle School. 1 Sept.
1998 <http://198.214.254.200/swift98/camp2.html>.

Sample Research Paper

Student writer Matt Korman researched the *Mir* space station by reading articles that he found in magazines and on the Internet. Then he wrote his research paper.

Korman 1

The writer provides a complete heading.

Matt Korman

Mr. Benjamin

Science 8

September 22, 1998

<u>Mir</u> Flies on for the Next Generation

BEGINNING

He introduces his topic and states his thesis (yellow highlight).

Captain Kirk of the <u>USS Enterprise</u> beams you aboard. As your molecules come back together, he gives you a tour of the spotless flight deck. It's filled with clean crew members working on equipment that's all in perfect shape. That's TV. The Russian <u>Mir</u> space station is reality, and life there isn't glamorous. <u>Mir</u> astronauts are more like the early pioneers who risked their lives but kept going and made their mission a success.

MIDDLE

The writer cites details that show conditions on *Mir*.

<u>Mir</u>'s struggles begin with the space station itself. <u>Mir</u> is an 11-year-old laboratory that made its 69,560th orbit of the earth on May 1, 1998. That's 1.83 billion miles! In addition to having high mileage, <u>Mir</u> has a computer system that is ancient. Since <u>Mir</u> blasted off in 1986, astronauts have had to fix 1,500 problems on the ship. Most were small, but a few were big. In February 1997, a fire shut down an oxygen generator. Then in June 1997, a spaceship carrying supplies to <u>Mir</u> crashed into a solar panel (Chien 97). Many times, the crew sits in the dark because there isn't enough power to work the computers or do experiments.

Korman 2

The writer repeats his analogy to pioneers.

Like the pioneers who headed west in covered wagons, Mir astronauts have learned to do the best they can with what they have. For example, Mir astronauts wear their cotton T-shirts, gym shorts, and socks for two weeks! The astronauts wear the clothes day and night and even exercise in them. After two weeks, astronauts just pitch the stinky stuff into space where it burns up in the earth's atmosphere (Hoversten).

He documents details gleaned from research, but not quoted directly.

Life on Mir isn't glamorous. In fact, it's not even healthy. The humid air makes molds grow, and the molds spoil the food. The crew can't wash well, and infections spread quickly, especially when new astronauts come onboard. After their bodies are weightless for a long time, the bones in their lower hips and spines get weaker (Chien 99). Then, when astronauts go back to Earth, they have more problems. They have poor balance, weak muscles, and severe soreness (Covault 76).

The living conditions on Mir would make even Captain Kirk return to Earth. Fans hum nonstop. The smell of gasoline hangs in the air, and food is served up freeze-dried. Right now, the shower is broken, so the crew have to take sponge baths. Even sleeping is hard.   Jerry Linenger is an astronaut who spent 132 days on Mir with these problems. He said, "There's something about it [life on Mir] that makes you feel, 'Yeah, I'm on the frontier' " (Hoversten).

ENDING

He restates his thesis and ends with a thoughtful sentence.

Even though life on Mir isn't glamorous, and equipment often fails, the Mir astronauts have had lots of success. Like the pioneers, the astronauts have found many useful things that help explorers who follow them. But maybe Mir's greatest success is that astronauts from Russia and the U.S., two old enemies, have worked together as friends (Chien 99).

Center "Works Cited" (or "Bibliography") one inch from the top.

Double-space this page.

Indent the second and subsequent lines of an entry by 5 spaces.

Korman 3

Works Cited

Chien, Phillip. "Space Jalopy." Popular Science May
          1998: 96-99.

Covault, Craig. "Mir 'Lessons' Preview Future ISS Flights."
          Aviation Week and Space Technology 9 Mar. 1998:
          76-78.

Hoversten, Paul. "Life on Mir, or roughing it on the 'frontier.'"
          Florida Today: Space Online. 20 Aug. 1997. 10 Sept. 1998
          <http://www.flatoday.com/space/explore/stories/1997b/
          082097c.htm>.

Wolf, David. Interview. NASA Shuttle-Mir Web. 14 Nov. 1997.
          NASA. 10 Sept. 1998 <http://shuttle-mir. nasa.gov/shuttle-
          mir/mir24/status/week14/wolf.html>.

Workplace Writing

Writing in the Workplace

People in the workplace write for many different reasons. They write letters to place orders, to offer jobs, and to discuss problems. They write reports to analyze budgets, to propose new projects, and to explain how their latest products work. They also write newsletters, memos, e-mail messages, want ads, bulletins, and so on.

In today's workplace, individuals who have good writing skills are best equipped to get their jobs done.

And guess what? Workplace writing skills are going to be even more important when you enter the workplace. According to a special workplace report, called the SCANS Report, writing is near the top of essential job skills that you will need to master.

WHAT'S AHEAD

This brief chapter lists the common forms of writing used in the workplace, forms you can also use now to communicate in your classes.

- ○ Types of Workplace Writing
- ○ Workplace Writing in School
- ○ Traits of Good Workplace Writing

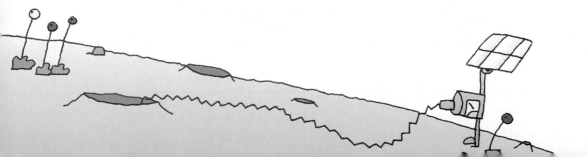

Types of Workplace Writing

Police officers, social workers, construction workers, doctors, and engineers—all of these workers write when they're on the job. Listed below are just a few of the types of writing done in the workplace.

LETTERS

Letters of Application   Letters of Request
Thank-You Letters   Informative Letters
Letters of Complaint   Letters Promoting Something
Bad News Letters

E-MAIL MESSAGES AND MEMOS

Brief Reminders   Announcements
Information Exchanges   Thank-You Notes
Recommendations

REPORTS

Sales Reports   Proposals for New Products
Minutes of Meetings   Progress Reports
Accident or Injury Reports   Research Reports
Job Completion Summaries   Case Studies

SPECIAL FORMS

News Releases   Advertisements
Product Brochures   Manuals
Newsletters

Workplace Writing in School

Writing letters, memos, and proposals can help you improve your communication skills, which in turn will help you become a better student . . . and give you a head start on valuable job skills. Here are some of the ways you can use workplace writing in school:

[LETTERS]

You might write . . .

- a **thank you letter** expressing your appreciation for the help a professional gave you for a school project.
- a **letter of complaint** to a school official stating your concern about a new or existing policy.

[E-MAIL MESSAGES AND MEMOS]

You might write . . .

- an **e-mail message** to your teacher updating your progress (or lack of it) on an important assignment.
- a **memo** to the principal reminding him or her about the next student-council meeting.

[REPORTS]

You might write . . .

- a **summary report** of a field trip or your own visit to a specific workplace.
- a **proposal** for a science project or a research paper.

[SPECIAL FORMS]

You might write . . .

- a **news release** about an upcoming classroom activity.
- a **pamphlet or brochure** telling new students about a particular club or organization.

Traits of Good Workplace Writing

For workplace writing to be effective, it must be clear, complete, smooth reading, and so on. In other words, it must exhibit the traits found in all effective writing. The six basic traits of good writing are listed below, along with examples of how student writers incorporated these qualities into their own writing. (Also see pages 19-24.)

Ideas (details and focus)

- In her job-application letter (see page 250), Andrea Rodriguez focuses on her qualifications for the job.

Organization (strong opening and clear divisions)

- To help readers understand his project, Brian Krygsman divides his project proposal (see page 259) into four sections.

Voice (tone, style, and attention to audience)

- In a memo (see page 253), Rebecca Ehly uses a friendly, informal voice in a mid-project update to her teacher.

Word Choice (language, phrasing)

- In order to present his complaint clearly (see page 249), Matt Visker uses precise computer terms.

Sentence Fluency (rhythm and readability)

- For rhythm and clarity, Emily Daniels states her request (see page 248) in three parallel questions.

Conventions (editorial correctness)

- Michael Vaughn carefully proofreads the student-council minutes (see page 257) for errors before submitting them to the council. He also has a trusted friend proofread them.

Writing Business Letters

People in the workplace still write traditional business letters, even in this era of e-mail messages and fax sheets. They write letters for many different reasons (sharing ideas, promoting products, asking for help). An effective business letter gets the reader's attention, and it gets things done, which is what business is all about.

Business letters can help you get things done, too—both in and out of school. Letters can connect you with fellow students, experts, organizations, and companies that can give you information, help you solve problems, and much more.

WHAT'S AHEAD

This chapter covers everything you need to know about writing business letters, from understanding the basic parts to sending the finished product. The last three pages offer sample letters for you to follow.

- Parts of a Business Letter
- Sample Basic Business Letter
- Writing Guidelines
- Using Clear, Fair Language
- Sending Your Letter
- Business-Letter Sampler

Parts of a Business Letter

The business letter is made up of six basic parts: the **heading, inside address, salutation, body, closing,** and **signature.**

1 The **heading** gives the writer's complete address, plus the date.

2 The **inside address** gives the name, title, and address of the person or organization you are writing to.

- If the person has a title, make sure to include it. (If the title is short, write it in the same line as the name, separated by a comma. If the title is long, write it on the next line.)

- If you are writing to an organization or a business, but not a specific person, begin the inside address with the name of the organization or business.

3 The **salutation** is the greeting. Always insert a colon after your salutation.

- Use Mr. or Ms. plus the person's last name. Do not guess at Miss or Mrs.

- If you don't know the name of the person who will read your letter, use a salutation like one of these:

    Dear Store Owner: (the person's title)
    Dear Sir or Madam:
    Dear Burlington Little League:
    Attention: Customer Service

4 The **body** is the main part of the letter. It should have single-spaced paragraphs with double spacing between each one. (Do not indent the paragraphs.) If the letter is longer than one page, make a heading on the second page. List vertically the reader's name, Page 2, and the date at the top left-hand margin.

5 The **closing** ends the letter politely. Use *Sincerely, Yours sincerely,* or *Yours truly* followed by a comma.

6 The **signature,** including the writer's handwritten and typed name, makes the letter official.

Be sure to use clear, fair language throughout your letter. (See page 245 for guidelines and examples.)

Sample Basic Business Letter

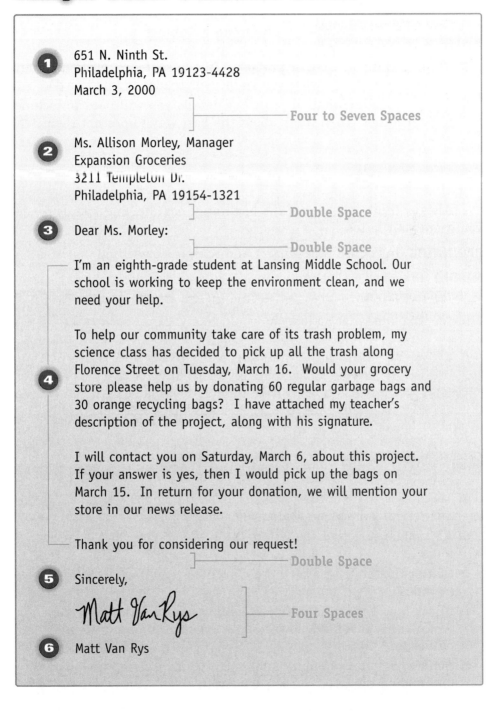

1 651 N. Ninth St.
Philadelphia, PA 19123-4428
March 3, 2000

Four to Seven Spaces

2 Ms. Allison Morley, Manager
Expansion Groceries
3211 Templeton Dr.
Philadelphia, PA 19154-1321

Double Space

3 Dear Ms. Morley:

Double Space

4 I'm an eighth-grade student at Lansing Middle School. Our school is working to keep the environment clean, and we need your help.

To help our community take care of its trash problem, my science class has decided to pick up all the trash along Florence Street on Tuesday, March 16. Would your grocery store please help us by donating 60 regular garbage bags and 30 orange recycling bags? I have attached my teacher's description of the project, along with his signature.

I will contact you on Saturday, March 6, about this project. If your answer is yes, then I would pick up the bags on March 15. In return for your donation, we will mention your store in our news release.

Thank you for considering our request!

Double Space

5 Sincerely,

Matt Van Rys

Four Spaces

6 Matt Van Rys

Writing Guidelines

Prewriting ----[Choosing a Subject]

- Think about your goal or purpose. In one sentence, write out your reason for writing—what you want your reader to know or do.
- Gather your information. List the details you will need to include in your letter. Then think about the best way to present them.

Writing ----[Writing the First Draft]

Always think in terms of the beginning, middle, and ending when you write your letter.

BEGINNING Introduce your subject and reason for writing.

MIDDLE Present all of the important facts and details in short, clearly stated paragraphs.

ENDING Explain what action you would like your reader to take.

State all of your ideas positively and politely. Your reader will more likely respond favorably to your letter if it has a positive tone. Also, make sure you choose words that treat both sexes fairly. (See page 245.)

Revising and **Editing**

- Make sure that your letter reads smoothly and clearly and answers any questions your reader might have.
- Also make sure that the letter states what you want the reader to do.
- Center the letter and keep the margins even (1 to 1-1/2 inches on all sides).
- Check your letter carefully for spelling and punctuation errors. Always check and double-check the spelling and accuracy of names and places.
- Send your letter promptly after correctly addressing the envelope and folding the letter. (See page 246.)

Using Clear, Fair Language

When you write, you have to make every effort to treat both sexes fairly. Avoid giving any special treatment to one of the sexes. Be especially careful of using male-only words.

■ Use equal language for both sexes:

The men and the women came through in the clutch.

Hank and Mimi

Mr. Bubba Gumm, Mrs. Lotta Gumm

Don't give special treatment to one of the sexes:

The men and the ladies came through in the clutch.

Hank and Miss Jenkins

Mr. Bubba Gumm, Mrs. Bubba Gumm

■ Use *he or she,* or make the antecedent and its pronoun plural:

Politicians lead public lives when they run for office.

Don't use male-only pronouns (*he, his, him*) when you want to refer to a human being in general:

A politician leads a public life when he runs for office.

■ Address a position:

Dear Personnel Officer:

Dear Members of the Big Bird Fan Club:

Don't use gender-specific references in the salutation of a business letter when you don't know the person's name:

Dear Sir: Dear Gentlemen:

■ Use gender-free words or titles:

YES	NO
chair	chairman
salesperson	salesman
mail carrier	mailman
police officer	policeman
flight attendant	stewardess
doctor	lady doctor
nurse	male nurse
housekeeper	maid

Sending Your Letter

ADDRESSING THE ENVELOPE

Place the return address (including your name) in the upper left corner, the destination address in the center, and the correct postage in the upper right corner.

```
MATT VAN RYS
651 N 9TH ST
PHILADELPHIA PA 19123-4428                          [postage]



        MS ALLISON MORLEY
        MANAGER
        EXPANSION GROCERIES
        3211 TEMPLETON DR
        PHILADELPHIA PA 19154-1321
```

There are two acceptable forms for addressing the envelope. In the traditional form, you use upper- and lowercase letters as well as punctuation and abbreviation. In the newer form preferred by the postal service, you use all caps and no punctuation.

Traditional Form	New Form
Mr. James Evans	MR JAMES EVANS
512 N. Adams Ave.	512 N ADAMS AVE
Winona, MN 55987-1386	WINONA MN 55987-1386

U.S. POSTAL SERVICE GUIDELINES

The guidelines preferred by the postal service for addressing an envelope follow:

1. Capitalize everything and leave out ALL punctuation.

2. Use the list of common abbreviations found in the National ZIP Code Directory. (See page 247.) Use numerals rather than words for numbered streets and avenues (9TH AVE NE, 3RD ST SW).

3. If you know the ZIP + 4 code, use it. You can get this information by phoning the postal service.

FOLDING THE LETTER

1. Fold the bottom third of the letter up, and crease.
2. Fold the top third of the letter down, and crease.
3. Insert the letter (with the open end at the top) into the envelope.

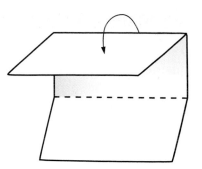

State Abbreviations

	Standard	Postal		Standard	Postal		Standard	Postal
Alabama	Ala.	AL	Kentucky	Ky.	KY	Ohio	Ohio	OH
Alaska	Alaska	AK	Louisiana	La.	LA	Oklahoma	Okla.	OK
Arizona	Ariz.	AZ	Maine	Maine	ME	Oregon	Ore.	OR
Arkansas	Ark.	AR	Maryland	Md.	MD	Pennsylvania	Pa.	PA
California	Calif.	CA	Massachusetts	Mass.	MA	Puerto Rico	P.R.	PR
Colorado	Colo.	CO	Michigan	Mich.	MI	Rhode Island	R.I.	RI
Connecticut	Conn.	CT	Minnesota	Minn.	MN	South		
Delaware	Del.	DE	Mississippi	Miss.	MS	Carolina	S.C.	SC
District			Missouri	Mo.	MO	South Dakota	S.D.	SD
of Columbia	D.C.	DC	Montana	Mont.	MT	Tennessee	Tenn.	TN
Florida	Fla.	FL	Nebraska	Neb.	NE	Texas	Tex.	TX
Georgia	Ga.	GA	Nevada	Nev.	NV	Utah	Utah	UT
Guam	Guam	GU	New			Vermont	Vt.	VT
Hawaii	Hawaii	HI	Hampshire	N.H.	NH	Virginia	Va.	VA
Idaho	Idaho	ID	New Jersey	N.J.	NJ	Virgin Islands	V.I.	VI
Illinois	Ill.	IL	New Mexico	N.M.	NM	Washington	Wash.	WA
Indiana	Ind.	IN	New York	N.Y.	NY	West Virginia	W.Va.	WV
Iowa	Iowa	IA	North Carolina	N.C.	NC	Wisconsin	Wis.	WI
Kansas	Kan.	KS	North Dakota	N.D.	ND	Wyoming	Wyo.	WY

Address Abbreviations

	Standard	Postal		Standard	Postal		Standard	Postal
Avenue	Ave.	AVE	Lake	L.	LK	Road	Rd.	RD
Boulevard	Blvd.	BLVD	Lane	Ln.	LN	Rural	R.	R
Court	Ct.	CT	North	N.	N	South	S.	S
Drive	Dr.	DR	Park	Pk.	PK	Square	Sq.	SQ
East	E.	E	Parkway	Pky.	PKY	Street	St.	ST
Expressway	Expy.	EXPY	Place	Pl.	PL	Terrace	Ter.	TER
Heights	Hts.	HTS	Plaza	Plaza	PLZ	Turnpike	Tpke.	TPKE
Highway	Hwy.	HWY	Ridge	Rdg.	RDG	Village	Vil.	VLG
Hospital	Hosp.	HOSP	River	R.	RV	West	W.	W

Business-Letter Sampler

On the following pages, you will find three different types of business letters. Turn here for help when you need to make a request, state a problem, or apply for something.

SAMPLE Request Letter

246 Fourth St. NE
Del Rio, TX 78840-2183
April 2, 2000

Ms. Jennifer Rosales
Vision Architecture Ltd.
Del Rio, TX 78840-3261

Dear Ms. Rosales:

BEGINNING
State your purpose.

I'm writing for information about the parking lot that you have planned for South Central Middle School.

MIDDLE
Explain your need.

For a math project, I have to figure out how many cars will fit on this new lot. To get the answer, I need the following questions answered:
1. How wide and long will the lot be?
2. How wide and deep is each car stall?
3. How wide are the lanes between the rows?

ENDING
Help the reader fulfill the request.

I would like to stop by your office after school on Friday, April 9 (around 4:00 p.m.), to collect this information. On Thursday, April 8, I will call to confirm this time with you.

Thank you.

Sincerely,

Emily Daniels

Emily Daniels

SAMPLE Letter Stating a Problem

311 Wishkah St.
Seattle, WA 98144-7328
February 2, 2000

Genius Entertainment
1037 58th St.
Detroit, MI 48210-1447

Attention: Customer Service Department

BEGINNING
Identify the problem.

On January 18, I bought your company's "GuitarWhiz 2000" program at a local store for $49.99. When I inserted the disk into my Power Mac G3 and tried to start the program, nothing happened. There was no icon on the screen, and no lights blinked on my CD-ROM to tell me the program was working.

MIDDLE
Supply the necessary details.

I used another disk to check my CD-ROM drive, and the drive worked fine. I then checked the instruction book to see if I had followed the directions properly. Still, I had no luck.

Identify the best solution.

I'm sending you the disk so you can check it. If it's okay, please send me instructions on how to fix my problem. If the disk is defective, I would like a replacement or a refund.

ENDING
Provide any final information.

If you have questions, please call me at 206-448-9133 after 3:30 p.m. I look forward to hearing from you soon.

Sincerely,

Matt Visker

Matt Visker

Application Letter

1983 Elm St. SW
Flagstaff, AZ 86001-3441
April 2, 2000

Dr. Heidi Larson
Larson Veterinary Clinic
9179 Highbury Ave.
Flagstaff, AZ 86001-3862

Dear Dr. Larson:

BEGINNING
Identify the position you are applying for.

Your accountant, Rusty Silhacek, is my neighbor. He mentioned that your office stays very busy, so I wondered if you could use some extra help. I would like to apply for a position as a part-time veterinary assistant.

MIDDLE
Discuss your qualifications.

As far as animal care goes, I'm experienced in feeding, bathing, exercising, and cleaning up after small and large animals. I truly love animals and have always given them special attention and care. I would be available to help after school and on weekends.

ENDING
Ask for an interview.

I would be happy to come in for an interview at your convenience. You can contact me any weekday after 3:00 p.m. at 523-4418. Thank you for considering my application.

Sincerely,

Andrea Rodriguez

Andrea Rodriguez

Special Forms of Workplace Writing

It's important to share your thoughts and feelings with family members and trusted friends. They need to know what's going on in your life so they can offer their support and advice. It's also a good idea to communicate with your teachers and classmates. They need to know your questions and concerns so they can help you do your best in school.

Maintaining open lines of communication is important now, and will remain important in the workplace. Just ask one of your parents. When people in the workplace regularly share their ideas, the business has a much better chance of operating efficiently. The bottom line is this: Effective communication can improve all aspects of your life.

WHAT'S AHEAD

This chapter contains guidelines and samples for different forms of workplace writing, including memos and e-mail messages. Use these forms in school or at home whenever you need to communicate with someone important in your life.

Writing Guidelines:

- Memos
- E-Mail
- Minutes
- Proposals

Writing Guidelines: Memos

A memo is a brief written message that you can share with a teacher, a coach, a principal, or a supervisor. Memos create a flow of information—asking and answering questions, giving instructions, describing work done, and reminding people about deadlines and meetings. You can use memos to connect with people in school, in the workplace, and at home.

Prewriting ----[Choosing a Subject]

- Write down your memo's goal. What's your reason for writing?
- Think about your reader. Decide what he or she needs to know.
- Gather the necessary details to include in the memo.

Writing ----[Writing the First Draft]

BEGINNING Start with a heading that includes the date, your reader's name, your name, and the subject of your memo. Then state your reason for writing and your main point.

MIDDLE Provide all of the details that explain or support your subject.

ENDING If necessary, identify follow-up action that needs to be taken. Otherwise, just end politely.

Revising and Editing

- Is your heading complete? Does your subject line clearly show your memo's topic?
- Have you answered the reader's questions: *What's your point, and why is it important? What do I need to do?*
- Have you organized the details so that they're easy to follow?
- Have you checked for spelling, punctuation, and usage errors?

SAMPLE Memo

BEGINNING
List the date, the reader, and the writer. State your subject clearly.

Date: March 14, 2000

To: Mr. Ortega

From: Rebecca Ehly

Subject: Mid-Project Report on Training Rats

The goal of my science fair project is to train my rat Carmel to play basketball. I want to teach him to do four things:

1. Go to the rubber ball (about 1" in diameter).

MIDDLE
Provide a full explanation.

2. Push the ball with his nose across the basketball court that I made in his cage.

3. Pick up the ball with his forepaws.

4. Put the ball through the hoop (about 2" above the floor of the cage).

Carmel has learned two steps: (1) go to the ball, and (2) push it. I taught him how to do these things by luring him with pieces of cheddar cheese (extra sharp).

ENDING
Focus on action that needs to take place.

Unfortunately, I haven't been able to get Carmel to do numbers 3 and 4. He won't lift the ball. I'm not sure what to do next. Do you have any suggestions?

Writing Guidelines: E-Mail

E-mail is a written message that a writer sends through a computer network to a reader. If you're already using e-mail, you know that it's fast and simple—letting you send, receive, reply to, and store many messages. E-mail is ideal for your school projects.

Prewriting ----[**Choosing a Subject**]

■ Write down the goal of your message. What's your purpose for writing?
■ Gather all the details you need to include.

Writing ----[**Writing the First Draft**]

BEGINNING Complete the e-mail's header as directed by your program. Then type a subject line that tells your reader your topic at a glance. At the beginning of your message, greet the reader and state your reason for writing.

MIDDLE Provide all the details that the reader needs, carefully organized and clearly stated.

ENDING If follow-up action is needed, spell it out. If not, just end politely.

Revising and **Editing**

Check your e-mail before sending it. Although e-mail can be informal, it shouldn't be messy, wordy, or full of careless errors.

■ Is your message **accurate**—from the reader's e-mail address to each fact or detail you've provided?
■ Is your message **complete**—providing all the information needed so that you don't have to send another message?
■ Is your message **clear**—written in short, double-spaced paragraphs with numbers, lists, and headings?
■ Have you kept your message **short**—one or two screens at the most?
■ Is your memo **correct**—have you checked for spelling, punctuation, and other errors?

SAMPLE E-Mail Message

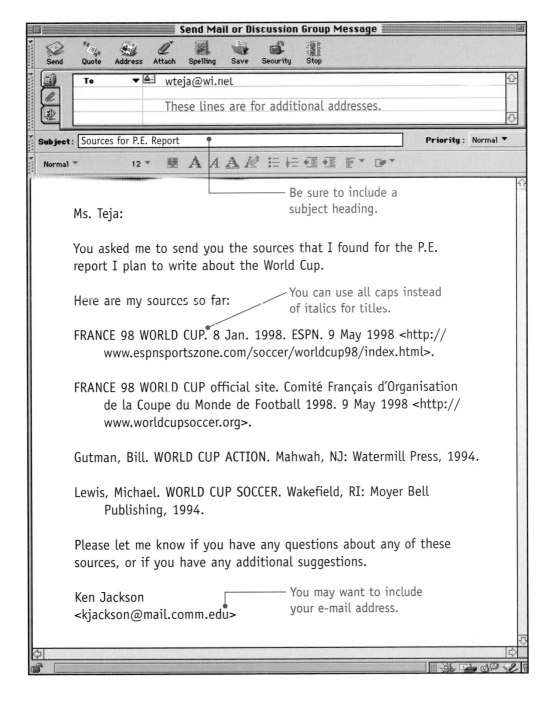

Send Mail or Discussion Group Message

Send Quote Address Attach Spelling Save Security Stop

To   ▼   wteja@wi.net

These lines are for additional addresses.

Subject: Sources for P.E. Report   Priority: Normal ▼

Normal ▼   12 ▼

Be sure to include a
subject heading.

Ms. Teja:

You asked me to send you the sources that I found for the P.E.
report I plan to write about the World Cup.

Here are my sources so far: You can use all caps instead
                                           of italics for titles.

FRANCE 98 WORLD CUP. 8 Jan. 1998. ESPN. 9 May 1998 <http://
        www.espnsportszone.com/soccer/worldcup98/index.html>.

FRANCE 98 WORLD CUP official site. Comité Français d'Organisation
        de la Coupe du Monde de Football 1998. 9 May 1998 <http://
        www.worldcupsoccer.org>.

Gutman, Bill. WORLD CUP ACTION. Mahwah, NJ: Watermill Press, 1994.

Lewis, Michael. WORLD CUP SOCCER. Wakefield, RI: Moyer Bell
        Publishing, 1994.

Please let me know if you have any questions about any of these
sources, or if you have any additional suggestions.

Ken Jackson   You may want to include
<kjackson@mail.comm.edu>   your e-mail address.

Writing Guidelines: Minutes

Minutes summarize a meeting—what was discussed, what was decided upon, and what action will be taken. The guidelines below should help you take good notes and write clear meeting minutes.

Prewriting ----[**Choosing a Subject**]

- Come to the meeting prepared with the proper materials—paper, pen, or even a laptop.
- Review the previous minutes and the meeting's agenda.
- Take notes of key points, speakers' names, and important decisions.

Writing ----[**Writing the First Draft**]

BEGINNING List details identifying the meeting—the group's name; the meeting's purpose, location, and time; and the names of those present. (Also name those people who are absent.)

MIDDLE Identify all issues discussed, any decisions made (sometimes called *motions*), and any follow-up actions needed (including names and deadlines).

ENDING Give details about the next meeting.

Revising and **Editing**

- Are all the details accurate—names, dates, item numbers, wording of decisions?
- Is your tone neutral? Have you left out feelings and judgments?
- Have you checked the spellings of all the names in your minutes?
- Have you checked all your punctuation carefully?

----[With minutes, timing is important. Draft the minutes *right after* the meeting, and distribute copies to all the group members *within a day or two.*]

SAMPLE Minutes

BEGINNING
Identify the group and its members.

--- Ulrich Middle School Student Council Meeting
Monday, February 1, 1999: Room 106

Present: Sarah Kramer, president; Dylan Brooks, vice
president; Stephanie Williams, Michael Vaughn,
Wade McCarthy, and Seth Donald, class reps;
Mrs. Christians, faculty rep.

MIDDLE
Number each topic with the year (99) and item number. Item numbers start over with a new year.

99.34   Sarah called the meeting to order. The agenda
was approved.

OLD BUSINESS

99.35   The secretary read the minutes of the January
25 meeting. They were accepted without
change.

99.36   The council took another look at motion 99.31
and voted to keep the candy machines.

NEW BUSINESS

99.37   Stephanie proposed that the school should
join in the "World Hunger Project" (February
27 and 28). These were her reasons:

1. The event would help students become
more aware of the hunger problem.

2. The money raised would be used to feed
hungry people through World Vision.

The motion to sponsor this event passed.
Details will be discussed in two weeks.

ENDING
List future business.

--- **NEXT MEETING**

99.38   The lunch-hour policy will be discussed.

99.39   The next meeting will be on Feb. 8 at 7:30
a.m. (Room 106).

Submitted by Michael Vaughn, secretary

Writing Guidelines: Proposals

Is there a project you want to do in one of your classes? Do you see a problem that needs fixing in your school or community? Then write it down in a proposal—a detailed plan for doing a project, solving a problem, or meeting a need.

Prewriting ----[Choosing a Subject]

- Study the problem, project, subject, or need. Define it, know its parts, and explore its background.
- Research your solution or idea. Will it work? Why or how?
- Think about your reader. How can you convince him or her of your idea's value.

Writing ----[Writing the First Draft]

BEGINNING Briefly introduce the problem, need, or idea that you're addressing. Then describe what you propose to do.

MIDDLE Provide convincing details supporting your proposal. Why is the problem, need, or idea important? Is your project workable? Why is your solution the best one? Include these details:

1. Equipment, material, and other resources needed
2. Steps to take and a schedule for completing them
3. Results expected

ENDING Focus on the benefits of the project and ask for its approval.

Revising and Editing

- Is your proposal detailed, specific, and accurate?
- Have you organized your points in an effective way? Will your reader say, *This will work!*
- Do you show that you care about the project?
- Have you used headings, lists, and white space?
- Have you checked your spelling, punctuation, and usage?

SAMPLE Proposal

Date: January 18, 2000
To: Mr. William Pasma
From: Brian Krygsman
Subject: Castle Construction for History Project

BEGINNING
Introduce your project's precise topic.

Project Description: For my history project on medieval life, I plan to build a scale model (2′ x 2′ x 2′) of an English castle and write an essay on the construction of castles for protection.

Materials Needed:

1. Books on medieval life and on castles
2. 3′ x 3′ plywood board (for base)
3. Clay (for walls)
4. Toilet paper rolls (for frame of towers)
5. Toothpicks and glue (for ladders, gates)
6. Popsicle sticks and string (for drawbridge)
7. Cloth (for banners and tapestries)
8. Lego people from castle sets

MIDDLE
Explain in detail how the project will be completed.

Deadlines and Procedure:

1. Jan. 25   Research medieval castles
2. Feb. 1   Choose a castle to build
3. Feb. 3   Design my model on paper as a blueprint
4. Feb. 10   Construct a scale model of castle
5. Feb. 16   Plan and write first draft of paper
6. Feb. 22   Complete paper and present project to class

Present your project schedule.

ENDING
Focus on results and ask for approval.

Outcome: My project will help the class understand how a castle was built and how it was used.

Is this project acceptable for this assignment? I would appreciate any suggestions.

Searching for Information

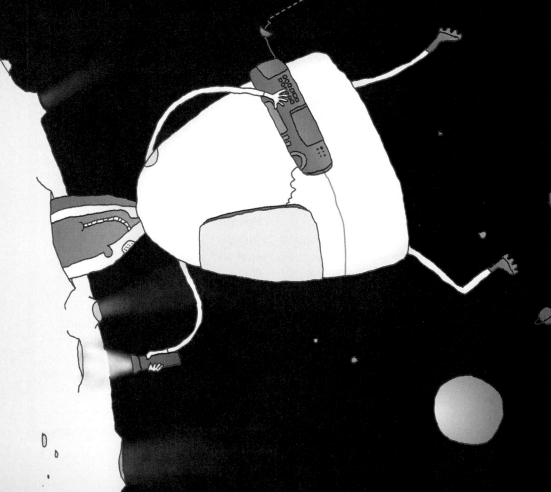

Types of Information

You've just been assigned a research project on health and fitness. You decide to investigate the work done by sports trainers. How do you get started? Well, you might refer to an encyclopedia CD-ROM at home or in the library for some background on the subject. Then there's the Internet—get on-line and you're bound to find some good information. You can also look through your health textbooks, read some sports and fitness magazines, contact trainers at the local college, and so on.

When you look for information, a world of possibilities awaits you. One source of information often leads you to another. In fact, you may find so much information that it will be hard to know what to do with it all. This is the information age, and you'll discover exactly what that means as you research subjects that really interest you.

WHAT'S AHEAD

There are two general sources of information—**primary** and **secondary.** This chapter will explain which is which, with special emphasis on examples of primary sources. You will also learn how to judge the quality of the information you find.

- Primary vs. Secondary Information Sources
- Types of Primary Sources
- Evaluating Sources of Information

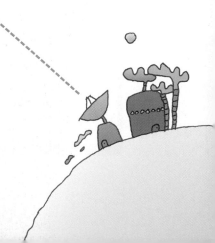

Primary vs. Secondary Information Sources

Primary sources of information are original sources. They give you firsthand knowledge—knowledge that you get personally by observing or participating in an activity. A primary source can also be someone else who has personally acquired knowledge and then shared his or her expertise with you in an interview or a written piece (letter, article, etc.). Primary sources are the originators of the information they share.

On the other hand, **secondary sources** share information that has been collected from primary sources. Facts and data have been gathered from other sources and then compiled, summarized, and maybe even changed. Most magazines, newspapers, encyclopedias, and some other nonfiction books are considered secondary sources of information.

A *primary source* of information can be traced no further than its author. A *secondary source* can be traced beyond its author to at least one or more other persons.

Primary Sources	**Secondary Sources**
1 Interview with a sports trainer	**1** Article that quotes a sport trainer
2 Visit to a training room	**2** Encyclopedia entry about sports training
3 Work with a sports trainer	**3** Television special about sports training

Types of Primary Sources

A primary source of information offers you firsthand details and ideas. Using primary sources will usually get you closer to the truth about a topic. This section discusses five types of primary sources.

OBSERVATION AND PARTICIPATION

Looking carefully at people, situations, things, and places is a common method of gathering information. So is actual participation in an event. If you were doing a report on reptiles, going to the zoo to watch the animals would be a primary source of details, as would assisting the zoo's veterinarian in an examination of an iguana.

SURVEYS AND FORMS

A survey or questionnaire can be a helpful form of research. Such forms can help you gather everything from simple facts to personal opinions and preferences. After some careful thinking, write down your questions and make up an easy-to-fill-in form. Deliver it to the "right" people and collect the finished surveys for the information you need. Surveys can be done over the phone, in person, through the mail, or with a computer.

INTERVIEWS

In an interview, you talk directly with someone who has expert knowledge about (or experience with) your topic. Interviews can be done in person, over the phone, by e-mail, or by exchanging letters. Make sure to write down your questions ahead of time. (See page 170.)

PRESENTATIONS

Going to lectures, museum displays, and exhibits can provide you with firsthand information about many different topics. So can listening to certain radio interviews. Remember to observe closely, think about what you are seeing and hearing, and write down your thoughts and details.

DIARIES, JOURNALS, AND LETTERS

Reading the thoughts of various experts or celebrities by reviewing letters and personal writings is an interesting way to gather facts and details for your assignments. These kinds of primary sources can be found in biographical writings, in secondhand bookstores, and at historical museums.

Evaluating Sources of Information

There is a great deal of information available to you on the Internet as well as in the media and in the library. However, before you use this information, you need to ask yourself questions (like those below) to judge whether or not your sources are trustworthy. If you use unreliable information, your report or project will also be unreliable.

- **Is the source primary or secondary?** Firsthand facts are often more trustworthy than secondhand facts. The simple reason is that information from a secondary source has been compiled by someone other than yourself. Should you trust the person who compiled it? Maybe and maybe not.

- **Is the source an expert?** An expert is someone regarded as an authority on a certain subject. If you aren't sure about someone's authority, ask your teacher, parent, guardian, or librarian for help in deciding.

- **Is the information accurate?** Accuracy is most likely to be found in a highly regarded source. For example, an article in the *Chicago Tribune* is probably more accurate than one in a supermarket tabloid.

> If two or three reliable sources of information all say the same thing, the information is probably trustworthy.

- **Is the information complete?** You can judge completeness by looking for all sides of an issue or a topic. If an author tells you only the facts that support his or her opinion about a subject, something important is probably missing. Look further.

- **Is the information current?** Generally, you want the very latest information on a subject, especially with science and technology topics. Look for books and articles with recent copyright dates.

- **Is the source biased?** A "bias" means literally a tilt toward one side. Biased sources—politicians, TV infomercials, and business people—have something to gain by using facts and emotions to put themselves in the best light. Obviously, you'll want to avoid using biased sources.

Using the Internet

The Internet can be an efficient source of information, or just another way to waste time. If, for the most part, you're checking out flashy ads, games, and chat rooms, you're not using the Internet as the valuable research tool it can be. But if you plan ahead and stay on track, you will find a wealth of up-to-date information for speeches, essays, reports, and research papers.

The Internet is a worldwide computer network. (Internet is short for "interconnected networks." People sometimes call it the "Net.") When you get on the Internet, you can search for information all over the world. You can also send messages to other users, no matter where they live. The World Wide Web, e-mail, and newsgroups are three important parts of the Internet.

WHAT'S AHEAD

In this chapter, you'll learn about the Internet and how to use it as a research tool. You will also learn some tips and strategies for making your time on the Internet as trouble free as possible.

- A Guide to the Internet
- Using the Internet
- Searching for Information
- Working with Your Research

A Guide to the Internet

A car is made up of many different systems—the transmission, the power train, the brake systems, etc.—all working together to make driving possible. The Internet also consists of several different systems, all working together to make on-line communication possible. These two pages show how all of these systems work together.

Internet Service Provider (ISP) ■ An Internet service provider connects a personal computer or local-area network to the Internet (much as a phone company gives telephone access to the world). It also saves your e-mail when you are off-line and usually furnishes other services, too. (A provider makes communication on the Internet possible.)

Personal Computer (PC) ■ A personal computer gives you access to the Internet via a provider.

Local-Area Network (LAN) ■ A school or business often interlinks its computers in a LAN so that users can share files and send interbuilding e-mail. Some LAN's are connected to the Internet; others are restricted to their own facility.

Electronic Mail (E-Mail) ■ E-mail is a message from one person to another, passed from computer to computer within a network. On the Internet, you can send e-mail to people all over the world. To receive e-mail, you need an e-mail account. You can set up an account through your Internet service provider.

World Wide Web ■ The World Wide Web is a part of the Internet consisting of pages that are interlinked. Before the Web, searching the Internet took a lot of time and patience. With the Web, however, a page of text at one site can be linked to other pages at other sites, making your on-line research much more effective.

Newsgroups ■ A newsgroup is a place to post messages about a particular topic and respond to messages. There are newsgroups on thousands of subjects, from *homework help* to *hiking*. Most newsgroups are collected together under one heading called *Usenet*.

If you have a question about the Internet, and can't find the answer anywhere else, ask your Internet provider. It's their business to help you with the Net. Just remember to phrase your e-mail message clearly and politely.

THE INTERNET AT A GLANCE

An Internet service provider (ISP) allows you to conduct research and communicate on-line. The provider gives you access, via a personal computer or a LAN, to the World Wide Web, e-mail, and newsgroups. (Study the chart below to see how the Net works.)

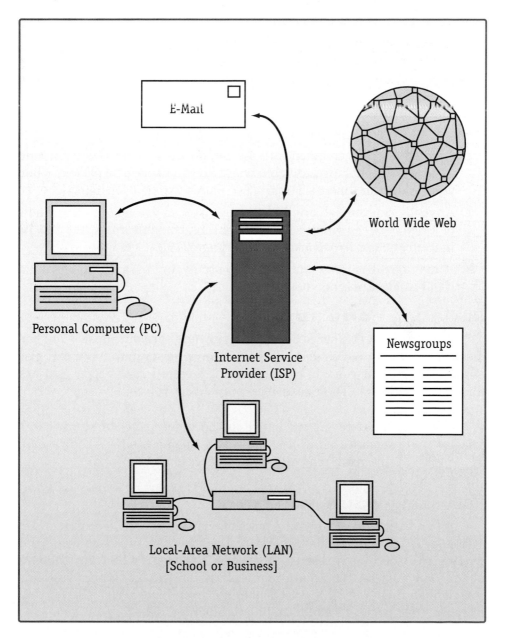

Using the Internet

When it comes to your class work, there are three reasons for using the Internet: conducting research, discussing your ideas, and publishing your finished writing.

Conducting RESEARCH

The main reason for using the Internet is research. The Net puts a world of information within your reach via a computer. At the outset of your searching, you can gain an overview of your subject. Then you can dig deeper for specific facts and details. What you find on the Net is often more up-to-date than the information in printed texts. But keep these three points in mind:

1. Because there is so much information on the Net, you may not find what you are looking for right away. So you need to be patient when you conduct on-line research. (See pages 270-271 for help.)

2. Anybody can publish anything on the Net, so you have to learn how to judge between what is accurate and responsible and what may be inaccurate and irresponsible. (See page 272.)

3. It may be difficult to know when to stop your research if you find a lot of information on your subject.

Discussing YOUR IDEAS

The Internet can serve as a testing ground for your ideas. You can discuss an idea in a chat room or post it for a newsgroup. You can also e-mail part of your work to other people interested in the topic and ask for their reactions. (Their responses may direct you to new sources.)

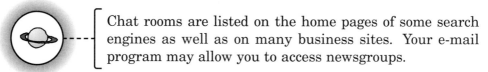

Chat rooms are listed on the home pages of some search engines as well as on many business sites. Your e-mail program may allow you to access newsgroups.

Publishing YOUR WRITING

When you're finished with a piece of writing (report, research paper, story, etc.), you can publish your work on the Net. In that way, your writing can serve as a resource for other Net users who want to learn about your subject. There are many places on the Net where students can publish their work. Your school might even have a Web site for that purpose. (See pages 42-43 for on-line publishing ideas.)

QUICK GUIDE

Surfing Tips

Here are some tips for surfing the Internet. ("Surfing" means riding Internet links from page to page in search of information.)

- **STAY FOCUSED:** When you're doing research, make sure to stay focused on your specific task. Otherwise, you may find yourself wasting a lot of time and have little, if anything, to show for your efforts.

- **CHECK YOUR FACTS:** The Internet is sometimes called a global town square because anyone can speak out. Some people are not always careful with their facts and opinions, so don't believe everything that is posted. (See page 272 for more about evaluating the quality of the information you find on the Net.)

- **PRESERVE YOUR PRIVACY:** You wouldn't stand in New York's Times Square with a bullhorn, shouting out your family's address, telephone number, and credit card number to every passerby. Nor should you reveal personal details on the Internet. Always check with your parents or a teacher before posting anything on the Net.

- **PROTECT YOURSELF:** If you find an Internet sight offensive, go somewhere else. Just about any newsgroup can get "spammed" with offensive messages.

- **USE NETIQUETTE:** Netiquette means being considerate of others when you are on-line. Follow these practices:

  Scout the Territory: When using a site, read its instructions. Check for a FAQ ("frequently asked questions") list before requesting help.

  Post Clear Messages: Don't assume your readers will understand; *make sure* they understand.

  Don't SHOUT: Use caps only when necessary—for titles, emphasis, and other special uses.

Searching for Information

There are millions of sites on the Internet. So how can you search for information and find what you are looking for? If you know the address for a specific site you want to visit, just key in the address. Otherwise, you can start your searching in one of these two ways:

1 CHECK YOUR PROVIDER

Each time you log onto the Internet, the first page you see is the *home page*. If your Internet provider is one of the major on-line services, it probably has an area devoted especially to young people and their schoolwork. This is a great place to start your research.

If your Internet provider is a smaller local service, it may not have an area devoted to students, but it probably has a list of Web links to help you. It may also list organizations and businesses that subscribe to the provider. Often, these groups are more than willing to help students in their research, either by e-mail or in person.

2 CARRY OUT WORD SEARCHES

Many providers list several different search engines you can use to explore the Internet. Search engines are programs that allow you to carry out word searches on the Net. For example, *Yahoo!* is a popular and effective search engine.

To do a word search, type in a keyword or phrase, and the search engine will find Web pages that fit the keyword. A *keyword* is a word that is related to the subject of your research. (See the next page.)

Your search engine may have a *searchable index*. To use this feature, read through the headings listed on the first page of the index and click on the ones that best fit your subject. New pages that appear may contain these headings divided into subheadings and the subheadings further divided. Eventually you will come to a list of specific sites to visit if you keep clicking on the proper headings and subheadings.

Word-Searching Guide

The key to carrying out a word search lies in how you phrase things.

- If you type in one word, the search engine will look for all sites that include that word in their description.

> **Try it!** Type *homework*; then start your search engine.

- If you type in more than one word, the search engine will look for all sites that contain any of those words.

> **Try it!** Type in *homework help*; then start your search engine.

- If you type a phrase in quotation marks, most search engines will look for all sites that contain exactly that phrase.

> **Try it!** Type *"homework help"*; then start your search engine.

- Most search engines allow you to use *Boolean* words (such as *and*, *or*, and *not)* and some use symbols (such as "+" for *and* and "-" for *not* to help control your searching.

> **Try it!** Type *homework and help;* then start your search engine.

- If your search turns up too many items, use a more specific phrase, possibly with quotation marks or Boolean words or symbols. You may also limit your search to a specific heading in a searchable index. (See "Helpful Hint" on previous page.)

> **Try it!** Click on a social studies heading; then type *homework* and start your search engine.

Working with Your Research

If you search long enough on the Internet, you should be able to find information on most topics. Your next job is to decide whether or not it is reliable.

Evaluating WHAT YOU FIND

Judging the accuracy of information on the Net is not always easy. The guidelines that follow will help you:

Consider the source. Government and educational sites are very reliable, as are most business sites. The sites you might question are the private, individual ones.

Compare more than one source. If multiple sources all say the same thing, chances are the information is accurate.

Check with a trusted adult. Ask a parent, teacher, librarian, or media specialist to help you judge the reliability of information.

Saving WHAT YOU FIND

Here are four ways to save information you find on the Internet.

1. **Bookmarking** When you bookmark a site, you save the Net address for future use.

2. **Printing** You can print out a hard copy of pages you visit. Make sure to note the Internet address, the author's name, and the date of the pages you copy.

3. **Copying on a Disk** Most Internet software lets you save pages either as text or as a source file. Saving as text preserves only the words; saving as a source file also preserves the Web links and formatting.

4. **E-Mailing** You can also save pages by e-mail. This can be helpful if you have no printer available, or if you want to send the copy to a different computer before you work with it.

Crediting WHAT YOU FIND

You will need to give credit for the information from the Net that you decide to use in your research papers and reports. (See "Documenting," page 229, for help.)

Using the Library

You have access to two main sources of information when you're conducting research for a report, a speech, or some other extended project. One source is the Internet, located somewhere out there in cyberspace, and the other is your school or city library, located down the hall or down the street in "real space."

The Net serves as a good starting point for research, offering plenty of up-to-date facts and ideas about almost any topic. (The trick, though, is finding this information and checking its accuracy.) The library, on the other hand, has thousands of books and other materials containing in-depth, reliable discussions on almost any topic. The library also offers at least one trained professional to help you with your research.

WHAT'S AHEAD

This chapter explains how to get the most out of your library. It tells you about the computer and card catalogs, call numbers, reference books, the *Readers' Guide,* and more. Basically, everything you need to feel at home in the library is included here. (See the previous chapter for guidelines about using the Net.)

- Searching for Information
- Using the Card Catalog
- Using the Computer Catalog
- Finding Books
- Using Reference Books
- Using the *Readers' Guide*
- Understanding the Parts of Books

ALM

ALM

Call Number
973.31
H

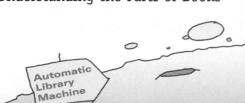

Automatic
Library
Machine

Searching for Information

Begin searching for what you need by exploring your library's catalog. Whether the catalog is contained on cards in file drawers or has been stored in a computer, you will find the same information—a list of all the books and materials held in that particular library, including their call numbers (addresses) or other tips for finding them.

Catalog Entries

There are three ways to approach your search in the catalog—by title, by author, or by subject.

1. Title entries begin with the book's title. In the card catalog, titles beginning with *A, An,* or *The* are filed under the next word in the title. Titles beginning with an abbreviation are filed as though the abbreviation were spelled out. (In a computer catalog, simply type in the title as you know it, whether or not it begins with an article or an abbreviation.)

> ### Vacation on the Unknown Planet, A

> ### Dr. Botanical's Backwoods Remedies
> (This title would be filed under *Doctor* in the card catalog.)

2. Author entries begin with the name of the book's author. In the card catalog, the author's last name is listed first. (In a computer catalog, you will probably find instructions about whether or not to type the last name first.)

> ### Russell, Theodore J.

3. Subject entries begin with the subject of the book.

> ### SPACE TRAVEL   FOLK MEDICINE

Using the Card Catalog

In the card catalog, you'll be able to find information about the same book in three ways:

1. Look up the **title card.**

2. Look up the **author card.** (If the library has more than one book by the same author, you will find more than one catalog card with that author's name at the top.)

3. Look up the **subject card.**

In addition to the title, author, and subject of the book, each card will offer additional information including the call number, which is the address that will lead you to the actual book on the shelf. (Each kind of card is filed separately in alphabetical order.)

S A M P L E Catalog Cards

Title Card

How to Get an Athletic Scholarship ———— **Title heading**
———— **Call number**

378.30973 Minnis, Whitney
How to get an athletic scholarship:
a student-athlete's guide to collegiate athletics

ASI Pub. (c1995) 104-pp. illus.

Author Card

378.30973 Minnis, Whitney ———————— **Author's name**
How to get an athletic scholarship: ————— **Title**
a student-athlete's guide to collegiate athletics

ASI Pub. (c1995) 104-pp. illus.

Everything high-school students need to know to
qualify and apply for athletic scholarships for

Subject Card

SPORTS ———————————— **Subject heading**
378.30973 Minnis, Whitney
How to get an athletic scholarship:
a student-athlete's guide to collegiate athletics

ASI Pub. (c1995) 104-pp. illus. ———————— **Publisher and copyright date**

Everything high-school students need to know to
qualify and apply for athletic scholarships for
college.

1 Sports 2 Scholarships

Using the Computer Catalog

In the computer catalog, you will also find information on the same book in three ways:

1. Enter the **title.**

2. Enter the **author's name.** (If the library has more than one book by the same author, you will find more than one entry with the author's name at the top.)

3. Enter the **subject,** or *keyword*, which is a word related to the subject.

If your subject is . . .	**your keyword might be . . .**
experimental spacecraft,	space travel, spaceship, or NASA.

When you need several books on the same subject, do a subject search. Either the librarian or instructions built into the computer catalog can help you figure out which keywords would be best to use.

SAMPLE Computer Catalog Entry

```
Author:      Minnis, Whitney
Title:       How to get an athletic
             scholarship: a student-athlete's
             guide to collegiate athletics
Published:   ASI, 1995
             104 pp.
Subjects:    Sports
             Scholarships
STATUS:                  CALL NUMBER:
Not checked out          378.30973
LOCATION:
General collection
```

Finding Books

NONFICTION BOOKS Many of the books you will use for classroom reports and research papers will be nonfiction. These books are assigned call numbers that are placed on the books' spines. Then the books are shelved in numerical order. This means that books on the same or related topics will be shelved near one another. Just by browsing, you can find several books on the same subject of interest.

- **Call numbers may contain decimals.**

  The number 932.167 is actually smaller than 932.2. This is true because 932.2 is really 932.200 without the two zeros. A book with the number 932.167 will be on the shelf before one with the number 932.2.

- **Call numbers may include letters.**

  A book with the number 932.2 will be on the shelf before one with the number 932.2F.

The **Dewey decimal classification** system is used by many libraries to catalog books and assign call numbers. In this system, information is divided into ten main categories, or classes.

The Ten Classes of the Dewey Decimal System

000 General Topics	500 Pure Science
100 Philosophy	600 Technology (Applied Science)
200 Religion	700 The Arts and Recreation
300 The Social Sciences	800 Literature and Rhetoric
400 Language	900 Geography and History

BIOGRAPHIES Biographies and autobiographies are assigned the call number 921 and arranged according to the last name of the subject of the book. A book about John Glenn would have the number 921GLENN on its spine and be shelved accordingly.

FICTION BOOKS Fictional books are shelved by the first three letters of the author's last name. If you have a favorite author, you can go directly to the fiction shelves and find some good reading.

Using Reference Books

Reference books are kept in their own section of the library. Here you will find encyclopedias, atlases, almanacs, indexes, dictionaries, thesauruses, and many other useful volumes.

Encyclopedias

- Encyclopedias are good starting points for gathering information.
- Articles are arranged alphabetically by topic.
- An index of topics (usually in the back of the last volume or in a separate volume) is available. You will find a list of places within the volumes in the set that contain more information.
- Related topics are listed at the end of most articles.
- Different sets of encyclopedias may include different information. Look in more than one set of encyclopedias.

SAMPLE Encyclopedia Index

Encyclopedia article and volume ——— **Nile River** [river, Africa] **N: 426** *with pictures and map*

    Egypt (the land) **E:123**

    Egypt, Ancient (the land) **E:133-134** *with picture and map*

    Irrigation (history) **I:459** — Page numbers

    Middle East (the land) **M:532**

    Mythology (Egyptian mythology) **M:976**

    River (table) **R:356**

    Sudan (land and climate) **So:954**

Related topic ——— **Nile Valley** [region, Egypt]

    City (ancient cities) **Ci:578**

    Egypt (the land) **E:123-124** *with picture*

    Nile River (the Nile Valley and Nile Delta) **N:426** *with map*

Atlases

- Some atlases include maps of the whole world; others cover only certain states, countries, or regions. Atlases may also contain facts about different countries.
- Atlases to look for:

  Webster's Concise World Atlas, World Facts and Maps, Discovery Atlas of Native Americans

Almanacs

- General almanacs contain facts and figures about many topics.
- Special-interest almanacs cover a single subject, such as movies or basketball.
- Look in the most recent edition for the latest facts. (Almanacs are usually published every year.)
- Almanacs to look for:

    The World Almanac and Book of Facts ■ Contains facts and figures about history, politics, business, sports, entertainment, etc.

    Information Please Almanac ■ A detailed index leads you to facts, statistics, and articles on astronomy, business, countries of the world, current events, inventions, space, famous people, etc.

    Kane's Famous First Facts ■ A large, single volume lists "firsts" in all areas of life by event, year, and date.

Periodical Indexes

- A periodical index lists articles in magazines and newspapers.
- These indexes are arranged alphabetically by subject.
- Indexes to look for:

    Readers' Guide to Periodical Literature ■ Lists articles from many publications. (See page 280.)

    New York Times Index ■ Lists articles from the *New York Times.*

Other Helpful Reference Books

Bartlett's Familiar Quotations ■ Contains 20,000 quotations arranged in chronological order from ancient times to the present.

Current Biography ■ Articles include a photo of the individual, a short biography, information about the person's work, address, and so on. Published monthly and annually.

Facts About the Presidents ■ A single volume contains important facts and dates about all the presidents.

Something About the Author: Facts and Pictures About Contemporary Authors and Illustrators of Books for Young People ■ Contains about 200 biographical sketches.

Webster's New Geographical Dictionary ■ This volume lists the world's most important places in alphabetical order. Includes geographical and historical information about each place.

Using the *Readers' Guide*

1. **Find the edition you want.** If you want magazine articles about an event that happened this past June, look in the guides for June and July.

2. **Look up the subject** alphabetically. If you can't find it, try a different word—"influenza" instead of "flu," "whale" instead of "orca," and so on.

3. **Look up an author's last name** if you want to find articles by that person.

4. **Check cross-references** (notes leading you to more information).

5. **Write down the facts** about the articles you want to read: the magazine's name, date published, title and page number of article.

6. **Find the magazines.** (The librarian may have to get them for you.)

SAMPLE FROM A *Readers' Guide* PAGE

BLOOD VESSELS ————————————————— | Subject Entry
         Transplantation
    Molecular plumbing [tissue engineering of vascular grafts] R. Peters and R.
      Sikorski. *Science* v279 no5354 p1230-1 F 20 '98 —————— | Name, Volume, and
BLOODLESS SURGERY | Number of Magazine
    "Bloodless" operations eliminate transfusions. il *USA Today (Periodical)*
    v126 no2633 p2-3 F '98
BLOOM, CAROLE ————————————————— | Author Entry
    The must-have desserts. il *Bon Appétit* v43 no1 p86-90 Ja '98
BLOOM, JENNIFER KINGSTON
    "Isn't he talking yet?" *Working Mother* v21 no5 p50-3 My '98 ———— | Title of Entry
BLUE GREEN ALGAE *See* Cyanobacteria
BLUE JAYS (BASEBALL TEAM) *See* Toronto Blue Jays (Baseball team)
BLUE JEANS *See* Jeans (Clothing) ————————————— | Cross-Reference
BLUE ORCHARD BEES *See* Bees
BLUEBONNETS (FLOWERS)
    Back roads & bluebonnets [wildflowers in Texas' Hill Country] M. Morris. —
    il map *Travel Holiday* v181 no3 p94-9 Ap '98 | Name of Author
BLUEFISH (BASEBALL TEAM) *See* Bridgeport Bluefish (Baseball team)
BLUEGILLS
    Breaming with bass [predator-prey relationship between largemouths
    and bluegills] J. Doggett. il *Field & Stream (Northeast ed.)* v102 no12
    p114+ Ap '98 ————————————————————— | Page Number/Date

HELPFUL HINT At the end of the year, all monthly issues of the *Readers' Guide* are published together in one book. Your library may also have the CD-ROM version. Ask the librarian for help.

Understanding the Parts of Books

If the book you have searched for and located in the library is a nonfiction or reference book, you need to know how to use that book efficiently. It is especially important, for instance, to make full use of the index and special glossaries and tables when using nonfiction books. Here is a list of book parts and tips to help you get the most out of the nonfiction books you find in the library.

- The **title page** is usually the first printed page in a book. It tells (1) the book's title, (2) the author's name, (3) the publisher's name, and (4) the place of publication.

- The **copyright page** follows the title page and gives the year the copyright was issued. When you are looking for up-to-date facts, be sure you use a book with a recent copyright date.

- A **preface**, a **foreword**, or an **introduction** sometimes follows the copyright page. This part usually tells something about the book and why it was written. It may also include an **acknowledgement**, or thank-you, to people who helped make the book possible.

- The **table of contents** gives the names and page numbers of chapters and sections in the book. Looking through this part will tell you the general topics covered in the text.

- The **body** of the book is the main part of the text.

- An **appendix** may follow the body. It contains information that supplements the main text—sometimes maps, charts, tables, copies of letters, official documents, or other special information.

- Some books also contain a **glossary** (minidictionary) of special terms that are used throughout the book. Whenever you don't understand a term, look it up in the glossary.

- If a book has a **bibliography,** a list of other books and articles about the same subject, you may use it to find more information.

- Finally, you will find the **index.** This is an alphabetical listing of all the important topics covered in the book.

 Note: The index is probably the most useful part of a reference book. It tells you, first, whether the book contains the information you need and, second, on which page you'll find it.

Thinking
to Learn

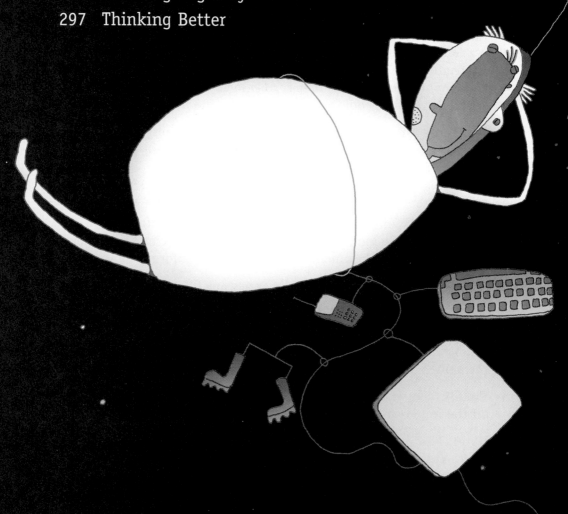

Thinking and Writing

Your assignments not only require you to do a lot of thinking, they require you to think in a lot of different ways. For example, taking a fill-in-the-blanks test calls for a different kind of thinking than writing a persuasive essay, just as defining a challenging term calls for a different kind of thinking than writing a letter analyzing a problem you are having with a product.

These different kinds of thinking are often divided into six levels: recalling, understanding, applying, analyzing, synthesizing, and evaluating. Recalling is the most basic level of thinking; evaluating is the most advanced level. All the levels of thinking are connected in one way or another, and you will rarely use one kind of thinking by itself.

WHAT'S AHEAD

This chapter explains the six levels of thinking. You'll also find example assignments for all the levels, plus a chart that reviews some basic guidelines for thinking and writing.

- Recalling Information
- Understanding Information
- Applying Information
- Analyzing Information
- Synthesizing Information
- Evaluating Information
- Guidelines for Thinking and Writing

Recalling Information

The most basic type of thinking you use in school is **recalling** information. This type of thinking is needed when you are asked to remember and repeat information you have learned in class.

To help you recall information, do the following:

- Listen carefully in class and take notes.
- Read your texts carefully.
- Review and study the information so that you know it well.

USING RECALLING

Your teachers will give you very few writing assignments in which they ask you simply to recall information. Instead, almost all writing assignments require that you combine recalling with other more advanced levels of thinking.

However, you may encounter questions that ask you only to recall information. For example, when you answer multiple-choice, matching, and fill-in-the-blank questions on a test, you must recall what you have learned. Imagine you've just studied the California gold rush in social studies class. Answering the questions below would require recalling.

Directions: Fill in the blanks to correctly complete the sentences below.

1. _John Marshall_ discovered gold in California in the year _1848_.

2. Miners who came to California were called _forty-niners_.

3. The gold rush brought immigrants from _Mexico_, _Spain_, _China_, and other countries.

Directions: Write three sentences, each telling an important fact about the gold rush.

1. San Francisco grew from 812 people to 25,000 people in two years because of the gold rush.

2. After all the surface gold had been taken from the streams, miners had to dig to find more gold.

3. Many shopkeepers got rich by selling food and supplies to miners.

Understanding Information

Your teachers will often ask you to do more than simply recall information. You will be asked to show that you **understand** the information well enough to write about it in your own words.

When your teachers ask you to explain something, tell what something means, or tell how something works, you need to display an understanding of a subject.

To help you understand information, do the following:

● Use study-reading and note-taking strategies. (See pages 307-322 and 361-368.)

● Rewrite the information in your own words.

● Explain the information to someone else.

USING UNDERSTANDING

Often, you will be asked to show understanding by writing a paragraph or an essay. To develop the paragraph below, the student had to recall important facts and details and use this information to show understanding.

Assignment: Explain how the gold rush changed John Sutter's life.

John Sutter owned the farm where James Marshall discovered gold in 1848. Ironically, Sutter did not get rich from the gold on his land. In fact, the gold rush ruined him. Before 1848, Sutter's farm was a large estate surrounded by adobe walls. Sutter and the Native Americans who worked for him grew crops, raised animals, and made everything they needed. Sutter had a reputation for being kind to everyone, including his workers and strangers who needed help. He was a successful, prosperous farmer. But when gold was discovered, greedy prospectors trampled Sutter's crops, killed and ate his livestock, and destroyed his house. Sutter's farm, his livelihood, was in shambles. He had no choice but to move to get away from the gold rush.

Note: You may also show your understanding of certain subjects by making a graphic organizer, chart, or map.

Applying Information

When you are asked to **apply** information, you must be able to use what you've learned to demonstrate, show, or complete something. For example, when you use your computer manual to help you set up your computer, you are applying the information in the manual to the job of setting up the computer.

To help you apply information, do the following:

- Select the most important facts and details.
- Think about how you could use the information.
- Organize the information in the best way to meet your specific needs. (See page 60.)

USING APPLYING

Many times, you will be asked to apply information to your own world. To do this, you need to know the important facts and main themes at the core of the information. Then you must apply this understanding to another situation in your own experience. The assignment below asks students to apply one of the gold rush themes to a personal situation.

Assignment: One of the main lessons we can learn from the gold rush of 1848 is that "opportunity is good, but greed can destroy." Relate this lesson to an action or experience in your own world.

I know someone who really wanted this new video game, but he didn't have the money to buy it. He said he would do anything to get the game, and he did; he tried to steal it from the store, but he got caught. He got in trouble with the police and with his parents. He was grounded for a month; plus he didn't get any allowance. If he had just saved up his allowance, he could have bought the game, and he would have it by now. But he was greedy, and it ruined everything.

Analyzing Information

When you are asked to compare and contrast, to rank things in order of importance, or to give reasons, you are **analyzing** information. Analyzing means breaking information down into smaller parts.

To help you analyze information, do the following:

- Identify the important parts that make up the whole.
- Determine how the parts are related to one another.

USING ANALYZING

When you must analyze information, first figure out what kind of analysis to do (compare and contrast, rank things, give reasons, etc.). Then decide which facts and details to use. Finally, decide how to organize the facts and details. The following assignment asks you to compare the gold rush to a contemporary get-rich-quick scheme.

Assignment: Louisa Clappe, who lived in a gold-mining camp, had this to say about the gold rush: "Gold mining is nature's great lottery scheme. A man may work . . . for many months, and be poorer . . . than when he commenced; or, he may take out thousands in a few hours. It is a mere matter of chance." Compare the gold rush of 1848 to today's state lotteries. How are the two alike?

There are some differences between the gold rush and today's lotteries, but they are alike in important ways. First, both the gold rush and today's lotteries attract people who hope to get rich quick. Second, succeeding at both depends on luck or chance, not on hard work. Third, a few people got rich in the gold rush, and a few people get rich in the lotteries. It was expensive to join the gold rush. If you didn't find gold, you could go broke. If people spend money they need for food, rent, or other necessities on lottery tickets, they can face bankruptcy.

 Note: A Venn diagram can help you organize your thoughts when you are asked to compare and contrast. (See page 313.)

Synthesizing Information

When you are asked to combine information with new ideas, or to use information to create something, you are **synthesizing.** To analyze, you break something down into its important parts; to synthesize, you put something together in a new way.

What often separates an advanced thinker from a basic thinker is his or her ability to synthesize information. Common ways of synthesizing information are *predicting, inventing,* and *redesigning.* In each case, you have to reshape the information you already have.

To help you synthesize information, do the following:

- Think of ways to combine the information with other ideas. (For example, information about the California gold rush plus your knowledge of space travel could turn into a science fiction story about a gold rush on another planet.)

- Put the information in a different form. (Turn what you know about the gold rush into a play, a poem, a children's story, a feature article, and so on.)

USING SYNTHESIZING

The same thing that makes synthesizing a challenge also makes it fun: You get to use your imagination. Suppose your teacher asks you to use information about a subject such as the gold rush to develop a creative piece of writing. Such an assignment asks you to synthesize— to use existing information in a new and creative way. The model that follows is a title-down poem.

Assignment: Write a poem, a story, or a series of journal entries about the gold rush.

Gold and greed lured thousands to the West,
On clipper ships, by wagon, and by long, hard hike.
Like ants digging tunnels, they worked without rest.
Despite dangers and costs, all hoped for a strike.

"Rush to the gold mines!" was the cry.
"Under the earth you'll get rich overnight!"
Some would get rich to be sure by and by.
However, most saw no nuggets in sight.

Evaluating Information

When you are asked to express your opinion about an important issue, or to discuss the good and bad points about something, you are **evaluating.** Evaluating is an advanced level of thinking requiring a thorough understanding and analysis of a subject.

To help you evaluate information, do the following:

- Learn as much as you can about a subject before you try to evaluate it.
- Recall, review, organize, and analyze the information as needed.

USING EVALUATING

A good evaluation is based on good information. Start with a sentence that identifies your overall opinion, or evaluation; then add facts and details that prove your evaluation is a good one. Note how the sample paragraph contains a great deal of supporting information.

Assignment: Write a paragraph in which you make a judgment about the overall effects of the gold rush of 1848.

While the immediate results (effects) of the gold rush were mostly negative, it did have some positive long-term effects on the area. Most prospectors failed to strike it rich and, in the process, wasted away all of their life savings. Others died in mining accidents or from severe weather or from snakebites. Those who did find gold were often victims of foul play—muggings, robberies, and even murder. There was little, if any, law enforcement in the mining camps, so all types of assaults and thievery were common. But, in the long run, the free spending of miners who did find gold helped establish cities such as San Francisco and Sacramento. In addition, ranchers and farmers followed the miners to California and made productive use of the land. The gold rush also brought enough people to the area to allow California to become a state and develop into an important part of the United States.

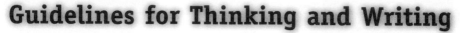

Guidelines for Thinking and Writing

Whenever you are asked to . . .		Be ready to . . .

RECALL----------------⌐ **Remember what you have learned** ⌐

underline	circle
list	match
name	label
cluster	define

- collect information
- list details
- identify or define key terms
- remember main points

UNDERSTAND-------⌐ **Explain what you have learned** ⌐

explain	review
summarize	restate
describe	cite

- give examples
- restate important details
- explain how something works

APPLY----------------⌐ **Use what you have learned** ⌐

change	illustrate
do	model
demonstrate	show
locate	organize

- select the most important details
- organize information
- explain a process
- show how something works

ANALYZE--------------⌐ **Break information down** ⌐

break down	rank
examine	compare
contrast	classify
tell why	

- carefully examine a subject
- break it down into important parts
- make connections and comparisons

SYNTHESIZE--------⌐ **Reshape information into a new form** ⌐

combine	connect
speculate	design
compose	create
predict	develop
invent	imagine

- invent a better way of doing something
- blend the old with the new
- predict or hypothesize (make an educated guess)

EVALUATE------------⌐ **Judge the worth of information** ⌐

recommend	judge
criticize	argue
persuade	rate
convince	assess

- point out a subject's strengths and weaknesses
- evaluate its clearness, accuracy, value, and so on.
- convince others of its value/worth

Thinking Logically

When you want to prove an important point, you must connect your ideas in just the right way—in a clear and logical way. For thinking to be logical, it has to be reasonable (*supported with enough good reasons*), reliable (*supported with solid evidence*), and believable.

Suppose that one of your teachers asks you to develop a persuasive essay related to some aspect of school life. After brainstorming for ideas, you decide to argue that all students should learn a second language. In order to develop a convincing argument, you would have to gather a great deal of information showing the value of second-language learning.

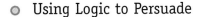

WHAT'S AHEAD

This chapter will help you use clear and logical thinking whenever you develop persuasive essays, research papers, and speeches. (Also see pages 115-122 for more on persuasive writing.)

- Using Logic to Persuade
- Avoiding Fuzzy Thinking
- Guidelines for Logical Thinking

Using Logic to Persuade

One of the most common types of logical thinking is persuasive thinking. When your teachers assign a persuasive speaking or writing assignment, they really are asking you to do two things: (1) form an opinion—a personal feeling or belief—about some important subject, and (2) support or prove your opinion.

Guidelines for Persuasive Assignments

When you know your opinion is a good one—and you have plenty of good facts to support it—you are ready to craft your piece of writing. If you find that you don't have many facts to support your opinion, you must modify or change it. Use the guidelines that follow to help you with persuasive assignments.

Know the difference between fact and opinion.

Make sure you understand the difference between an opinion and a fact before you start a persuasive writing assignment. An *opinion* is a view or belief held by a person. A good opinion is based on fact, but it is not a fact itself. A *fact* is a specific statement that can be checked or proven to be true. *Note:* The examples below show the difference between an opinion and the supporting facts. The opinion states a personal view. The facts are specific and can be proven; they support the opinion.

> **Opinion:** Yellowstone Park is a great place to go on vacation.
>
> **Supporting Facts:** Most of the world's geysers are located in Yellowstone.
>
> The park has many wild animals, including bison, elk, and bear.
>
> The park also contains deep canyons, clean lakes, and beautiful waterfalls.

Form an opinion.

Make sure you understand and believe the opinion you are trying to support. You cannot write or speak in a sincere, honest style if you don't believe in your topic. *Note:* Don't be afraid to form an opinion about a controversial issue or topic.

Write an opinion statement.

Make sure that your opinion statement is worded effectively. For help, follow the simple formula given below.

Formula: A specific subject (*Wild animals in the park*)
+ a specific opinion (*should be protected from hunters*)

= a good opinion statement.

Opinions that include words that are strongly positive or negative—such as *all, best, every, never, none,* or *worst*—may be difficult to support. For example, an exaggerated opinion statement like "All wild animals are a nuisance in the park campgrounds" would certainly be impossible to support.

Support your opinion.

Whenever you support or defend an opinion, make sure you do so with clear, provable facts. Otherwise, your reader probably won't agree with your opinion. Let's say you are supporting the opinion that "Wild animals in Yellowstone, even the most dangerous species, should be protected from hunters." Note the following supporting facts.

Provable Fact: "Some of the dangerous species, such as grizzly bears, are endangered." (You can look up official lists of endangered species to prove that this is true.)

Not a Provable Fact: "Grizzly bears attack humans only when they are afraid." (This statement would be hard to prove.)

Organize your facts.

You can develop a persuasive speech or essay in two basic ways: (1) You can state your opinion or belief in the topic sentence or thesis statement and then support it with specific facts; or (2) you can start your assignment by presenting a number of specific facts that lead to a believable concluding or ending statement in which your opinion or belief is made clear.

Avoiding Fuzzy Thinking

Make sure that all ideas in a persuasive assignment are well thought out. Some thinking shortcuts lead to misleading ideas. Read the descriptions that follow to learn about different types of fuzzy thinking, and avoid these in your own writing.

- **Avoid statements that jump to a conclusion.**

    Because wolves kill elk in Yellowstone Park, wolves must be eliminated.

    This statement jumps to a conclusion. In fact, if wolves did not kill some elk, the elk could overpopulate the park and cause other species to become extinct.

- **Avoid statements that are supported with nothing more than the simple fact that most people agree with them.**

    It is okay to feed black bears because most people don't think they are dangerous.

    This type of statement suggests that if a group of people believe something, it must be true. In reality, black bears are wild animals; it is not safe to feed them.

> "The whole of science is nothing more than a refinement of everyday thinking."
> – Albert Einstein

- **Avoid statements that contain a weak or misleading comparison.**

    A mountain lion, which weighs about 150 pounds, is no match for an elk, which weighs about 1,000 pounds.

    This statement makes a misleading comparison. Although elk are much larger, mountain lions use their speed, strength, and stalking ability to overpower elk.

- **Avoid statements that exaggerate the facts or mislead the reader.**

    If you meet a bear in the wild, the best thing to do is play dead.

    This statement is misleading. Sometimes playing dead may actually work. If, however, you play dead in between a mother and her cubs, you may be in real trouble. Never use information that could mislead your reader.

● **Avoid statements that appeal only to the reader's feelings and contain no factual information.**

> Baby bears are not dangerous because they are small and cute.

This statement appeals to our feelings about baby bears, rather than the actual facts. Even small bears can injure a person. Also, a mother bear who finds a human near her cubs may attack the person. The fact is, baby bears can be dangerous.

● **Avoid statements that contain part of the truth, but not the whole truth. These statements are called half-truths.**

> At one time, people almost drove the coyote to extinction.

This statement is only partly true. In spite of people's efforts to drive coyotes to extinction, the animals have actually multiplied. While coyotes used to live only in some western states, they now are found in all parts of the country.

● **Avoid statements that reduce a solution to two possible extremes: "America: Love it or leave it." "Put up or shut up." This type of statement eliminates every possibility in the middle.**

> Either grizzlies must be allowed to roam free in wilderness
> areas, or they will become extinct.

This statement doesn't allow for a logical discussion of the issue. Surely there are protection plans besides free roaming that could be considered.

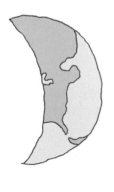

Guidelines for Logical Thinking

Follow these basic guidelines whenever you are using logic to persuade.

- Decide on your purpose and state it clearly.
- Gather whatever information you can on the subject. (See below.)
- Focus on a main point that you can logically support.
- Support your main point with reliable evidence.
- Consider any objections your audience may have.
- Admit that some arguments against your point may be true.
- Restate your central claim or point.

ASKING QUESTIONS

Asking questions is one of the most effective ways to gather information about a subject. You can use the questions in the chart below to fit many different types of subjects, including problems (like teenage smoking), policies (like a new dress code), or concepts (like community service).

	Description	Function	History	Value
Problems	What is the problem? What are the signs of the problem?	Who or what is affected by it? What new problems may it cause in the future?	What is the current status of the problem? What or who caused it?	What is its significance? Why is it more (or less) important than other problems?
Policies	What type of policy is it? What are its most important features?	What is the policy designed to do? What is needed to make it work?	What brought this policy about? What are the alternatives to this policy?	Is the policy workable? What are its advantages and disadvantages?
Concepts	What type of concept is it? Who or what is related to it?	Who has been influenced by this concept? Why is it important?	When did it originate? How has it changed over the years?	What practical value does it hold? What is its social worth?

Thinking Better

Would you like to be a faster thinker . . . a more logical thinker . . . a more creative thinker? Would you like to be able to think longer and harder? How about learning to keep more thoughts in mind without becoming confused? In short, would you like to learn how to think better? Then read on.

Thinking begins with careful observation—noticing the details of a situation or setting, and storing them for later use. Thinking requires that you become personally involved in the things going on around you. It requires that you make connections—working with the details of your experience to form new understandings and original ideas. These new ideas, in turn, will make everything you do (from writing and talking to drawing and designing) more creative, logical, and thoughtful.

WHAT'S AHEAD

The first part in this short chapter offers suggestions for becoming a better, stronger thinker. The second part shows you how to move efficiently through the writing and thinking process.

○ Becoming a Better Thinker
○ Basic Writing and Thinking Moves

Becoming a Better Thinker

There is no magic formula for becoming a better thinker. Like every-thing worthwhile, it takes time and practice. However, the suggestions that follow should get you off on the right track.

1 **Be patient . . .** don't expect quick, easy solutions to every problem or challenge you face; good thinking often takes time and requires you to plan, listen, discuss, etc.

2 **Set goals . . .** think about what you can do now (short-term goals) and what you have to patiently work on step-by-step to accomplish (long-term goals).

3 **Get involved . . .** read books, magazines, and newspapers; watch documentaries; participate in sports, join a club, volunteer; look at art—do your own art.

4 **Think logically . . .** think beyond your "knee-jerk" emotions or the first answer that pops into your head; look at all sides of a prob-lem and consider all the possible solutions. (See pages 291-296.)

5 **Ask questions . . .** ask questions about what you read, what you hear, even what you see; if you think you know "what" it is, then ask "why, who, when, where, how, how much, why not, what if?"

6 **Be creative . . .** do not settle for the obvious answer or the usual way of doing things; look at things in a new way—redesign, reinvent, reenact, rewrite. (See "Offbeat Questions," page 55.)

7 **Make connections . . .** pay attention to the details and how they are tied together; use what you have learned to help you solve new problems; use comparisons, analogies, metaphors.

8 **Write things down . . .** writing can help you clarify ideas and remember them longer; it can help you discover things you didn't know you knew; it can help you sort through your thoughts and "see" them in a new light. (See "Journal Writing," pages 145-148.)

Your Basic Writing and Thinking Moves: What follows on the next page is a "process chart" showing the kinds of thinking (from simple to complex) that go on when you write. Don't expect, however, to think in a straight line. Thinking goes up and down, backward and forward.

Basic Writing and Thinking Moves

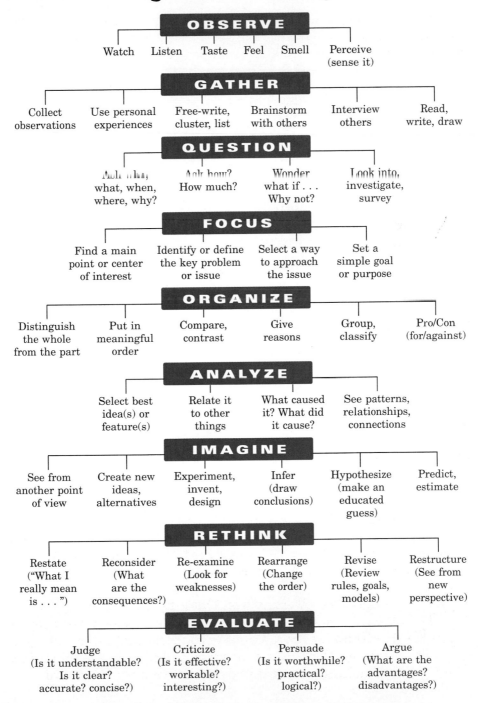

OBSERVE

Watch   Listen   Taste   Feel   Smell   Perceive (sense it)

GATHER

Collect observations | Use personal experiences | Free-write, cluster, list | Brainstorm with others | Interview others | Read, write, draw

QUESTION

Ask who, what, when, where, why? | Ask how? How much? | Wonder what if . . . Why not? | Look into, investigate, survey

FOCUS

Find a main point or center of interest | Identify or define the key problem or issue | Select a way to approach the issue | Set a simple goal or purpose

ORGANIZE

Distinguish the whole from the part | Put in meaningful order | Compare, contrast | Give reasons | Group, classify | Pro/Con (for/against)

ANALYZE

Select best idea(s) or feature(s) | Relate it to other things | What caused it? What did it cause? | See patterns, relationships, connections

IMAGINE

See from another point of view | Create new ideas, alternatives | Experiment, invent, design | Infer (draw conclusions) | Hypothesize (make an educated guess) | Predict, estimate

RETHINK

Restate ("What I really mean is . . .") | Reconsider (What are the consequences?) | Re-examine (Look for weaknesses) | Rearrange (Change the order) | Revise (Review rules, goals, models) | Restructure (See from new perspective)

EVALUATE

Judge (Is it understandable? Is it clear? accurate? concise?) | Criticize (Is it effective? workable? interesting?) | Persuade (Is it worthwhile? practical? logical?) | Argue (What are the advantages? disadvantages?)

Reading to Learn

Reading Charts

Imagine trying to find a new store in a large mall without that handy map with the arrow that says *You Are Here!* Imagine trying to put together a new computer system without any diagrams to show each step.

A good chart can help you understand complex information at a glance. For example, if you wanted to identify the number of female and male eighth-grade band students in each state, you could write out 50 sentences. But, oh, how tedious they would be to write . . . and to read!

A better choice would be to put the information in a simple table. The first column could list all of the states, the second column could give the number of female students per state, and so on. Information displayed in this way would be far easier to read and analyze. Remember the old saying: A picture is worth a thousand words.

WHAT'S AHEAD

The basic job of all charts is to show how facts relate to one another. Different kinds of charts show different kinds of relationships. This chapter will help you read and understand the most common kinds of charts.

- Understanding Graphs
- Understanding Tables
- Understanding Diagrams

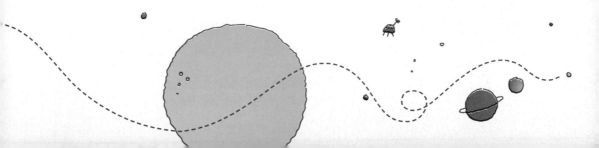

Understanding Graphs

Graphs are pictures of information, not pictures of things. The information in graphs is often called *data*. The most common kinds of graphs are *line graphs, pie graphs,* and *bar graphs*.

LINE GRAPH When you think of a graph, you probably think of a line graph. A line graph shows how things change over time. It starts with an L-shaped grid. The horizontal line of the grid stands for *passing time* (seconds, minutes, years, or even centuries). The vertical line of the grid shows the *subject* of the graph. The subject of the graph below is immigration to the United States; the time is 1910-1990.

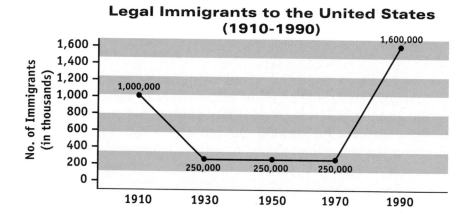

Legal Immigrants to the United States (1910-1990)

PIE GRAPH A pie graph shows proportions and how each proportion or part relates to the other parts and to the whole "pie." In the sample pie graph, you can see what percentage of all legal immigrants come from particular regions of the world.

If percentages are used, they should add up to 100%; if numbers are used, the graphs may add up to some other total.

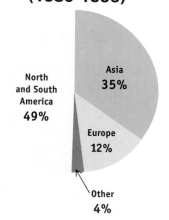

U.S. Legal Immigrants: Regions of Origin (1980-1996)

BAR GRAPH   A bar graph uses bars (sometimes called *columns*) to show how different things compare to one another at the same time. Unlike line graphs, bar graphs do not show how things change over time. A bar graph is like a snapshot that shows how things compare at one point in time.

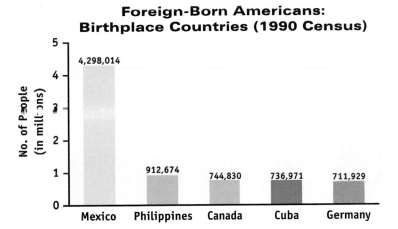

**Foreign-Born Americans:
Birthplace Countries (1990 Census)**

STACKED BAR GRAPH   A stacked bar graph gives more detailed information than a regular bar graph. Besides comparing the bars, it compares parts within the bars themselves.

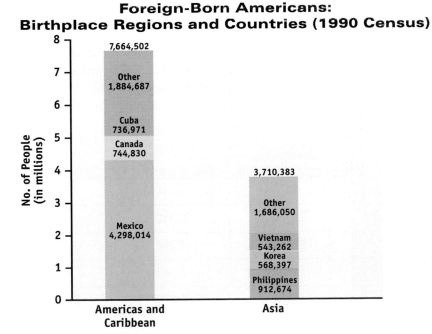

**Foreign-Born Americans:
Birthplace Regions and Countries (1990 Census)**

Understanding Tables

Tables organize words and numbers so that it's easy to see how they relate to one another. Each table has *rows* (going across) and *columns* (going down). Rows contain one kind of information, while columns contain another kind of information. Some common kinds of tables include comparison tables, distance tables, and conversion tables. Tables can also be custom-made to meet your special needs.

COMPARISON TABLE The table below is a comparison table that makes it easy to see the bloom color of different plants. The rows show kinds of plants; the columns show colors. (A ● means that a plant has flowers of that color.)

Plant	Bloom Colors				
	yellow-orange	pink-red	blue-purple	white	multi
Aster		●	●	●	
Begonia	●	●		●	
Dianthus		●	●	●	●
Gazania	●	●		●	●

DISTANCE TABLE Another common kind of table is a distance, or mileage, table. To read a distance table, find your starting point in one row or column. Then find your destination in the other direction. Where the row and column meet, you find the distance between locations.

Mileage Table			
	Los Angeles	Seattle	Baltimore
Los Angeles	0	1,141	2,701
New York	2,787	2,912	197
Tampa	2,591	3,096	997
Chicago	1,989	2,043	697
Houston	1,581	2,498	1,420

CONVERSION TABLE Another very useful table is a conversion table. This is a table that converts (changes) information from one form to another. The table below converts degrees Fahrenheit to degrees Celsius (centigrade).

Degrees Fahrenheit* to	Degrees Centigrade
0	-17.9
32	0
40	4.5
50	10.1
60	15.7
70	21.3
80	26.9
90	32.5
100	38.1

*Multiply Fahrenheit by .56 after subtracting 32

CUSTOM-MADE TABLES Tables can show all kinds of information. They are a good way to record information you gather. Imagine that you need to gather facts about several different countries and compare some of the information you have gathered. You could make a custom-made table like the one below.

Comparing Countries			
	Canada	Mexico	U.S.
Size (Sq. Miles)	3.85 million	759,000	3.8 million
Type of Government	Parliamentary	Republic	Republic
Voting Age	18	18	18
Literacy	99%	87%	98%

Understanding Diagrams

A diagram is a drawing of something that shows how it is put together, how its parts relate to one another, or how it works. The two most common types of diagrams are the picture diagram and the line diagram.

PICTURE DIAGRAM A picture diagram is just that—a picture or drawing of the subject being discussed. Some parts of the subject may be left out of the diagram to emphasize the parts the writer wants to show. For example, this picture diagram of a cell shows only the largest, most important parts.

Parts of a Cell

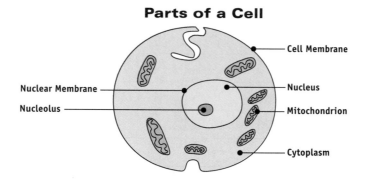

LINE DIAGRAM Another type of diagram is a line diagram. A line diagram uses lines, symbols, and words to help you show the relationship among ideas. The problem-solving diagram below is a common kind of line diagram that helps you understand how to solve a scientific problem. *Note:* When a diagram shows a process, it usually shows the steps from top to bottom (as in the sample below) or from left to right.

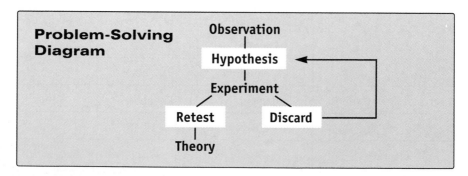

Study-Reading Skills

Study-reading is reading for understanding. It's all about reading efficiently and remembering what you read. It's the kind of reading you do when you read your textbooks, and it's also the kind you do when you gather information for a report or research paper. By study-reading, you can find out . . .

- **who** is doing or has done significant things in this world,
- **what** natural and social changes have occurred,
- **why** certain events are important,
- **how** different things work, and
- much more.

WHAT'S AHEAD

The information in this chapter will help you improve your reading skills. You will learn about common patterns of nonfiction, such as description and comparison. You will also learn about two important study-reading strategies and some ideas for adjusting your reading rate. (Also see pages 361-365.)

- Patterns of Nonfiction
- Study-Reading Strategies
- Adjusting Your Reading Rate

Patterns of Nonfiction

Knowing the common patterns of nonfiction makes it easier to understand your assigned reading. Six of these patterns are reviewed in this chapter: *description, main idea / supporting details, comparison / contrast, chronological order, cause and effect,* and *process.*

Description

This article from a book about valuable food sources explains the benefits of rice. It follows the **description** pattern, telling how rice grows, what its nutritional value is, and its other uses.

For over half of the world's population, rice is the staple food; for some it is the only source of protein. Rice is a native plant of Asia, perhaps specifically of India, and came (via shipwreck) to the New World in the seventeenth century. Rice plants thrive in warm, moist climates and must be submerged for much of their growing period.

Rice, like wheat and barley, is a grain that is all too often eaten in a highly refined, less nourishing state. Most of its nutrients are in the bran layer that surrounds each kernel. Unfortunately, most of the people for whom rice is a primary food are guilty of consuming it with much of its value milled away. Rice is easily digested, contains very little fat or sodium, and has no gluten, so it is a good carbohydrate choice for people on restrictive diets. When eaten in its less refined forms, it is a good source of protein, vitamins, and minerals. Rice is also used to make vinegar, beer, and wine.

Note Taking

WEB: Use a web to help you organize important information that follows a description pattern.

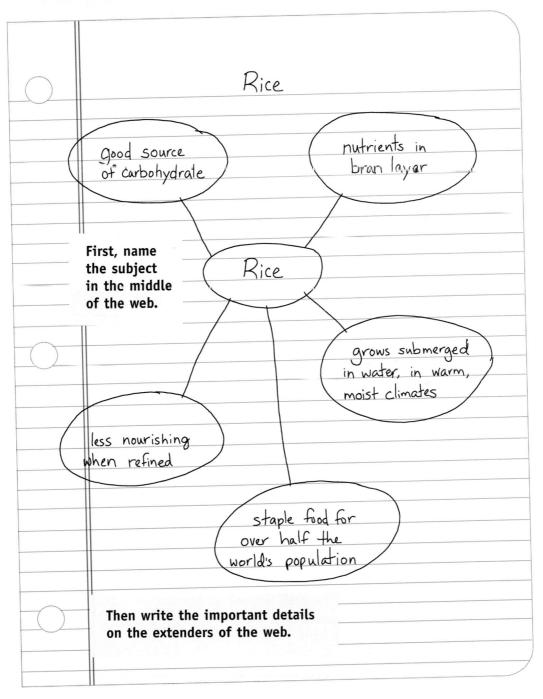

Rice

good source of carbohydrate

nutrients in bran layer

First, name the subject in the middle of the web.

Rice

grows submerged in water, in warm, moist climates

less nourishing when refined

staple food for over half the world's population

Then write the important details on the extenders of the web.

Main Idea/Supporting Details

This information from a book about new sports activities follows the **main idea/supporting details** pattern. The heading at the top of the page introduces the subject, the first couple of sentences share the main idea, and the rest of the page gives details that support this idea.

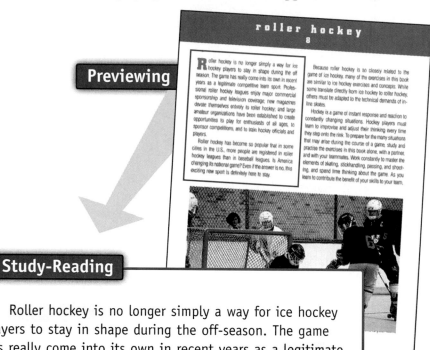

Previewing

roller hockey
8

Roller hockey is no longer simply a way for ice hockey players to stay in shape during the off season. The game has really come into its own in recent years as a legitimate competitive team sport. Professional roller hockey leagues enjoy major commercial sponsorship and television coverage; new magazines devote themselves entirely to roller hockey; and large amateur organizations have been established to create opportunities to play for enthusiasts of all ages, to sponsor competitions, and to train hockey officials and players.

Roller hockey has become so popular that in some cities in the U.S., more people are registered in roller hockey leagues than in baseball leagues. Is America changing its national game? Even if the answer is no, this exciting new sport is definitely here to stay.

Because roller hockey is so closely related to the game of ice hockey, many of the exercises in this book are similar to ice hockey exercises and concepts. While some translate directly from ice hockey to roller hockey, others must be adapted to the technical demands of in-line skates.

Hockey is a game of instant response and reaction to constantly changing situations. Hockey players must learn to improvise and adjust their thinking every time they step onto the rink. To prepare for the many situations that may arise during the course of a game, study and practise the exercises in this book alone, with a partner, and with your teammates. Work constantly to master the elements of skating, stickhandling, passing, and shooting, and spend time thinking about the game. As you learn to contribute the benefit of your skills to your team,

Study-Reading

Roller hockey is no longer simply a way for ice hockey players to stay in shape during the off-season. The game has really come into its own in recent years as a legitimate competitive team sport. Professional roller hockey leagues enjoy major commercial sponsorship and television sponsorship; new magazines devote themselves entirely to roller hockey; and large amateur organizations have been established to create opportunities to play for enthusiasts of all ages, to sponsor competitions, and to train hockey officials and players.

Roller hockey has become so popular that in some cities in the U.S., more people are registered in roller hockey leagues than in baseball leagues. Is America changing its national game? Even if the answer is no, this exciting new sport is definitely here to stay.

Note Taking   **TABLE ORGANIZER:** When a selection follows the main idea/supporting details pattern, use a table organizer to help you sort out the important details.

Roller Hockey

The tabletop names the main idea.

Roller Hockey is a legitimate team sport.			
professional leagues have commercial and TV sponsorships	new magazines are devoted to the sport	amateur organizations sponsor competitions and train officials and players	more registered in roller hockey leagues than some baseball leagues

The legs of the table list supporting details.

Comparison/Contrast

Comparison/contrast is another important pattern of nonfiction. The information below, from an article in a student magazine, compares solar power and fossil fuels. The first part of the article describes fossil fuels, and the rest of the article discusses the use of solar power. The article also gives some advantages and disadvantages for both kinds of fuel.

Previewing

Why Solar POWER?

The gasoline that ordinary cars use is made from oil, a fossil fuel. Fossil fuels—oil, coal, and natural gas—formed underground when pressure and heat acted on plants and animals that died millions of years ago. The supply of fossil fuels is limited, and when they're burned to produce energy to run cars and heat homes, they pollute the air.

Sunlight is free. It can't be used up, and it doesn't pollute. A

solar car uses many solar cells to convert sunlight into electricity. Light striking the cells produces an electric current. The electric energy is then stored in a battery to be used as needed.

Some homes use active solar heating systems. A liquid is pumped to the roof, where it's heated by sunlight as it passes over solar collectors. The hot liquid returns to a special heating system inside the house.

Solar energy has disadvantages as well as advantages. Solar cells supply less power than gasoline, so solar cars cannot weigh very much—if they were heavy, they wouldn't move! Also, they travel much more slowly that gasoline-powered cars. And there's one major problem with harnessing solar energy—the sun doesn't shine all day, every day, everywhere!

Study-Reading

The gasoline that ordinary cars use is made from oil, a fossil fuel. Fossil fuels—oil, coal, and natural gas—were formed underground when pressure and heat acted on plants and animals that died millions of years ago. The supply of fossil fuels is limited, and when they're burned to produce energy to run cars and heat homes, they pollute the air.

Sunlight is free. It can't be used up, and it doesn't pollute. A solar car uses many solar cells to convert sunlight into electricity. Light striking the cells produces an electric current. The electric energy is then stored in a battery to be used as needed.

Some homes use active solar heating systems. A liquid is pumped to the roof, where it's heated by sunlight as it passes over solar collectors. The hot liquid returns to a special heating system inside the house.

Solar energy has disadvantages as well as advantages. Solar cells supply less power than gasoline, so solar cars cannot weigh very much—if they were heavy, they wouldn't move! Also, they travel much more slowly than gasoline-powered cars. And there's one major problem with harnessing solar energy— the sun doesn't shine all day, every day, everywhere!

Note Taking   **VENN DIAGRAM:** A Venn diagram is an effective way to organize important information that compares two subjects.

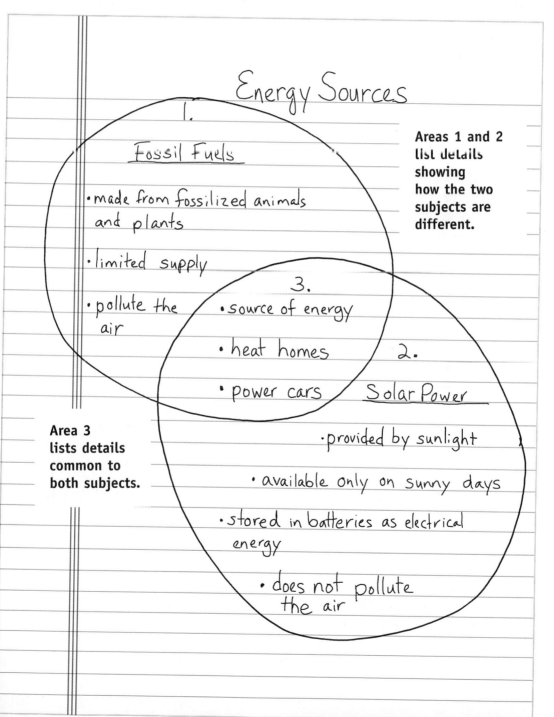

Energy Sources

1.

Fossil Fuels

• made from fossilized animals and plants

• limited supply

• pollute the air

3.

• source of energy

• heat homes

• power cars

2.

Solar Power

• provided by sunlight

• available only on sunny days

• stored in batteries as electrical energy

• does not pollute the air

Areas 1 and 2 list details showing how the two subjects are different.

Area 3 lists details common to both subjects.

Chronological Order

This article taken from a history textbook follows the **chronological** (time order) pattern of organization. The article gives the basic facts about the Lewis and Clark expedition that opened up the western part of the United States.

Previewing

Lewis and Clark Expedition   223

In January of 1803, President Thomas Jefferson asked Congress for $2,500 to pay for an expedition to the Louisiana Territory. Congress quickly agreed to the request. Jefferson appointed his secretary, Meriwether Lewis, to recruit the other members of the expedition and to plan the trip.

On May 14, 1804, the expedition, led by Mr. Lewis and William Clark, left St. Louis, Missouri, on its journey up the Missouri River. Their destination was the Pacific Ocean, but to reach it they would have to travel through a wilderness that no white person had ever seen and that appeared on no map.

The Corps of Discovery, as the expedition was called, spent the winter of 1804-1805 at a village they built near today's Bismarck, North Dakota. They

called the village Fort Mandan, because it was near a Mandan tribal settlement. It was here that Lewis and Clark met Sacagawea, the Shoshone teenager who would be an invaluable interpreter for them on the rest of the journey.

On November 7, 1805—a year and a half after leaving St. Louis— the expedition reached its goal. Clark wrote in his journal: "Great joy in camp. We are in view of the ocean, this great Pacific Ocean which we [have] been so long anxious to see."

Nearly a year later, on September 23, 1806, the explorers returned to St. Louis, where they were welcomed as heroes.

Study-Reading

In January of 1803, President Thomas Jefferson asked Congress for $2,500 to pay for an expedition to the Louisiana Territory. Congress quickly agreed to the request. Jefferson appointed his secretary, Meriwether Lewis, to recruit the other members of the expedition and to plan the trip.

On May 14, 1804, the expedition, led by Mr. Lewis and William Clark, left St. Louis, Missouri, on its journey up the Missouri River. Their destination was the Pacific Ocean, but to reach it they would have to travel through a wilderness that no white person had ever seen and that appeared on no map.

The Corps of Discovery, as the expedition was called, spent the winter of 1804-1805 at a village they built near today's Bismarck, North Dakota. They called the village Fort Mandan, because it was near a Mandan tribal settlement. It was here that Lewis and Clark met Sacagawea, the Shoshone teenager who would be an invaluable interpreter for them on the rest of the journey.

On November 7, 1805—a year and a half after leaving St. Louis— the expedition reached its goal. Clark wrote in his journal: "Great joy in camp. We are in view of the ocean, this great Pacific Ocean which we [have] been so long anxious to see."

Nearly a year later, on September 23, 1806, the explorers returned to St. Louis, where they were welcomed as heroes.

Note Taking

TIME LINE: A time line is an efficient way to show the chronological order of events.

Lewis and Clark Expedition

January 1803 — Jefferson asked Congress for funds for an expedition to explore the Louisiana Territory.

May 14 1804 — Lewis and Clark headed up the Missouri River from St. Louis—then west toward the Pacific Ocean.

Winter, 1804-1805 — Lewis and Clark expedition spent the winter in North Dakota at Fort Mandan. There they met Sacagawea, a Native American interpreter.

November 7, 1805 — Expedition reached the Pacific Ocean.

September 23, 1806 — Expedition returned to St. Louis.

Cause and Effect

This information about Easter Island, found on the Internet, follows the **cause and effect** pattern. It discusses a change in the food chain that may have been the reason for the ancient Easter Islanders deserting their home.

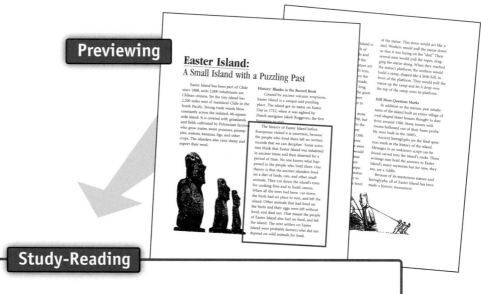

Previewing

Study-Reading

The history of Easter Island before Europeans visited it is uncertain because the people who lived there left no written records that we can decipher. Some scientists think that Easter Island was inhabited in ancient times and then deserted for a period of time. No one knows what happened to the people who lived there. One theory is that the ancient islanders lived on a diet of birds, rats, and other small animals. They cut down the island's trees for cooking fires and to build canoes. When all the trees had been cut down, the birds had no place to nest and left the island. Other animals that had lived on the birds and their eggs were left without food and died out. That meant the people of Easter Island also had no food and left the island. The next settlers on Easter Island were probably farmers who did not depend on wild animals for food.

Note Taking   **CAUSE AND EFFECT:** Use the following type of organizer to keep track of important information that shows cause and effect.

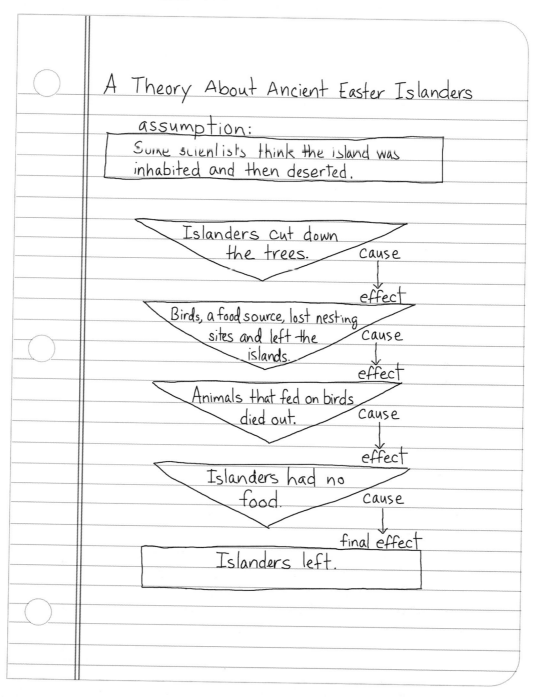

A Theory About Ancient Easter Islanders

assumption:
Some scientists think the island was inhabited and then deserted.

Islanders cut down the trees.   Cause

↓ effect

Birds, a food source, lost nesting sites and left the islands.   Cause

↓ effect

Animals that fed on birds died out.   Cause

↓ effect

Islanders had no food.   Cause

↓ final effect

Islanders left.

Process

The text in this later part of the Easter Island article (page 316) follows a **process** pattern. It describes how some scientists think the large statues of Easter Island were built over time.

Easter Island:
A Small Island with a Puzzling Past

Easter Island has been part of Chile since 1888, anits 2,000 inhabitants are Chilean citizens. Yet the tiny island lies 2,200 miles west of mainland Chile in the South Pacific. Strong trade winds blow

History: Blanks in the Record Book
Created by ancient volcanic eruptions, Easter Island is a unique and puzzling place. The island got its name on Easter Day in 1722, when it was sighted by Dutch navigator Jakob Roggeven, the first

land before certain, because left no written her. Some scien- ind was inhabited deserted for a nows what hap- lived there. One islanders lived nd other small the island's trees uild canoes. een cut down, nest, and left the at had lived on were left without meant the people no food, and left ers on Easter ners who did not for food.

The Biggest Mystery of All
The biggest mystery of Easter Island is a puzzle carved in stone: Hundreds of huge stone statues of human heads and torsos, carved centuries ago out of the island's gray volcanic rock. The statues are 10 to 40 feet tall and weigh up to 85 tons. No one knows for sure exactly when the statues were made, why they were made, or how their creators moved them long distances from inland quarries to the giant stone platforms along the coast where they still stand, seeming to stare out to

Scientists think that the earliest stone platforms were built in about AD 700, but that the first statues weren't added to the platforms until the 1100's. The largest statues probably were built around 1300. Scientists theorize that the statues were carved inside volcanoes, where there were massive walls of stone. The carvers would complete the front and sides of a statue while it was still part of the wall. Then they would chip away at its back to sepa- rate it from the rock wall. Once the statue was finished, workers would use rope to tie a large, flat, V-shaped stone to the front

of the statue. This stone would act like a sled. Workers would pull the statue down so that it was laying on the "sled." Then several men would pull the ropes, drag- ging the statue along. When they reached the statue's platform, the workers would build a ramp, shaped like a little hill, in front of the platform. They would pull the statue up the ramp and let it drop over the top of the ramp onto its platform.

Still More Question Marks
In addition to the statues, past inhabi- tants of the island built an entire village of oval-shaped stone houses thought to date from around 1500. Stone towers with rooms hollowed out of their bases proba- bly were built in the 1600's.
Ancient hieroglyphs are the final ques- tion mark in the history of the island. Messages in an unknown script can be found carved into the island's rocks. These writings may hold the answers to Easter Island's many mysteries but for now, they too, are a riddle.
Because of its mysterious statues and hieroglyphs, all of Easter Island has been made a historic monument.

Previewing

Study-Reading

Scientists think that the earliest stone platforms were built in about AD 700, but that the first statues weren't added to the platforms until the 1100's. The largest statues probably were built around 1300. Scientists theorize that the statues were carved inside volcanoes, where there were massive walls of stone. The carvers would complete the front and sides of a statue while it was still part of the wall. Then they would chip away at its back to separate it from the rock wall. Once the statue was finished, workers would use rope to tie a large, flat, V-shaped stone to the front of the statue. This stone would act like a sled. Workers would pull the statue down so that it was lying on the "sled." Then several people would pull the ropes, dragging the statue along. When they reached the statue's platform, the workers would build a ramp, shaped like a little hill, in front of the platform. They would pull the statue up the ramp and let it drop over the top of the ramp onto its platform.

Note Taking

PROCESS LIST: Important information that follows the process pattern can be arranged in a list.

Easter Island's Statues: A Theory

1. First, stone platforms were built.
   ↓
2. Statues were carved out of walls inside volcanoes.
   ↓
3. Workers tied a V-shaped stone "sled" to front of statue.
   ↓
4. Workers pulled statue down and dragged it, on sled, to the platform.
   ↓
5. Workers built a hill-shaped ramp in front of the platform.
   ↓
6. Finally, workers pulled the statue up the ramp and let it drop onto its platform.

This list shows the steps, or stages, in the order that they are given in the reading.

Study-Reading Strategies

Learning to be a good reader saves you time, adds to your understanding, and may result in better grades. When you are doing a reading assignment related to social studies, science, or another content subject, try using either the **Think and Read** or the **KWL** strategy.

Think and Read

Reading is thinking prompted by print. Under each of the sections below, choose one or more of the suggestions to help you become more thoughtful in your reading.

THINK before READING . . .

- Ask yourself what you already know about the topic.
- Skim over the text. (See "Skimming," page 322.)

PAUSE during READING . . .

- Write out questions, definitions, and important things you need to remember. You can use sticky tabs or strips of paper for this.
- Reread difficult parts aloud. Then continue reading.
- To discover the definition of a word you don't know, use context clues, a dictionary, or a glossary, or ask someone.

REFLECT after READING . . .

- Tell yourself (or someone else) what you learned.
- Write a list of things you want to remember.
- Write a summary of your reading.
- Determine which pattern of nonfiction the text follows. (See pages 308-319.) Create your own graphic organizer and take notes on the piece.

Turn to "Taking Reading Notes" on page 364 for more tips on reading to learn.

KWL

KWL is a good study-reading strategy to use when you already know something about the topic. KWL stands for what I "know," what I "want" to know, and what I "learned."

How to Use a KWL Chart

1 Write the topic of your reading at the top of a sheet of paper. Then divide the sheet into three columns and put a *K*, a *W*, and an *L* above the columns.

2 List what you already know in the *K* column.

3 Fill in the *W* column with questions you want to explore.

4 When you finish reading, fill in the *L* column with things you learned or still hope to learn.

The Milky Way

K (What do I know?)	W (What do I want to know?)	L (What I learned or still want to know.)
It's very big.	What's a galaxy?	A galaxy is a family of stars.
Earth is a part of it.	How big is the Milky Way?	The Milky Way is more than 100,000 light years across.
It's a galaxy.	Are there other suns in the Milky Way?	There are other suns, and they might have planets orbiting around them.

Adjusting Your Reading Rate

Many students think they'll do better in school if they read faster. But reading faster doesn't always mean reading better. Depending on the purpose for your reading and what you are reading, you'll have to adjust your speed.

Let's compare two things you might read—a math chapter about percentages and a chapter in a novel. The purpose for reading the math chapter is to pass a test and apply the information to your life. You will probably have to read this chapter very slowly, and then reread it a number of times, stopping to take notes or do certain calculations. The purpose for reading the novel chapter is to enjoy the story and find out what the characters are up to. You will probably read this material rather quickly.

Just remember that not all reading is done at the same rate. Adust your rate according to *what* and *why* you're reading.

TECHNIQUES FOR ADJUSTING RATE

When you are reading for *specific facts* or *information*, there are two techniques you can use to adjust your reading rate: skimming and scanning.

- Use skimming to get a quick overview of reading material.
- Use scanning to find specific information like important dates and vocabulary definitions.

Skimming

When you skim, you look at the headings, boldfaced words and phrases, first and last sentences—just the key points. Skimming is a good way to preview material before you read it carefully, and also a good way to review material after you read it.

Scanning

When you scan, you look for key words. Browse or look through each page, searching only for the key words and skipping all others. Use your finger to scroll down the page. When you find a key word, stop and read to determine if this is the information you want.

Improving Your Vocabulary

Your vocabulary is all the words you know and use. Increasing your vocabulary will improve your ability to learn—better understand what you read and hear—and to communicate more effectively.

One of the best ways to improve your vocabulary is to read. Books, magazines, newspapers, and the Internet are filled with all kinds of new words and ideas. When you come across an unfamiliar word, find out its meaning, and then begin to use the word in your daily work. This is a sure way to increase your vocabulary.

WHAT'S AHEAD

As you read and write, there are a number of vocabulary-building strategies available to you. This chapter explains several of these strategies so that you can try them for yourself.

- Using Context Clues
- Referring to a Thesaurus
- Checking a Dictionary
- Keeping a Personal Dictionary
- Using Prefixes, Suffixes, and Roots
- Understanding the Levels of Diction

Using Context Clues

When you come across a word you don't know, you can often figure out its meaning from the other words in the sentence. The other words form a familiar context, or setting, for the unfamiliar word. Looking closely at these surrounding words will give you hints, or clues, about the meaning of the new word. Seven common types of context clues are listed below with examples.

TYPES OF CONTEXT CLUES

Clues from synonyms:

Sara had an **ominous** feeling when she woke up, but the feeling was less threatening when she saw she was in her own room.

Clues from antonyms:

Boniface had always been quite heavy, but he looked **gaunt** when he returned from the hospital.

Clues contained in comparisons and contrasts:

Riding a mountain bike in a **remote** area is my idea of a great day. I wonder why some people like to ride motorcycles on busy six-lane highways.

Clues contained in a definition or description:

Manatees, large aquatic mammals (sometimes called sea cows), can be found in the warm coastal waters of Florida.

Clues that appear in a series:

The campers spotted sparrows, chickadees, cardinals, and **indigo buntings** on Saturday morning.

Clues provided by the tone and setting:

It was a cool and breezy fall afternoon. Hundreds of fans were gathering for the last game of the season, and the student jazz band was entertaining the crowd. It was an **auspicious** event.

Clues derived from cause and effect:

The amount of traffic at 6th and Main doubled last year, so crossing lights were placed at that corner to **avert** an accident.

Referring to a Thesaurus

A thesaurus is a reference book that gives synonyms and antonyms for words. A thesaurus helps you in two ways:

1. It helps you find just the right word for a specific sentence.

2. It keeps you from using the same words again and again.

If a thesaurus is organized alphabetically, look up the word as you would in a regular dictionary. If you have a traditional thesaurus, look for your word in the book's index.

FINDING THE BEST WORD

A thesaurus would be helpful if you needed one effective word to mean *very cold* in the following sentence:

Because of the _____ weather, none of the cars in our neighborhood would start.

SAMPLE THESAURUS ENTRY

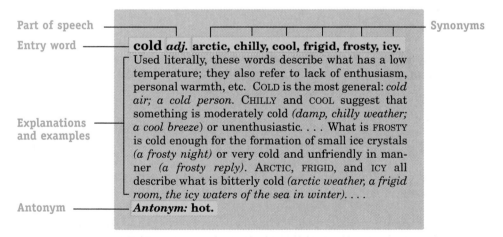

Part of speech ——

Entry word ——

cold *adj.* **arctic, chilly, cool, frigid, frosty, icy.**
Used literally, these words describe what has a low temperature; they also refer to lack of enthusiasm, personal warmth, etc. COLD is the most general: *cold air; a cold person.* CHILLY and COOL suggest that something is moderately cold *(damp, chilly weather; a cool breeze)* or unenthusiastic. . . . What is FROSTY is cold enough for the formation of small ice crystals *(a frosty night)* or very cold and unfriendly in manner *(a frosty reply).* ARCTIC, FRIGID, and ICY all describe what is bitterly cold *(arctic weather, a frigid room, the icy waters of the sea in winter).* . . .

Explanations and examples ——

Antonym ——   ***Antonym:* hot.**

Synonyms

After reading the list of synonyms, you decide on *arctic* because it describes very cold weather.

Because of the ___arctic___ weather, none of the cars in our neighborhood would start.

Checking a Dictionary

The dictionary is, of course, your most reliable source for learning the meanings of new words. Remember, too, that a word often has more than one meaning, so read them all. In addition to the meanings of words, the dictionary offers the following aids and information:

Guide words are words located at the top of every page. They list the first and last entry words on a page, and they help you know which words fall in alphabetical order between the entry words.

Entry words are the bold words that are defined on the dictionary page. Entry words are listed in alphabetical order.

Syllable divisions show where you can divide a word into syllables. Some dictionaries use heavy black dots to divide the syllables. Other dictionaries put extra space between syllables.

Parts of speech labels tell you the different ways a word can be used. For example, the word *grief* is used only as a noun. On the other hand, the word *griddle* can be used as a noun (*The griddle was ready for the pancakes*) or as a verb (*I'll griddle the pancakes*).

Pronunciations are phonetic respellings of a word.

Spelling and **capital letters** (if appropriate) are given for every entry word. If an entry is capitalized, capitalize it in your writing, too.

Illustrations are often provided to make the definition clearer.

Accent marks show which syllable or syllables should be stressed when you say a word.

Synonyms are words with similar meanings. **Antonyms** (words with opposite meanings) may be listed last.

Etymology gives the history of a word [in brackets]. Knowing a little about its history can make a word easier to remember.

Pronunciation key gives symbols to help you pronounce the entry words.

Remember each word may have several definitions. That's why it's important to read all of the meanings and then select the one that is best for you.

MODEL Dictionary Page

Entry word — grid·dle (grĭd′l) n. A flat metal surface used for cooking by dry heat. [ME gridel, gridiron < ONFr. gredil < Lat. craticula, dim. of cratis, hurdle, lattice.] —grid′dle v.

grid·dle·cake (grĭd′l-kāk′) n. See pancake.

Syllable divisions — grid·i·ron (grĭd′i ′ərn) n. 1. Football. a. The field of play b. The game itself. 2. A metal structure high above the stage of a theater, from which ropes or cables are strung to scenery and lights.

Definition with two closely related meanings — 3.a. A flat framework of parallel metal bars for broiling food. b. An object resembling a griddle. [ME gridirne, alteration of gridere, alteration of gridal. See GRIDDLE.]

grid·lock (grĭd′lŏk′) n. 1. A traffic jam in which no vehicular movement is possible. 2. A complete lack of movement or progress. —grid′lock′ v. —grid′locked′ adj.

Pronunciation — grief (grēf) n. 1. Deep mental anguish, as from bereavement. See Syns at regret. 2. A source of deep mental anguish. 3. Annoyance or frustration. 4. Trouble or difficulty. 5. Archaic. A grievance. [ME < OFr. < grever, to harm. See GRIEVE.]

Spelling and capital letters — Grieg (grēg, grĭg), Edvard Hagerup. 1843-1907. Norwegian composer known for his works incorporating folk music.

Grier (grîr), Robert Cooper. 1794-1870. Amer. jurist; associate justice of the U.S. Supreme Court (1846-70).

Accent mark — griev·ance (grē′vəns), n. 1.a. A circumstance seen as just cause for protest. b. A complaint or protestation based on a grievance. 2. Indignation or resentment stemming from feeling wronged. 3. Obsolete. a. The act of inflicting hardship or harm. b. The cause of hardship or harm. [ME grevaunce < OFr. grevance < grever, to harm. See GRIEVE.]

Parts of speech (principle parts of the verb) — grieve (grēv), v. grieved, griev·ing, grieves. —tr. 1. To cause to be sorrowful; distress. 2. Archaic. To hurt or harm. —intr. To experience or express grief. [ME greven < OFr. grever, to harm < Lat. gravāre, to burden < gravis, heavy. See gʷere- 1°.] —griev′er n. — greiv′·ing·ly adv.

Synonyms — Syns: grieve, lament, mourn, sorrow. The central meaning shared by these verbs is "to feel, show, or express grief, sadness, or regret": grieved over the loss; lamenting over declining standards; mourning for lost hopes; sorrowed over our poverty. Ant: rejoice. ← **Antonyms**

griev·ous (grē′vəs), adj. 1. Causing grief, pain, or anguish. 2. Serious or dire; grave: a grievous crime. —griev′ous·ly adv. —griev′ous·ness n.

grif·fin also grif·fon or gryph·on (grĭf′ən), n. A fabulous beast with the head and wings of an eagle and the body of a lion.

Etymology — [ME griffoun < OFr. griffon < grif < LLat. grȳphus, var. of Lat. grȳps, grȳph- < Gk. grups.]

Guide words —

griffin

Pronunciation key

ă	pat	oi	boy
ā	pay	ou	out
âr	care	ŏŏ	took
ä	father	ōō	boot
ĕ	pet	ŭ	cut
ē	be	ûr	urge
ĭ	pit	th	thin
ī	pie	th	this
îr	pier	hw	which
ŏ	pot	zh	vision
ō	toe	ə	about,
ô	paw		item

Stress marks:
′ (primary);
′ (secondary), as in
dictionary (dĭk′shə-nĕr′ē)

Keeping a Personal Dictionary

You can improve your vocabulary by keeping a personal dictionary. Put each new word in a notebook, in a section of your journal, or on a note card. You may also find it helpful to put your words into groups according to topic. Include the following items for each entry:

- pronunciation key
- a definition
- a sentence using the word
- synonyms for the word

<u>Social Studies</u>

ratify (răt′ə fī)
to approve

Will congress ratify the new tax law?

Synonyms: approve, support, confirm

<u>Literature</u>

furtive (fûr′-tĭv)
done in a sneaky or sly manner

Huck gave Tom a furtive look.

Synonyms: secret, sly, sneaky

<u>Music</u>

libretto (lĭ-brĕt′-ō)
the text of an opera or a musical

We found the libretto for Joseph's Amazing Technicolor Dreamcoat on the Internet.

Using Prefixes, Suffixes, and Roots

You can figure out the meanings of new words by using the three word parts: prefixes, suffixes, and roots. Before you can do this, however, you must become familiar with a number of common word parts.

Prefixes

Prefixes are those "word parts" that come *before* the root word. (*Pre-* means "before.") Prefixes often change the intent or meaning of the root word.

a, an [*not, without*] amoral (without a sense of moral responsibility), atypical, atom (not cutable), apathy (without feeling)

ab, abs, a [*from, away*] abnormal, avert (turn away), abduct (lead away)

acro [*high*] acropolis (high city), acrobat, acronym, acrophobia (fear of height)

ambi, amphi [*both*] ambidextrous (skilled with both hands), ambiguous, amphibious (living on both land and water)

ana [*on, up, backward*] analysis (loosening up or taking apart for study), anatomy

ante [*before*] antedate, anteroom, antebellum, antecedent (happening before)

anti [*against*] anticommunist, antidote, anticlimax

be [*on, away*] bedeck, belabor, bestow, beloved

bene, bon [*well*] benefit, bonus, benefactor, benevolent, benediction, bonanza

bi [*both, double, twice*] bicycle, biweekly, binoculars, bilateral

by [*side, close, near*] bypass, bystander, by-product, bylaw, byline

cata [*down, against*] catalog, catapult, catastrophe, cataclysm

cerebro [*brain*] cerebral, cerebellum, cerebrum, cerebrospinal

circum, circ [*around*] circumference, circumnavigate, circumspect

co, con, col, cor, com [*together, with*] copilot, conspire, collect, correspond, compose

contra, counter [*against*] controversy, contradict, counterpart

de [*from, down*] demote, depress, degrade, deject, deprive

deca [*ten*] decade, decathlon, decapod (ten feet)

di [*two, twice*] divide, dilemma, dilute

dia [*through, between*] diameter, diagonal, diagram, dialogue (speech between people)

dis [*apart, away, reverse*] dismiss, distort, distinguish

dys [*badly, ill*] dyspepsia (digesting badly, indigestion), dystrophy, dysentery

em, en [*in, into*] embrace, enslave

epi [*upon*] epidermis (upon the skin, outer layer of skin), epitaph, epithet

eu [*well*] eulogize (speak well of, praise), eupepsia, euphony, eugenics

ex, e [*out*] expel (drive out), ex-mayor, exit, exorcism, eject, emit

extra [*beyond*] extraordinary (beyond the ordinary), extracurricular

fore [*before in time*] forecast, foretell (to tell beforehand), foreshadow, forefather, foregone, foreleg, foreground

hemi, demi, semi [*half*] semicircle (half of a circle), hemisphere, hemicycle, demitasse, semigloss

hex [*six*] hexameter, hexagon

homo [*man*] Homo sapiens, homicide (man killing)

hyper [*over, above*] hypersensitive (overly sensitive), hypertensive, hyperactive

hypo [*under*] hypodermic (under the skin), hypothesis

il, ir, in, im [*not*] illegal, irregular, incorrect, immoral

in, im [*into*] inject, inside, impose, implant, imprison

infra [*beneath*] infrared

inter [*between*] intercollegiate, interfere, intervene, interrupt (break between)

intra [*within*] intravenous (within the veins), intramural (within the walls)

intro [*into, inward*] introduce, introvert (turn inward)

macro [*large, excessive*] macrodent (having large teeth), macrocosm

mal [*badly, poor*] maladjusted, malnutrition, malfunction, malady

meta [*beyond, after, change*] metabolism, metaphor, metamorphosis (change in form), metaphysical

mis [*incorrect, bad*] misuse, misprint

miso [*hatred*] misanthropist (one who hates people), misogamy

mono [*one*] monoplane, monotone, monochrome, monocle

multi [*many*] multiply, multiform

neo [*new*] neopaganism, neoclassic, neologism, neophyte

non [*not*] nontaxable (not taxed), nontoxic, nonexistent, nonsense

ob, of, op, oc [*toward, against*] obstruct, offend, oppose, occur

oct [*eight*] octagon, octameter, octave

paleo [*ancient*] paleoanthropology (pertaining to ancient man), paleontology (study of ancient life-forms)

para [*beside, almost*] parasite (one who eats beside or at the table of another), paraphrase, parody, parachute, paramedic, parallel

penta [*five*] pentagon (figure or building having five angles or sides), pentameter, pentathlon

per [*throughout, completely*] pervert (completely turn wrong, corrupt), perfect, perceive, permanent, persuade

peri [*around*] period, periphery, perimeter (measurement around an area), periscope, pericardium

poly [*many*] polygon (figure having many angles or sides), polygamy, polyglot

post [*after*] postpone, postwar, postscript, posterity

pre [*before*] prewar, preview, premonition, precede, prevent

pro [*forward, in favor of*] project (throw forward), progress, promote, prohibition

pseudo [*false*] pseudonym (assumed or false name), pseudo, pseudopodia

quad [*four*] quadruple (four times as much), quadriplegic, quadratic, quadrant

quint [*five*] quintuplet, quintuple, quintet, quintile

re [*back, again*] reclaim, revive, revoke, rejuvenate, retard, reject, return

retro [*backward*] retroactive, retrospective (looking backward), retrorocket

se [*aside*] seduce (lead aside), segregate, secede, secrete

self [*by oneself*] self-determination, self-employed, self-service, selfish

sesqui [*one and a half*] sesquicentennial (one and one-half centuries)

sex, sest [*six*] sexagenarian (sixty years old), sexennial, sextant, sextuplet, sestet

sub [*under*] submerge (put under), submarine, subhuman, substitute, subsoil, suburb

suf, sup, sus [*from under*] suffer, support, suspect, suspend

super, supr [*above, over, more*] superman, supervise, supreme, supernatural, superior

syn, sym, sys, syl [*with, together*] sympathy, system, synthesis, symphony, syllable, synchronize (time together), synonym

trans, tra [*across, beyond, through*] transoceanic, transmit (send across land, sea, or space), transfusion, traverse

tri [*three*] tricycle, triangle, tripod, tristate

ultra [*beyond, exceedingly*] ultraconservative, ultramodern, ultraviolet

un [*not, release*] unfair, unnatural, unbutton

under [*beneath*] underground, underlying

uni [*one*] unicycle, uniform, unify, universe, unique (one of a kind)

vice [*in place of*] vice president, viceroy, vice admiral

Numerical Prefixes

Prefix	Symbol	Multiples and Submultiples	Equivalent
tera	T	10^{12}	trillionfold
giga	G	10^9	billionfold
mega	M	10^6	millionfold
micro	u	10^{-6}	millionth part
nano	n	10^{-9}	billionth part
pico	p	10^{-12}	trillionth part

Suffixes

Suffixes come at the end of a word. Sometimes a suffix will tell you what part of speech a word is. For example, many adverbs end in the suffix *ly*. Study suffixes carefully.

able, ible [*able, can do*] capable, agreeable, edible, visible (can be seen)

age [*act of, collection of*] salvage (act of saving), storage, forage

al [*relating to*] gradual, industrial, manual, natural (relating to nature)

an, ian [*native of, relating to*] Canadian (native of Canada), African

ance, ancy [*action, process, state*] assistance, allowance, defiance, resistance

ant [*performing, agent*] assistant, servant

ar, er, or [*one who, that which*] doctor, baker, miller, teacher, racer, amplifier

ary, ery, ory [*relating to, quality, place where*] dictionary, dietary, bravery, dormitory (a place where people sleep)

asis, esis, osis [*action, process, condition*] hypnosis, neurosis, osmosis

ate [*cause, make*] segregate (cause a group to be set aside), liquidate

cian [*having a certain skill or art*] musician, beautician, magician, physician

cide [*kill*] homicide, pesticide, genocide (killing a certain group of people)

cule, ling [*very small*] molecule (a small particle), duckling, sapling

cy [*action, function*] hesitancy, prophecy, normalcy (function in a normal way)

dom [*quality, realm, office*] boredom, freedom, wisdom (quality of being wise)

ee [*one who receives the action*] employee, nominee (one who is nominated), refugee

en [*made of, make*] silken, frozen, oaken (made of oak), wooden, lighten

ence, ency [*action, state of, quality*] difference, conference, urgency

ese [*a native of, the language of*] Japanese, Vietnamese

fic [*making, causing*] scientific, specific

ful [*full of*] frightful, careful, helpful (full of help)

fy [*make*] fortify (make strong), simplify, amplify

hood [*time or period*] manhood, womanhood, childhood, adulthood

ic [*nature of, like*] metallic (of the nature of metal), heroic, poetic, acidic

ice [*condition, state, quality*] justice, malice

ile [*relating to, suited for, capable of*] juvenile, senile (related to being old), missile

ion, sion, tion [*act of, state of, results of*] action, injection, infection (state of being infected)

ish [*origin, nature, characteristic of*] Irish, Finnish, clownish, foolish

ism [*system, manner, condition*] alcoholism, heroism, Communism

ist [*one who, that which*] artist, dentist, violinist

ite [*nature of, quality of, mineral product*] Israelite, dynamite, graphite, sulfite

ity, ty [*state of, quality*] captivity, clarity

ive [*causing, making*] abusive (causing abuse), exhaustive

ize [*make*] emphasize, publicize (make public), idolize, penalize

less [*without*] baseless, careless (without care), artless, fearless, helpless

ly [*like, manner of*] carelessly, fearlessly, hopelessly, shamelessly

ment [*act of, process, result of*] contentment, amendment (act of amending), achievement (result of achieving)

ness [*state of*] carelessness, restlessness, lifelessness

ology [*study, science, theory*] anthropology, biology, geology, neurology

ous [*full of, having*] gracious, nervous, spacious, vivacious (full of life)

ship [*office, state, quality, skill*] friendship, authorship, dictatorship

tude [*state of, condition of*] gratitude, aptitude, multitude (condition of being many)

ure [*state of, act, process*] culture, literature, rupture (state of being broken)

ward [*in the direction of*] eastward, forward, backward

y [*inclined to, tend to*] cheery, crafty, itchy

Roots

Knowing the **root** of a word—especially a difficult word—can help you understand and remember it much better. This can be very useful when learning new words in all your classes. Because vocabulary is so important to success in all areas, knowing the following roots will be very valuable.

acer, acid, acri [*bitter, sour, sharp*] acerbic (sour or bitter), acidity, acrid, acrimony

acu [*sharp*] acute, acupuncture

ag, agi, ig [*do, move, go*] agent (doer), agenda (things to do), navigate (move by sea), ambiguous (going both ways, not clear), agitate

ali, alter [*other*] alias (a person's other name), alternative, alibi, alien (from another country or planet), alter (change to another form)

altus [*high, deep*] altimeter (a device for measuring heights), altitude

am, amor [*love, liking*] amorous, enamored, amiable

anni, annu, enni [*year*] anniversary, annually (yearly), centennial (occurring once in 100 years)

anthrop [*man*] anthropology (study of mankind), misanthrope (hater of mankind), philanthropic (love of mankind)

arch [*chief, first, rule*] archangel (chief angel), architect (chief worker), archaic (first; very early), archives, monarchy (rule by one person), matriarchy (rule by the mother), patriarchy (rule by the father)

aster, astr [*star*] aster (star flower), asterisk, asteroid, astrology (lit., star-speaking; study of the influence by stars and planets), astronomy (star law), astronaut (lit., star traveler; space traveler)

aud [*hear, listen*] audible (can be heard), auditorium, audio, audition, auditory, audience

aug, auc [*increase*] auction, augur, augment (add to; increase)

auto, aut [*self*] automobile (self-moving vehicle), autobiography (lit., self-life writing), automatic (self-acting), autograph (self-writing; signature)

belli [*war*] rebellion, belligerent (warlike or hostile)

bibl [*book*] Bible, bibliography (writing, list of books), bibliomania (craze for books), bibliophile (book lover)

bio [*life*] biology (study of life), biography, biopsy (cutting living tissue for examination), microbe (small, microscopic living thing)

breve [*short*] abbreviate, brief, brevity

calor [*heat*] calorie (a unit of heat), calorify (to make hot), caloric

cap, cept [*take*] capable, capacity, capture, accept, except, forceps

capit, capt [*head*] decapitate (to remove the head from), capital, captain, caption

carn [*flesh*] carnivorous (flesh-eating), incarnate, reincarnation

caus, caut [*burn, heat*] cauterize (to make hot; burn), cauldron, caustic

cause, cuse, cus [*cause, motive*] because, excuse (to attempt to remove the blame or cause), accusation

ced, ceed, cede [*move, yield, go, surrender*] proceed (move forward), cede (yield), secede (move aside from), accede, concede, intercede, precede, recede

centri [*center*] concentric, centrifugal, centripetal, eccentric (out of center)

chrom [*color*] chromosome (color body in genetics), Kodachrome, monochrome (one color), polychrome (many colors)

chron [*time*] chronological (in order of time), chronometer (time-measured), chronicle (record of events in time), synchronize (make time with, set time together)

cide [*kill*] suicide (self-killer), homicide (human killer), pesticide (pest killer), germicide (germ killer), insecticide (insect killer)

cise [*cut*] decide (cut off uncertainty), precise (cut exactly right), concise, incision, scissors

cit [*to call, start*] incite, citation, cite

civ [*citizen*] civic (relating to a citizen), civil, civilian, civilization

clam, claim [*cry out*] exclamation, clamor, proclamation, reclamation, acclaim

clud, clus, claus [*shut*] include (to take in), recluse (one who shuts himself away from others), claustrophobia (abnormal fear of being shut up, confined), conclude

cognosc, gnosi [*know*] prognosis (forward knowing), diagnosis (thorough knowledge), recognize (to know again), incognito (not known)

cord, cor, card [*heart*] cordial (hearty, heart-felt), accord, concord, discord, record, courage, encourage (put heart into), discourage (take heart out of), core, coronary, cardiac

corp [*body*] corporation (a legal body), corpse, corpulent

cosm [*universe, world*] cosmos (the universe), cosmic, cosmology, cosmopolitan (world citizen), cosmonaut, microcosm, macrocosm

crat [*rule, strength*] autocracy, democratic

cred [*believe*] creed (statement of beliefs), credo (a creed), credence (belief), credit (belief, trust), credulous (believing too readily, easily deceived), credentials (statements that promote belief, trust), incredible

cresc, cret, crease, cru [*rise, grow*] crescendo (growing in loudness or intensity), crescent (growing, like the moon in first quarter), concrete (grown together, solidified), increase, decrease, accrue (to grow)

cur, curs [*run*] current (running or flowing), concurrent, concur (run together, agree), curriculum (lit., a running, a course), incur (run into), precursor (forerunner), recur, occur, courier

cura [*care*] manicure (caring for the hands), curator, curative

cus, cuse (see *cause*)

cycl, cyclo [*wheel, circular*] Cyclops (a mythical giant with one eye in the middle of his forehead), cyclone (a wind blowing circularly; a tornado), unicycle, bicycle

deca [*ten*] decade, decalogue, decathlon

dem [*people*] demography (vital statistics of the people: deaths, births, etc.), democracy (people-rule), epidemic (on or among the people)

dent, dont [*tooth*] dental (relating to teeth), orthodontist, denture, dentifrice

derm [*skin*] hypodermic (under skin; injected under the skin), dermatology (skin study), epidermis (on skin; outer layer), taxidermy (arranging skin; mounting animals)

dic, dict [*say, speak*] diction (how one speaks, what one says), dictionary, dictate, dictator, dictaphone, dictatorial, edict, predict, verdict, contradict, benediction

doc [*teach*] indoctrinate, documentation, doctrine

domin [*master*] domain, dominion, dominate, predominant

don [*give*] donate (make a gift), condone

dorm [*sleep*] dormant, dormitory

dox [*opinion, praise*] orthodox (having the correct, commonly accepted opinion), heterodox (differing opinion; contrary, to the standard), paradox (self-contradictory)

duc, duct [*lead*] duke (leader), induce (lead into, persuade), seduce (lead aside), aquaduct (water leader, artificial channel), subdue, viaduct, conduct, conduit, produce, reduce

dura [*hard, lasting*] durable, duration, endurance

dynam [*power*] dynamo (power producer), dynamic, dynamite, hydrodynamics (lit., water power)

end, endo [*within*] endoral (within the mouth), endocardial (within the heart), endoskeletal

equi [*equal*] equinox, equilibrium

erg [*work*] energy, erg (unit of work), allergy, ergophobia (morbid fear of work), ergometer, ergograph

fac, fact, fic [*do, make*] factory (the place where workmen are employed in making goods of various kinds), manufacture, faculty, amplification

fall, fals [*deceive*] fallacy, falsify

fer [*bear, carry*] ferry (carry by water), coniferous (bearing cones, as a pine tree), fertile (bearing richly), defer, infer, refer, referee, referendum, circumference

fic, fect (see *fac*)

fid, feder [*faith, trust*] fidelity, confident, confidante, infidelity, infidel, federal, confederacy, Fido

fila, fili [*thread*] filament (a threadlike conductor heated by electrical current), filter, filet

fin [*end, ended, finished*] final, finite, finish, confine, fine, refine, define, finale

fix [*attach*] fixation (the state of being attached), fixture, affix, prefix, suffix

flex, flect [*bend*] flex (bend), reflex (bending back), flexible, flexor (muscle for bending), inflexibility, reflect, deflect, genuflect (bend the knee)

flu, fluc, fluv [*flowing*] influence (to flow in), fluctuate (to wave in an unsteady motion), fluviograph (instrument for measuring the flow of rivers), fluid, flue, flush, fluently

form [*shape, structure*] form, uniform, conform, deform, reform, perform, formative, formation, formal, formula

fort, forc [*strong*] fort, fortress (a strong point, fortified), fortify (make strong), forte (one's strong point), forte (strong, loud in music), fortitude (strength for endurance), force

fract, frag [*break*] fragile (easy to break), fracture (a break), infraction, fraction (result of breaking a whole into equal parts), refract (to break or bend, as a light ray), fragment

fum [*smoke*] fume (smoke; odor), fumigate (destroy germs by smoking them out), perfume

gam [*marriage*] bigamy (two marriages), monogamy, polygamy (literally, many marriages)

gastro [*stomach*] gastric, gastronomic, gastritis (inflammation of the stomach)

gen [*birth, race, produce*] genesis (birth, beginning), genus, genetics (study of heredity), genealogy (lineage by race, stock), generate, genitals (the reproductive organs), congenital (existing as such at birth), indigenous (born, or produced naturally in a region or country), genetic

geo [*earth*] geometry (earth measurement), geography (lit., earth-writing), geocentric (earth centered), geology

germ [*vital, part*] germination (to grow), germ (seed; living substance, as the germ of an idea), germane

gest [*carry, bear*] congest (bear together, clog), suggestion (mental process by which one thought leads to another), congestive (causing congestion), gestation, suggestion

gloss, glot [*tongue*] epiglottis, polyglot (many tongues), glossary

glu, glo [*lump, bond, glue*] glue, conglomerate (bond together), agglutinate (make to hold in a bond)

grad, gress [*step, go*] grade (step, degree), gradual (step by step), graduate (make all the steps, finish a course), graduated (in steps or degrees), aggressive (stepping toward, pushing), congress (a going together, assembly)

graph [*write, written*] graph, graphic (written; vivid), photography (light-writing), graphite (carbon used for writing), autograph (self-writing; signature), phonograph (sound-writing), bibliography

grat [*pleasing*] congratulate (express pleasure over success), gratuitous (gratis), gratuity (mark of favor, a tip), grateful, gracious, ingrate (not thankful; hence, unpleasant)

grav [*heavy, weighty*] grave, gravity, aggravate, gravitate

greg [*herd, group, crowd*] congregation (a group functioning together), gregarian (belonging to a herd), segregate (tending to group aside or apart)

hab, habit [*have, live*] habitat (the place in which one lives), inhabit (to live in; to establish as residence), rehabilitate, habitual

helio [*sun*] heliograph (an instrument for using the sun's rays), heliotrope (a plant that turns to the sun)

hema, hemo [*blood*] hematid (red blood corpuscle), hemotoxic (causing blood poisoning), hemorrhage, hemoglobin, hemophilia

here, hes [*stick*] adhere, cohere, cohesion

hetero [*different*] heterogeneous (different in composition), heterograft (a tissue graft taken from a different species)

homo [*same*] homogeneous (the same in composition), homonym (word with same name or pronunciation as another), homogenize

hum, human [*earth, ground, man*] humility (quality of lowliness), humane (marked by sympathy, compassion for other human beings and animals), humus, exhume (to take out of the ground)

hydr, hydro, hydra [*water*] dehydrate (take water out of; dry), hydrant (water faucet), hydraulic (pertaining to water or to liquids), hydraulics, hydrophobia (fear of water), hydrogen

hypn [*sleep*] hypnosis, Hypnos (god of sleep), hypnotherapy (treatment of disease by hypnosis)

ignis [*fire*] ignite, igneous, ignition

ject [*throw*] deject, inject, project (throw forward), eject, object

join, junct [*join*] junction (act of joining), enjoin (to lay an order upon; to command), juncture, conjunction, adjoining, joiner, injunction

jud, judi, judic [*judge, lawyer*] judge (a public officer who has the authority to give a judgement), judicial (relating to administration of justice), judicious, prejudice

jur, jus [*law*] justice (a just judgement), conjure (to swear together), jurisdiction, juror

juven [*young*] juvenile, rejuvenate (to make young again)

later [*side, broad*] lateral, latitude

leg [*law*] legal (lawful; according to law), legislate (to enact a law), legislature (a body of persons who can make laws), legitimize (make legal)

lic, licit [*permit*] license (freedom to act), illicit (not permitted), licit (permitted; lawful)

lit, liter [*letters*] literary (concerned with books and writing), literature, literal, alliteration, obliterate

liver, liber [*free*] liberal (relating to liberty), delivery (freedom; liberation), liberalize (to make more free: as, to liberalize the mind from prejudice), deliverance

loc, loco [*place*] locomotion (act of moving from place to place), locality (locale; neighborhood), allocate (to assign; to place), relocate (to put back into place)

log, logo, ology [*word, study, speech*] zoology (animal study), psychology (mind study), logic (orig., speech; then reasoning), prologue, epilogue, dialogue, catalogue, logorrhea (a flux of words; excessively wordy)

loqu, locut [*talk, speak*] eloquent (speaking out well and forcefully), loquacious (talkative), colloquial (talking together; conversational or informal), circumlocution (talking around a subject), soliloquy

luc, lum [*light*] lumen (a unit of light), luminary (a heavenly body; someone who shines in his profession), translucent (letting light come through)

lude [*play*] ludicrous, prelude (before play), interlude

magn [*great*] magnificent, magnify (make great, enlarge), magnanimous (great of mind or spirit), magnate, magnitude, magnum

man [*hand*] manual, manage, manufacture, manacle, manicure, manifest, maneuver, emancipate

mand [*command*] remand (order back), mandatory (commanded), countermand (order against, cancelling a previous order), mandate

mania [*madness*] mania (insanity; craze), monomania (mania on one idea), kleptomania (thief mania; abnormal tendency to steal), pyromania (insane tendency to set fires), maniac

mar, mari, mer [*sea, pool*] mermaid (fabled marine creature, half fish), marine (a sailor serving on shipboard), marsh (wetland, swamp), maritime (relating to the sea and navigation)

matri, mater [*mother*] matrimony (state of wedlock), maternal (relating to the mother), matriarch

medi [*half, middle, between, halfway*] mediate (come between, intervene), medieval (pertaining to the Middle Ages), mediterranean (lying between lands), mediocre

mega [*great*] megaphone (great sound), megalopolis (great city; an extensive urban area including a number of cities), megacycle (a million cycles), megaton

mem [*remember*] commemoration (the act of remembering by a memorial or ceremony), memo (a note; a reminder), memento, memoir, memorable

meter [*measure*] meter (a measure), voltmeter (instrument to measure volts in an electric circuit), barometer, thermometer

micro [*small*] micron (a millionth of a meter), microscope, microfilm, microcard, microwave, micrometer (device for measuring very small distance), microbe (small living thing), omicron (small)

migra [*wander*] migrate (to wander), emigrant (one who leaves a country), immigrate (to come into the land to settle)

mit, miss [*send*] emit (send out, give off), remit (send back, as money due), submit, admit, commit, permit, transmit (send across), omit, mission, missile

mob, mot, mov [*move*] mobile (capable of moving), motionless (without motion), motor (that which imparts motion; source of mechanical power), emotional (moved strongly by feelings), motivate, promotion

mon [*warn, remind*] admonish (warn), monument (a reminder or memorial of a person or event), monitor, premonition (forewarning)

mori, mort, mors [*mortal, death*] mortal (causing death or destined for death), immortal (not subject to death), mortality (rate of death), immortality, mortician (one who buries the dead), mortuary (place for the dead, a morgue)

morph [*form*] amorphous (with no form, shapeless), Morpheus (the shaper, god of dreams), metamorphosis (a change of form, as a caterpillar into a butterfly), morphology

multi, multus [*many, much*] multifold (folded many times), multilinguist (one who speaks many languages), multiped (an organism with many feet), multiply

nat [*to be born, to spring forth*] nature (the essence of a person a thing), innate (inborn), natal, native, nativity

neur [*nerve*] neuritis (inflammation of a nerve), neuropathic (having a nerve disease), neurologist (one who practices neurology), neural, neurosis, neurotic

nom [*law, order*] autonomy (self-law, self-government), economy (household law, management), astronomy

nomen, nomin [*name*] nominate (name someone for an office), nomenclature

nounce, nunci [*warn, declare*] announcer (one who makes announcements publicly), enunciate (to declare carefully), pronounce (declare; articulate), denounce

nov [*new*] novel (new; strange; not formerly known), renovate (to make like new again), novice, nova, innovate

nox, noc [*night*] nocturnal, equinox (equal nights), noctilucent (something that shines by night)

numer [*number*] numeration (act of counting), numeral (a figure expressing a number), enumerate (count out, one by one), innumerable

omni [*all, every*] omnipotent (all-powerful), omnipresent (present everywhere), omniscient (all-knowing), omnivorous (all-eating)

onym [*name*] pseudonym (false name), anonymous (without a name), antonym (against name; word of opposite meaning), synonym

oper [*work*] operate (to labor; function), cooperate (work together)

ortho [*straight, correct*] orthodox (of the correct or accepted opinion), orthodontist (one who straightens teeth), orthopedic (originally pertaining to straightening a child), unorthodox

pac [*peace*] pacifist (one for peace only; opposed to war), pacify (make peace, quiet), Pacific Ocean (peaceful ocean)

pan [*all*] Pan American, panacea (cure-all), pandemonium (place of all the demons; wild disorder), pantheon (place of all the gods)

pater, patr [*father*] patriarch (head of the tribe, family), patron (a wealthy person who supports as would a father), paternity (fatherhood, responsibility, etc.), patriot

path, pathy [*feeling, suffering*] pathos (feeling of pity, sorrow), sympathy, antipathy (against feeling), empathy (feeling or identifying with another), telepathy (far feeling; thought transference)

ped, pod [*foot*] pedal (lever for a foot), impede (get the feet in a trap, hinder), pedestal (foot or base of a statue), pedestrian (foot traveler), centipede, tripod (three-footed support), podiatry (care of the feet), antipodes (opposite feet)

pedo [*child*] orthopedic, pedagogue (child leader; teacher), pediatrics (medical care of children)

pel, puls [*drive, urge*] compel, dispel, expel, repel, propel, pulse, impulse, pulsate, compulsory, expulsion, repulsive, compulsive

pend, pens [*hang, weigh*] pendant (a hanging object), pendulum, depend, impend, suspend, perpendicular, pending, dispense, pensive (weighing thought)

phil [*love*] philosophy (love of wisdom), philanthropy, philharmonic, bibliophile, Philadelphia (city of brotherly love)

phobia [*fear*] claustrophobia (fear of closed spaces), acrophobia (fear of high places), hydrophobia (fear of water)

phon [*sound*] phonograph, phonetic (pertaining to sound), symphony (sounds with or together)

photo [*light*] photograph (light-writing), photoelectric, photogenic (artistically suitable for being photographed), photosynthesis (action of light on chlorophyll to make carbohydrates), photometer (light meter)

plac, plais [*please*] placid (calm, peaceful), placebo, placate, complacent (self-satisfied)

plenus [*full*] replenish (to fill again), plentiful, plenteous, plenary

pneuma, pneumon [*breath*] pneumatic (pertaining to air, wind or other gases), pneumonia (disease of the lungs)

pod (*see ped*)

poli [*city*] metropolis (mother city; main city), police, politics, Indianapolis, megalopolis, Acropolis (high city, upper part of Athens)

pon, pos [*place, put*] postpone (put afterward), component, opponent (one put against), proponent, expose, impose, deposit, posture (how one places oneself), position

pop [*people*] population (the number of people in an area), populous (full of people), popular

port [*carry*] porter (one who carries), portable, transport (carry across), report, export, import, support, transportation

portion [*part, share*] portion (a part; a share, as a portion of pie), proportion (the relation of one share to others)

potent [*power*] potent, omnipotent, impotent (without power)

prehend [*seize*] apprehend (seize a criminal), comprehend (seize with the mind), comprehensive (seizing much, extensive)

prim, prime [*first*] primacy (state of being first in rank), primitive (from the earliest or first time), primary, primal

proto [*first*] prototype (the first model made), protocol, protagonist, protozoan

psych [*mind, soul*] psyche (soul, mind), psychic (sensitive to forces of the mind or soul), psychiatry (hearing of the mind), psychology, psychosis (serious mental disorder), psychotherapy (mind treatment)

punct [*point, dot*] punctual (being exactly on time), punctuation, puncture, acupuncture, punctilious

put [*think*] computer (a thinking machine), dispute, repute

que, qui [*ask, seek*] question, inquire, acquire, inquisitive

reg, recti [*straighten*] correct, direct, regular, rectify (make straight), regiment, rectangle

ri, ridi [*laughter*] ridicule (laughter at the expense of another; mockery), deride (make mock of; jeer at), ridiculous

rog, roga [*ask*] prerogative (privilege; asking before), interrogation (questioning; the act of questioning), derogatory

rupt [*break*] rupture (break), interrupt (break into), abrupt (broken off), disrupt (break apart), erupt (break out), incorruptible (unable to be broken down)

sacr, secr [*scared*] sacred, consecrate, desecrate, sacrosanct

salv, salu [*safe, healthy*] salvation (act of being saved), salvage (that which is saved after appearing to be lost), salutary (promoting health), salute (wish health to)

sangui [*blood*] sanguine, sanguinity, sanguinaria (bloodroot)

sat, satis [*enough*] satisfy (to give pleasure to; to give as much as is needed), satient (giving pleasure, satisfying), saturate

sci [*know*] science (knowledge), conscious (knowing, aware), omniscient (knowing everything)

scope [*see, watch*] telescope, microscope, kaleidoscope (instrument for seeing beautiful forms), periscope, stethoscope

scrib, script [*write*] scribe (a writer), manuscript (written by hand), scribble, inscribe, describe, subscribe, prescribe

sed, sess, sid [*sit*] preside (sit before), president, reside, subside, sediment (that which sits or settles out of a liquid), session (a sitting), obsession (an idea that sits stubbornly in the mind), possess

sen [*old*] senior, senator, senile (old; showing the weakness of old age)

sent, sens [*feel*] sentiment (feeling), consent, resent, dissent, sentimental (having strong feeling or emotion), sense, sensation, sensitive, sensory, dissension

sequ, secu [*follow*] sequence (following of one thing after another), sequel, consequence, subsequent, consecutive (following in order)

serv [*save, serve*] servant, service, subservient, servitude, reservation, preserve, conserve, deserve, observe, conservation

sign, signi [*sign, mark, seal*] signal (a gesture or sign to call attention), signature (the mark of a person written in his own handwriting), design, insignia (distinguishing marks)

simil, simul [*like, resembling*] simulate (pretend; put on an act to make a certain impression), similar, assimilate (to make similar to), simile

sist, sta, stit, stet [*stand*] assist (to stand by with help), circumstance, stamina (power to withstand, to endure), persist (stand firmly; unyielding; continue), substitute (to stand in for another), status (standing), state, static, stable, stationary

solus [*alone*] solo, soliloquy, solitaire, solitude, solitary

solv, solu [*loosen*] solvent (a loosener, a dis-solver), solve, absolve (loosen from, free from), resolve, soluble, solution, resolution, resolute, dissolute (loosened morally)

somnus [*sleep*] insomnia (not being able to sleep), somnambulist (a sleepwalker)

soph [*wise*] sophomore (wise fool), philosophy (love of wisdom), sophisticated (world wise)

spec, spect [*look*] specimen (an example to look at, study), specific, spectator (one who looks), spectacle, speculate, aspect, expect, inspect, respect, prospect, retrospective (looking backward), introspective

sphere [*ball, sphere*] sphere (a planet; a ball), stratosphere (the upper portion of the atmosphere), hemisphere (half of the earth), spheroid

spir [*breath*] spirit (lit., breath), conspire (breathe together; plot), inspire (breathe into), aspire (breathe toward), expire (breathe out; die), perspire, respiration

spond, spons [*pledge, answer*] sponsor (one who pledges responsibility to a project), correspond (to communicate by letter; sending and receiving answers), irresponsible, respond

strict [*draw tight*] strict, restrict, constrict (draw tightly together), boa constrictor (snake that constricts its prey)

stru, struct [*build*] structure, construct, instruct, obstruct, construe (build in the mind, interpret), destroy, destruction

sume, sump [*take, use, waste*] consume (to use up), assume (to take; to use), presume (to take upon oneself before knowing for sure), sump pump (a pump that takes up water)

tact, tang, tag [*touch*] contact (touch), contagious (transmission of disease by touching), intact (untouched, uninjured), intangible (not able to be touched), tangible, tactile

tele [*far*] telephone (far sound), telegraph (far writing), telegram, telescope (far look), television (far seeing), telephoto (far photography), telecast, telepathy (far feeling)

tempo [*time*] tempo (rate of speed), temporary, pro tem (for the time being), extemporaneously, contemporary (those who live at the same time)

ten, tin, tain [*hold*] contain, tenacious (holding fast), tenant, detention, retentive, content, pertinent, obstinate, abstain, pertain, detain, obtain, maintain

tend, tens [*stretch, strain*] tension (a stretching, strain), tendency (a stretching; leaning), extend, intend, contend, pretend, superintend, tender, tent

terra [*earth*] territory, terrestrial, terrain, terrarium

test [*to bear witness*] testament (a will; bearing witness to someone's wishes), detest, attest (certify; affirm; bear witness to), testimony

therm [*heat*] thermometer, therm (heat unit), thermal, thermos bottle, thermostat (a device for keeping heat constant), hypothermia (low body temperature)

tom [*cut*] atom (not cutable; smallest particle of matter), appendectomy (cutting out an appendix), tonsillectomy, dichotomy (cutting in two; a division), anatomy (cutting to study structure)

tort, tors [*twist*] torsion (act of twisting, as a torsion bar), torture (twisting to inflict pain), retort (twist back, reply sharply), extort (twist out), distort (twist out of shape), contort, tortuous (full of twists)

tox [*poison*] toxic (poisonous), intoxicate, antitoxin

tract, tra [*draw, pull*] tractor, attract, subtract, tractable (can be led or handled), abstract (to draw away), subtrahend (the number to be drawn away from another), traction

trib [*pay, bestow*] tribute (to pay honor to), contribute (to give money to a cause), attribute, retribution, tributary

tui, tut [*guard, teach*] tutor (one who teaches a pupil), tuition (payment for instruction or teaching fees), intuition

turbo [*disturb*] turbulent, turmoil, disturb, turbid

typ [*print*] type, prototype (first print, model), typical, typography, typewriter, typology (study of types, symbols), typify

uni [*one*] unicorn (a legendary creature with one horn), unify (make into one), university, unanimous, universal

vac [*empty*] vacate (to make empty), vacuum (a space entirely devoid of matter), evacuate (to remove troops or people), vacation, vacant

val [*strength, worth*] valor, (value; worth), validity (truth; legal strength), equivalent (of equal worth), evaluate (find out the value; appraise actual worth), valiant, value

ven, vent [*come*] convene (come together, assemble), intervene (come between), circumvent (coming around), convention, venture, venue, event, avenue, prevent

vert, vers [*turn*] reverse (turn back), avert (turn away), divert (turn aside, amuse), invert (turn over), introvert (turn inward, one interested in his or her own reactions), controversy (a turning against; a dispute)

vict, vinc [*conquer*] victor (conqueror, winner), victorious, evict (conquer out, expel), convict (prove guilty), convince (conquer mentally, persuade), invincible (not able to be conquered)

vid, vis [*see*] video (television), vision, evident, provide, providence, visible, revise, supervise (oversee), vista, visit

viv [*alive, life*] revive (make live again), survive (live beyond, outlive), vivid (full of life), vivisection (surgery on a living animal), vivacious (full of life)

voc [*call*] vocation (a calling), avocation (occupation not one's calling), convocation (a calling together), invocation (calling in), evoke, provoke, revoke, advocate, provocative, vocal, vocabulary

vol [*will*] malevolent, benevolent (one of goodwill), volunteer, volition

volcan, vulcan [*fire*] Vulcan (Roman god of fire), volcano (a mountain erupting fiery lava), volcanize (to undergo volcanic heat)

vor [*eat greedily*] voracious, carnivorous (flesh-eating), herbivorous (plant-eating), omnivorous (eating everything), devour

zo [*animal*] zoology (study of animal life), zodiac (circle of animal constellations), protozoa (first animals; one-celled animals), zoo (short for zoological garden), zoomophism (attributing animal form to God)

The Human Body

arthral	joint	**gastro**	stomach	**oral**	mouth
audio	hearing	**glos**	tongue	**osteo**	bone
capit	head	**hem**	blood	**ped**	foot
card	heart	**man**	hand	**pneuma**	lungs
corp	body	**myo**	muscle	**psych**	mind
dactyl	finger	**nephro**	kidney	**rhino**	nose
dent	tooth	**neur**	nerve	**sarco**	flesh
derm	skin	**oculo**	eye	**spir**	breath

Understanding the Levels of Diction

Knowing about the different levels of diction helps you use the most appropriate language in your writing. (*Diction* is a writer's choice of words.)

FORMAL ENGLISH

Your research papers, reports, informational essays, and business letters should meet the standards of **formal English**. This level of language pays careful attention to word choice, contains many complex sentences, follows all of the basic conventions of grammar and usage, and maintains a serious, objective (factual) tone throughout. The following sample meets the standards of formal English.

> **The appearance of swans on the White River signals the arrival of spring. They are impossible to miss because of their large size and pure white color. Since swans mate for life, they usually arrive in pairs. They tend to stay in this area for three to four weeks, and then one day, without warning, they will be gone.**

INFORMAL ENGLISH

You may write many other pieces, such as personal narratives, personal essays, and feature articles using a more informal level of language. **Informal English** usually includes some personal references (*I, you, he, she*), a few popular expressions or colloquialisms (page 138), and shorter sentences. In addition, informal English sounds friendly in tone and follows all of the basic conventions of grammar and usage. It makes readers feel comfortable and at ease with the writing. The sample below is written using informal English.

> **The swans are here again, just as they are at the beginning of every spring. What a sight! They're so big and graceful and white. I love watching them swimming around in pairs. It's too bad that these beautiful birds stay for such a short time. They should "set up house" here for much longer.**

You may also use slang (page 140) in your stories and plays and jargon, or technical language, (page 142) in your reports and essays.

Understanding Literature

Literature is writing that is excellent in form and packed with meaning. It usually deals with events, emotions, and ideas that are common to all people. That's why you will find yourself nodding in agreement, laughing, and sometimes crying when you read good literature. And always, you will be left with something to think about. We'll let you in on a little secret, too. Good books usually hold more than one truth, which means that the message may be different from one reader to the next.

To get the most out of your reading, become familiar with the different types of literature—each shares its message in a slightly different way. Also learn about the parts or elements of literature— plot, characterization, theme, and so on.

WHAT'S AHEAD

This chapter includes two lists of terms and definitions. The first will acquaint you with the various types of literature; the second with the elements or parts that will enable you to discuss and write about your assigned reading.

- Types of Literature
- Elements of Fiction
- Discussing Literature

Types of Literature

This list will give you brief descriptions of some of the most common types of literature. If you need more information, see the index in this handbook.

Allegory: A story in which the characters and action represent an idea or a truth about life.

Autobiography: A writer's story of his or her own life.

Biography: A writer's account of some other person's life.

Comedy: Writing that deals with life in a humorous way, often poking fun at people's mistakes.

Drama: Also called a play, this writing form uses dialogue to share its message and is meant to be performed in front of an audience.

Essay: A short piece of nonfiction that expresses the writer's opinion or shares information about a subject.

Fable: A short story that often uses talking animals as the main characters and teaches an explicit moral, or lesson.

Fantasy: A story set in an imaginary world in which the characters usually have supernatural powers or abilities.

Folktale: A story originally passed from one generation to another by word of mouth only. The characters are usually all good or all bad and in the end are rewarded or punished as they deserve.

Historical Fiction: A made-up story that is based on a real time and place in history, so fact is mixed with fiction.

Myth: A traditional story intended to explain some mystery of nature, religious doctrine, or cultural belief. The gods and goddesses of mythology have supernatural powers, but the human characters usually do not.

Novel: A book-length, fictional prose story. Because of its length, a novel's characters and plot are usually more developed than those of a short story.

Parable: A short story that explains a belief or moral principle.

Play: (See *drama*.)

Poetry: A literary work that uses concise, colorful, often rhythmic language to express ideas or emotions. Examples: ballad, blank verse, free verse, elegy, limerick, sonnet.

Prose: A literary work that uses the familiar spoken form of language, sentence after sentence.

Realism: Writing that attempts to show life as it really is.

Science Fiction: Writing based on real or imaginary scientific developments and often set in the future.

Short Story: Shorter than a novel, this piece of literature can usually be read in one sitting. Because of its length, it has only a few characters and focuses on one problem or conflict.

Tall Tale: A humorous, exaggerated story often based on the life of a real person. The exaggerations build until the character can accomplish impossible things.

Tragedy: Literature in which the hero is destroyed because of some tragic flaw in his or her character.

Elements of Fiction

This list includes many terms used to describe the elements or parts of literature. The information will enable you to discuss and write about the novels, poetry, essays, and other literary works you read.

Action: Everything that happens in a story.

Antagonist: The person or force that works against the hero of the story. (See *protagonist.*)

Character: One of the people (or animals) in a story.

Characterization: The ways in which a writer develops a character, making him or her seem believable. Here are three methods:

○ Sharing the character's thoughts, actions, and dialogue.

○ Describing his or her appearance.

○ Revealing what others in the story think of this character.

Conflict: A problem or struggle between two opposing forces in a story. Here are the five basic conflicts:

○ **Person Against Person** A problem between characters.

○ **Person Against Self** A problem within a character's own mind.

○ **Person Against Society** A problem between a character and society, school, the law, or some tradition.

○ **Person Against Nature** A problem between a character and some element of nature—a blizzard, a hurricane, a mountain climb, etc.

○ **Person Against Fate (God)** A problem or struggle that appears to be well beyond a character's control.

Dialogue: The conversations that characters have with one another.

Foil: A character who serves as a contrast or challenge to the main character.

Mood: The feeling a piece of literature creates in a reader.

Moral: The lesson a story teaches.

Narrator: The person or character who actually tells the story, filling in the background information and bridging the gaps between dialogue. (See *point of view.*)

Plot: The action that makes up the story, following a plan called the plot line.

Plot Line: The planned action or series of events in a story. There are five parts: exposition, rising action, climax, falling action, and resolution.

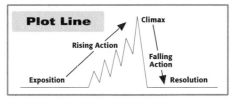

○ **Exposition** The part of the story, usually near the beginning, in which the characters are introduced, the background is explained, and the setting is described.

○ **Rising Action** The central part of the story during which various problems arise.

○ **Climax** The high point or climax in the action of a story.

○ **Falling Action** The action and dialogue following the climax that lead the reader into the story's end.

○ **Resolution** The part of the story in which the problems are solved and the action comes to a satisfying end.

Point of View: The angle from which a story is told. The angle depends upon the narrator, or person telling the story.

○ **First-Person Point of View**

This means that one of the characters is telling the story: "Linda is my older sister, beautiful and popular, and so I've given up on being noticed at all."

○ **Third-Person Point of View**

In this case, someone from the outside of the story is telling it: "Linda is her older sister, beautiful and popular, and so she's given up on being noticed at all." There are three third-person points of view: *omniscient, limited omniscient,* and *camera view.* (See illustration.)

Protagonist: The main character in a story, often a good or heroic type.

Setting: The place and the time frame in which a story takes place.

Theme: The message about life or human nature that is "hidden" in the story that the writer tells.

Tone: The attitude or feeling that comes across in a piece of literature, revealed by the characters, the word choice, and the general writing style. The tone can be serious, funny, satiric, etc.

Total Effect: The total impact or influence that a story has on a reader.

Third-Person Points of View

Omniscient point of view allows the narrator to share the thoughts and feelings of all the characters.

Limited omniscient point of view allows the narrator to share the thoughts and feelings of only one character.

Camera view (objective view) allows the story-teller to record the action from his or her own point of view, being unaware of any of the characters' thoughts or feelings.

Discussing Literature: A Book Group

One interesting way to get the most out of a piece of literature is to read and discuss it with others. You can do this by forming a book group. Begin by finding five or six people who enjoy reading and talking about books. Find a place where you can gather, and set up a regular meeting time. Then choose a good book, making sure everyone can get a copy. Finally, assign a certain number of chapters or sections for each session.

Book groups can meet during the school day, after school, and even during summer vacation.

Ideas for Discussion

THE PLOT

What events from the story (book) stand out in your mind? Why?
What is the basic conflict in the story?
What parts of the story remind you of your own life? In what way?
What other books have you read with similar plots?

THE CHARACTERS

Who are your favorite characters?
Do any of the characters remind you of people you know?

OVERALL EFFECT

What is your opinion of the book?
How does the title fit the book?
What is the tone of the book?
What is the theme of the book?
Who else do you think would like to read this book?

Guidelines for Sharing in a Book Group

- Listen respectfully to one another. Ask questions and give reactions after a group member has shared.

- Add to what the others say about the book.

Note: After you have discussed the book, you might take time to read favorite parts to each other.

Learning to Learn

Preparing a Speech

No doubt, you enjoy talking to your friends as often as you can. It's just as certain, though, that you do not enjoy giving a speech in front of your classmates. For one thing, giving a speech is such a formal activity—you have to have all of your thoughts and ideas worked out ahead of time. For another thing, everyone is just sitting there, waiting for you to say something brilliant or funny or . . .

There are three main things you can do to present an effective speech and make the whole experience as painless as possible. First, choose a subject that genuinely interests you and will appeal to your listeners. Second, collect and organize plenty of interesting details to share. And third, practice your speech until giving it is almost as easy as talking to a trusted friend.

WHAT'S AHEAD

This chapter will help you plan and present effective speeches. As you follow the guidelines, you will also see how a middle-school student named Aaron Stalzer prepared a speech for his social studies class.

- Planning Your Speech
- Writing Your Speech
- Practicing and Giving Your Speech

Planning Your Speech

To get started, you need to do the following things: understand the purpose of your speech, select a specific subject, and collect plenty of interesting details.

Understand your purpose. There are three main purposes for formal speaking: *to inform, to persuade,* and *to demonstrate.*

- **Informing:** If your purpose is to inform, or to educate, you are preparing an informational or *informative* speech. (Collecting plenty of details is essential.)
- **Persuading:** If your purpose is to argue for or against something, you are preparing a *persuasive* speech. (Developing a convincing and logical argument is your main job. See pages 121-122.)
- **Demonstrating:** If your purpose is to show how to do something or to show how something works, you are preparing a *demonstration* speech. (Putting together a clear, step-by-step explanation is the key.)

Select a specific subject. A good speech starts with a good subject—one that you think will interest your audience. Here are some important points to consider when selecting a subject:

- **Know your subject:** Make sure that you know your subject well or that you can learn about it in a short time.
- **Choose the right subject:** Make sure that your subject meets the requirements (and purpose) of the assignment.
- **Choose a specific subject:** Make sure that your subject is specific enough to cover in the time allowed for your speech.

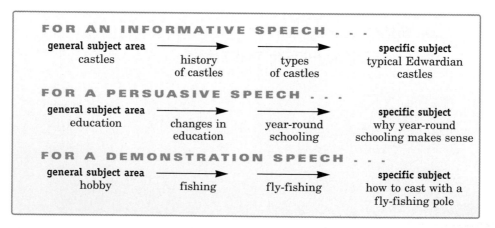

FOR AN INFORMATIVE SPEECH . . .

general subject area			specific subject
castles	history of castles	types of castles	typical Edwardian castles

FOR A PERSUASIVE SPEECH . . .

general subject area			specific subject
education	changes in education	year-round schooling	why year-round schooling makes sense

FOR A DEMONSTRATION SPEECH . . .

general subject area			specific subject
hobby	fishing	fly-fishing	how to cast with a fly-fishing pole

Collect interesting details. Listed below are different sources of information for your research. Always consult as many sources as time permits.

- **Tap your memory:** If your speech is based on an experience, write down the facts, details, and feelings as you remember them.

- **Talk with people:** Discuss your subject with a variety of people who may be able to provide details from their experiences.

- **Get firsthand experience:** Experiencing (or trying out) your subject is especially important for demonstration speeches.

- **Search the library:** Make sure to check different library resources, including books, magazines, pamphlets, videos, and so on.

- **Explore the Internet:** Check out appropriate Web sites and news-groups for information.

Collecting Tips

- Gather more facts and details than you need. You can decide which ones to use as you write your speech.

- Take good notes and make sure to write down all the sources of your information. You can write each main point or fact on a separate note card. This will help you later on when you are ready to write your speech. (See page 352.)

- Look for photographs, maps, models, artifacts, charts, and so on. Showing such items can make any speech more interesting and helpful, especially a demonstration speech.

- Create your own graphics or charts if you can't find ones that meet your needs.

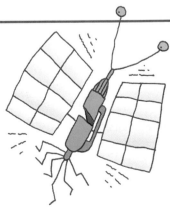
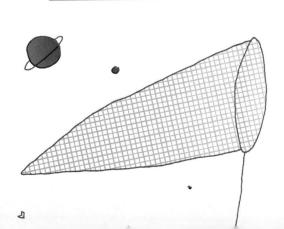

Writing Your Speech

As you write your speech, remember that your ideas will be heard, not read; so let your personality come through.

I would like to tell you about a typical Edwardian castle built in Wales in the late 1200's. We'll call it Lord Aaron's Castle.

In addition, use specific words that help listeners picture in their minds what you are saying.

Slabs of gray stone are chiseled into blocks and cemented with mortar to build a mighty tower. This is the heart of the castle.

1 AN ATTENTION-GETTING BEGINNING

The beginning of your speech must get your listeners' attention and, of course, tell what your speech is about. Here are five ways to begin:

- ○ Ask a question.
- ○ Give a surprising fact.
- ○ Tell an interesting or a surprising story.
- ○ Ask listeners to imagine something.
- ○ Repeat a famous quotation.

In the model speech (page 353), Aaron Stalzer uses two of these starting methods. First, he asks listeners to imagine something; then he asks a question.

Imagine that you are an engineer at the time of King Edward I of England. The French army is about to invade, and the king hires you to build a castle that will keep them out. The king will give you 1,500 workers to build your castle, but you have to design it. How will you make the castle strong and safe?

Review the facts and details you have gathered to find the best way of capturing your audience's attention. Write two or more beginnings, and see which one you like best.

2 A CONVINCING MAIN PART

Once you decide upon the beginning part, turn your attention to the body of your speech. If you have written your information on note cards, move them around until you get everything in the best order. (See page 60 for help.)

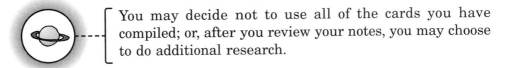

You may decide not to use all of the cards you have compiled; or, after you review your notes, you may choose to do additional research.

As you write, turn each fact or detail into an interesting, smooth-reading sentence. Explain or describe each part of your topic clearly so that your audience can follow along easily and enjoy what you say. If you are giving your opinion about something, support your point of view with enough reasons to convince your listeners.

3 A STRONG ENDING

Remember that your ending must say more than "That's it" or "There's nothing more to say." In fact, it should be just as interesting as the beginning. Here are different ways to end a speech:

- Tell one last interesting fact or story.
  (This is a good way to end an informative speech.)
- Explain why the topic is important.
  (This is a good way to end a persuasive speech.)
- Sum up the most important ideas in your speech.
  (This is a good way to end a demonstration speech.)
- Share a final idea that will keep the topic in your listeners' thoughts.

Aaron ended his speech with an interesting story about castles.

If you're wondering about the dungeon, here is an interesting story: At the time of King Edward, "donjon" was another name for the tower. It was also called a "keep" because it was the best place to keep people and treasure safe from invaders. Later, when people didn't live in castles anymore, someone had the idea to use the towers, or donjons, as prisons. That's where the word "dungeon" comes from.

Sample Note Cards

Aaron wrote out the beginning and ending parts on note cards. The other cards contained only main ideas. (See below.)

BEGINNING:

Imagine that you are an engineer at the time of King Edward I of England. The French army is about to invade, and the king hires you to build a castle that will keep them out. The king will give you 1,500 workers to build your castle, but you have to design it.

- gray stones chiseled into blocks and cemented with mortar into a tower

- around the moat is a large, grassy courtyard with a wall, gardens, stables, and farm animals

ENDING:

If you're wondering about the dungeon, here is an interesting story: At the time of King Edward, "donjon" was another name for the tower. It was used to keep people and treasure safe from invaders. Later, when people didn't live in castles anymore, someone had the idea to use the towers, or donjons, as prisons. That's where the word "dungeon" comes from.

Model Speech

Here is Aaron Stalzer's complete informative speech. He also included one poster-sized illustration, showing the castle design.

Lord Aaron's Castle

Imagine that you are an engineer at the time of King Edward I of England. The French army is about to invade, and the king hires you to build a castle that will keep them out. The king will give you 1,500 workers to build your castle, but you have to design it. How will you make the castle strong and safe?

The castles built at the time of King Edward I of England were the strongest ones ever built. Based on the latest building techniques of the time, you've created the following design. We'll call it Lord Aaron's Castle, and it will be located in Wales.

The castle rises from the top of a hill. This is so the defenders of the castle can easily see the enemies approaching. Slabs of gray stone are chiseled into bricks and cemented with mortar to build a mighty tower. This is the heart of the castle. The tower is surrounded by a moat that is about 10 feet deep. A heavy wooden drawbridge can be lowered over the moat. But when it is raised, enemies have no way to get across.

Around the moat is a large, grassy courtyard with a well (so the defenders will have water if the enemy lays siege to the castle), gardens, horse stables, and farm animals. Surrounding the courtyard is a stone wall that is 10 feet high. There is only one gate in the wall. This gate is on a different side of the tower than the drawbridge. That way, if enemies get through the gate, they still can't easily get into the tower. As they walk or ride around the courtyard toward the drawbridge, defending soldiers can shoot arrows down at them.

The tower is divided into four levels or stories. Lord Aaron's wife will have her room on the top floor. Below that will be the lord's quarters, and below that will be the dining rooms and servants' quarters, and then the treasure rooms.

If you're wondering about the dungeon, here is an interesting story: At the time of King Edward, "donjon" was another name for the tower. It was used to keep people and treasure safe from invaders. Later, when people didn't live in castles anymore, someone had the idea to use the towers, or donjons, as prisons. That's where the word "dungeon" comes from.

Practicing and Giving Your Speech

1 MAKE A FINAL COPY

- Key in your speech on a computer or neatly write it out.
- If you key it in, make sure to use a type font that is easy to read.
- Double- or triple-space, and use wide margins.
- Never run a sentence from one page to another.
- Never use abbreviations unless you plan to say them as they are written. For example, don't write "A.M." when you intend to say "morning."
- Number each page to help keep things in order.

2 PRACTICE, PRACTICE, PRACTICE

- Start practicing your speech at least two days ahead of time.
- Practice by yourself at first. If possible, record yourself.
- Then get friends or family members to listen to your speech. (Ask for honest, constructive advice.)
- Practice until you know your speech inside and out.

3 GIVE YOUR SPEECH

- Stand straight and tall.
- Speak loudly and clearly.
- Take your time, and use your voice to add color and interest to your speech.
- Look up as often as you can. (You don't have to make direct eye contact if that makes you nervous. Just scan the audience as you look up.)
- Use your hands in a planned way. At the very least, hold your note cards or written speech. But don't tap your fingers on the speaker's stand or make any nervous movements with your hands.
- Keep your feet firmly on the floor. Don't sway from side to side.
- Show interest in your topic all the way through your speech, and wait a few seconds after you are done before you sit down.

Viewing Skills

Most of us have never personally seen the president, a volcano erupting, or a space shuttle roaring off its launching pad. Still, we know exactly what all three look like because we've seen them on television. TV can bring the whole world into our homes.

In a way, TV is like a teacher. It has a big impact on what we know and on how we think about life. Consequently, it's important to be a thoughtful viewer, watching with a critical eye and questioning what you see.

For starters, think about the purpose of each program. Situation comedies and dramas are supposed to entertain, not necessarily show you what life is really like. On the other hand, documentaries and news programs are supposed to inform, so they should be accurate and true to life. Finally, commercials are supposed to persuade us to buy something, so we should view them with caution.

WHAT'S AHEAD

This chapter will tell you more about how to be a smart viewer, helping you learn from what you watch on television, instead of allowing TV to turn off your brain.

- Watching the News
- Watching Documentaries
- Watching Commercials

Watching the News

You tune in to the news to find out what is happening in your city and around the world. There are ways for you to judge whether a news story is complete and correct, but you need to watch and listen carefully.

WATCH FOR completeness

A good news story is complete. It answers the basic questions *who, what, when, where, why,* and sometimes *how.* Here is the beginning of a news story that was read by Peter Jennings on ABC's *World News Tonight* on June 3, 1998. Notice that all **5 W's** are answered in the first sentence:

> The secretary of state is on her way to Geneva
> who   what   where
>
> tomorrow   to talk to America's allies about trying
> when   why
>
> to keep India and Pakistan from getting into a
>
> nuclear conflict. . . .

When viewing the news, always listen carefully for the context of each story. This story went on to explain why India and Pakistan are often in conflict (religious differences are a big part of the problem) and why the threat of a nuclear war was especially strong (both countries had just tested nuclear weapons). This kind of background information is called "context." It gives you a better understanding of the meaning and importance of a story.

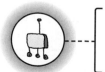

Viewing Tip: Remember to watch the *entire* news story before you come to any conclusions about its importance or relevance for you. The last few facts in the story may be the ones that tie everything together for you.

WATCH FOR correctness

A good news story must be correct. If reporters are unsure of all the facts, they must carefully word their stories to indicate this. Compare the following two news clips, for example. The first gives information that was available just after the event. The second gives information that only became available later in the day.

First report: A high-speed train derailed in Germany today, and early reports are that as many as 30 people may have been killed.

Second report: The death toll now stands at 100 in the derailment of a German train. Rescuers continue to search the wreckage.

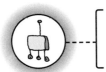

Viewing Tip: Remember that early reports about a news event often are not complete or correct. Keep checking until all the facts are in.

WATCH FOR point of view

No two people ever tell the same story exactly the same way. This is also true of news reporters. When you watch a TV news story, you are getting the news team's point of view. They have made decisions that shape what you see and hear. Here are two ways that this is done:

1 News teams decide which facts to tell and which pictures to show. A story about a high-crime area may show houses with broken windows and littered yards, but may neglect to show any of the well-kept homes in the same neighborhood.

2 News teams decide which people to interview. Telling both sides of a story is important, but the individuals chosen to speak for each side will affect your opinion. For example, interviewing a popular police chief who supports a new law, and a gang leader who is against it, would have a definite persuasive affect.

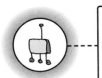

Viewing Tip: Notice the facts, pictures, and people included in a news story. Think about what may have been left out. Consider how these choices may affect your opinion about a situation.

Watching Documentaries

Documentaries are programs that tell about one subject in depth. Their main purpose is to inform, although many are interesting enough to entertain as well. If you are an active, thoughtful viewer, you can learn a lot from a good documentary. Here are some tips:

Before you watch . . .

- Find out what the program is about.
- Make a list of your questions after thinking about what you already know about the subject and what you'd like to learn. Leave room between questions for notes.
- Make sure you understand any questions your teacher may have given you to answer.

While you watch . . .

- Take a few brief notes. Spend most of your time watching; just write down key words that will help you compose complete answers later.
- Watch for completeness, correctness, and point of view.
- Jot down any additional questions you think of.

After you watch . . .

- Write complete answers to your questions while the program is fresh in your mind.
- Talk with someone else who watched the program. Individuals notice and remember different things. Ask each other, "What did you find most interesting? What was the name of that red bird? Did you understand the part about . . . ?" and so on.
- Write or talk about your feelings about the program. Did anything make you laugh, upset you, or confuse you? Exploring your feelings will help you remember more about the subject.
- Write a summary to help you remember the main points and ideas in the program. (See the next page.)

SAMPLE Summary

What follows is a summary based on one student's understanding of a documentary about the Nile River. It was written after the student talked about the program and reviewed her notes.

Nile: River of Gods

Main Idea — This video showed why civilization first appeared on the banks of the Nile River in Africa. The Nile provided everything needed to build the wealthy, advanced Egyptian society.

Most importantly, the Nile provided rich soil and water for farming. Every year, the river would flood. Afterward, a layer of mud was left behind. It contained all the nutrients needed to grow crops such as barley, millet, rice, wheat, and flax. The Nile also provided irrigation water for the crops. This combination of good soil, water, and lots of sun meant that Egyptians could grow more food than they needed.

Important Details — The Nile River also provided transportation, giving the people a way to trade their extra grain for other goods and materials needed to build cities and develop the Egyptian culture. The Nile's mud was also used to make bricks and pottery.

The Nile River has been called the "river of gods" because the ancient Egyptians found inspiration for their gods from the animals that lived in and around it. The lion, buffalo, falcon, crocodile, hippo, and ibis are just some of the animals that became gods to the people. The ibis became the

Interesting Final Fact — god of knowledge because these birds always seemed to know when the river would flood, arriving just beforehand.

Watching Commercials

News programs and documentaries have the same main purpose: to inform you. But commercials have a completely different purpose: to persuade you to buy something. People who create TV commercials have several tried-and-true techniques for making people want to buy products. Here are a few of their favorite selling methods.

Slice of Life

A slice-of-life commercial looks like it was filmed with someone's home video camera. It seems to show a bunch of real people having a great time drinking Brand X cola or wearing Brand X athletic shoes. These commercials can be convincing, but the people in them are actors. Each scene is carefully staged and rehearsed. It's very possible that the actors holding cans of Brand X cola have never even tasted it!

Famous Faces

A famous-face commercial shows a celebrity using Brand X. This selling method is effective because many people want to be like their favorite celebrities. The idea is to make people think that if they buy Brand X cola, they will be more like the beautiful movie star or the superstar athlete who is in the commercial.

Just the Facts

A just-the-facts commercial uses facts and figures to sell a product. For example, it may say, "Nine out of ten teenagers say Brand X is the best cola." But the commercial may not tell you anything about the survey that produced these results. Since you can't be sure the survey is trustworthy, it's difficult to believe the commercial.

Problem-Solution

A problem-solution commercial shows someone with a problem, and then shows the product solving the problem. For example, a new kid moves to town. His problem is that he doesn't know anybody or have any friends. Then he has an idea: He buys a few cans of Brand X cola and offers them to the guys playing basketball in the park. The guys love Brand X cola, so they decide the new guy is cool. Brand X solved his problem. Of course, this only happens in the world of TV commercials!

Classroom Skills

When you're in school, your main job is to learn. You learn by listening to your teachers, reading your textbooks, talking about ideas, and doing your homework. This is why having good classroom skills will help you. Taking good notes and writing in a learning log are two important classroom skills.

Taking notes helps you in three ways:

1. Taking notes helps you **pay attention.**

2. Taking notes helps you **understand.**

3. Taking notes helps you **remember.**

Writing in a learning log helps you by giving you **a chance to think carefully** about the subjects you are studying.

WHAT'S AHEAD

In this chapter, you will learn how to practice note taking and writing in a learning log. *Remember:* Using good classroom skills will help you do your best work now . . . and for years to come.

- Setting Up Your Notes
- Taking Lecture Notes
- Taking Reading Notes
- Reviewing Your Notes
- Keeping a Learning Log

Setting Up Your Notes

Use a notebook or a three-ring binder for your notes and write on only one-half of each page. (A three-ring binder allows you to add and remove pages when you need to.)

Flies   Feb. 3   p. 21

Leave room to write more notes later.

- Order: Diptera

di = two   pteron = wing

- Diptera - only flying insects w/2 wings (rest have 4)
- halteres instead of hind wings; used for balance
- 120,000+ species, including mosquitoes

"stabbing" mouth parts

antennae

thorax

halteres

Effects on humans
spread disease:
- carry viruses and bacteria
- "inject" them into humans
- malaria, yellow fever

Taking Lecture Notes

The following tips will help you take lecture notes. (A *lecture* is a talk that teaches you something.) Your teacher may present a lecture when he or she introduces a new unit or reviews important information for a test. Your ability to remember and understand a lecture increases greatly if you take good notes.

- **Write the topic and the date at the top of each page.** You may also want to number each page of notes. Then, if a page gets out of order, you'll know exactly where it belongs.

- **Listen carefully when the teacher introduces the topic.** You may hear important clues. Your teacher may say, "I'm going to explain the three branches of the federal government." Then you can listen for the three subtopics.

- **Write your notes in your own words.** Don't try to write down everything the teacher says.

- **When you hear a word that is new to you, write it down.** Don't worry about spelling. Just make your best guess.

- **Draw pictures to help you remember things better.**

- **Listen for key words such as** *first, second, last, most important,* **and so on.**

- **Copy what the teacher writes on the board or overhead projector.**

The real secret to taking good notes is listening. Don't get so busy writing that you forget to listen. If you listen carefully, you will hear details that you can add to your notes later.

Taking Reading Notes

Taking notes while you are reading is easier than taking notes while you are listening to a lecture. As you read, you can stop anytime to write a note or to look up additional information. Here are some tips for taking reading notes:

1 **Preview the assignment.** Read the title, introduction, section headings or subtitles, and summary. Look at any pictures, charts, and maps. This information will tell you what the reading is about.

2 **Skim through the whole assignment once** before you take any notes. Also, if there are questions that go with the reading, look them over before you begin.

3 **Take notes** as you read over the material again—this time reading more slowly and thoroughly.

- **Write down only the important information and ideas.**

- **Try to write your notes in your own words.** Don't just copy from the book.

- **You may write down each heading or subtopic,** and then write the most important facts under each heading. (Pay close attention to words in **boldface** or *italics*.)

- **Remember to take notes about any important pictures, charts, or maps.** You may also make drawings of your own.

- **Use graphic organizers.** (See page 56.)

- **Make a list of new words.** Also write down the page number where you found each word. Look up each word in a glossary or dictionary. Choose the meaning that best fits the way the word is used. Write that meaning in your notes.

- **Summarize difficult or important material** out loud before taking notes on it.

- **Write down any questions you have for your teacher.**

 Turn to "Study-Reading Skills," beginning on page 307, for more ways to take notes when you read.

Reviewing Your Notes

Look over your reading and lecture notes each day. Circle the words and phrases that you don't understand. Look up these words in a dictionary or the glossary of your textbook. Then write each word (spelled correctly) and its meaning in the margin of your notes.

- **Write any questions you may have in the margins of your notes.** Talk over your questions with a classmate or your teacher. Make sure to write down what you learn.
- **Use a highlighter to mark important parts of your notes.**
- **Rewrite your notes if they are sloppy or if you want to reorganize them.**
- **Review your notes again before the next class.**

Flies   Feb. 3   p. 21

- Order: Diptera

          di = two   pteron = wing

halteres: - Diptera - only flying insects
modified wings   w/2 wings (rest have 4)
used to   - halteres instead of hind wings;
stabilize flight   used for balance
               - 120,000+ species, including
                 mosquitoes

Keeping a Learning Log

A learning log is a place to write down your thoughts, feelings, and questions about what you are studying. Learning-log notes are different from lecture and reading notes. Here are some tips:

- **Keep a learning log for any subject,** but especially for one that is hard for you. This will help you learn the subject better.

- **Use graphic organizers and drawings.** (See page 56.)

- **Write freely.** Don't worry about getting every word correct.

- **Write about any of the following ideas:**
  - the most important thing you learned from a reading assignment or lecture
  - your thoughts about a group project
  - what you learned from an experiment
  - a list of key words that come to mind after a lesson
  - your feelings about something you learned
  - your feelings about how you are doing in the subject

WRITING-TO-LEARN ACTIVITIES

You might be perfectly satisfied with writing freely in a learning log. If, however, you want to try something a little different, use one of the following activities:

First Thoughts: List your first impressions about something you are studying or reading.

Nutshelling: Try writing down in one sentence the importance of something you are studying or reading.

Stop 'n' Write: Stop whatever you are studying or reading and start writing about it. This will help you keep on task.

Admit Slips/Exit Slips: Submit brief writings to your teacher before or after class. Write about an idea related to the class that confuses you, interests you, makes you angry, and so on. Ask your teacher to react to your comments.

Synergizing: Generate ideas in pairs. Take turns writing statements (or questions and answers) with a classmate. This is especially effective when reviewing.

Sample Science Log

Learning logs work in any class and for any subject. The sample log below was written as a reaction to a lecture on flies and mosquitoes. Keep in mind that a learning log works best if you think and write freely, "personalizing" each piece of information.

Feb. 5   Flies

Key words: Diptera
            halteres
            viruses, bacteria, protozoa
            malaria

I thought flies and mosquitoes were a pain just because they bite. But it turns out that you can get more than an itchy bump from a mosquito. They can carry germs that cause serious diseases such as malaria. (Fortunately, mosquitoes in the United States do not carry malaria.) Doctors think that, in all of history, more people have died of malaria than any other disease. Malaria was even one of the reasons why the Roman Empire fell. That means that mosquitoes have had a pretty big effect on history.

History-making pest!

Sample Math Log

Students in Mr. Manzo's algebra class keep learning logs to help them think through math concepts. Each day they write down a question about a concept discussed in class; then they answer the question in their journals. Below are two entries from Paul Scholl's journal.

Mon., Sept. 13
Question: Why should I "show my work" in algebra class?
Answer: I know why Mr. Manzo wants me to show my work. That way he knows that I did the problem myself, and he can see how I did it. If I get stuck, my writing helps him understand how to help me. Most times, showing work makes sense.

But sometimes it doesn't. Sometimes I can figure a problem in my head. Then what? Why can't I just write the answer? Why do I have to write all the stuff about how I got the answer?

Thurs., Sept. 16
Question: What are two meanings of the minus sign?
Answer: One meaning of the minus sign is "subtraction." Another meaning is "negative number."

For example, the minus sign in the left side of the equation below means "subtract 3." But the minus sign in the right side means "negative 3."

$$7 - 3 = 7 + (-3)$$

Group Skills

Collaborate means "to work together." You have probably collaborated on many school projects in the past, and will certainly collaborate on many more in the future. But, as you know, working in small groups or teams can sometimes be difficult—not everything always goes smoothly.

The following skills will help you work and learn better in groups: **listening, observing, cooperating, responding,** and **clarifying.** These skills are often called "people skills" because they help people work together successfully in groups, teams, and families. Another common term is "team skills" or "group skills."

Whatever name they go by, it is now obvious that the ability to use these skills in teams or groups is very important for success in school, at home, and later on the job.

WHAT'S AHEAD

This chapter will help you improve your group skills, from the time the group first *gets* together until everyone begins to *work* together.

- ○ Skills for Listening
- ○ Skills for Observing, Cooperating, Clarifying
- ○ Skills for Responding

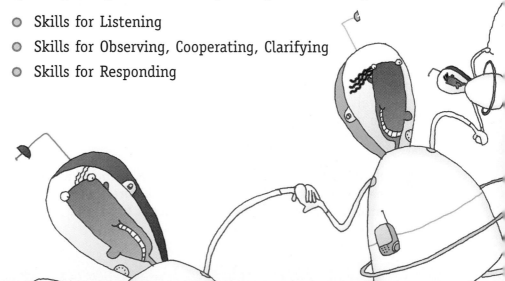

Skills for Listening

Good listening requires skill and practice. People tend to listen in spurts. A spurt may last from a few seconds to a few minutes, but no one can listen with complete attention for very long. This is why it's important to know how to listen effectively when you work in a group.

Listen actively.

To be a good listener, you must be an active listener. This means you should let the speaker know you are listening. You can make eye contact, nod your head, and remain attentive. You can also let the speaker know you have listened by asking a good question, by summarizing, or by offering a compliment or comment.

Listen accurately.

Hearing is not the same as listening. Hearing involves your ears; listening involves your ears and your mind. You need to think about what you hear. Listen with pen in hand. Jot down a word, phrase, or question to help you remember what is being said and what you want to add. Then, when the speaker stops, you can offer your ideas.

Know when—and how—to interrupt.

If you are a good listener, you will sooner or later have a comment, a question, or an important fact to add. Even so, interrupting someone who is speaking is not usually a good idea. If you feel you must interrupt the discussion, say, "Excuse me, Janet, when you finish I have something to add."

Sometimes it is also necessary to interrupt a group member who has wandered off the topic. When that happens, you can say, "Excuse me, but I think we should get back to the main point of our discussion."

Learn how to respond when you are interrupted.

When you are interrupted without good reason by a group member, you can say, "I wasn't finished making my point yet" or "Could you please wait until I'm finished?" Whatever you say, say it courteously. (You can discourage interruptions by keeping what you say short and to the point.)

 It's important for all listeners to keep an open mind about the speaker and the topic. Do not judge beforehand whether you are going to like—or not like—what is about to be said.

Skills for Observing

Being observant is an important group skill. People "say" as much with their actions and tone of voice as with their words.

Watch body language.

At times you can "see" what a person is saying or feeling. Such *body language* includes facial expressions, hand gestures, and body positions.

Offer words of encouragement.

When you encourage someone, you show your appreciation of that person's ideas. All of us are more likely to participate in groups if we feel that what we say will be accepted.

Skills for Cooperating

Offer compliments.

We too often forget to compliment or thank others when we work in groups. Simply say, "I really like your suggestion," or "That's a great idea." Offering compliments helps to build stronger groups.

Never use put-downs.

Put-downs must be avoided in group work. They not only disrupt the group, but destroy members' self-confidence as well.

Cooperating means "working together." It means using common sense and common courtesy—and sharing a common goal.

Skills for Clarifying

Clarifying means "making something clear." It means you make something easy for others to understand.

Offer to explain or clarify.

If what you say is long or complex, you can end by asking, "Are there any questions?"

Request help or clarification when needed.

Summarize what you heard and end with a question like, "Is that about it, or did I miss something?"

Skills for Responding

When you work in a group, nearly everything you say and do is a response to what someone else has said or done. **First,** you hear others' statements or observe their behavior. **Second,** you take a moment to think about the ways you could respond. **Third,** you choose your response.

Think before responding.

Someone may make a statement like, "The Pumpkinheads is a dumb group." Before you knew about group skills, you might respond by saying, "Yeah, well I think you're dumb." If you respond in this way, the other person has dragged you into a dead-end argument instead of a discussion.

But, you can choose how you will respond. You can avoid an argument by saying, "Everyone is entitled to his or her own opinion." You can look for some details by asking, "Why do you feel they're dumb?" Or you can seek clarification by asking, "What do you mean by 'dumb'?"

Learn how to disagree.

Never say, "I disagree with you." Say instead, "I disagree. I think the Pumpkinheads is a great group." This is disagreeing with the idea, not the speaker. You can continue by listing some reasons for disagreeing. Also, instead of saying "I disagree," you can ask the speaker a few questions, questions showing that important points have been left out. After trying to answer the questions, the speaker may change his or her position—or you may change yours.

Communicating with Respect

Whenever you work with a group, you must use respect and common courtesy.

1. Respect yourself by
- believing that your own thoughts and feelings have value,
- taking responsibility for what you say, and
- getting others to respect what you think and feel.

2. Respect others by
- encouraging everyone to participate,
- listening openly to what they have to say, and
- using compliments whenever you can.

Taking Tests

Taking a test is a little bit like giving a speech: no matter how well prepared you are, you always feel a little queasy about what lies ahead. And that's okay. A little tension can help you stay mentally alert. But you don't want things to get out of hand. You want to remain cool, calm, and focused. So, keep up with all your class work and study smart. That way, there will be no surprises the next time you sit down to take a test.

To do well on a test, you need to do a variety of things. You need to pay attention in class, take good notes, ask the right questions, and study efficiently. You also need to know how to be a good test taker.

WHAT'S AHEAD

This chapter gives you all the tips you need to improve your test-taking skills. We hope they help!

- Preparing for a Test
- Taking a Test
- Taking Objective Tests
- Taking Essay Tests

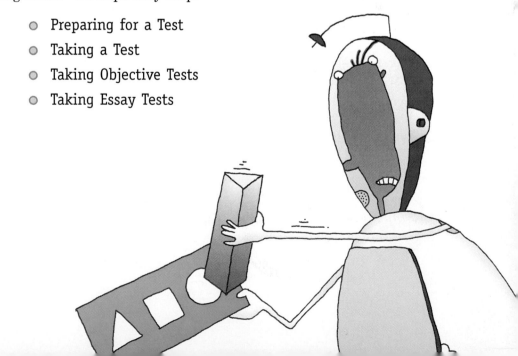

Preparing for a Test

1 ASK QUESTIONS

- What material will be covered on the test?
- What kind of questions will be on the test?

2 REVIEW THE MATERIAL

- Start reviewing a few days before the test.
- Review all the material. Then focus on the difficult parts.
- Divide your study time into two or three sessions if there is a lot to cover.

3 STUDY YOUR NOTES

- Reread the material. Then put it in your own words.
- Make lists, flash cards, or rhymes to help you remember.
- Use graphic organizers to help you organize your thoughts. (See page 56.)
- Picture the material in your mind (or draw pictures).
- Explain the material to someone else.

Taking a Test

1. **Listen carefully to directions.** Be sure you know the amount of time you have, what kind of markings to use, and so on.
2. **Ask for help.** If there is anything unclear or confusing about the test, ask your teacher to explain.
3. **Look over the whole test quickly.** First answer the questions you are sure of; then answer the other questions.
4. **When you finish, use any extra time you have to check your test.** Make sure you answered all the questions.

HELPFUL HINT

If you want to remember a list of words, make up a silly sentence. Here's a sentence to help you remember the planets listed in order of distance from the sun.

My very **e**nergetic **m**other **j**ust **s**lid **u**nder **N**ellie's **p**orch.

(Mercury, Venus, Earth, Mars, Jupiter, Saturn, Uranus, Neptune, Pluto)

Taking Objective Tests

There are four common kinds of objective tests. (Objective means "based on facts.") These tests are called objective because you must answer the questions with facts, not opinions. Here are some tips to help you do well on each kind of objective test.

True/False Test

A true/false test is a list of sentences or statements. You decide if each statement is true or false.

- Read the whole statement carefully. If any part of the statement is false, the answer is false.

    __*false*__ **Tom Sawyer, Becky Thatcher, and David Copperfield are characters in the novel *The Adventures of Tom Sawyer*.**

- Be careful when you see words such as *always, all, never,* and *no.* Very few things are *always* true or *never* true.

- Watch for words that mean "not." These words include *no, not, nothing, don't, doesn't, didn't, isn't, wasn't,* and *weren't.* Make sure you understand what the statement means.

    __*true*__ **Tom isn't happy when his aunt makes him paint the fence.**

Matching Test

A matching test has two lists. You match a word in one list to a word or phrase that goes with it in another list.

- Read both lists before you begin answering.

- Read the directions carefully. Should you use each answer once . . . more than once . . . or not at all? If an answer can be used only once, mark it off after using it. This makes it easy to see which answers you have left.

    1. _____ Sid   A. was lost in the cave with Tom

    2. _____ Huck   B. never took part in Tom's schemes

    3. _____ Becky   C. was Tom's best friend

Multiple-Choice Test

A multiple-choice test gives several answers for each question. You decide which answer is correct, and mark it.

- On most multiple-choice tests, you mark only one answer for each question or statement. However, watch for directions that may tell you to mark all answers that are correct.

  Which of the following people are Tom's friends?

  A. Huck Finn   **C. Willie Mufferson**

  B. Becky Thatcher   **D. Both A and B**

- You may be asked to mark the *best* answer, or the *most* correct answer. This means that there may be more than one correct answer, but there is only one *best* answer.

- Read the question carefully. One word can change the meaning of the whole question.

  Tom's adventures take him to every imaginable scary place except

  A. a graveyard   **C. a pirate ship**

  B. a cave   **D. a haunted house**

- Read all the answers before you mark the one you think is correct.

Fill-in-the-Blanks Test

A fill-in-the-blanks test is made up of sentences or paragraphs with some words left out. You fill in the missing words.

- Each blank probably stands for one word. If there are three blanks in a row, you need to write in three words.

  Tom finds twelve thousand dollars' worth of _____

  _____ _____ in the cave.

- If the word just before the blank is "an," the word that fills in the blank probably begins with *a, e, i, o,* or *u.*

  Tom has an _____ named Polly and a _____

  named Sid.

Taking Essay Tests

In an essay test, you write a short essay that answers a specific question. This kind of test involves several steps. You read the question, think about what you know, plan your answer, and, finally, you write your answer. It's a big job. But you can write a good essay answer if you take it one step at a time.

① UNDERSTAND THE QUESTION

Read the question carefully—at least two times. As you read, look for the *key word* or words that tell you exactly what to do. Here are some key words you will often find in essay questions.

Compare means "tell how these things are alike."

Contrast means "tell how these things are different." Some essay questions ask you to compare *and* contrast.

Define means "tell what a word or subject means, what its function or role is, what group or category it belongs to, and how it is different from other members of the group."

Describe means "tell how something looks, sounds, or feels." In some cases, you may even describe how something smells and tastes.

Evaluate means "give your opinion." Write about good points and bad points. It is very important to tell why you have this opinion and to give facts and details that support it.

Explain means "tell how something happens or how it works." You should give reasons, causes, or step-by-step details.

Identify means "answer who? what? when? where? and why? about a subject."

List means "include a specific number of examples, reasons, or causes."

Outline means "organize your answer into main points and specific examples." In some cases, you will use an actual outline.

Prove means "present facts and details that show something is true."

Review means "give an overall picture of the main points about a subject."

Summarize means "tell the important points in a shortened form."

2 PLAN YOUR ANSWER

Find the key word in the question and underline it. Copy the word onto your paper and write what it means. Begin writing down facts and details that support the key word. You may use a graphic organizer or just make a list.

HELPFUL HINT

It's not necessary to write down everything you know about the subject. Instead, think carefully about what the question is asking and write down the information that answers the question.

Science Test — Chapter 18

Question: <u>Describe</u> the sun. Give as many details as you can.

<u>Describe:</u> Tell how it looks, sounds, or feels.

THE SUN
* size, age
  - yellow dwarf
  - medium size
  - 4.6 billion years old
  - over a million kilometers in diameter
  - more than 99% of mass in solar system
  - creates strong gravitational pull
* kinds of gases
  - 4 layers: photosphere, convection zone, radiation zone, core
  - core temperature: more than 15,000,000 degrees centigrade
  - hydrogen changed to helium = energy

3 WRITE A ONE-PARAGRAPH ANSWER

If you can answer the question in one paragraph, use all of your main points and supporting details in that one paragraph. Remember to arrange the information in the best possible way.

Science Test — Chapter 18

Question: Describe the sun. Give as many details as you can.

Science Test -- Chapter 18

The sun is a yellow dwarf star that scientists think is about 4.6 billion years old. It is over 1 million kilometers in diameter and contains more than 99 percent of the mass in the whole solar system. Because of its huge mass, the sun has a strong gravitational pull. The sun is made up of gases and has four layers. The surface is called the photosphere. The next layer is the convection zone, then the radiation zone, and at the center is the core. The core temperature is more than 15 million degrees centigrade. At the core, hydrogen is turned into helium by a process called nuclear fusion. This process creates many forms of energy, including heat and light. Without the heat and light of the sun, we could not exist on planet Earth.

WRITE A MULTIPARAGRAPH ANSWER

Sometimes you will need to write a multiparagraph answer. For example, the question below asks students to describe two different things. Notice that the first paragraph has a topic sentence that addresses the first part of the question. The second paragraph has a topic sentence covering the second part of the question.

Question: Describe the sun and its effects on the planets in our solar system.

The sun is a yellow dwarf star that scientists think is about 4.6 billion years old. Even though the sun is only a medium-size star, it is 1,392,000 kilometers in diameter. The sun is made up of four layers of gases. The surface is called the photosphere. The next layer is the convection zone, then comes the radiation zone, and at the center is the core. At the core, which is more than 15 million degrees centigrade, hydrogen is turned into helium by a process called nuclear fusion. This process creates many forms of energy, including heat and light.

The sun has many powerful effects on the planets in our solar system. Because of its huge mass, the sun has a strong gravitational pull. This is what keeps the planets orbiting around the sun. The sun's light and heat travel through space to the planets, making nearby planets such as Mercury and Venus very hot, while leaving faraway planets such as Pluto and Neptune extremely cold.

To sum up, without the sun and its gravitational pull, our solar system would not exist. Without the heat and light from the sun, we would not exist.

Planning Skills

You probably know people who are very good at something—like drawing or playing basketball or singing. These people obviously have natural gifts, but most of them also work very hard at improving their skills. The same thing applies to you when it comes to planning skills. You may already do a pretty good job of planning your school and home life. You may already know how to set goals, budget your time, and complete your assignments. But, if you're like most people, there's room for improvement.

The planning skills that you use in school are the same kinds of skills you use at home. Just as importantly, you can use these skills for years to come. Now is the perfect time to take the next step toward a lifelong goal of managing your time and talent as efficiently as possible.

WHAT'S AHEAD

This chapter offers you a number of different ways to improve your planning skills. You'll learn about setting realistic goals, budgeting your time wisely, completing assignments on time, and managing stress in your daily life. We hope you find it helpful.

- Setting Goals
- Planning Your Time
- Completing Assignments
- Managing Stress

Setting Goals

Can you think of any projects you would like to undertake, any skills you would like to improve, any resolutions you would like to keep? The guidelines that follow will give you insights into setting long-range goals and planning how to reach them.

GOAL-SETTING GUIDELINES

- **Set realistic goals.** What would be a realistic goal for you? Are you capable of writing a novel or setting out to break the state record in the mile run? Probably not, but what you can do is this: Plan to write one full page each day in a personal journal—maybe for two months or even longer. Each time you run in a track meet, plan to run a faster race than the time before. These are reasonable goals.

- **Be flexible enough to accept occasional setbacks.** There will be times when you just can't write—although there should almost always be time for at least one page of writing. There will be track meets when it will be difficult for you to run your best time— maybe you're running in a monsoon, or you're just not feeling well.

- **Plan how you will accomplish your goal.** Set aside a specific time to write and stick to it. Make it a point to talk to your coach after every race. Find out from him or her what you can do to improve your time, and then work on that aspect of your running between meets.

- **Divide your goal into manageable parts.** Take things one part or one day at a time. Keep track of how you're doing and reward yourself when you do well.

- **Give each of your goals a chance.** There's a lot to be gained by dedicating yourself to a long-range goal. If you write one page every day for two months, you'll have written 61 pages. That's quite an accomplishment. If you train hard and make steady improvements in your running, that, too, is an accomplishment to be proud of.

"The world stands aside to let anyone pass who knows where he or she is going."
—Jordan Allister

Planning Your Time

If you can't seem to get things done, or if you procrastinate—put off doing something—you should practice time management. Time management is an important lifelong skill.

STEPS IN THE PROCESS

- **Turn big jobs into smaller jobs.** When you're faced with a major project or some other important task, don't look at it as one big job. Break it down into smaller, more manageable parts. Studying or working 15 minutes a day for two weeks beats 2 or 3 hours of work the night before your science project is due.

- **Keep a weekly schedule.** A weekly planner shows you at a glance what you have coming up and helps you plan time for activities, studying, and fun. A model weekly planner follows. Design your own planner to meet your personal needs.

WEEKLY PLANNER

Day/Date	Assignment	Due Date	Activities, Meetings	Study Times
Monday 10/30				
Tuesday 10/31				

- **Make a "Daily List."** Write down things you need to do today and must do tomorrow. Number them in order of importance; then cross each item off as it is completed.

- **Plan your study time realistically.** Time slots of 15-20 minutes followed by 5-minute breaks work well for most students.

- **Keep a flexible schedule.** Plans change and new things pop up daily. Be ready to change your schedule if necessary.

Find out when you are the most productive. Reserve this time for your most challenging assignments and projects. Also make time for relaxation and exercise so that you have a good balance between work and play.

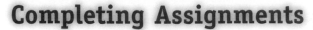

Completing Assignments

One of the challenges you and your classmates face each day is completing your assignments correctly and on time. If you have good study habits, it's a challenge you've probably already met, something you do automatically. But if you do need some help in organizing yourself to get assignments done, the following guidelines will help.

PLANNING AHEAD

- **Know exactly what the assignment is,** when it is due, and what you must do to complete it successfully.
- **Plan how much time you will need** to complete the assignment.
- **Decide when and where** (library, study hall, home) you will do your assignment.
- **Gather any materials you may need** to complete your assignment.

If you are having trouble getting started on your assignments, try doing them at the same time and place each day. This will help you control the urge to wait until you are "in the mood" before starting. Also avoid doing your assignments when you are overly hungry or tired.

GETTING IT DONE

- **Go over all the directions** your teacher has given you for each assignment.
- **Plan to take breaks** only after completing a certain amount of each assignment and stick to that schedule. If necessary, ask your family not to disturb you and hold any phone calls you may get.
- **Keep a list of things you need to check** on or ask your teacher about. You must clearly understand a problem before you can solve it.
- **Use study-reading or note-taking techniques** to help you complete the reading and studying parts of your assignment. (See 307-322 and 361-368.)
- **Turn in your assignment on time** and welcome any suggestions your teacher may give you for future improvement. (Make sure your assignment is neat and free of careless errors.)

Managing Stress

You are the best person to identify signs and causes of stress or pressure in your daily life. Stress can produce many different symptoms—from simply feeling uptight to feeling angry, from getting headaches to eating too little or too much. The information below points out possible causes and symptoms of stress in your life, and suggests ways to deal with them.

CAUSES OF STRESS

- Moving
- Doing poorly in school
- Performing in front of others
- Doing something you know is wrong
- Peer pressure
- Birth of a sibling
- High expectations
- Divorce of parents

SYMPTOMS OF STRESS OVERLOAD

- Unusual mood swings
- Withdrawal from activities
- Overdoing an activity
- Withdrawal from family or friends
- No interest in school
- Loss of concentration
- Low self-esteem
- Sleeping too much

WAYS TO REDUCE STRESS

There are a number of things you can do. First you must identify whatever it is in your life that is causing the stress; then you must create a plan for dealing with the situation.

- **Eliminate the problem that is causing stress:** Getting to the root of the problem is the best long-term solution for dealing with stress. Working to improve your grades and challenging yourself to change your attitude are both good examples of long-term solutions.

- **Avoid the problem:** While this is not an ideal solution, it can be temporarily useful. Going to a movie, reading a good book, playing piano, and going for a walk or run are all good ways to "put off" stressful situations. Temporarily avoiding a problem can sometimes give you the space you need to come up with a long-term solution.

- **Take part in stress-reducing activities:** Stress is a natural part of life. Eating a healthy diet, exercising regularly, talking to a friend, and doing something enjoyable are ways to keep stress levels low.

Proofreader's Guide

Marking Punctuation

Period

A period is used to end a sentence. It is also used after initials, after abbreviations, and as a decimal point.

387.1 At the End of a Sentence

A period is used to end a sentence that makes a statement or a request, or that gives a command that is not used as an exclamation.

Homes in the future will have many high-tech features. [statement]

Check your video doorbell to see who stopped by while you were gone. [request]

Don't worry. [command]

Your household robot will not reveal your whereabouts unless programmed to do so. [statement]

Note: It is not necessary to place a period after a statement that has parentheses around it and is part of another sentence.

387.2 After an Initial

A period should be placed after an initial.

E. L. Konigsburg [author]
Marie A. Smith [politician]

387.3 After Abbreviations

A period is placed after each part of an abbreviation—unless the abbreviation is an acronym. An acronym is a word formed from the first (or first few) letters of words in a set phrase. (See 409.5.)

Abbreviations:
Mr.   Mrs.   Ms.   Dr.   B.C.E.   C.E.
Acronyms:
AIDS   NASA

Note: When an abbreviation is the last word in a sentence, only one period should be used at the end of the sentence.

In the twenty-first century, we'll get more of our energy from renewable sources, such as the sun, the wind, ocean water, etc.

387.4 As a Decimal

Use a period as a decimal point and to separate dollars and cents.

For $2.99 on Tuesdays, I can rent three videos. But is it a bargain to spend 33.3 percent of my allowance on videos that I won't have time to watch anyway?

388

Ellipsis

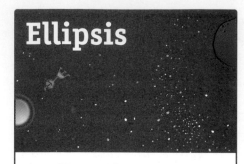

An ellipsis (three periods) is used to show a pause in dialogue or to show that words or sentences have been left out. (Leave one space before, after, and between each period.)

To Show a Pause

An ellipsis is used to show a pause in dialogue.

> "My report," said Reggie, "is on . . . ah . . . cars of the future. One place that I . . . ah . . . checked out on the Internet said that cars would someday run on sunshine. Is this . . . ah . . . a plot to keep teenage drivers home at night?"

To Show Omitted Words

An ellipsis is used to show that one or more words have been left out of a quotation. Read this prediction from www.futurist.com:

> "The human life span has nearly tripled in the last 200 years, from an average of 30 years to nearly 85 years. If you reach 65 and are healthy, you can expect to live another 20 years."

Here's how you would type part of this quotation, leaving some of the words out.

> "The human life span has nearly tripled . . . from an average of 30 years to nearly 85 years."

At the End of a Sentence

If the words left out are at the end of a sentence, use a period followed by three dots.

> "The human life span has nearly tripled in the last 200 years. . . . If you reach 65 and are healthy, you can expect to live another 20 years."

SCHOOL DAZE

Max, where is your project? Today is the last day to turn it in!

Well . . . ah . . . can I fax it to you before midnight?

Comma

Commas are used to indicate a pause or a change in thought. Commas are used to keep words and ideas from running together, making writing easier to read. No other form of punctuation is more important to understand than the comma.

389.1 ┤ Between Items in a Series

Commas are used between words, phrases, or clauses in a series. (A series contains at least three items.)

Spanish, French, and German are the languages most often taught in schools today, but Chinese, English, and Hindi are the languages spoken by the most people in the world. [words]

Being comfortable with technology, working well with others, and knowing another language and culture are important skills for today's workers. [phrases]

389.2 ┤ To Keep Numbers Clear

Commas are used to separate the digits in a number in order to distinguish hundreds, thousands, millions, etc.

In 1995 the total number of immigrants to the United States was 720,461. The greatest number of immigrants came from Mexico (89,932), the Philippines (50,984), and Vietnam (41,752).

Note: Commas are not used in years. Also, it is often easier to use a combination of numerals and words for certain large numbers in the millions and billions. (See 410.2 for more information.)

389.3 ┤ In Dates and Addresses

Commas are used to distinguish items in an address and items in a date.

In June our family is moving to 2727 Telluride Avenue, Denver, Colorado 81435, for a year.

In January 2029 we will celebrate the 100th birthday of Rev. Martin Luther King, Jr. On August 28, 1963, he gave his famous "I Have a Dream" speech.

The address of the Martin Luther King, Jr., Center for Nonviolent Social Change, Inc., is 449 Auburn Ave. N., Atlanta, GA 30312-1503.

390.1 | To Set Off Dialogue

Commas are used to set off the exact words of the speaker from the rest of the sentence.

> The electronics executive said, "Did you know that computers can now speak with a Texas drawl?"

Note: When you are reporting or summarizing what someone said, use no comma (or quotation marks) as in the example below. The words *if* and *that* often signal dialogue that is being reported rather than quoted.

> The electronics executive said that computers can now speak with a Texas drawl.

390.2 | To Set Off Interruptions

Commas are used to set off a word, phrase, or clause that interrupts the main thought of a sentence. Such expressions usually can be identified through the following tests:

1. They may be omitted without changing the meaning of the sentence.
2. They may be placed nearly anywhere in the sentence without changing the meaning of the sentence.

> Computers, *as we all know,* are getting smaller. You may someday, *for example,* own a wristwatch computer.

390.3 | To Set Off Interjections

A comma is used to separate an interjection or a weak exclamation from the rest of the sentence.

> No kidding, you mean someday computers may be sewn into our clothing?

> Yes, and don't be surprised if that piece of clothing reminds you about your dentist appointment and your homework assignments.

390.4 | In Direct Address

Commas are used to separate a noun of direct address from the rest of the sentence. (A noun of direct address is the noun that names the person spoken to in the sentence.)

> Jill, listen to this. With a touch of a key, an interior decorator can change wallpaper and fabrics on his computer screen.

> That's nothing, Jack. An architect can, with the touch of a key, see how light will fall in different parts of the building.

390.5 | To Enclose Information

Commas are used to enclose a title, a name, or initials that follow a person's last name.

> Melanie Prokat, M.D., and Gerald Sahn, Ph.D., admitted that they can't program their VCR's. Then Mereick, B., and Abrams, J. D., confessed that they can't either.

391.1 | Between Two Independent Clauses

A comma may be used between two independent clauses that are joined by coordinate conjunctions such as *and*, *but*, *or*, *nor*, *for*, *so*, and *yet*.

Many businesses are selling their products on the Internet, and on-line buying has become popular with millions of people.

Avoid Comma Splices

A comma splice results when two independent clauses are "spliced" together with only a comma— and no conjunction. (See page 86.)

391.2 | To Separate Clauses and Phrases

A comma should separate an adverb clause or a long modifying phrase from the independent clause that follows it.

If everyone shops on the Internet, what will happen to shopping malls? [adverb clause]

According to the experts, shopping malls may one day be as hard to find as drive-in movie theaters. [long modifying phrase]

In time "malling" may be just a fond memory of the good old days that you can tell your grandchildren about. [Commas are usually omitted after short introductory phrases, and when the adverb clause follows the independent clause.]

391.3 | To Separate Adjectives

Commas are used to separate two or more adjectives that equally modify the same noun.

Many intelligent, well-educated scientists think that one of Jupiter's 16 moons shows signs of life.

Intelligent and *well-educated* are separated by a comma because they modify *scientists* equally.

Note: No comma is used between the last adjective (*well-educated*) and the noun (*scientists*).

In 2004 scientists hope to send a space probe to this cold Jovian moon.

Cold and *Jovian* do not modify *moon* equally; therefore, no comma separates the two.

Use these tests to help you decide if adjectives modify equally:
1. **Switch the order** of the adjectives; if the sentence is clear, the adjectives modify equally.
2. **Put the word** *and* between the adjectives; if the sentence reads well, use a comma when *and* is taken out.

391.4 | To Set Off Phrases

Commas are used to separate an explanatory phrase from the rest of the sentence.

English, the language computers speak worldwide, is also the most widely used language in science and medicine.

392.1 To Set Off Appositives

An appositive is a word or phrase that identifies or renames a noun or pronoun. (Do not use commas with restrictive appositives because they are necessary to the basic meaning of the sentence.)

COBOL, a programming language that is based on English words and phrases, was invented by Grace Hopper, a U.S. Navy admiral. [The two appositive phrases are set off with commas.]

U.S. Navy Admiral Grace Hopper invented COBOL.

[The restrictive appositive, *Grace Hopper,* is not set off because it's needed to make the sentence clear.]

392.2 To Set Off Nonrestrictive Phrases and Clauses

Commas are used to punctuate **nonrestrictive** phrases and clauses (those phrases or clauses that are not necessary to the basic meaning of the sentence).

Ninety-seven percent of the earth's water supply is contained in our oceans, and 2 percent is frozen. We get our water from the 1 percent that is left, which comes from the earth's surface or groundwater.

The clause—*which comes from the earth's surface or groundwater*—is additional information; it is non-restrictive (not required). If the clause were left out, the meaning of the sentence would remain clear.

Restrictive phrases or clauses (those that are needed in the sentence) restrict or limit the meaning of the sentence and are not set off with commas.

Groundwater that is free from harmful liquids and chemicals is rare.

The clause—*that is free from harmful liquids and chemicals*—is restrictive; it is needed to complete the meaning in the basic sentence and is not, therefore, set off with commas.

SCHOOL DAZE

Sarah, we've completed two-thirds of the quarter, and you haven't turned in one assignment. What do you have to say for yourself?

Ah . . . is there anything I can do for extra credit?

Semicolon

A semicolon is a cross between a period and a comma. It is sometimes used in place of a period; other times it serves the same function as a comma.

393.1 To Join Two Independent Clauses

A semicolon is used to join two independent clauses that are not connected with a coordinate conjunction. (This means that each of the two clauses could stand alone as a separate sentence.)

> My dad bought a robot-operated lawn mower; I was anxious to see the thing work.

393.2 To Set Off Two Independent Clauses

Use a semicolon to separate independent clauses if they are long, or if they already contain commas.

> After I "set the route," the robot mower was ready to cut the grass; but when I checked on it later, I discovered that our high-tech mower had also cut Mrs. Crabb's yard—and all of her flowers.

393.3 With Conjunctive Adverbs

A semicolon is also used to join two independent clauses when the clauses are connected only by a conjunctive adverb (*also, as a result, for example, however, therefore, instead*).

> I apologized for the robot's slipup; however, Mrs. Crabb continued to scream about careless teenagers and dumb machines.

393.4 To Separate Groups That Contain Commas

A semicolon is used to distinguish groups of items within a list.

> Here's a list of things we should be recycling: aluminum cans; cardboard, newspapers, and other paper products; glass bottles, jars, and other glass items.

> Certain items are still difficult to recycle: foam cups, plates, and cartons; plastic bags, diapers, and wrappers; used tires and chemicals.

See 436.3 for an explanation and examples of independent clauses.

Colon

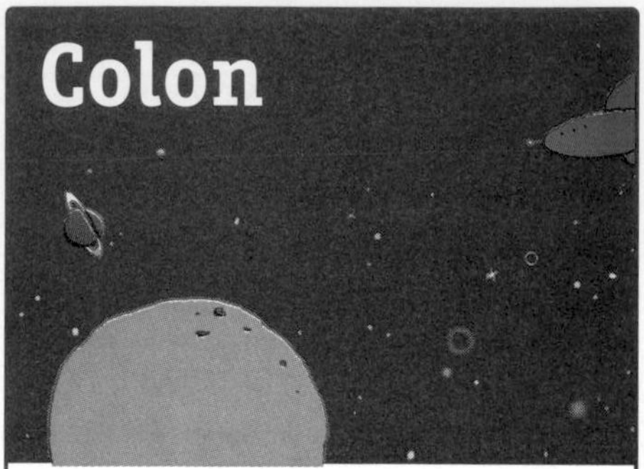

A colon may be used to introduce a letter, a list, or an important point. Colons are also used between the numbers in time.

394.1 After a Salutation

A colon may be used after the salutation of a business letter.

Dear Ms. Manners:

394.2 As a Formal Introduction

A colon may be used to formally introduce a sentence, a question, or a quotation.

One scientist explained why it's important to protect the environment: "It's like pulling bricks from a wall; everything will seem fine until the wall suddenly collapses."

394.3 For Emphasis

A colon is used to emphasize a word or phrase.

Experts worry about one creature that is mysteriously dying off in great numbers: the frog.

394.4 Between Numerals Indicating Time

A colon is used between the parts of a number that indicates time.

Come to think of it, I rarely hear frogs croaking anymore between 4:00 a.m. and 8:00 a.m.

394.5 To Introduce a List

A colon is used to introduce a list.

We produce enough foam cups annually to circle the earth 436 times. Here's how we can begin to control this problem: use paper picnic products, buy eggs in paper cartons, and ask for paper food containers at fast-food restaurants.

Note: When introducing a list, the colon usually comes after summary words—*the following, these things*—or after words describing the subject of the list.

Correct:
To conserve water you should do the *following three things:* install a low-flow showerhead, turn the water off while brushing your teeth, and fix drippy faucets.

Incorrect:
To conserve water you should: install a low-flow showerhead, turn the water off while brushing your teeth, and fix drippy faucets.

Correct:
Other ideas come to mind: take shorter showers, run only full dishwashers, and stop worrying about brown lawns.

Dash

The dash can be used to show a sudden break in a sentence, to emphasize a word or clause, and to show that someone's speech is being interrupted.

395.1 ┤ To Indicate a Sudden Break

A dash can be used to show a sudden break in a sentence.

> There is one thing—actually several things—that I find hard to believe about the superphone of the future. Push a few buttons, and it will print out everything from the news to sports scores to concert information.

395.2 ┤ For Emphasis

A dash may be used to emphasize a word, series of words, a phrase, or a clause.

> High-tech jobs—ones that require both technical education and on-the-job training—are hot.

> I think that one of these career choices—computer science, computer programming, or systems analyst—is my ticket to employment in the future.

395.3 ┤ To Indicate Interrupted Speech

A dash is used to show that someone's speech is being interrupted by another person.

> Why, hello—yes, I understand—
> no, I remember—oh—of course,
> I won't—why, no, I—why, yes,
> I—why don't I just fax it to you.

Note: A dash is indicated by two hyphens--without spacing before or after the hyphens--in all typed material.

Parentheses

Parentheses are used around words that are included in a sentence to add information or to help make an idea clearer.

395.4 ┤ To Add Information

Use parentheses when adding or clarifying information.

> Cures for diseases (from arthritis to AIDS) may be found in plants in the rain forest. Fewer than 10 percent of the plant species in the world have been studied (a total of over 250,000 species).

Hyphen

The hyphen is used to divide words at the end of a line, to join the words in compound numbers from twenty-one to ninety-nine, and to form compound words. It is also used to join numbers that indicate the life span of an individual, the scores of a game, and so on.

396.1 To Divide a Word

The hyphen is used to divide a word when you run out of room at the end of a line. A word may be divided only between syllables. Here are some additional guidelines:

✦ Never divide a one-syllable word: *raised, through.*

✦ Avoid dividing a word of five letters or less: *paper, study.*

✦ Never divide a one-letter syllable from the rest of the word: *omit-ted,* not *o-mitted.*

✦ Never divide abbreviations or contractions.

✦ Never divide the last word in more than two lines in a row or the last word in a paragraph.

✦ When a vowel is a syllable by itself, divide the word after the vowel: *epi-sode,* not *ep-isode.*

396.2 In Compound Words

The hyphen is used to make some compound words.

e-mail

baby-sitter

toll-free number

retro-rocket

three-story building

ice-skating

all-star

396.3 To Avoid Confusion or Awkward Spelling

Use a hyphen with prefixes or suffixes to avoid confusion or awkward spelling.

Re-collect (not *recollect*) the reports we distributed last week.

It has a shell-like (not *shelllike*) texture.

396.4 Between Numbers in a Fraction

A hyphen is used between the numbers in a fraction, but not between the numerator and denominator when one or both are already hyphenated.

four-tenths

five-sixteenths

seven thirty-seconds (7/32)

397.1 To Create New Words

A hyphen is used to form new words beginning with the prefixes *self, ex, all, great,* etc. A hyphen is also used with suffixes such as *elect* and *free.*

> A special mesh seeded with live cells may induce self-generating skin for burn victims.

> Despite high-tech health care, we have not created a germ-free world. Some bacteria no longer respond to all-purpose antibiotics.

397.2 To Join Letters and Words

A hyphen is used to join a capital letter to a noun or participle.

> U-turn
>
> T-bar lift
>
> X-ray therapy
>
> PG-rated movie

397.3 To Form an Adjective

Use the hyphen to join two or more words that work together to form a single-thought adjective before a noun.

> voice-recognition software
>
> heat-and-serve meals
>
> microwave-safe cookware

Note: When words forming the adjective come after the noun, do not hyphenate them.

> These dishes are microwave safe.

Caution: When the first of the words ends in *ly,* do **not** use a hyphen; also, do not use a hyphen when a number or letter is the final part of a one-thought adjective.

> newly designed computer
>
> grade A milk

SCHOOL DAZE

Gee Ms. Roberts, if I have to cut any more **misspelled** words, the only thing left will be my name!

Question Mark

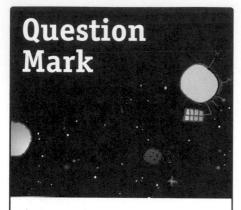

A question mark is used after an interrogative sentence and to show doubt about the correctness of a fact or figure.

398.1 | Direct Question

A question mark is used at the end of a direct question (an interrogative sentence).

How long will it be before deep-diving vehicles will be able to search the deepest ocean floor for deposits of manganese, silver, and cobalt?

398.2 | Indirect Question

No question mark is used after an indirect question.

Because I love dolphins and seals, I'm often asked if I want to be a marine biologist.

I asked if marine biologists will one day be required to live on the ocean floor.

398.3 | To Show Doubt

The question mark is placed within parentheses to show that the writer isn't sure a fact or figure is correct.

By the year 2050 (?) we will be able to explore the ocean floor without attachment to any support vehicle.

Exclamation Point

The exclamation point may be placed after a word, a phrase, or a sentence to show emotion. (The exclamation point should not be overused.)

398.4 | To Express Strong Feeling

The exclamation point is used to show excitement or strong feeling.

Yeah! Wow! Oh my!

Surprise! You've won the million-dollar sweepstakes!

Caution: Never use more than one exclamation point; such punctuation is incorrect and looks foolish.

Don't ever do that to me again!

Quotation Marks

Quotation marks are used to set off the exact words of a speaker, to show what a writer has "borrowed" from another book or magazine, to set off the titles of certain publications, and to show that certain words are used in a special way.

399.1 To Set Off Direct Quotations

Quotation marks are placed before and after direct quotations. Only the exact words quoted are placed within quotation marks.

> Futurist Don Reynolds says, "Today's students will go through an average of four careers in one life span."

399.2 For Quoting a Quotation

Single quotation marks are used to punctuate a quotation within a quotation.

> "When Mr. Kurt said, 'Read this book by tomorrow,' I was stunned," said Sung Kim.

399.3 For Long Quotations

If more than one paragraph is quoted, quotation marks are placed before each paragraph and at the end of the last paragraph.

In research papers or reports, quotations that are more than four lines on a page are usually set off from the rest of the paper by indenting 10 spaces from the left.

Note: Longer quotations that are set off require no quotation marks either before or after the quoted material, unless quotation marks appear in the original copy.

400.1 Placement of Punctuation

Periods and commas are always placed **inside** quotation marks.

> "I don't know," said Albert.
> Albert said, "I don't know."

An exclamation point or a question mark is placed **inside** the quotation marks when it punctuates the quotation; it is placed **outside** when it punctuates the main sentence.

> Ms. Wiley asked, "Can you actually tour the Smithsonian on the Internet?"

> Did I hear you say, "Now we can tour the Smithsonian on the Internet"?

Semicolons or colons are placed **outside** quotation marks.

> First, I will read "The Masque of the Red Death"; then, I will read "The Raven."

400.2 For Special Words

Quotation marks also may be used (1) to set apart a word that is being discussed, (2) to indicate that a word is slang, or (3) to point out that a word or phrase is being used in a special way.

1. Daria's mom works in a "cube farm" in Palo Alto, California, a place where rows of cubicles take the place of private offices.

2. I'd say that group was really "bad."

3. This electronic lure is really going to "light up" some fish's life.

400.3 To Punctuate Titles

Quotation marks are used to punctuate titles of songs, poems, short stories, lectures, episodes of radio or television programs, chapters of books, and articles found in magazines, newspapers, or encyclopedias.

> "Change the World" [song]

> "The Raven" [poem]

> "The Pearls of Parlay" [short story]

> "A House Is Not a Home " [a television episode]

> "We'll Never Conquer Space" [a chapter in a book]

> "The Robot's Role in Space" [lecture]

> "Teen Rescues Stranded Dolphin" [newspaper article]

Note: When you punctuate a title, capitalize the first word, last word, and every word in between except for articles, short prepositions, and coordinating conjunctions.

Other Titles
For help punctuating titles not listed above, turn to 401.3.

Italics and Underlining

Italics is slightly slanted type. In this sentence, the word *happiness* is typed in italics. In handwritten material, each word or letter that should be in italics is underlined.

401.1 | Handwritten

Underline words that should be italicized.

In Tuck Everlasting, the author explores what it would be like to live forever.

401.2 | Printed

Put words in italics before they are printed.

In *Tuck Everlasting*, the author explores what it would be like to live forever.

401.3 | In Titles

Underline (or *italicize*) the titles of books, plays, book-length poems, magazines, radio and television programs, movies, videos, cassettes, CD's, the names of aircraft and ships, and newspapers.

Walk Two Moons [book]

Discover [magazine]

Law and Order [television program]

Titanic [movie]

The Joshua Tree [CD]

U.S.S. Arizona [ship]

Columbia [space shuttle]

New York Times or **New York Times** [newspaper]

Note: When the name of a city is used as part of the name of a newspaper, the name of the city need not be underlined.

Exceptions: Do not underline or put in quotation marks your own title at the top of your written work.

401.4 | For Foreign Words

Underline foreign words that are not commonly used in everyday English. Also underline scientific names.

E pluribus unum appears on most U.S. currency.

Humankind is also known as Homosapiens.

401.5 | For Special Uses

Underline any number, letter, or word that is being discussed or used in a special way. (Sometimes quotation marks are used for this same reason. See 400.2.)

I hope that this letter I stands for incredible instead of incomplete.

Apostrophe

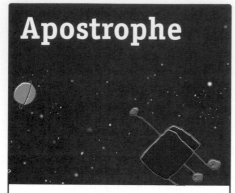

An apostrophe is used to show possession, to form plurals, or to show that one or more letters have been left out of a word.

402.1 | In Contractions

An apostrophe is used to show that one or more letters have been left out of a word to form a contraction.

don't [*o* is left out]

she'd [*woul* is left out]

it's [*i* is left out]

402.2 | In Place of Omitted Letters or Numbers

An apostrophe is used to show that one or more digits have been left out of a number, or that one or more letters have been left out of a word to show its special pronunciation.

class of '99 [*19* is left out]

g'bye [the letters *ood* are left out]

Note: Letters and numbers are usually not omitted in formal writing. They are, however, often left out in dialogue because dialogue needs to sound like real people talking.

402.3 | To Form Plurals

An apostrophe and *s* are used to form the plural of a letter, a sign, a number, or a word discussed as a word.

A's   8's   +'s   to's

"Don't use too many *and*'s in your writing."

402.4 | To Express Time or Amount

An apostrophe is used with an adjective that is part of an expression indicating time or amount.

Tomorrow's school lessons may be taught over the Internet.

My father lost an entire day's work when that thunderstorm knocked out our power.

402.5 | To Form Possessives in Compound Nouns

The possessive of a compound noun is formed by placing the possessive ending after the last word.

her sister-in-law's hip-hop music [singular]

her sisters-in-law's tastes in music [plural]

the secretary of state's wife [singular]

the secretaries of state's wives [plural]

403.1 To Form Possessives With Indefinite Pronouns

The possessive of an indefinite pronoun is formed by adding an apostrophe and *s*.

> **everyone's   anyone's**

Note: For two-word pronouns, add an apostrophe and *s* to the second word.

> **somebody else's**

403.2 To Form Singular Possessives

To form the possessive of a singular noun, add an apostrophe and *s*.

> **Dr. Mill's theory is that the world's population will double in 20 years.**

Note: For a singular noun ending with an *s* or *z* sound, the possessive may be formed by adding just an apostrophe.

> **Texas' oil (or) Texas's oil**

Note: When the singular noun is a one-syllable word, however, the possessive is usually formed by adding both an apostrophe and *s*.

> **boss's request**

403.3 To Form Plural Possessives

The possessive form of plural nouns ending in *s* is usually made by adding just an apostrophe. For plural nouns not ending in *s*, an apostrophe and *s* must be added.

> **Joneses' great-grandfather**
> **children's book**

Remember! The word immediately before the apostrophe is the owner.

> **boss's office** [*boss* is the owner]
> **bosses' office** [*bosses* are the owners]

403.4 To Show Shared Possession

When possession is shared by more than one noun, add an apostrophe and *s* to the last noun in the series.

> **VanClumpin, VanDiken, and VanTulip's air band.** [All three are members of the band.]
> **VanClumpin's, VanDiken's, and VanTulip's air guitars.** [Each person owns an air guitar.]

Punctuation Marks

´	Accent	,	Comma	( )	Parentheses
'	Apostrophe	—	Dash	.	Period
*	Asterisk	/	Diagonal/Slash	?	Question mark
[ ]	Brackets	ä	Dieresis	" "	Quotation marks
^	Caret	. . .	Ellipsis	;	Semicolon
ç	Cedilla	!	Exclamation point	ñ	Tilde
:	Colon	-	Hyphen	__	Underscore

Editing for Mechanics

Capitalization

404.1 | Proper Nouns, Adjectives

Capitalize all proper nouns and all proper adjectives. A proper noun is the name of a particular person, place, thing, or idea. A proper adjective is an adjective formed from a proper noun.

Common Noun . . . . country, president, continent

Proper Noun . . . . Canada, Andrew Jackson, Asia

Proper Adjective . . . . . . Canadian, Jacksonian, Asian

404.2 | Names of People

Capitalize the names of people and also the initials or abbreviations that stand for those names.

Colin L. Powell, Frances McDormand, Aung San Suu Kyi, Mary Sanchez-Gomez

Note: If a woman uses both her maiden name and married name, the maiden name is listed first, and both are capitalized.

404.3 | Historical Events

Capitalize the names of historical events, documents, and periods of time.

World War I, the Bill of Rights, the Magna Carta, the Middle Ages, the Paleozoic Era

404.4 | Abbreviations

Capitalize abbreviations of titles and organizations.

U.S.A., FBI, M.D., B.C.E., C.E., NATO (North Atlantic Treaty Organization), M.A., Ph.D.

404.5 | Organizations

Capitalize the name of an organization, an association, or a team and its members.

New York State Historical Society, the Red Cross, General Motors Corporation, the Miami Dolphins, Republicans, the Democratic Party

404.6 | Names of Subjects

Capitalize the name of a specific course, but not the name of a general subject. (Exception—the names of all languages are proper nouns and are always capitalized: *French, Hindu, German, Latin.*)

Our summer recreation program offers an art course called Paint a Pet Dish.

405.1 | First Words

Capitalize the first word of every sentence and the first word in a direct quotation. Do not capitalize the first word in an indirect quotation.

In many families, pets are treated like people, according to an article in the *Kansas City Star*. [sentence]

Marty Becker, co-author of *Chicken Soup for the Pet Lover's Soul*, says that in the last 10 years, pets have moved out of kennels and basements and into living rooms and bedrooms. [indirect quotation]

Becker reports, **"Seven out of ten people let their pets sleep on the bed."** [direct quotation]

"I get my 15 minutes of fame," he says, **"every time I come home."**
[Notice that *every* is not capitalized because the word does not begin a new sentence.]

"It's like being treated like a rock star," says Becker. **"I have to tell you that feels pretty good."**
[*I* is always capitalized, but in this case it also begins a new sentence.]

405.2 | Capitalize Geographic Names

Planets and heavenly bodies . . . . **Earth, Jupiter, Milky Way**

Continents. . . . . **Europe, Asia, South America, Australia, Africa**

Countries . . . . **Morocco, Haiti, Greece, Chile, United Arab Emirates**

States . . . . **New Mexico, Alabama, West Virginia, Delaware, Iowa**

Provinces . . . . **Alberta, British Columbia, Quebec, Ontario**

Counties . . . . **Sioux County, Kandiyohi County, Wade County**

Cities . . . . **Montreal, Baton Rouge, Albuquerque, Portland**

Bodies of water . . . . **Delaware Bay, Chickamunga Lake, Indian Ocean, Gulf of Mexico, Skunk Creek**

Landforms . . . . **Appalachian Mountains, Bitterroot Range, Capitol Reef**

Public areas . . . . **Tiananmen Square, Sequoia National Forest, Mount Rushmore, Eiffel Tower, Statue of Liberty, Open Space Park, Vietnam Memorial**

Roads and highways. . . . . **New Jersey Turnpike, Interstate 80, Central Avenue, Chisholm Trail, Mutt's Road**

Buildings . . . . **Pentagon, Te Paske Theatre, Empire State Building**

406.1 Particular Sections of the Country

Capitalize words that indicate particular sections of the country; words that simply indicate a direction are not capitalized.

> Having grown up on the hectic West Coast, I find life in the South to be refreshing. My little block in northern Los Angeles had more residents than my entire county located east of Memphis.

Also capitalize proper adjectives formed from names of specific sections of a country. Do not capitalize adjectives formed from words that simply indicate direction.

> Here in western Tennessee, Southern hospitality is a way of life.

406.2 Names of Languages, Races, Nationalities, Religions

Capitalize the names of languages, races, nationalities, and religions, as well as the proper adjectives formed from them.

> Arab
>
> Spanish
>
> Judaism
>
> Catholicism
>
> African art
>
> Irish linen
>
> Swedish meatballs

406.3 Words Used as Names

Capitalize words such as *mother*, *father*, *aunt*, and *uncle* when these words are used as names.

> Uncle Marius started to sit on the couch.
> [*Uncle* is a name; the speaker calls this person "Uncle Marius"]

> Then Uncle stopped in midair.
> [*Uncle* is used as a name.]

> My aunt had just called him.
> [The word *aunt* describes this person but is not used as a name.]

> Then my dad and mom walked into the room.
> [The words *dad* and *mom* are not used as names in this sentence.]

> "Mom, what is everyone doing in here?" I asked.
> [*Mom* is used as a name.]

Note: Words such as *aunt, mom, dad, grandma,* etc., are not usually capitalized if they come after a possessive pronoun (*my, his, our*).

406.4 Days, Months, Holidays

Capitalize the names of days of the week, months of the year, and special holidays.

> Thursday, Friday, Saturday
>
> July, August, September
>
> Independence Day, Arbor Day

Note: Do not capitalize the names of seasons.

> winter, spring, summer, fall

407.1 Official Names

Capitalize the names of businesses and the official names of their products. (These are called *trade names.*) Do not, however, capitalize a general, descriptive word like *toothpaste* when it follows the trade name.

The Gap, Radio Shack, Microsoft

Levis, Kodak, Reebok

Tombotono pizza, Crest toothpaste

407.2 Titles Used with Names

Capitalize titles used with names of persons and abbreviations standing for those titles.

President Jiang Zemin

Governor Christine Whitman

Senator John Glenn

Dr. Irina Zelinsky

Rev. James Offutt

407.3 Titles

Capitalize the first word of a title, the last word, and every word in between except articles (*a, an, the*), short prepositions, and coordinate conjunctions. Follow this rule for titles of books, newspapers, magazines, poems, plays, songs, articles, movies, works of art, pictures, stories, and essays.

Where the Red Fern Grows [book]

Miami Herald [newspaper]

Sports Illustrated [magazine]

"The Cremation of Sam McGee" [poem]

Someone to Watch over Me [play]

Titanic [movie]

"Bridge over Troubled Water" [song]

Mona Lisa [work of art]

Capitalize	Do Not Capitalize
American . . . . un-American
January, February . . . . winter, spring
Missouri and Ohio Rivers . . . . the rivers Missouri and Ohio
The South is quite conservative. . . . . . . Turn south at the stop sign.
Duluth Central High School . . . . a Duluth high school
Governor George E. Pataki . . . . George E. Pataki, our governor
President Ezer Weizman . . . . Ezer Weizman, Israel's president
Ford Mustang GT . . . . a Ford automobile
The planet Earth is egg shaped. . . . . . The earth we live on is good.
I'm taking History 101. I'm taking history.

Plurals

Nouns Ending in a Consonant

The plurals of most nouns are formed by adding *s* to the singular.

cheerleader — cheerleaders
wheel — wheels

The plural form of nouns ending in *ch, sh, s, z,* and *x* is made by adding *es* to the singular.

lunch — lunches   dish — dishes
mess — messes   buzz — buzzes
fox — foxes

408.2 Nouns Ending in *o*

The plurals of nouns ending in *o* with a vowel just before the *o* are formed by adding *s*.

radio — radios   studio — studios
rodeo — rodeos

The plurals of most nouns ending in *o* with a consonant letter just before the *o* are formed by adding *es*.

echo — echoes   hero — heroes
tomato — tomatoes

Exception: Musical terms always form plurals by adding *s*.

alto — altos   banjo — banjos
solo — solos   piano — pianos

408.3 Nouns Ending in *ful*

The plurals of nouns that end with *ful* are formed by adding an *s* at the end of the word.

three platefuls   six tankfuls
four cupfuls   five pailfuls

408.4 Nouns Ending in *f* or *fe*

The plurals of nouns that end in *f* or *fe* are formed in one of two ways: If the final *f* sound is still heard in the plural form of the word, simply add *s;* if the final sound is a *v* sound, change the *f* to *ve* and add *s*.

roof —roofs   chief — chiefs
[plural ends with *f* sound]

wife — wives   loaf — loaves
[plural ends with *v* sound]

408.5 Nouns Ending in *y*

The plurals of common nouns that end in *y* with a consonant letter just before the *y* are formed by changing the *y* to *i* and adding *es*.

fly — flies   jalopy — jalopies

The plurals of common nouns that end in *y* with a vowel before the *y* are formed by adding only *s*.

donkey — donkeys
monkey — monkeys

The plurals of proper nouns ending in *y* are formed by adding *s:*

There are three Circuit Citys in our metro area.

409.1 | Compound Nouns

The plurals of some compound nouns are formed by adding *s* or *es* to the main word in the compound.

brothers-in-law

maids of honor

secretaries of state

409.2 | Irregular Spelling

Some words (including many foreign words) form a plural by taking on an irregular spelling; others are now acceptable with the commonly used *s* or *es* ending.

child . . . . children

goose . . . . . . geese

cactus . . . . . . cacti or cactuses

409.3 | Adding an 's

The plurals of symbols, letters, figures, and words discussed as words are formed by adding an apostrophe and an *s*.

My mom has three Ph.D.'s and loves running 440's on the high-school track.

What state name has two sets of *s*'s and one set of *p*'s?

You've got too many *but*'s and *so*'s in that sentence.

For information on forming plural possessives, see 403.3.

Abbreviations

409.4 | Abbreviations

An abbreviation is the shortened form of a word or phrase. The following abbreviations are always acceptable in any kind of writing:

Mr., Mrs., Ms., Dr., a.m., p.m. (A.M., P.M.), B.C.E. (Before the Common Era), C.E. (Common Era), B.A., M.A., Ph.D., M.D.

Caution: Do **not** abbreviate the names of states, countries, months, days, or units of measure in formal writing. Also, do not use signs or symbols (%, &) in place of words.

409.5 | Acronyms

Most abbreviations are followed by a period. Acronyms are exceptions. An acronym is a word formed from the first (or first few) letters of words in a phrase.

ROM — read-only memory

WHO — world health organization

409.6 | Initialisms

An initialism is similar to an acronym except that it cannot be pronounced as a word.

PBS — Public Broadcasting System

MTV — Music Television

Numbers

410.1 Numbers Under 10

Numbers from one to nine are usually written as words; all numbers 10 and over are usually written as numerals.

two	seven	nine
10	25	106

410.2 Very Large Numbers

You may use a combination of numerals and words for very large numbers.

1.3 million   17 million

You may spell out large numbers that can be written as two words.

two thousand; but 2001

410.3 Sentence Beginnings

Use words, not numerals, to begin a sentence.

Eleven students said they were unable to finish the assignment.

410.4 Numerals Only

Use numerals to express money, decimals, percentages, chapters, pages, time, telephone numbers, dates, identification numbers, zip codes, addresses, and statistics.

$2.39	Highway 36
26.2	July 6, 1942
8 percent	44 B.C.E.
chapter 7	C.E. 79
pages 287-89	a vote of 23 to 4
4:30 P.M.	34 mph
2125 Cairn Road	1-800-555-1212

410.5 Comparing Numbers

If you are comparing two or more numbers in a sentence, write all of them as numerals or as words.

Students from 9 to 14 years old are invited.

Students from nine to fourteen years old are invited.

410.6 Numbers in Compound Modifiers

Numbers that come before a compound modifier that includes a numeral should be written as words.

We need twelve 10-foot lengths to finish the floor.

Within the last year, Don wrote twenty-five 12-page reports.

Improving Spelling

Spelling

411.1 — *i before e*

Write *i* before *e* except after *c,* or when sounded like *a* as in *neighbor* and *weigh.*

Exceptions to the Rule: *counterfeit, either, financier, foreign, height, heir, leisure, neither, seize, sheik, species, their, weird.*

Note: Eight of the exceptions are in this sentence:

Neither sheik dared leisurely seize either weird species of financiers.

411.2 — Silent *e*

If a word ends with a silent *e,* drop the *e* before adding a suffix that begins with a vowel.

state	stating	statement
like	liking	likeness
use	using	useful
nine	ninety	nineteen

Note: You do not drop the *e* when the suffix begins with a consonant. Exceptions include *truly, argument,* and *ninth.*

411.3 — Words Ending in *y*

When *y* is the last letter in a word and the *y* comes just after a consonant, change the *y* to *i* before adding any suffix except those beginning with *i.*

fly	flies	flying
hurry	hurried	hurrying
lady	ladies	
happy	happiness	
beauty	beautiful	

When forming the plural of a word that ends with a *y* that comes just after a vowel, add *s.*

toy	toys
play	plays
monkey	monkeys

411.4 — Consonant Ending

When a one-syllable word ends in a consonant (*bat*) preceded by one vowel (*ba̱t*), double the final consonant before adding a suffix that begins with a vowel (*batt̲ing*).

sum	summary
god	goddess

When a multi-syllable word ends in a consonant (*contro̲l*) preceded by one vowel (*contro̲l*), the accent is on the last syllable (*control*), and the suffix begins with a vowel (*ing*)— the same rule holds true: double the final consonant (*contro̲lling*).

prefer	preferred
begin	beginning

Yellow Pages Guide to Improved Spelling

Be patient. Learning to become a good speller takes time.

Check your spelling by using a dictionary or list of commonly misspelled words (like the list that follows).

Learn the correct pronunciation of each word you are trying to spell. Knowing the correct pronunciation of a word will help you remember how it's spelled.

Look up the meaning of each word as you are checking the dictionary for pronunciation. (Knowing how to spell a word is of little use if you don't know what it means.)

Practice spelling the word before you close the dictionary. Look away from the page and try to see the word in your mind's eye. Write the word on a piece of paper. Check the spelling in the dictionary and repeat the process until you are able to spell the word correctly.

Keep a list of the words that you misspell.

Write often. As noted educator Frank Smith said, "There is little point in learning to spell if you have little intention of writing."

A

ab-bre-vi-ate
a-board
a-bout
a-bove
ab-sence
ab-sent
ab-so-lute (-ly)
a-bun-dance
ac-cel-er-ate
ac-ci-dent
ac-ci-den-tal (-ly)
ac-com-pa-ny
ac-com-plice
ac-com-plish
ac-cord-ing

ac-count
ac-cu-rate
ac-cus-tom (ed)
ache
a-chieve (-ment)
a-cre
a-cross
ac-tu-al
a-dapt
ad-di-tion (-al)
ad-dress
ad-e-quate
ad-just (-ment)
ad-mire
ad-ven-ture
ad-ver-tise (-ment)
ad-ver-tis-ing
a-fraid

af-ter
af-ter-noon
af-ter-ward
a-gain
a-gainst
a-gree-a-ble
a-gree (-ment)
ah
aid
airy
aisle
a-larm
al-co-hol
a-like
a-live
al-ley
al-low-ance
all right

al-most
al-ready
al-though
al-to-geth-er
a-lu-mi-num
al-ways
am-a-teur
am-bu-lance
a-mend-ment
a-mong
a-mount
an-a-lyze
an-cient
an-gel
an-ger
an-gle
an-gry
an-i-mal

an-ni-ver-sa-ry
an-nounce
an-noy-ance
an-nu-al
a-non-y-mous
an-oth-er
an-swer
ant-arc-tic
an-tic-i-pate
anx-i-ety
anx-ious
any-body
any-how
any-one
any-thing
any-way
any-where
a-part-ment
a-piece
a-pol-o-gize
ap-par-ent (-ly)
ap-peal
ap-pear-ance
ap-pe-tite
ap-pli-ance
ap-pli-ca-tion
ap-point-ment
ap-pre-ci-ate
ap-proach
ap-pro-pri-ate
ap-prov-al
ap-prox-i-mate
ar-chi-tect
arc-tic
aren't
ar-gu-ment
a-rith-me-tic
a-round
a-rouse
ar-range (-ment)
ar-riv-al
ar-ti-cle

ar-ti-fi-cial
a-sleep
as-sas-sin
as-sign (-ment)
as-sis-tance
as-so-ci-ate
as-so-ci-a-tion
as-sume
ath-lete
ath-let-ic
at-tach
at-tack (ed)
at-tempt
at-ten-dance
at-ten-tion
at-ti-tude
at-tor-ney
at-trac-tive
au-di-ence
Au-gust
au-thor
au-thor-i-ty
au-to-mo-bile
au-tumn
a-vail-a-ble
av-e-nue
av-er-age
aw-ful (-ly)
awk-ward

bag-gage
bak-ing
bal-ance
bal-loon
bal-lot
ba-nan-a
ban-dage
bank-rupt
bar-ber

bar-gain
bar-rel
base-ment
ba-sis
bas-ket
bat-te-ry
beau-ti-ful
beau-ty
be-cause
be-come
be-com-ing
be-fore
be-gan
beg-gar
be-gin-ning
be-have
be-hav-ior
be-ing
be-lief
be-lieve
be-long
be-neath
ben-e-fit (-ed)
be-tween
bi-cy-cle
bis-cuit
black-board
blan-ket
bliz-zard
both-er
bot-tle
bot-tom
bough
bought
bounce
bound-a-ry
break-fast
breast
breath (n.)
breathe (v.)
breeze
bridge

brief
bright
bril-liant
broth-er
brought
bruise
bub-ble
buck-et
buck-le
bud-get
build-ing
bul-le-tin
buoy-ant
bu-reau
bur-glar
bury
busi-ness
busy
but-ton

cab-bage
caf-e-te-ria
cal-en-dar
cam-paign
ca-nal
can-cel (ed)
can-di-date
can-dle
can-is-ter
can-non
can-not
ca-noe
can't
can-yon
ca-pac-i-ty
cap-tain
car-bu-re-tor
card-board
ca-reer

care-ful
care-less
car-pen-ter
car-riage
car-rot
cash-ier
cas-se-role
cas-u-al-ty
cat-a-log
ca-tas-tro-phe
catch-er
cat-er-pil-lar
cat-sup
ceil-ing
cel-e-bra-tion
cem-e-ter-y
cen-sus
cen-tu-ry
cer-tain (-ly)
cer-tif-i-cate
chal-lenge
cham-pi-on
change-a-ble
char-ac-ter (-is-tic)
chief
chil-dren
chim-ney
choc-o-late
choice
cho-rus
cir-cum-stance
cit-i-zen
civ-i-li-za-tion
class-mates
class-room
cli-mate
climb
clos-et
cloth-ing
coach
co-coa
co-coon

cof-fee
col-lar
col-lege
colo-nel
col-or
co-los-sal
col-umn
com-e-dy
com-ing
com-mer-cial
com-mis-sion
com-mit
com-mit-ment
com-mit-ted
com-mit-tee
com-mu-ni-cate
com-mu-ni-ty
com-pan-y
com-par-i-son
com-pe-ti-tion
com-pet-i-tive (-ly)
com-plain
com-plete (-ly)
com-plex-ion
com-pro-mise
con-ceive
con-cern-ing
con-cert
con-ces-sion
con-crete
con-demn
con-di-tion
con-duc-tor
con-fer-ence
con-fi-dence
con-grat-u-late
con-nect
con-science
con-scious
con-ser-va-tive
con-sti-tu-tion
con-tin-ue

con-tin-u-ous
con-trol
con-tro-ver-sy
con-ve-nience
con-vince
cool-ly
co-op-er-ate
cor-po-ra-tion
cor-re-spond
cough
couldn't
coun-ter
coun-ter-feit
coun-try
coun-ty
cour-age
cou-ra-geous
court
cour-te-ous
cour-te-sy
cous-in
cov-er-age
co-zy
crack-er
crank-y
crawl
cred-i-tor
cried
crit-i-cize
cru-el
crumb
crum-ble
cup-board
cu-ri-os-i-ty
cu-ri-ous
cur-rent
cus-tom
cus-tom-er
cyl-in-der

dai-ly
dair-y
dam-age
dan-ger (-ous)
daugh-ter
dealt
de-ceive
de-cided
de-ci-sion
dec-la-ra-tion
dec-o-rate
de-fense
def-i-nite (-ly)
def-i-ni-tion
de-li-cious
de-pen-dent
de-pot
de-scribe
de-scrip-tion
de-sert
de-serve
de-sign
de-sir-a-ble
de-spair
des-sert
de-te-ri-o-rate
de-ter-mine
de-vel-op (-ment)
de-vice
de-vise
di-a-mond
di-a-phragm
di-a-ry
dic-tio-nar-y
dif-fer-ence
dif-fer-ent
dif-fi-cul-ty
din-ing
di-plo-ma

di-rec-tor
dis-agree-a-ble
dis-ap-pear
dis-ap-point
dis-ap-prove
dis-as-trous
dis-ci-pline
dis-cov-er
dis-cuss
dis-cus-sion
dis-ease
dis-sat-is-fied
dis-tin-guish
dis-trib-ute
di-vide
di-vine
di-vis-i-ble
di-vi-sion
doc-tor
does-n't
dol-lar
dor-mi-to-ry
doubt
dough
du-al
du-pli-cate

ea-ger (-ly)
e-con-o-my
edge
e-di-tion
ef-fi-cien-cy
eight
eighth
ei-ther
e-lab-o-rate
e-lec-tric-i-ty
el-e-phant
el-i-gi-ble

el-lipse
em-bar-rass
e-mer-gen-cy
em-pha-size
em-ploy-ee
em-ploy-ment
en-close
en-cour-age
en-gi-neer
e-nor-mous
e-nough
en-ter-tain
en-thu-si-as-tic
en-tire-ly
en-trance
en-vel-op (v.)
en-ve-lope (n.)
en-vi-ron-ment
e-quip-ment
e-quipped
e-quiv-a-lent
es-cape
es-pe-cial-ly
es-sen-tial
es-tab-lish
ev-ery
ev-i-dence
ex-ag-ger-ate
ex-ceed
ex-cel-lent
ex-cept
ex-cep-tion-al (-ly)
ex-cite
ex-er-cise
ex-haust (-ed)
ex-hi-bi-tion
ex-is-tence
ex-pect
ex-pen-sive
ex-pe-ri-ence
ex-plain
ex-pla-na-tion

ex-pres-sion
ex-ten-sion
ex-tinct
ex-traor-di-nar-y
ex-treme (-ly)

fa-cil-i-ties
fa-mil-iar
fam-i-ly
fa-mous
fas-ci-nate
fash-ion
fa-tigue (d)
fau-cet
fa-vor-ite
fea-ture
Feb-ru-ar-y
fed-er-al
fer-tile
field
fierce
fi-ery
fif-ty
fi-nal-ly
fi-nan-cial (-ly)
fo-li-age
for-ci-ble
for-eign
for-feit
for-mal (-ly)
for-mer (-ly)
forth
for-tu-nate
for-ty
for-ward
foun-tain
fourth
frag-ile
freight

friend (-ly)
fright-en
ful-fill
fun-da-men-tal
fur-ther
fur-ther-more

gad-get
gauge
gen-er-al-ly
gen-er-ous
ge-nius
gen-tle
gen-u-ine
ge-og-ra-phy
ghet-to
ghost
gnaw
gov-ern-ment
gov-er-nor
grad-u-a-tion
gram-mar
grate-ful
grease
grief
gro-cery
grudge
grue-some
guar-an-tee
guard
guard-i-an
guess
guid-ance
guide
guilt-y
gym-na-si-um

H

ham-mer
hand-ker-chief
han-dle (d)
hand-some
hap-haz-ard
hap-pen
hap-pi-ness
ha-rass
hast-i-ly
hav-ing
haz-ard-ous
head-ache
height
hem-or-rhage
hes-i-tate
his-to-ry
hoarse
hol-i-day
hon-or
hop-ing
hop-ping
hor-ri-ble
hos-pi-tal
hu-mor-ous
hur-ried-ly
hy-drau-lic
hy-giene
hymn

I

i-ci-cle
i-den-ti-cal
il-leg-i-ble
il-lit-er-ate
il-lus-trate
im-ag-i-nar-y
im-ag-i-na-tive

im-ag-ine
im-i-ta-tion
im-me-di-ate (-ly)
im-mense
im-mi-grant
im-mor-tal
im-pa-tient
im-por-tance
im-pos-si-ble
im-prove-ment
in-con-ve-nience
in-cred-i-ble
in-def-i-nite-ly
in-de-pen-dence
in-de-pen-dent
in-di-vid-u-al
in-dus-tri-al
in-fe-ri-or
in-fi-nite
in-flam-ma-ble
in-flu-en-tial
in-i-tial
ini-ti-a-tion
in-no-cence
in-no-cent
in-stal-la-tion
in-stance
in-stead
in-sur-ance
in-tel-li-gence
in-ten-tion
in-ter-est-ed
in-ter-est-ing
in-ter-fere
in-ter-pret
in-ter-rupt
in-ter-view
in-ves-ti-gate
in-vi-ta-tion
ir-ri-gate
is-land
is-sue

J

jeal-ous (-y)
jew-el-ry
jour-nal
jour-ney
judg-ment
juic-y

K

kitch-en
knew
knife
knives
knock
knowl-edge
knuck-les

L

la-bel
lab-o-ra-to-ry
la-dies
lan-guage
laugh
laun-dry
law-yer
league
lec-ture
le-gal
leg-i-ble
leg-is-la-ture
lei-sure
length
li-a-ble
li-brar-y
li-cense
lieu-ten-ant

light-ning
lik-a-ble
like-ly
li-quid
lis-ten
lit-er-a-ture
liv-ing
loaves
lone-li-ness
loose
lose
los-er
los-ing
lov-a-ble
love-ly

M

ma-chin-er-y
mag-a-zine
mag-nif-i-cent
main-tain
ma-jor-i-ty
mak-ing
man-u-al
man-u-fac-ture
mar-riage
ma-te-ri-al
math-e-mat-ics
max-i-mum
may-or
meant
mea-sure
med-i-cine
me-di-um
mes-sage
mile-age
min-i-a-ture
min-i-mum
min-ute
mir-ror

mis-cel-la-neous
mis-chie-vous
mis-er-a-ble
mis-sile
mis-spell
mois-ture
mol-e-cule
mo-not-o-nous
mon-u-ment
mort-gage
moun-tain
mus-cle
mu-si-cian
mys-te-ri-ous

na-ive
nat-u-ral (-ly)
nec-es-sar-y
ne-go-ti-ate
neigh-bor (-hood)
nei-ther
nick-el
niece
nine-teen
nine-teenth
nine-ty
nois-y
no-tice-a-ble
nu-cle-ar
nui-sance

o-be-di-ence
o-bey
ob-sta-cle
oc-ca-sion
oc-ca-sion-al (-ly)

oc-cur
oc-curred
of-fense
of-fi-cial
of-ten
o-mis-sion
o-mit-ted
op-er-ate
o-pin-ion
op-po-nent
op-por-tu-ni-ty
op-po-site
or-di-nar-i-ly
o-rig-i-nal
out-ra-geous

pack-age
paid
pam-phlet
par-a-dise
par-a-graph
par-al-lel
par-a-lyze
pa-ren-the-ses
par-tial
par-tic-i-pant
par-tic-i-pate
par-tic-u-lar (-ly)
pas-ture
pa-tience
pe-cu-liar
peo-ple
per-haps
per-ma-nent
per-pen-dic-u-lar
per-sis-tent
per-son-al (-ly)
per-son-nel
per-spi-ra-tion

per-suade
phase
phy-si-cian
piece
pitch-er
planned
pla-teau
play-wright
pleas-ant
plea-sure
pneu-mo-nia
pol-i-ti-cian
pos-sess
pos-si-ble
prac-ti-cal (-ly)
prai-rie
pre-cede
pre-cious
pre-cise (-ly)
pre-ci-sion
pref-er-a-ble
pre-ferred
prej-u-dice
prep-a-ra-tion
pres-ence
pre-vi-ous
prim-i-tive
prin-ci-pal
prin-ci-ple
pris-on-er
priv-i-lege
prob-a-bly
pro-ce-dure
pro-ceed
pro-fes-sor
prom-i-nent
pro-nounce
pro-nun-ci-a-tion
pro-tein
psy-chol-o-gy
pump-kin
pure

quar-ter
ques-tion-naire
qui-et
quite
quo-tient

raise
re-al-ize
re-al-ly
re-ceipt
re-ceive
re-ceived
rec-i-pe
rec-og-nize
rec-om-mend
reign
re-lieve
re-li-gious
re-mem-ber
rep-e-ti-tion
rep-re-sen-ta-tive
res-er-voir
re-sis-tance
re-spect-ful-ly
re-spon-si-bil-i-ty
res-tau-rant
re-view
rhyme
rhythm
ri-dic-u-lous
route

safe-ty
sal-ad
sal-a-ry
sand-wich
sat-is-fac-to-ry
Sat-ur-day
scene
sce-ner-y
sched-ule
sci-ence
scis-sors
scream
screen
sea-son
sec-re-tar-y
seize
sen-si-ble
sen-tence
sep-a-rate
sev-er-al
sher-iff
shin-ing
sim-i-lar
since
sin-cere (-ly)
ski-ing
sleigh
sol-dier
sou-ve-nir
spa-ghet-ti
spe-cif-ic
sphere
sprin-kle
squeeze
squir-rel
stat-ue
stat-ure
stat-ute
stom-ach

stopped
straight
strength
stretched
study-ing
sub-tle
suc-ceed
suc-cess
suf-fi-cient
sum-ma-rize
sup-ple-ment
sup-pose
sure-ly
sur-prise
syl-la-ble
sym-pa-thy
symp-tom

tar-iff
tech-nique
tem-per-a-ture
tem-po-rar-y
ter-ri-ble
ter-ri-to-ry
thank-ful
the-ater
their
there
there-fore
thief
thor-ough (-ly)
though
through-out
tired
to-bac-co
to-geth-er
to-mor-row
tongue

touch
tour-na-ment
to-ward
trag-e-dy
trea-sur-er
tried
tries
tru-ly
Tues-day
typ-i-cal

un-con-scious
un-for-tu-nate (-ly)
u-nique
uni-ver-si-ty
un-nec-es-sary
un-til
us-a-ble
use-ful
us-ing
usu-al (-ly)
u-ten-sil

va-ca-tion
vac-u-um
val-u-a-ble
va-ri-e-ty
var-i-ous
veg-e-ta-ble
ve-hi-cle
very
vi-cin-i-ty
view
vil-lain
vi-o-lence

vis-i-ble
vis-i-tor
voice
vol-ume
vol-un-tary
vol-un-teer

wan-der
weath-er
Wednes-day
weigh
weird
wel-come
wel-fare
whale
where
wheth-er
which
whole
whol-ly
whose
width
wom-en
worth-while
wreck-age
writ-ing
writ-ten

yel-low
yes-ter-day
yield

Using the Right Word

a, an

A is used before words that begin with a consonant sound; *an* is used before words that begin with a vowel sound.

a heap, *a* cat, *an* idol, *an* elephant, *an* honor, *a* historian

419.2 **accept, except**

The verb *accept* means "to receive"; the preposition *except* means "other than."

Melissa graciously *accepted* defeat. [verb]

All the boys *except* Zach were here. [preposition]

419.3 **affect, effect**

Affect is always a verb; it means "to influence." *Effect* can be a verb, but it is most often used as a noun that means "the result."

How does population growth *affect* us?

What are the *effects* of population growth?

419.4 **allowed, aloud**

The verb *allowed* means "permitted" or "let happen"; *aloud* is an adverb that means "in a normal voice."

We weren't *allowed* to read *aloud* in the library.

419.5 **allusion, illusion**

An *allusion* is a brief reference or mention of a famous person, place, thing, or idea. An *illusion* is a false impression or idea.

As he made an *allusion* to the great magicians of the past, Houdini created the *illusion* of having sawed his assistant in half.

419.6 **a lot**

A lot is not one word, but two; it is a general descriptive phrase (meaning "plenty") that should be avoided in formal writing.

419.7 **already, all ready**

Already is an adverb that tells when. *All ready* is a phrase meaning "completely ready."

We are *already* awake and *all ready* for breakfast.

419.8 **alright, all right**

Alright is the incorrect spelling of *all right*, a phrase meaning "satisfactory" or "okay." (Please note, the following are spelled correctly: *always, altogether, already, almost.*)

420.1 altogether, all together

Altogether is always an adverb meaning "completely." *All together* is used to describe people or things that are gathered in one place at one time.

> "No," said the principal. "There is *altogether* too much goofing around whenever seventh graders have assemblies *all together*."

420.2 among, between

Among is used when speaking of more than two persons or things. *Between* is used when speaking of only two.

> The three friends talked *among* themselves as they tried to choose *between* trumpet or trombone lessons.

420.3 amount, number

Number is used when you can actually count the persons or things. *Amount* is used to describe things that you cannot count, but can measure according to their whole effect.

> In most classes, the *number* of *A*'s and *B*'s received is directly proportional to the *amount* of effort put forth.

420.4 annual, biannual, semiannual, biennial, perennial

An *annual* event happens once every year.

A *biannual* (or *semiannual*) event happens twice a year.

A *biennial* event happens every two years.

A *perennial* event happens year after year.

SCHOOL DAZE

John, I've got the projects **all together**. Now which one is yours?

I'm not **altogether** sure. See if there's one with a missing piece.

421.1 ant, aunt

Aunt is a relative. *Ant* is an insect.

My favorite *aunt* is an entomologist, a scientist who studies *ants* and other insects.

421.2 ascent, assent

Ascent is the act of rising; *assent* is agreement.

The pilot *assented* that the plane's *ascent* was unusually bumpy.

421.3 bare, bear

The adjective *bare* means "to be naked." A *bear* is a large, heavy animal with shaggy hair.

He chased the polar *bear* across the snow though his feet were *bare*.

The verb *bear* means "to put up with" or "to carry."

Dwayne could not *bear* another of his older brother's lectures.

421.4 base, bass

Base is the foundation or the lower part of something. *Bass* is a deep sound or tone.

Our speakers sit atop a *base* so solid that even the loudest *bass* tones don't rattle it.

Bass (rhymes with *mass*) is a fish.

Jim hooked a record-setting *bass,* but it got away . . . so he says.

421.5 beat, beet

The verb *beat* means "to strike, to defeat"; a *beet* is a carrot-like vegetable (often red).

After our team *beat* Tom's team four games to one, I was as red as a *beet*.

421.6 berth, birth

Berth is a space or compartment. *Birth* is the process of being born.

We pulled aside the curtain in our train *berth* to view the *birth* of a new day outside our window.

421.7 beside, besides

Beside means "by the side of." *Besides* means "in addition to."

Besides a flashlight, Kedar likes to keep his pet boa *beside* his bed at night.

421.8 billed, build

Billed means either "to be given a bill" or "to have a beak." The verb *build* means "to construct."

We asked the carpenter to *build* us a birdhouse. She *billed* us for time and materials.

421.9 blew, blue

Blew is the past tense of "blow." *Blue* is a color and is also used to mean "feeling low in spirits."

As the smoke *blew* through the dark *blue* room, I felt more *blue* than ever.

422.1 board, bored

A *board* is a piece of wood. *Board* also means "a group or council that helps run an organization."

The school *board* approved the purchase of 50 pine *boards*.

Bored may mean "to make a hole by drilling" or "to become weary or tired of something."

Trying to catch fish *bored* Joe, so he took a stick and *bored* a hole in his tennis shoe.

422.2 brake, break

A *brake* is a device used to stop a vehicle. *Break* means "to split, crack, or destroy."

I hope my *brakes* never *break*.

422.3 bring, take

Use *bring* when the action is moving toward the speaker; use *take* when the action is moving away from the speaker.

***Take* this toy poodle away and *bring* me a real dog.**

422.4 by, buy, bye

By is a preposition meaning "near or through." *Buy* is a verb meaning "to purchase."

***By* tomorrow I hope to *buy* tickets for the concert.**

Bye is the position of being automatically advanced to the next tournament round without playing.

Our soccer team received a *bye* because of our winning record.

422.5 can, may

Can means "able to" while *may* means "permitted to."

"*Can* I go to the library?" actually means, "Do you think my mind and body are strong enough to get me there?"

"*May* I go?" means, "Do I have your permission to go?"

422.6 cannon, canon

A *cannon* is a big gun; a *canon* is a rule or law made by an authority in a church or organization.

422.7 canvas, canvass

Canvas is a heavy cloth; *canvass* means "to go among the people asking them for votes or opinions."

422.8 capital, capitol

Capital can be either a noun, referring to a city or to money, or an adjective, meaning "major or important." *Capitol* is used only when talking about a building.

The *capitol* building is in the *capital* city for a *capital* [major] reason.

The city government contributed the *capital* [money] for the building project.

422.9 cell, sell

Cell means "a small room" or "a small unit of life that makes up all plants and animals." *Sell* is a verb meaning "to give up for a price."

423.1 | cent, sent, scent

Cent is a coin; *sent* is the past tense of the verb "send"; *scent* is an odor or smell.

> After our car hit a skunk, we *sent* our friends a postcard that said, "A single *cent* doesn't go very far, but skunk *scent* lasts forever."

423.2 | chord, cord

Chord may mean "an emotion or feeling," but it is more often used to mean "the sound of three or more musical tones played at the same time." A *cord* is a string or rope.

> The band struck a *chord* at the exact moment the mayor pulled the *cord* on the drape covering the new statue.

423.3 | chose, choose

Chose (chōz) is the past tense of the verb *choose* (chooz).

> This afternoon Mom *chose* tacos and hot sauce; this evening she will *choose* an antacid.

423.4 | coarse, course

Coarse means "rough or crude." *Course* means "a path or direction taken"; *course* also means "a class or series of studies."

> The chef teaching the cooking *course* taught her students to use *coarse* salt and freshly ground pepper in salads.

423.5 | complement, compliment

Complement means "to complete or go with." *Compliment* is an expression of admiration or praise.

> I *complimented* Aunt Athena by saying that her new hat *complemented* her coat and dress.

423.6 | continual, continuous

Continual refers to something that happens again and again; *continuous* refers to something that doesn't stop happening.

> Sunlight hits Peoria, Iowa, on a *continual* basis; but sunlight hits the earth *continuously*.

423.7 | counsel, council

When used as a noun, *counsel* means "advice"; when used as a verb, *counsel* means "to advise." *Council* refers to a group that advises.

> The student *council* asked for *counsel* from its trusted adviser.

423.8 | creak, creek

A *creak* is a squeaking sound; a *creek* is a stream.

> The old willow leaning over the *creek, creaks* in the wind.

424.1 cymbal, symbol

A *cymbal* is a metal instrument shaped like a plate. A *symbol* is something (usually visible) that stands for or represents another thing or idea (usually invisible).

The damaged *cymbal* lying on the stage was a *symbol* of the band's final concert.

424.2 dear, deer

Dear means "loved or valued"; *deer* are animals.

People who love the movie *Bambi* believe that every *deer* is *dear* to the heart.

424.3 desert, dessert

A *desert* is a barren wilderness. *Dessert* is a food served at the end of a meal.

In the *desert,* cold water is more inviting than even the richest *dessert.*

The verb *desert* means "to abandon"; the noun *desert* (pronounced like the verb) means "deserving reward or punishment."

A spy who *deserts* his country will receive his just *deserts* if he is caught.

424.4 die, dye

Die (dying) means "to stop living." *Dye* (dyeing) is used to change the color of something.

424.5 faint, feign, feint

Faint means "to be feeble, without strength." *Feign* is a verb that means "to pretend or make up." *Feint* is a noun that means "a move or activity that is pretended in order to divert attention."

The actors *feigned* a duel. One man staggered and fell in a *feint.* The audience gave *faint* applause.

424.6 farther, further

Farther is used when you are writing about a physical distance. *Further* is used when you are not referring to distances; it can also mean "additional."

Alaska reaches *farther* north than Iceland. *Further* information can be obtained at your local library.

424.7 fewer, less

Fewer refers to the number of separate units; *less* refers to bulk quantity.

I have *less* money than you have, but I have *fewer* worries.

424.8 fir, fur

Fir refers to a type of evergreen tree; *fur* is animal hair.

424.9 flair, flare

Flair means "a natural talent"; *flare* means "to light up quickly or burst out."

425.1   for, fore, four

For is a preposition meaning "because of" or "directed to"; *fore* means "earlier" or "the front." *Four* is the number 4.

The dog had stolen one of the *four* steaks Mary had grilled *for* the party and was holding the bone in his *fore*paws when she found him.

425.2   good, well

Good is an adjective; *well* is nearly always an adverb.

The strange flying machines flew *well*. (The adverb *well* modifies *flew*.)

They looked *good* as they flew overhead. (The adjective *good* modifies *they*.)

When used in writing about health, *well* is an adjective.

The pilots did not feel *well*, however, after the long, hard race.

425.3   hare, hair

Hair refers to the growth covering the head and body of animals and human beings; *hare* refers to an animal similar to a rabbit.

The *hair* on my head stood up as the *hare* darted out in front of our car.

425.4   heal, heel

Heal means "to mend or restore to health." *Heel* is the back part of a human foot.

The arrow pierced Achilles' *heel*, and the wound would not *heal*.

425.5   hear, here

You *hear* with your ears. *Here* is the opposite of *there* and means "nearby."

425.6   heard, herd

Heard is the past tense of the verb "hear"; *herd* is a group of animals.

The *herd* of grazing sheep raised their heads when they *heard* the collie barking in the distance.

SCHOOL DAZE

I don't care how **well** they perform. You're not using activity money for that!

But, Mr. McGair, a **good** Wrestlemania match will build school spirit.

426.1 heir, air

Heir is a person who inherits something; *air* is the stuff we breathe.

Will the next generation be *heir* to terminally polluted *air*?

426.2 hole, whole

A *hole* is a cavity or hollow place. *Whole* means "entire or complete."

The *hole* in the ozone layer is a serious problem requiring the attention of the *whole* world.

426.3 immigrate, emigrate

Immigrate means "to come into a new country or area." *Emigrate* means "to go out of one country to live in another."

Martin Ulferts *immigrated* to this country in 1882. He was only three years old when he *emigrated* from Germany.

426.4 imply, infer

Imply means "to suggest indirectly"; *infer* means "to draw a conclusion from facts."

A writer or speaker *implies*; a reader or listener *infers*.

426.5 it's, its

It's is the contraction of "it is." *Its* is the possessive form of "it."

It's a fact that a minnow has teeth in its throat.

426.6 knew, new

Knew is the past tense of the verb "know." *New* means "recent or modern."

If we *knew* what the future had in store, would we be less or more afraid of *new* experiences?

426.7 know, no

Know means "to understand." *No* means "the opposite of yes."

Don't you *know* that *no* always means *no*?

426.8 later, latter

Later means "after a period of time." *Latter* refers to the second of two things mentioned.

Ruth Bader Ginzburg was appointed to the Supreme Court *later* than Sandra Day O'Connor.

The *latter* was appointed by President Ronald Reagan in 1981.

426.9 lay, lie

Lay means "to place." (*Lay* is a transitive verb; that means it needs a word to complete the meaning.) *Lie* means "to recline." (*Lie* is an intransitive verb.)

Lay your sleeping bag on the floor before you lie down on it. (*Bag* completes the meaning of *lay* by answering the question *what*.)

427.1 | lead, led

Lead is a present tense verb meaning "to guide." The past tense of the verb is *led*. When the words are pronounced the same, then *lead* is the metal.

"Hey, Nat, get the *lead* out!"

"Hey, ease off! Who gave you a ticket to *lead* me around?"

427.2 | learn, teach

Learn means "to get information"; *teach* means "to give information."

What I *learn* today, I will *teach* tomorrow.

427.3 | leave, let

Leave means "to allow something to remain behind." *Let* means "to permit."

Rozi wanted to *leave* her boots at home, but Jorge wouldn't *let* her.

427.4 | like, as

Like is a preposition meaning "similar to"; *as* is a conjunction meaning "to the same degree" or "while." *Like* usually introduces a phrase; *as* usually introduces a clause.

The glider floated *like* a bird.
The glider floated *as* the pilot had hoped it would.

As we circled the airfield, we saw maintenance carts moving *like* ants below us.

427.5 | loose, lose, loss

Loose (lüs) means "free or untied"; *lose* (lüz) means "to misplace or fail to win"; *loss* means "something lost."

Even though he didn't want to *lose* the *loose* tooth, it was no big *loss*.

427.6 | made, maid

Made is the past tense of "make," which means "to create." A *maid* is a female servant; *maid* is also used to describe an unmarried girl or young woman.

The *maid* asked if our beds needed to be *made*.

427.7 | mail, male

Mail refers to letters or packages handled by the postal service. *Male* refers to the masculine sex.

427.8 | main, mane

Main refers to the principal or most important part or point. *Mane* is the long hair growing from the top or sides of the neck of certain animals such as the horse, lion, etc.

427.9 | meat, meet

Meat is food or flesh; *meet* means "to come upon or encounter."

I'd like you to *meet* the butcher who sells the leanest *meat* in town.

428.1 metal, meddle, medal, mettle

Metal is an element like iron or gold. *Meddle* means "to interfere." *Medal* is an award. *Mettle*, a noun, refers to quality of character.

> For showing his *mettle* in battle, the soldier received a shiny *medal* made of a gold-plated *metal*. Most soldiers do not *meddle* in politics.

428.2 miner, minor

A *miner* digs in the ground for valuable ore. A *minor* is a person who is not legally an adult. A *minor* problem is one of no great importance.

> The use of *minors* as *miners* is no *minor* problem.

428.3 moral, morale

Moral relates to what is right or wrong or to the lesson to be drawn from a story. *Morale* refers to a person's attitude or mental condition.

> The *moral* of this story is "Everybody loves a winner."

> After the unexpected win at football, *morale* was high throughout the town.

428.4 morning, mourning

Morning refers to the first part of the day before noon; *mourning* means "showing sorrow."

> Abby was *mourning* her test grades all *morning*.

428.5 oar, or, ore

An *oar* is a paddle used in rowing or steering a boat. *Or* is a conjunction indicating choice. *Ore* refers to a mineral made up of several different kinds of material, as in iron ore.

428.6 pain, pane

Pain is the feeling of being hurt. *Pane* is a section or part of something, as in a framed section of glass in a window or door.

428.7 pair, pare, pear

A *pair* is a couple (two); *pare* is a verb meaning "to peel"; *pear* is the fruit.

428.8 past, passed

Passed is always a verb. *Past* can be used as a noun, as an adjective, or as a preposition.

> A motorcycle *passed* my 'Vette. [verb] The old man won't forget the *past*. [noun] I'm sorry, but I'd rather not talk about my *past* life. [adjective] Old Blue walked *past* the cat and never saw it. [preposition]

428.9 peace, piece

Peace means "harmony or freedom from war." *Piece* is a part or fragment of something.

> Someone once observed that *peace* is not a condition, but a process—a process of building goodwill one *piece* at a time.

429.1 — **personal, personnel**

Personal means "private." *Personnel* are people working at a job.

429.2 — **plain, plane**

Plain means "an area of land that is flat or level"; it also means "clearly seen or clearly understood."

It's *plain* to see why the early settlers had trouble crossing the Great *Plains*.

Plane means "flat, level, and even"; it is also a tool used to smooth the surface of wood.

I used a *plane* to make the board *plane* and smooth.

429.3 — **pore, pour, poor**

A *pore* is an opening in the skin. *Pour* means "to cause a constant flow or stream." *Poor* means "needy."

Pour a bowl of water for the *poor* mutt. Dogs perspire through the *pores* on their noses.

429.4 — **principal, principle**

As an adjective, *principal* means "primary." As a noun, it can mean "a school administrator" or "a sum of money." *Principle* means "idea or doctrine."

His *principal* gripe is lack of freedom.

"Hey, Charlie, I hear the *principal* chewed you out!"

After 20 years, the amount of interest was higher than the *principal*.

The *principle* of freedom is based on the *principle* of self-discipline.

429.5 — **quiet, quit, quite**

Quiet is the opposite of "noisy." *Quit* means "to stop." *Quite* means "completely or entirely."

I *quit* mowing, even though I wasn't *quite* finished, so the neighborhood could *quiet* down.

SCHOOL DAZE

At first Mrs. Warren was really **quiet**.

She couldn't **quit** looking at my project. Finally, she said, "Gloria, I've never seen sardines used in **quite** that way before."

430.1 raise, rays, raze

Raise is a verb meaning "to lift or elevate." *Rays* are thin lines or beams, as in rays of sunlight. *Raze* is a verb that means "to tear down completely."

As I *raised* the shade, bright *rays* of sunlight streamed into the room.

Across the street, I could see the old theater that will soon be *razed* to make room for a parking lot.

430.2 real, very, really

Do not use *real* in place of the adverbs *very* or *really*.

Pimples are *very* (not *real*) embarrassing.

Her nose is *really* (not *real*) small.

430.3 red, read

Red is a color; *read* is a verb meaning "to understand the meaning of written words and symbols."

430.4 right, write, rite

Right means "correct or proper"; it also refers to anything that a person has a legal claim to, as in "copyright." *Write* means "to record in print." *Rite* is a ritual or ceremonial act.

Did you *write* that it is the *right* of the referee to perform the *rite* of tossing a coin before each game?

430.5 scene, seen

Scene refers to the setting or location where something happens; it also means "sight or spectacle." *Seen* is a form of the verb "see."

An actor likes to be *seen* making a *scene*.

430.6 seam, seem

Seam is a line formed by connecting two pieces of material. *Seem* means "to appear to exist."

It *seems* as though every Thanksgiving I stuff myself so much that my *seams* threaten to burst.

430.7 sew, so, sow

Sew is a verb meaning "to stitch"; *so* is a conjunction meaning "in order that." The verb *sow* means "to plant."

430.8 sight, cite, site

Sight means "the act of seeing" or "something that is seen." *Cite* means "to quote or refer to." A *site* is a location or position.

The Alamo at night was a *sight* worth the trip. I was also able to *cite* my visit to this historical *site* in my history paper.

430.9 sit, set

Sit means "to put the body in a seated position." *Set* means "to place."

How can you just *sit* there and watch as I *set* up all these chairs?

431.1 | sole, soul

Sole means "single, only one"; sole also refers to the bottom surface of a foot or shoe. *Soul* refers to the spiritual part of a person.

Peoples' *soles* develop blisters on a two-mile hike while their *souls* walk on eternally.

431.2 | some, sum

Some means "a certain unknown number or part." *Sum* means "an amount."

The total *sum* was stolen by *some* thieves.

431.3 | sore, soar

Sore means "painful"; to *soar* means "to rise or fly high into the air."

Craning to watch the eagle *soar* overhead, our necks soon grew *sore*.

431.4 | stationary, stationery

Stationary means "not movable"; *stationery* is the paper and envelopes used to write letters.

431.5 | steal, steel

Steal means "to take something without permission"; *steel* is a metal.

Early ironmakers had to *steal* recipes for producing *steel*.

431.6 | than, then

Than is used in a comparison; *then* tells when.

He cried and said that his big brother was bigger *than* my big brother. *Then* I cried.

431.7 | their, there, they're

Their is a possessive pronoun, one that shows ownership. *There* is a pronoun used to point out location. *They're* is the contraction for "they are."

They're upset because *their* son dumped garbage over *there*.

431.8 | threw, through

Threw is the past tense of "throw." *Through* means "passing from one side of something to the other" or "a period of time."

The ball went *through* the strike zone. *Through* his long career in baseball, Nolan Ryan *threw* more strikeouts (5,715) than any other pitcher in history.

431.9 | to, too, two

To is the preposition that can mean "in the direction of." (*To* also is used to form an infinitive.) *Too* is an adverb meaning "very or excessive." (*Too* is often used to mean "also.") *Two* is the number 2.

Only *two* of Columbus's first three ships returned *to* Spain from the New World.

Columbus was *too* restless *to* stay there long.

432.1 vain, vane, vein

Vain means "worthless." It may also mean "thinking too highly of one's self; stuck-up." *Vane* is a flat piece of material set up to show which way the wind blows. *Vein* refers to a blood vessel or a mineral deposit.

The weather *vane* indicates the direction of wind; the blood *vein* determines the direction of flowing blood; the *vain* mind moves in no particular direction and thinks only about itself.

432.2 vary, very

Vary is a verb that means "to change."

The weather can *vary* from snow to sleet to sunshine in a single day.

Very can be an adjective meaning "in the fullest sense" or "complete."

Garon's story was the *very* opposite of the truth.

Very can also be an adverb meaning "extremely."

The story was *very* interesting.

432.3 waist, waste

Waist is the part of the body just above the hips. The verb *waste* means "to wear away, decay"; the noun *waste* refers to material that is unused or useless.

432.4 wait, weight

Wait means "to stay somewhere expecting something." *Weight* is the measure of heaviness.

432.5 ware, wear, where

Ware means "a product that is sold"; *wear* means "to have on or to carry on one's body"; *where* asks the question "in what place or in what situation?"

Where can you buy the best cooking *ware* and the best rain gear to *wear* on a camp-out?

432.6 way, weigh

Way means "path or route." *Weigh* means "to measure weight."

What is the correct *way* to *weigh* liquid medicines?

432.7 weather, whether

Weather refers to the condition of the atmosphere. *Whether* refers to a possibility.

The *weather* will determine *whether* I go fishing.

432.8 week, weak

A *week* is a period of seven days; *weak* means "not strong."

432.9 which, witch

Which is a pronoun used to refer to or point out something. A *witch* is a woman believed to have supernatural powers.

Which of the women accused of being *witches* in Salem in the 1600s were actually guilty of any crime?

433.1 | who, which, that

Who is used to refer to people. *Which* refers to animals and non-living things but never to people. *That* can refer to people, animals, or things.

Who said you could order pizza, which is classified by some as junk food, for dinner?

It was the new baby-sitter *that* you hired.

433.2 | who, whom

Who is used as the subject in a sentence; *whom* is used as the object of a preposition or as a direct object.

Who ordered this pizza? The pizza was ordered by *whom*?

Note: To test for *who/whom,* arrange the parts of the clause in a subject-verb-object order. (*Who* works as the subject, *whom* as the object.)

433.3 | who's, whose

Who's is the contraction for "who is." *Whose* is a possessive pronoun, one that shows ownership.

Who's the writer *whose* books for young readers have sold more copies than any other U.S. author? (Judy Blume)

433.4 | wood, would

Wood is the material that trees are made of; *would* is a form of the verb "will."

Sequoia trees live practically forever, but *would* you believe that the *wood* from these giants is practically useless? (It's too brittle.)

433.5 | your, you're

Your is a possessive pronoun, one that shows ownership. *You're* is the contraction for "you are."

SCHOOL DAZE

David, **you** know **you're** supposed to be doing **your** homework.

I am, Mom. I'm doing firsthand research on energy conservation.

Understanding Sentences

Sentence

434.1 — Sentence

A sentence is made up of one or more words that express a complete thought. A sentence begins with a capital letter; it ends with a period, a question mark, or an exclamation point.

This book should help you write. It explains many things.

How do you plan to use it? I hope you find it helpful!

Composing Sentences

For more information on sentences, turn to pages 85-92.

PARTS OF A SENTENCE

434.2 — Subject and Predicate

A sentence must have a subject and predicate in order to express a complete thought. Either the subject or the predicate (or both) may not be stated, but both must be clearly understood.

[*You*] Get involved!
[*You* is the understood subject.]

Who needs your help?
Wildlife. [*do*].
[*Do* is the understood predicate.]

What do many animals face?
[*They face*] Extinction. [*They* is the understood subject, and *face* is the understood predicate.]

434.3 — Subject

A subject is the part of a sentence that is doing something or about which something is said.

***Humans* have caused 75 percent of the extinctions that have occurred in the last 500 years.**

434.4 — Simple Subject

The simple subject is the subject without the words that describe or modify it.

An animal *species* becomes extinct when the last of its kind dies.

435.1 — Complete Subject

The complete subject is the simple subject and all the words that modify it.

An animal species becomes extinct when the last of its kind dies.

435.2 — Compound Subject

A compound subject has two or more simple subjects.

Elephants, tigers, and *lions* have been killed in great numbers.

435.3 — Predicate

The predicate is the part of the sentence that says something about the subject.

Hunting *has reduced the tiger population significantly in India.*

435.4 — Simple Predicate

The simple predicate is the predicate (verb) without the words that describe or modify it.

Before 1990, about 100,000 African elephants *were killed* every year for their ivory tusks.

435.5 — Complete Predicate

The complete predicate is the simple predicate with all the words that modify or describe it.

Before 1990, about 100,000 African elephants *were killed every year for their ivory tusks.*

435.6 — Compound Predicate

A compound predicate is composed of two or more simple predicates.

In 1990 the countries of the world *met* and *banned* the sale of ivory.

435.7 — Compound Subject and Predicate

A sentence may have a compound subject and a compound predicate.

Public *awareness* and new *laws* can *protect* and *save* endangered species.

Using Subjects and Verbs

For more information on how subjects and verbs work together in a sentence, see pages 88-89.

435.8 — Direct Object

The **direct object** is the noun or pronoun that receives the action of the predicate—*directly.* (The direct object answers the question *what* or *whom.*)

Many smaller and less well-known animals need *friends* who will speak up for them.

The direct object may be compound.

We all need *animals, plants, wetlands, deserts, rain forests,* and *woodlands* to survive on this planet.

436.1 | Indirect Object

An **indirect object** is the noun or pronoun that receives the action of the predicate—*indirectly*. An indirect object names the person *to whom* or *for whom* something is done.

> **I gave the *class* my report on earthquakes.** [*Class* is the indirect object because it says to whom the report was given.]

When the indirect object follows a preposition, it becomes the object of the preposition and is no longer considered an indirect object.

> **I gave a report to the *class*.** [*Class* is the object of the preposition *to*.]

> For additional examples and more information on direct and indirect objects, see 450.1.

436.2 | Modifier

A modifier is a word or a group of words that changes or adds to the meaning of another word. (See page 136.)

CLAUSES

A clause is a group of related words that has both a subject and a predicate.

436.3 | Independent and Dependent Clauses

An independent clause presents a complete thought and can stand as a sentence; a dependent clause does not present a complete thought and cannot stand as a sentence.

In the following sentences, the dependent clauses are in red and the independent clauses are in boldface.

> If this ancient oak tree were cut down, **it might affect more than 200 different species.**

> **A whole chain of plants and animals is affected** when one species dies out completely.

SCHOOL DAZE

Boy, are you guys in for a real blockbuster next hour!

Ya . . . Mr. Runge is showing a movie called *A Day in the Life of a Dependent Clause.*

PHRASES

437.1 | Phrase

A phrase is a group of related words that lacks either a subject or a predicate (or both).

has nothing on it
[The predicate lacks a subject.]

this guy's desk
[The subject lacks a predicate.]

except two dead plants
[The phrase lacks both a subject and a predicate.]

This guy's desk has nothing on it except two dead plants.
[Together, the three phrases form a complete thought.]

437.2 | Types of Phrases

Phrases usually take their names from the main words that introduce them (prepositional phrase, verb phrase, etc.). They are also named for the function they serve in a sentence (adverb phrase, adjective phrase).

The ancient oak tree
[noun phrase]

with crooked old limbs
[prepositional phrase]

has stood its guard,
[verb phrase]

very stubbornly,
[adverb phrase]

protecting the little house.
[verbal phrase]

TYPES OF SENTENCES

437.3 | Simple Sentence

A simple sentence is a sentence with only one independent clause (one complete thought). It may have either a simple subject or a compound subject. It may also have either a simple predicate or a compound predicate.

My back aches.
[simple subject; simple predicate]

My muscles and my eyes hurt.
[compound subject; simple predicate]

My *face* and *hair look* and *feel* terrible.
[compound subject; compound predicate]

A simple sentence may also contain one or more phrases, but no dependent clauses.

I must be getting a case of the flu.
[simple subject: *I;*
simple predicate: *must be getting;*
phrase: *a case of the flu*]

437.4 | Compound Sentence

A compound sentence is made up of two or more simple sentences (also called independent clauses) that are joined by a coordinate conjunction, punctuation, or both.

I try to avoid illness, but the flu bug always finds me.

I drink plenty of liquids; I get plenty of sleep.

438.1 Complex Sentence

A complex sentence contains one independent clause (in **boldface**) and one or more dependent clauses (in red).

Even though I feel down, I plan to carry on. [dependent clause followed by independent clause]

It isn't easy, though, when my nose runs until it turns red. [independent clause followed by two dependent clauses]

438.2 Compound-Complex Sentence

A compound-complex sentence contains two or more independent clauses (in **boldface**) and one or more dependent clauses (in red).

The Statue of Liberty was sculpted by Frédéric-Auguste Bartholdi, but the internal framework was designed by Alexandre-Gustave Eiffel, who later designed the Eiffel Tower in Paris.

Effective Sentences

For more on writing effective sentences, turn to pages 85-92.

KINDS OF SENTENCES

438.3 Declarative Sentence

A declarative sentence makes a statement. It tells something about a person, a place, a thing, or an idea.

The Statue of Liberty is a grand old monument that stands in New York Harbor as a symbol of our freedom.

438.4 Interrogative Sentence

An interrogative sentence asks a question.

Could you tell me Miss Liberty's measurements?

438.5 Imperative Sentence

An imperative sentence gives a command. It often contains an understood subject (you).

Check out these statistics.

438.6 Exclamatory Sentence

An exclamatory sentence communicates strong emotion or surprise.

Miss Liberty weighs more than 200 tons and is 300 feet tall! That's big!

Understanding Our Language

Noun

A **noun** is a word used as the name of something: a person, a place, a thing, or an idea.

John Ulferts, uncle
Mississippi, river
"Star-Spangled Banner," song
Labor Day, holiday

KINDS OF NOUNS

439.1 — Proper Noun

A **proper noun** is the name of a specific person, place, thing, or idea. Proper nouns are capitalized.

Brett Favre, *Maniac McGee*,
Rock and Roll Hall of Fame,
Cobblestone Publishing, Sunday

439.2 — Common Noun

A **common noun** is any noun that does not name a specific person, place, thing, or idea. Common nouns are not capitalized.

child, country, rainbow, winter,
blockhead, happiness, north

439.3 — Concrete Noun

A **concrete noun** names a thing that is physical (can be touched or seen). Concrete nouns can be either proper or common.

space shuttle, *Super Nintendo*

439.4 — Abstract Noun

An **abstract noun** names something you can think about but cannot see or touch. Abstract nouns can be either common or proper.

Christianity, Judaism, poverty,
satisfaction, illness, love

439.5 — Collective Noun

A **collective noun** names a group or *collection* of persons, animals, places, or things.

PERSONS ... tribe, congregation,
family, class, team

ANIMALS ... flock, herd, gaggle,
clutch, litter

THINGS ... batch, cluster, bunch

> Use specific nouns when you write—they add color and clarity. See page 135 for more information.

NUMBER OF NOUNS

Nouns are classified according to their number. The number of a noun tells us whether the noun is singular or plural.

440.1 — Singular Noun

A **singular noun** names one person, place, thing, or idea.

> boy, group, audience, stage,
> rock concert, hope

440.2 — Plural Noun

A **plural noun** names more than one person, place, thing, or idea.

> boys, groups, audiences, stages,
> rock concerts, hopes

For information on how to create the plural form of a number of special words, turn to 408.1-409.3.

440.3 — Compound Noun

A **compound noun** is made up of two or more words.

> **football**
> [written as one word]
>
> **high school**
> [written as two words]
>
> **brother-in-law**
> [written as a hyphenated word]

GENDER OF NOUNS

Nouns have **gender;** that is, they are grouped according to sex: *feminine, masculine, neuter,* and *indefinite.*

Turn to page 245 for more information on using gender properly when writing.

440.4 — Types of Gender

Feminine .... mother, sister, women, cow, hen [female]

Masculine .... father, men, bull, rooster [male]

Neuter ... tree, cobweb, closet [without sex]

Indefinite .... president, duckling, doctor, lawyer, assistant [male or female]

USES OF NOUNS

Nouns are classified according to their use in a sentence.

440.5 — Subject Nouns

A noun becomes the subject of a sentence when it does something or is being talked about.

> The guidance *counselor* looked the eighth-grade student in the eye and warned him, "The high-school *principal* won't allow you to take more than one study hall."

441.1 Predicate Nouns

A noun is considered a **predicate noun** when it follows a form of the *be* verb (*is, are, was, were, been*) and repeats or renames the subject. In the examples below, *place* renames *study hall*, and *waste* renames *hours*.

> "A *study hall* is a good *place* to work on your assignments, but two *hours* of study hall is a *waste* of your valuable time."

441.2 Possessive Nouns

A noun becomes a **possessive noun** when it shows possession or ownership.

> The *student's* face showed concern. "But I need an *hour's* rest every day in order to do well in my classes."

> Turn to 403.2-403.4 for more about possessive nouns.

441.3 Object Nouns

A noun becomes an **object noun** when it is used as the direct object, the indirect object, or the object of the preposition.

> "Don't worry. You'll enjoy *high school* with only one study hall."
> [*High school* is a direct object.]
> "High-school teachers give *students plenty* of *time* to work."
> [*Students* is an indirect object; *plenty* is a direct object; *time* is the object of the preposition *of.*]

Pronoun

A **pronoun** is a word used in place of a noun.

> I, you, he, she, it, we, they, his, hers, her, its, me, myself, us, yours, etc.

> Amanda tweaked *her* uncle's nose after *he* teased the kids about *their* dancing to rock "noise."

441.4 Antecedent

An **antecedent** is the noun that the pronoun refers to or replaces. All pronouns have antecedents.

> The *speaker* coughed and reached for the glass of water. When the glass reached his lips, he noticed a *fly* that was "swimming" in the water.
> [*Speaker* is the antecedent of *his* and *he*; *fly* is the antecedent of *that*.]

All pronouns must agree with their antecedents in number, person, and gender. See pages 89-90.

442.1 — Personal Pronouns

Personal pronouns take the place of nouns in a sentence; they come in many shapes and sizes.

SIMPLE .... I, you, he, she, it, we, they

COMPOUND ... myself, yourself, himself, herself, ourselves

PHRASAL .... one another, each other

NUMBER OF PRONOUNS

442.2 — Singular/Plural

Pronouns can be either singular or plural in **number.**

SINGULAR ... I, you, he, she, it

PLURAL .... we, you, they

Note: The pronouns *you, your,* and *yours* may be singular or plural.

PERSON OF A PRONOUN

The **person** of a pronoun tells us whether the pronoun is speaking, being spoken to, or being spoken about.

442.3 — First Person

A **first-person pronoun** is used in place of the name of the speaker.

I am speaking.

We are speaking.

442.4 — Second Person

A **second-person pronoun** is used to name the person or thing spoken to.

Eliza, will *you* please listen.

You dogs better stop growling and listen, too.

442.5 — Third Person

A **third-person pronoun** is used to name the person or thing spoken about.

Bill better listen if *he* ever wants to use the car again.

USES OF PRONOUNS

A pronoun can be used as a subject, an object, or to show possession.

442.6 — Subject Pronouns

A **subject pronoun** is used as the subject of a sentence (*I, you, he, she, it, we, they*).

I like myself when things go well.

A subject pronoun is also used after a form of the *be* verb (*am, is, are, was, were, being, been*) if it repeats the subject.

"It is *I,*" growled the big wolf from under Grandmother's bonnet.

"It is *he!*" shrieked Little Red as she twisted his snout into a corkscrew.

443.1 | Object Pronouns

An **object pronoun** can be used as the object of a verb or preposition (*me, you, him, her, it, us, them*).

"You saved *me!*" shouted Grandmother, as she leaped from the closet. [*Me* is the direct object of the verb *saved* because it receives the action of the verb.]

Grandmother told *us* the story of her narrow escape. [*Us* is the indirect object of the verb *told* because it indirectly receives the action of the verb.]

Is this fairy tale too scary for *you?* [*You* is the object of the preposition *for.*]

443.2 | Possessive Pronouns

A **possessive pronoun** shows possession or ownership.

my, mine, our, ours,
his, her, hers,
their, theirs,
its, your, yours

Note: You do not use an apostrophe with a personal pronoun to show possession.

To make a noun possessive, add an apostrophe. See 403.2-403.4 for more details.

Singular Pronouns			
	Subject Pronouns	Possessive Pronouns	Object Pronouns
First Person	I	my, mine	me
Second Person	you	your, yours	you
Third Person	he	his	him
	she	her, hers	her
	it	its	it

Plural Pronouns			
	Subject Pronouns	Possessive Pronouns	Object Pronouns
First Person	we	our, ours	us
Second Person	you	your, yours	you
Third Person	they	their, theirs	them

OTHER TYPES OF PRONOUNS

In addition to the commonly used personal pronouns, there are a number of other types of pronouns that you should know about. (See the chart on the next page.)

444.1 | Relative Pronouns

A **relative pronoun** is both a pronoun and a connecting word. It connects a subordinate clause to the main clause.

China is the country *that has the largest population in the world.*
[*That* relates to *country.*]

The Chinese, *who have one of the world's oldest civilizations,* have worked hard to modernize their country in little more than 20 years. [*Who* relates to *Chinese.*]

The Chinese, *who boast of having 40 cities with more than a million people each,* can also point to the fact *that every sixth person in the world is Chinese.* [*Who* relates to *Chinese* and *that* relates to *fact.*]

444.2 | Interrogative Pronouns

An **interrogative pronoun** asks a question.

Who wants to go?

Which star would you visit?

Whom would you take along for company?

Whose company could you stand for that long?

444.3 | Demonstrative Pronouns

A **demonstrative pronoun** points out or identifies a noun without naming the noun. When used together in a sentence, *this* and *that* distinguish one item from another, and *these* and *those* distinguish one group from another.

This was a great idea; *that* was a nightmare.

Caution: Do not add *here* or *there* to a demonstrative pronoun.

This here was a great idea; *that there* was a nightmare. [incorrect]

Who? Which? That?

If you have trouble figuring out which of these pronouns to use when, turn to 433.1.

444.4 | Intensive Pronouns

An **intensive pronoun** emphasizes or *intensifies* the noun or pronoun it refers to. Common intensive pronouns include *itself, myself, himself, herself,* and *yourself.*

Though the chameleon's quick-change act protects it from predators, the lizard *itself* can catch insects 10 inches away with its long, sticky tongue.

Note: The sentence would be complete without the intensive pronoun. The pronoun simply emphasizes *lizard.*

445.1 ┤ Reflexive Pronouns

A **reflexive pronoun** is a pronoun that throws the action back upon the subject of a sentence.

A chameleon protects *itself* from danger by changing colors.
[direct object]

A chameleon can give *itself* tasty meals of unsuspecting insects.
[indirect object]

I wish I could claim some of its amazing powers for *myself*.
[object of the preposition]

Note: These sentences would not be complete without the reflexive pronouns.

445.3 ┤ Indefinite Pronouns

An **indefinite pronoun** is a pronoun that does not specifically name its antecedent (the noun or pronoun it replaces).

Will *somebody* reach the stars some day? If *anybody* could travel at the speed of light (186,400 miles per second), it would still take more than four years to reach the nearest star.

See page 89 for details on using indefinite pronouns properly in a sentence.

445.2 ┤ Kinds of Pronouns

Relative
who, whose, whom, which, what, that, whoever, whomever, whatever, whichever

Interrogative
who, whose, whom, which, what

Demonstrative
this, that, these, those

Intensive and Reflexive
myself, himself, herself, itself, yourself, themselves, ourselves

Indefinite Pronouns

all	both	everything	nobody	several
another	each	few	none	some
any	each one	many	no one	somebody
anybody	either	most	nothing	someone
anyone	everybody	much	one	something
anything	everyone	neither	other	such

Verb

A **verb** is a word that shows action or existence (state of being).

> **Tornadoes** *cause* **tremendous damage.** [action]
>
> **The weather** *is* **often calm before a storm.** [existence]

TYPES OF VERBS

446.1 — Action Verb

An action verb tells what the subject is doing.

> **Natural disasters** *hit* **the globe nearly every day.**

446.2 — Linking Verb

A **linking verb** connects or *links* a subject to a noun or an adjective in the predicate.

> **I** *feel shakey* **whenever I hear about earthquakes.**
> [*Shakey* is a predicate adjective because it is linked by the verb *feel* to the subject *I*.]
>
> **There** *is* **no** *need* **to worry.**
> [*Need* is a predicate noun because it is linked by the verb *is* to the subject *there*.]

Linking Verbs

The most common linking verbs are forms of the verb *be*—**is, are, was, were, being, been, am**—and verbs such as **smell, look, taste, feel, remain, turn, appear, become, sound, seem, grow, stand.**

446.3 — Helping Verb

Helping verbs *help* to form some of the tenses and voice of the main verb. (Helping verbs are also called *auxiliary verbs*.)

> **One thing we** *do know* **is that shooting stars are really meteors that** *have burned* **up while entering the earth's atmosphere.**

Helping Verbs

The most common helping verbs are **shall, will, should, would, could, must, can, may, have, had, has, do, did,** and the forms of the verb *be*—**is, are, was, were, am, being, been.**

NUMBER OF VERBS

Verbs have **number,** which means they are singular or plural. The number of a verb depends on the number of its subject.

446.4 — Singular/Plural

A singular subject needs a **singular verb.** A plural subject needs a **plural verb.**

> **She** *wonders* **if there is life on other planets.** [singular]
>
> **They** *wonder* **if there is life on other planets.** [plural]

PERSON OF VERBS

447.1 — Point of View

Verbs will also differ in form depending upon the point of view or *person* of the pronouns being used with them:

first person (*I*)
I write [singular]
we write [plural]

second person (*you*)
you write [singular]
you write [plural]

third person (*he, she, it*)
he/she/it writes [singular]
they write [plural]

VOICE OF VERBS

The **voice** of a verb tells you whether the subject is doing the action or is receiving the action.

447.2 — Active Voice

A verb is in the **active voice** if the subject is doing the action in a sentence.

> I *dream* of going to galaxies light-years from Earth.

447.3 — Passive Voice

A verb is in the passive voice if the subject is receiving the action instead of personally doing the action.

> My daydreams *are* often *shattered* by reality.

TENSE	Active Voice		Passive Voice	
	SINGULAR	**PLURAL**	**SINGULAR**	**PLURAL**
Present Tense	I find you find he/she/it finds	we find you find they find	I am found you are found he/she/it is found	we are found you are found they are found
Past Tense	I found you found he found	we found you found they found	I was found you were found he was found	we were found you were found they were found
Future Tense	I will find you will find he will find	we will find you will find they will find	I will be found you will be found he will be found	we will be found you will be found they will be found
Present Perfect	I have found you have found he has found	we have found you have found they have found	I have been found you have been found he has been found	we have been found you have been found they have been found
Past Perfect	I had found you had found he had found	we had found you had found they had found	I had been found you had been found he had been found	we had been found you had been found they had been found
Future Perfect	I will have found you will have found he will have found	we will have found you will have found they will have found	I will have been found you will have been found he will have been found	we will have been found you will have been found they will have been found

TENSES OF VERBS

A verb has three principal parts: the ***present, past,*** and ***past participle.*** All six of the tenses are formed from these principal parts.

✦ The past and past participle of regular verbs are formed by adding *-ed* to the present form.

✦ Irregular verbs are formed with different spellings. (See the chart on page 449.)

448.1 — Present Tense

A verb is in the **present tense** when it expresses action (or existence) that is happening *now* or that happens *continually, regularly.*

The universe *is* gigantic.

It *takes* my breath away to think about it.

448.2 — Past Tense

A verb is in the **past tense** when it expresses action (or existence) that is completed at a *particular* time in the past.

Galileo, an Italian scientist, *was* the first scientist to use a telescope. This only *landed* him in hot water with the Flat Earth Society.

448.3 — Future Tense

A verb is in the **future tense** when it expresses action that *will* take place.

When *will* the universe end? What mysteries *will be solved* in the twenty-first century?

448.4 — Present Perfect Tense

A verb is in the **present perfect tense** when it expresses action that *began in the past but continues or is completed in the present.*

I *have wondered* for some time how the stars got their names. Many stars *have been named* after the gods of ancient times.

Note: To form the present perfect tense, add *has* or *have* to the past participle.

448.5 — Past Perfect Tense

A verb is in the **past perfect tense** when it expresses action that *began in the past and was completed in the past.*

I *had hoped* to see a shooting star on our camping trip.

Note: To form the past perfect tense, add *had* to the past participle.

448.6 — Future Perfect Tense

A verb is in the **future perfect tense** when it expresses action or existence that *will begin in the future and will be completed by a specific time in the future.*

By the twenty-first century, we *will have found* the answers to many of our questions.

Note: To form the future perfect tense, add *will have* to the past participle.

Common Irregular Verbs and Their Principal Parts

The principal parts of the common irregular verbs are listed below. The part used with the helping verbs *has, have,* or *had* is called the **past participle**.

PRESENT TENSE	I write.	She hides.
PAST TENSE	Earlier I wrote.	Earlier she hid.
PAST PARTICIPLE	I have written.	She has hidden.

Present Tense	Past Tense	Past Participle	Present Tense	Past Tense	Past Participle
am, be	was, were	been	lead	led	led
begin	began	begun	lie (recline)	lay	lain
bid (offer)	bid	bid	lie (deceive)	lied	lied
bid (order)	bade	bidden	raise	raised	raised
bite	bit	bitten	ride	rode	ridden
blow	blew	blown	ring	rang	rung
break	broke	broken	rise	rose	risen
bring	brought	brought	run	ran	run
burst	burst	burst	see	saw	seen
catch	caught	caught	set	set	set
come	came	come	shake	shook	shaken
dive	dived	dived	shine		
do	did	done	(polish)	shined	shined
drag	dragged	dragged	(light)	shone	shone
draw	drew	drawn	shrink	shrank	shrunk
drink	drank	drunk	sing	sang, sung	sung
drive	drove	driven	sink	sank, sunk	sunk
drown	drowned	drowned	sit	sat	sat
eat	ate	eaten	slay	slew	slain
fall	fell	fallen	speak	spoke	spoken
fight	fought	fought	spring	sprang, sprung	sprung
flee	fled	fled	steal	stole	stolen
flow	flowed	flowed	strive	strove	striven
fly	flew	flown	swear	swore	sworn
forsake	forsook	forsaken	swim	swam	swum
freeze	froze	frozen	swing	swung	swung
give	gave	given	take	took	taken
go	went	gone	tear	tore	torn
grow	grew	grown	throw	threw	thrown
hang			wake	woke, waked	woken, waked
(execute)	hanged	hanged	wear	wore	worn
(dangle)	hung	hung	weave	wove	woven
hide	hid	hidden, hid	wring	wrung	wrung
know	knew	known	write	wrote	written
lay (place)	laid	laid			

USES OF ACTION VERBS

450.1 — Transitive Verbs

Transitive verbs are verbs that transfer their action to an object. An object must receive the action of a transitive verb for the meaning of the verb to be complete.

> The earthquake *shook* San Francisco with a fury. [*Shook* transfers its action to *San Francisco*. Without *San Francisco* the meaning of the verb *shook* is incomplete.]

> San Francisco *was shaken* by the earthquake. [The subject of the sentence, *San Francisco*, receives the action of the verb, *was shaken*.]

A transitive verb throws the action directly to a **direct object** and indirectly to an **indirect object.** For a sentence to have an indirect object, it must have a direct object. A sentence can, however, have only a direct object.

Note: Direct and indirect objects are always nouns or pronouns.

> Fires destroyed *San Francisco* after the 1906 earthquake. [direct object: *San Francisco*]

> Our teacher gave *us* the *details*. [indirect object: *us*; direct object: *details*]

> See 435.8–436.1 for more about direct and indirect objects.

450.2 — Intransitive Verbs

An **intransitive verb** completes its action without an object.

> Her stomach *felt* queasy. [*Queasy* is a predicate adjective; there is no direct object.]

> She *looked* for a mint. [Again, there is no direct object. *Mint* is the object of the preposition *for*.]

450.3 — Transitive/Intransitive

Some verbs can be either **transitive** or **intransitive.**

> She *read* my note. [transitive]

> She *read* aloud. [intransitive]

SCHOOL DAZE

Who can give me an example of a **gerund** used as a subject?

Hanging upside down refreshes my brain.

VERBALS

A **verbal** is a word that is made from a verb, has the power of a verb, but acts as another part of speech. **Gerunds, participles,** and **infinitives** are verbals.

451.1 Gerund

A **gerund** is a verb form that ends in -*ing* and is used as a noun.

Worrying **is useless.**
[The noun *worrying* is the subject.]

You should stop *worrying* **about things you can't change.** [The noun *worrying* is the direct object.]

451.2 Participle

A **participle** is a verb form ending in -*ing* or -*ed*. A participle is used as an adjective.

The idea of the earth *shaking* **and** *splitting* **both fascinates and frightens me.**
[*Shaking* and *splitting* modify *earth.*]

Why doesn't this *tired* **earth just stand still?** [*Tired* modifies *earth.*]

451.3 Infinitive

An **infinitive** is a verb form introduced by *to;* it may be used as a noun, an adjective, or an adverb.

To conquer **my fears is one of my goals.**
[*To conquer* is used as a noun and is the subject of this sentence.]

In the past, I was terrified *to climb* **a mountain.**
[*To climb* is an adverb modifying the adjective *terrified.*]

Adjective

An **adjective** is a word used to describe a noun or pronoun.

Why did *ancient* **dinosaurs become** *an extinct* **species?**

Were they wiped out by *a catastrophic* **flood or** *a deadly* **epidemic?**

451.4 Articles

The **articles** *a, an,* and *the* are adjectives.

A brontosaurus was *an* **animal about 70 feet long.**

The **huge dinosaur lived on land and ate plants.**

451.5 Proper Adjective

A **proper adjective** is formed from a proper noun, and it is always capitalized.

A *Chicago* **museum is home to the skeleton of one of these ancient beasts.**
[*Chicago* functions as a proper adjective describing the noun *museum.*]

452.1 Common Adjective

A **common adjective** is any adjective that is not proper, and it is not capitalized (unless it is the first word in a sentence).

> *Ancient* mammoths were *huge, woolly* creatures whose *complete* bodies have been found *frozen* deep in the *ice* fields of Siberia.

SPECIAL KINDS OF ADJECTIVES

452.2 Demonstrative Adjective

A **demonstrative adjective** is one that points out a particular noun. *This* and *these* point out something nearby; *that* and *those* point out something at a distance.

> *This* mammoth is huge, but *that* mammoth is even bigger.

Note: When a noun does not follow *this, these, that,* or *those,* they are pronouns, not adjectives.

452.3 Compound Adjective

A **compound adjective** is made up of two or more words. (Sometimes it is hyphenated.)

> The stomachs of these *quick-frozen, fur-covered* mammoths contained the animals' last meals, perfectly preserved.

452.4 Indefinite Adjective

An **indefinite adjective** is one that gives us approximate or *indefinite* information. It does not tell *exactly* how many or how much. (See "indefinite pronouns" on page 445.)

> *Some* mammoths were heavier than today's elephants.

452.5 Predicate Adjective

A **predicate adjective** is an adjective that follows a linking verb and describes the subject.

> Mammoths were once *abundant,* but now they are *extinct.*

SCHOOL DAZE

Jerry, haven't you finished your paper yet?

No, Mrs. Wright told me to add a **few** new twists and wrinkles.

FORMS OF ADJECTIVES

453.1 Positive Form

The **positive form** describes a noun or pronoun without comparing it to anyone or anything else.

> The Eurostar is a *fast* train that runs between London and Paris.
>
> It is an *impressive* train.

453.2 Comparative Form

The **comparative form** of an adjective (*-er*) compares two persons, places, things, or ideas.

> The Eurostar is *faster* than the Orient Express.
>
> This train is *more impressive* than my commuter train.

453.3 Superlative Form

The **superlative form** (*-est*) compares three or more persons, places, things, or ideas.

> In fact, the Eurostar is the *fastest* train in Europe.
>
> It is the *most impressive* commuter train in the world.

453.4 Two-Syllable Adjective

Some two-syllable adjectives show comparisons by their *er/est* suffixes, or by modifiers like *more* and *most*.

> For example, you may say, *"clumsy, clumsier, clumsiest."*
>
> But, you may also say, *"clumsy, more clumsy, most clumsy."*

453.5 Three- (or More) Syllable Adjective

When adjectives are **three or more syllables long,** they usually require the words *more/most, less/least* to express comparison.

> *ridiculous, less ridiculous, least ridiculous*

Note: You would NOT say, "ridiculousless, ridiculousleast."

453.6 Irregular Forms

Some adjectives use completely **different words** to express comparison.

> good, better, best
>
> bad, worse, worst

Interjection

An **interjection** is a word or phrase used to express strong emotion or surprise. Punctuation (a comma or an exclamation point) is used to separate an interjection from the rest of the sentence.

> *Wow,* would you look at that!
>
> *Oh, no!* He's falling!
>
> *Whoops!* So am I!

Adverb

An **adverb** is a word used to modify a verb, an adjective, or another adverb. An adverb tells *how, when, where, why, how often,* and *how much.*

> **Dad snores *loudly.*** [*Loudly* modifies the verb *snores.*]
>
> **His snores are *really* explosive.** [*Really* modifies the adjective *explosive.*]
>
> **Dad snores *very* loudly.** [*Very* modifies the adverb *loudly.*]

454.1 — Forms of Adverbs

Adverbs, like adjectives, have three forms: **positive, comparative,** and **superlative.** (See the chart below.)

positive . . . . describes
comparative . . . . compares two things
superlative . . . . . compares three or more things

454.2 — Types of Adverbs

There are four basic types of adverbs: *time, place, manner,* and *degree.*

TIME . . . . Adverbs of time tell *when, how often,* and *how long.*
  tomorrow, often, never

PLACE . . . . Adverbs of place tell *where, to where,* or *from where.*
  there, backward, outside

MANNER . . . Adverbs of manner often end in *-ly* and tell how something is done.
  unkindly, gently, well

Note: Some adverbs can be written with or without the *-ly* ending. When in doubt, use the *-ly* form.
  slow, slowly; deep, deeply

DEGREE . . . . Adverbs of degree tell *how much* or *how little.*
  scarcely, entirely, generally

Note: Adverbs often end in *-ly,* but not *always.* Words like *very, quite,* and *always* are adverbs that modify other adverbs or adjectives.

Caution: Not all words ending in *-ly* are adverbs. "Lovely," for example, is an adjective.

Positive	Comparative	Superlative
well	better	best
badly	worse	worst
fast	faster	fastest
loudly	more loudly	most loudly
dramatically	less dramatically	least dramatically

Preposition

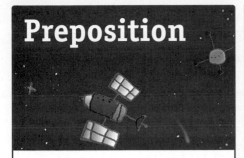

A **preposition** is a word (or group of words) that shows position, direction, or how two words or ideas are related to each other. Specifically, a preposition shows the relationship between its object and some other word in the sentence.

> The caterpillar hung *under* Natasha's nose.
>
> [*Under* shows the relationship between the verb *hung* and the object of the preposition *nose.*]

455.1 | Prepositional Phrase

A **prepositional phrase** includes the *preposition*, the *object* of the preposition, and the *modifiers* of the object.

> Natasha's friends ran *away from a big caterpillar.*
>
> [preposition: *away from;*
> object: *caterpillar;* modifier: *big*]

A prepositional phrase may function as an adjective or as an adverb.

> But Natasha *with a wiggly mustache* enjoyed the hairy critter. [The prepositional phrase, *with a wiggly mustache,* functions as an adjective and modifies *Natasha.*]

455.2 | Object of Preposition

A preposition never appears alone—it needs an object. If a word found in the list of prepositions appears in a sentence, but has no object, it is not a preposition. It is probably an adverb.

> Natasha never had a mustache *before.* [*Before* is used as an adverb in this sentence because it modifies *had,* a verb.]

455.3 | Prepositions

aboard	considering	onto
about	despite	opposite
above	down	out
according to	down from	out of
across	during	outside
across from	except	outside of
after	except for	over
against	excepting	over to
along	for	owing to
alongside	from	past
alongside of	from among	prior to
along with	from between	regarding
amid	from under	round
among	in	round about
apart from	in addition to	save
around	in behalf of	since
aside from	in front of	through
at	in place of	throughout
away from	in regard to	till
back of	in spite of	to
because of	inside	together with
before	inside of	toward
behind	instead of	under
below	into	underneath
beneath	like	until
beside	near	unto
besides	near to	up
between	of	up to
beyond	off	upon
but	on	with
by	on account of	within
by means of	on behalf of	without
concerning	on top of	

N

Conjunction

A **conjunction** connects individual words or groups of words. There are three kinds of conjunctions: *coordinating*, *correlative*, and *subordinating*.

Polluted lakes, rivers, *and* streams can be cleaned up.

[The conjunction *and* connects the word *rivers* to the word *streams*.]

456.1 | **Coordinating Conjunction**

A **coordinating conjunction** connects a word to a word, a phrase to a phrase, or a clause to a clause. The words, phrases, or clauses joined by a coordinating conjunction must be *equal* or of the *same type*.

If you want to reduce pollution, ride a bike *or* plant a tree. [Two equal phrases are connected by *or*.]

Even small things, like turning off lights you're not using *and* turning off the water while you're brushing your teeth, add up to energy savings.
[*And* connects the phrases *turning off lights you're not using* and *turning off the water while you're brushing your teeth*.]

456.2 | **Correlative Conjunction**

Correlative conjunctions are conjunctions used in pairs.

***Either* you're part of the problem, *or* you're part of the solution.**

456.3 | **Subordinating Conjunction**

A **subordinating conjunction** is a word or group of words that connects two clauses that are *not* equally important. A subordinating conjunction connects a dependent clause to an independent clause in order to complete the meaning of the dependent clause.

More people will get involved *when they realize that Earth is "Home Sweet Home."*
[The clause *when they realize that Earth is "Home Sweet Home"* is dependent. It cannot stand alone.]

456.4 | **Conjunctions**

Coordinating: and, but, or, nor, for, so, yet

Correlative: either, or; neither, nor; not only, but also; both, and; whether, or; as, so

Subordinating: after, although, as, as if, as long as, as though, because, before, if, in order that, provided that, since, so, so that, that, though, till, unless, until, when, where, whereas, while

Note: Conjunctive adverbs and relative pronouns can also connect clauses. (See pages 393 and 444.)

QUICK GUIDE

Parts of Speech

In the English language there are eight parts of speech. They help you understand words and how to use them in sentences. Every word in every sentence is a part of speech—a noun, a verb, an adjective, etc. The chart below lists the eight parts of speech.

- **NOUN:** A word that names a person, a place, a thing, or an idea

  Alex Moya   Belize   ladder   courage

- **PRONOUN:** A word used in place of a noun

  I   he   it   they   you   anybody   some

- **VERB:** A word that shows action or links a subject to another word in the sentence

  sing   shake   catch   is   are

- **ADJECTIVE:** A word that describes a noun or a pronoun

  stormy   red   rough   seven   grand

- **INTERJECTION:** A word (set off by commas or an exclamation point) that shows strong emotion

  Stop! Hey, how are you?

- **ADVERB:** A word that describes a verb, an adjective, or another adverb

  quickly   today   now   bravely   softer

- **PREPOSITION:** A word that shows position or direction or introduces a prepositional phrase

  around   up   under   over   between   to

- **CONJUNCTION:** A word that connects other words or groups of words

  and   but   or   so   because   when

Student Almanac

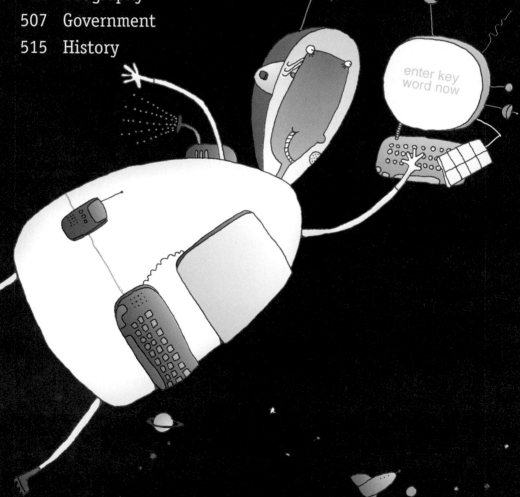

enter key
word now

Language

The language lists in this section of your handbook should be both interesting and helpful. You can look through this section when you want to work on your handwriting, when you want to explore other languages, or when you need to send a "signed" message across a noisy room.

Manual Alphabet (Sign Language)

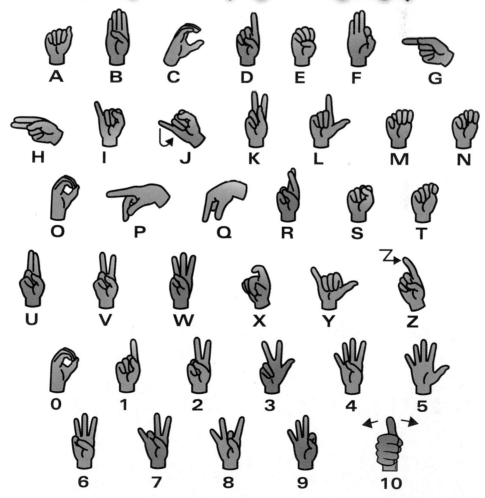

How to Write in Cuneiform

A	⠀	N	⠀
B	⠀	O	⠀
C	⠀	P	⠀
D	⠀	Q	⠀
E	⠀	R	⠀
F	⠀	S	⠀
G	⠀	T	⠀
H	⠀	U	⠀
I	⠀	V	⠀
J	⠀	W	⠀
K	⠀	X	⠀
L	⠀	Y	⠀
M	⠀	Z	⠀

Foreign Words

Language	HELLO	GOOD-BYE
Chinese (Mandarin dialect)	dzǎu	dzàihyàn
Danish	hallo	farvel
Farsi (Iran)	salaam	khoda hafez
	سلام	خدا حافظ
French	bonjour	au revoir
German	Guten Tag	Auf Wiedersehen
Hawaiian	aloha	aloha
Hebrew	shalom	shalom
Italian	buon giorno	addio
Polish	hallo	żegnam
Portuguese	alô	adeus
Russian	Здравствуйте	

pronunciation **ZDRAHST**-vooy-tyeh

До свидания
pronunciation daw svee-**DA**-nee-ya

Spanish	hola	adiós
Swahili	neno la kusalimu rafiki au mtani	kwa heri
Swedish	god dag	adjö
Tagalog (Philippines)	kumusta	paalám
Thai	sa wat dee ka	la kone na ka

Braille Alphabet and Numbers

Numbers 1–0 correspond to letters a–j: 1=a, 2=b, 3=c, 4=d, 5=e, 6=f, 7=g, 8=h, 9=i, 0=j

a b c d e f g h i j k l m n o
p q r s t u v w x y z   CAPITAL SIGN   NUMERAL SIGN

English from Around the World

Words from many languages have been added to English. This chart shows you some of these words. The chart on the next two pages shows you even more about language from around the world.

Old English	man, woman, morning, night, day, month, year, cat, dog, house, red, yellow, at, in, by, from, cow, calf, pig
Scandinavian	they, them, their, knife, sky, ski, happy, scare, egg
French	constitution, city, state, nation, congress, mayor, poetry, art, court, medicine, dance, fashion, tailor, physician, beef, veal, pork
Greek	paragraph, school, alphabet, stomach
Latin	camp, wine, paper, perfume, umbrella, mile, senator, legislator
Native American	canoe, toboggan, opossum, moose, chipmunk, pecan, hickory, igloo, kayak
Spanish	cigar, mosquito, tornado, rodeo, canyon
Italian	spaghetti, pizza, macaroni, balcony, bank, piano, balloon, tarantula, volcano
Dutch	cookie, coleslaw, deck, dock, boss, pump
German	hamburger, kindergarten, pretzel, book
Asian	pepper, panther, shampoo, silk, tea, jungle, ketchup
Australian	kangaroo, boomerang, koala, outback
African	chimpanzee, banana, banjo, okra
Middle Eastern	candy, cotton, coffee, sugar, spinach, tiger

Language Families

Language families are groups of languages. Within a specific group, the languages are related because they all developed from the same language. English belongs to the **Indo-European** language family, as do many other languages. (See the chart below.)

The map shows all of the major language families plus the main languages in each family. (See the key on the next page.)

THE INDO-EUROPEAN FAMILY TODAY

Albanian

Armenian

Balto-Slavic —
- Bulgarian
- Czech
- Latvian
- Lithuanian
- Polish
- Russian
- Serbo-Croatian
- Slovak
- Slovenian
- Ukrainian

Celtic —
- Breton
- Irish (Celtic)
- Scots (Celtic)
- Welsh

Germanic —
- Dutch
- English
- German
- Scandinavian —
  - Danish
  - Icelandic
  - Norwegian
  - Swedish

Greek

Indo-Iranian —
- Bengali
- Farsi
- Hindi
- Pashto
- Urdu

Romance —
- French
- Italian
- Portuguese
- Romanian
- Spanish

MAJOR LANGUAGE FAMILIES

- Indo-European
- Sino-Tibetan
- Afro-Asian
- Uralic and Altaic
- Japanese and Korean
- Dravidian
- Malayo-Polynesian
- Mon-Khmer
- Niger-Kordofanian
- Nilo-Saharan
- Khoisan
- All others

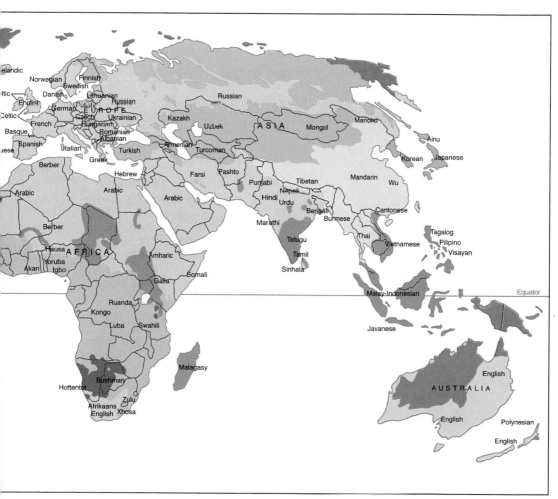

Cursive Alphabet

Aa Bb Cc Dd Ee Ff
Gg Hh Ii Jj Kk
Ll Mm Nn Oo Pp
Qq Rr Ss Tt Uu
Vv Ww Xx Yy Zz

Editing and Proofreading Marks

Mark	Meaning
agr.	agreement problem
awk.	awkward expression
cap. (≡)	capitalization
⁀‿	close up space
c.f.	comma fault
CS	comma splice
d.m.	dangling modifier
ꝺ	delete
d. neg.	double negative
frag.	sentence fragment
gen.	be more specific
inc.	incomplete
˅' ˅" ˅"	insert apostrophe or quotation marks
∧, ∧; ∧:	insert comma, semicolon, or colon
∧	insert here
⊙	insert period
? ! ∧ ∧	insert question mark or exclamation point
l.c. (/)	lowercase
m.m.	misplaced modifier
n.c.	not clear
no ¶	no paragraph
¶	paragraph
pro. ref.	pronoun reference
?	questionable idea
red.	redundant
RO	run-on sentence
shift	shift in agreement
◯ *sp.*	spelling
stet.	let it stand
t.	verb tense
TS	topic sentence
∩∪	transpose (switch)
u.	usage
〰	use boldface
____	use italics
w.c.	word choice
w.o.	word order
wordy	more words than needed
X	wrong; correct error

Science

The science facts that follow should be both interesting to use and helpful to have at your fingertips. "Animal Facts," "Periodic Table of the Elements," "The Metric System," and "Planet Profusion" all hold useful information that may be expected of you in other classes at various times.

Animal Facts

Animal	Male	Female	Young	Group	Gestation (days)	Longevity (years)
Bear	He-bear	She-bear	Cub	Sleuth	180-240	18-20 (34)*
Cat	Tom	Queen	Kitten	Clutter/Clowder	52-65	10-17 (30)
Cattle	Bull	Cow	Calf	Drove/Herd	280	9-12 (25)
Chicken	Rooster	Hen	Chick	Brood/Flock	21	7-8 (14)
Deer	Buck	Doe	Fawn	Herd	180-250	10-15 (26)
Dog	Dog	Bitch	Pup	Pack/Kennel	55-70	10-12 (24)
Donkey	Jack	Jenny	Foal	Herd/Pace	340-385	18-20 (63)
Duck	Drake	Duck	Duckling	Brace/Herd	21-35	10 (15)
Elephant	Bull	Cow	Calf	Herd	515-760	30-60 (98)
Fox	Dog	Vixen	Cub/Kit	Skulk	51-60	8-10 (14)
Goat	Billy	Nanny	Kid	Tribe/Herd	135-163	12 (17)
Goose	Gander	Goose	Gosling	Flock/Gaggle	30	25-30
Horse	Stallion	Mare	Filly/Colt	Herd	304-419	20-30 (50+)
Lion	Lion	Lioness	Cub	Pride	105-111	10 (29)
Monkey	Male	Female	Boy/Girl	Band/Troop	149-179	12-15 (29)
Rabbit	Buck	Doe	Bunny	Nest/Warren	27-36	6-8 (15)
Sheep	Ram	Ewe	Lamb	Flock/Drove	121-180	10-15 (16)
Swan	Cob	Pen	Cygnet	Bevy/Flock	30	45-50
Swine	Boar	Sow	Piglet	Litter/Herd	101-130	10 (15)
Tiger	Tiger	Tigress	Cub		105	19
Whale	Bull	Cow	Calf	Gam/Pod/Herd	276-365	37
Wolf	Dog	Bitch	Pup	Pack	63	10-12 (16)

* ( ) Record for oldest animal of this type

Periodic Table of the Elements

Key:
Atomic Number — 2
Symbol — He
Helium
Atomic Weight (or Mass Number of most stable isotope if in parentheses) — 4.00260

Legend:
- Alkali metals
- Alkaline earth metals
- Transition metals
- Lanthanide series
- Actinide series
- Other metals
- Nonmetals
- Noble gases

(Of elements 110–121, some are still unknown, and some are recently claimed but unnamed. They have temporary systematic names.)

1a	2a	3b	4b	5b	6b	7b	8	8	8	1b	2b	3a	4a	5a	6a	7a	0
1 H Hydrogen 1.00797																	2 He Helium 4.00260
3 Li Lithium 6.941	4 Be Beryllium 9.0128											5 B Boron 10.811	6 C Carbon 12.01115	7 N Nitrogen 14.0067	8 O Oxygen 15.9994	9 F Fluorine 18.9984	10 Ne Neon 20.179
11 Na Sodium 22.9898	12 Mg Magnesium 24.305											13 Al Aluminum 26.9815	14 Si Silicon 28.0855	15 P Phosphorus 30.9738	16 S Sulfur 32.064	17 Cl Chlorine 35.453	18 Ar Argon 39.948
19 K Potassium 39.0983	20 Ca Calcium 40.08	21 Sc Scandium 44.9559	22 Ti Titanium 47.88	23 V Vanadium 50.94	24 Cr Chromium 51.996	25 Mn Manganese 54.9380	26 Fe Iron 55.847	27 Co Cobalt 58.9332	28 Ni Nickel 58.69	29 Cu Copper 63.546	30 Zn Zinc 65.39	31 Ga Gallium 69.72	32 Ge Germanium 72.59	33 As Arsenic 74.9216	34 Se Selenium 78.96	35 Br Bromine 79.904	36 Kr Krypton 83.80
37 Rb Rubidium 85.4678	38 Sr Strontium 87.62	39 Y Yttrium 88.905	40 Zr Zirconium 91.224	41 Nb Niobium 92.906	42 Mo Molybdenum 95.94	43 Tc Technetium (98)	44 Ru Ruthenium 101.07	45 Rh Rhodium 102.906	46 Pd Palladium 106.42	47 Ag Silver 107.868	48 Cd Cadmium 112.41	49 In Indium 114.82	50 Sn Tin 118.71	51 Sb Antimony 121.75	52 Te Tellurium 127.60	53 I Iodine 126.905	54 Xe Xenon 131.29
55 Cs Cesium 132.905	56 Ba Barium 137.33	57–71* Lanthanides	72 Hf Hafnium 178.49	73 Ta Tantalum 180.948	74 W Tungsten 183.85	75 Re Rhenium 186.207	76 Os Osmium 190.2	77 Ir Iridium 192.22	78 Pt Platinum 195.08	79 Au Gold 196.967	80 Hg Mercury 200.59	81 Tl Thallium 204.383	82 Pb Lead 207.19	83 Bi Bismuth 208.980	84 Po Polonium (209)	85 At Astatine (210)	86 Rn Radon (222)
87 Fr Francium (223)	88 Ra Radium 226.025	89–103** Actinides	104 Rf Rutherfordium (261)	105 Db Dubnium (262)	106 Sg Seaborgium (263)	107 Bh Bohrium (262)	108 Hs Hassium (265)	109 Mt Meitnerium (266)	110 (269)	111 (272)							

*Lanthanides

57 La Lanthanum 138.906	58 Ce Cerium 140.12	59 Pr Praseodymium 140.908	60 Nd Neodymium 144.24	61 Pm Promethium (145)	62 Sm Samarium 150.36	63 Eu Europium 151.96	64 Gd Gadolinium 157.25	65 Tb Terbium 158.925	66 Dy Dysprosium 162.50	67 Ho Holmium 164.930	68 Er Erbium 167.26	69 Tm Thulium 168.934	70 Yb Ytterbium 173.04	71 Lu Lutetium 174.967

**Actinides

89 Ac Actinium 227.028	90 Th Thorium 232.038	91 Pa Protactinium 231.036	92 U Uranium 238.029	93 Np Neptunium 237.048	94 Pu Plutonium (244)	95 Am Americium (243)	96 Cm Curium (247)	97 Bk Berkelium (247)	98 Cf Californium (251)	99 Es Einsteinium (252)	100 Fm Fermium (257)	101 Md Mendelevium (258)	102 No Nobelium (259)	103 Lr Lawrencium (260)

The Metric System

Even though the metric system is not the official system of measurement in the United States, it is used in science, medicine, and some other fields.

The metric system is a form of measurement based on the decimal system (units of 10), so there are no fractions. The table below lists the basic measurements in the metric system.

Linear Measure | Length or distance

1 centimeter............... =	10 millimeters................. =	....0.3937 inch
1 decimeter..................	10 centimeters................... =	.................................0.007 inches
1 meter........................ =	10 decimeters................... =	................39.37 inches or 3.28 feet
1 dekameter............... =	10 meters .... =	....393.7 inches
1 kilometer................. =	1,000 meters .... =	....0.621 mile

Square Measure | Area

1 square centimeter ... =	100 square millimeters ... =	..............................0.155 square inch
1 square decimeter..... =	100 square centimeters... =	.... 15.5 square inches
1 square meter .... =	100 square decimeters ..... –	1,549.9 sq. inches or 1.196 sq. yards
1 square dekameter ... =	100 square meters........... =	...............................119.6 square yards
1 square kilometer ..... =	100 square hectometers .. =	..............................0.386 square mile

Capacity Measure

1 centiliter .... =	10 milliliters .... =	.... 0.338 fluid ounce
1 deciliter.................... =	10 centiliters................... =	...............................3.38 fluid ounces
1 liter .... =	10 deciliters .... =	.......1.057 liquid qts. or 0.908 dry qt.
1 kiloliter .... =	1,000 liters...................... =	...264.18 gallons or 35.315 cubic feet

Land Measure

1 centare .... =	1 square meter................ =	.... 1,549.9 square inches
1 hectare .... =	100 ares........................... =	.... 2.471 acres
1 square kilometer ..... =	100 hectares.................... =	.... 0.386 square mile

Volume Measure

1 cubic centimeter...... =	1,000 cubic millimeters... =	.... 0.061 cubic inch
1 cubic decimeter .... =	1,000 cubic centimeters .. =	..........................61.023 cubic inches
1 cubic meter .... =	1,000 cubic decimeters.... =	...............................35.314 cubic feet

Weights

1 centigram................. =	10 milligrams................... =	....0.1543 grain
1 decigram .... =	10 centigrams .... =	....1.5432 grains
1 gram........................ =	10 decigrams................... =	....15.432 grains
1 dekagram................. =	10 grams .... =	....0.3527 ounce
1 kilogram................... =	1,000 grams .... =	.... 2.2046 pounds

American to Metric Table

The following table shows you what the most common U.S. measurements are in the metric system. You probably already know that 1 inch equals 2.54 centimeters. But, did you know that 1 gallon equals 3.7853 liters?

Linear Measure Length or Distance

1 inch		=	2.54 centimeters
1 foot	= 12 inches	=	0.3048 meter
1 yard	= 3 feet	=	0.9144 meter
1 mile	= 1,760 yards or 5,280 feet	=	1,609.3 meters

Square Measure Area

1 square inch		=	6.452 square centimeters
1 square foot	= 144 square inches	=	929 square centimeters
1 square yard	= 9 square feet	=	0.8361 square meter
1 acre	= 4,840 sq. yards	=	0.4047 hectare
1 square mile	= 640 acres	=	259 hectares or 2.59 sq. kilometers

Cubic Measure

1 cubic inch		=	16.387 cubic centimeters
1 cubic foot	= 1,728 cubic inches	=	0.0283 cubic meter
1 cubic yard	= 27 cubic feet	=	0.7646 cubic meter
1 cord	= 8 cord feet	=	3.625 cubic meters

Dry Measure

1 pint		=	0.5505 liter
1 quart	= 2 pints	=	1.1012 liters
1 peck	= 8 quarts	=	8.8096 liters
1 bushel	= 4 pecks	=	35.2383 liters

Liquid Measure

4 fluid ounces	= 1 gill	=	0.1183 liter
1 pint	= 4 gills	=	0.4732 liter
1 quart	= 2 pints	=	0.9463 liter
1 gallon	= 4 quarts	=	3.7853 liters

Some Ways to Measure When You Don't Have a Ruler

1. A standard sheet of paper is 8-1/2 by 11 inches (21.59 x 27.94 cms).
2. A quarter is approximately 1 inch wide (2.54 cms).
3. A penny is approximately 3/4 inch wide (1.9 cms).
4. U.S. paper currency is 6-1/8 by 2-5/8 inches (15.56 x 6.67 cms).

Conversion Table

TO CHANGE	TO	MULTIPLY
acres	square miles	0.001562
Celsius	Fahrenheit	*1.8

*(Multiply Celsius by 1.8; then add 32.)

cubic meters	cubic yards	1.3079
cubic yards	cubic meters	0.7646
Fahrenheit	Celsius	*0.55

*(Multiply Fahrenheit by .55 after subtracting 32.)

feet	meters	0.3048
feet	miles	0.0001894
feet/sec.	miles/hr.	0.6818
grams	ounces	0.0353
grams	pounds	0.002205
hours	days	0.04167
inches	centimeters	2.5400
liters	gallons (U.S.)	0.2642
liters	pints (dry)	1.8162
liters	pints (liquid)	2.1134
liters	quarts (dry)	0.9081
liters	quarts (liquid)	1.0567
meters	miles	0.0006214
meters	yards	1.0936
metric tons	tons	1.1023
miles	kilometers	1.6093
miles	feet	5,280
miles/hr.	feet/min.	88
millimeters	inches	0.0394
ounces	grams	28.3495
ounces	pounds	0.0625
pounds	kilograms	0.45359
pounds	ounces	16
quarts (dry)	liters	1.1012
square feet	square meters	0.0929
square kilometers	square miles	0.3861
square meters	square feet	10.7639
square miles	square kilometers	2.5900
square yards	square meters	0.8361
tons	metric tons	0.9072
tons	pounds	2,000
yards	meters	0.9144
yards	miles	0.0005682

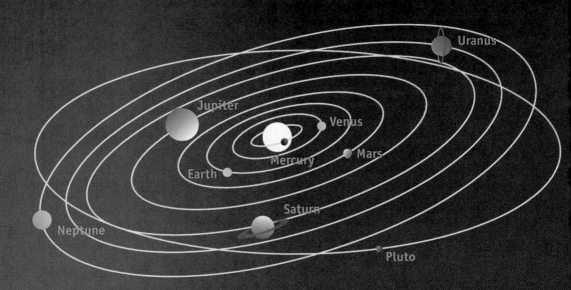

Planet Profusion

There are thousands of galaxies in the universe. Our solar system is located in the Milky Way galaxy, which is 150,000 light-years in diameter. Even though this galaxy contains an estimated 250 billion to one trillion stars, our solar system contains only one star—the sun. The sun, which is the center of our solar system, has nine planets and a myriad of asteroids, meteorites, and comets orbiting it. The planets are large, nonluminous bodies that follow fixed elliptical orbits about the sun. (See the illustration above.)

Some of the planets are considered terrestrial planets—Mercury, Venus, Earth, and Mars—which resemble Earth in size, chemical composition, and density. They have rocky bodies and distinct atmospheres. Some planets are considered Jovian planets—Jupiter, Saturn, Uranus, and Neptune—which are much larger in size and have thick, gaseous atmospheres, low densities, and only a small hidden rocky core. Pluto is not in either group; rather it is a large icy body with a number of similar miniplanets like it in a belt beyond Neptune called the "Kuiper belt." (See the table on the next page.)

	Sun	Moon	Mercury	Venus	Earth	Mars	Jupiter	Saturn	Uranus	Neptune	Pluto
Orbital Speed (in miles per second)		.6	29.8	21.8	18.5	15.0	8.1	6.0	4.2	3.4	3.0
Rotation on Axis	24 days 16 hrs. 48 min.	27 days 7 hrs. 38 min.	59 days	243 days	23 hrs. 56 min.	24 hrs. 37 min.	9 hrs. 55 min.	10 hrs. 39 min.	17 hrs. 8 min.	16 hrs. 7 min.	6 days
Mean Surface Gravity (Earth = 1.00)		0.16	0.38	0.9	1.00	0.38	2.53	1.07	0.91	1.14	0.07
Density (times that of water)	100 (core)	3.3	5.4	5.3	5.5	3.9	1.3	0.7	1.27	1.6	2.03
Mass (times that of Earth)	333,000	0.012	0.055	0.82	6×10^{21} metric tons	0.10	318	95	14.5	17.2	0.0026
Approx. Weight of a 150-Pound Human		24	59	135	150	57	380	161	137	171	11
Number of Satellites	9 planets	0	0	0	1	2	16	23	15	8	1
Mean Distance to Sun (in millions of miles)		93.0	36.0	67.24	92.96	141.7	483.8	887.1	1,783.9	2,796.4	3,666
Revolution Around Sun		365.25 days	88.0 days	224.7 days	365.25 days	687 days	11.86 years	29.46 years	84.0 years	165 years	248 years
Approximate Surface Temperature (degrees Fahrenheit)	10,000° (surface) 27,000,000° (center)	lighted side 200° dark side -280°	-346° to 950°	850°	-126.9° to 136°	-191° to -24°	-236°	-203°	-344°	-360°	-342° to -369°
Diameter (in miles)	865,400	2,155	3,032	7,519	7,926	4,194	88,736	74,978	32,193	30,775	1,423

Additional Units of Measure

Below are some additional units of measure that you may come across in or out of school. They are used to measure everything from boards to "light." The ones at the bottom of the page are used in shipbuilding, in the military, and with horses.

Astronomical Unit (A.U.) ● 93,000,000 miles, the average distance of the earth from the sun (Used in astronomy).

Board Foot (bd. ft.) ● 144 cubic inches or 12 in. x 12 in. x 1 in. (Used for measuring lumber).

Bolt ● 40 yards (Used for measuring cloth).

Btu ● British thermal unit—amount of heat needed to increase the temperature of one pound of water by one degree Fahrenheit (252 calories).

Gross ● 12 dozen or 144.

Knot ● A rate of speed—one nautical mile per hour (Used on boats).

Light, Speed of ● 186,281.7 miles per second.

Light-year ● 5,878,000,000,000 miles—the distance that light travels in a year.

Pi (π) ● 3.14159265+—the ratio of the circumference of a circle to its diameter.

Roentgen ● Dosage of unit of radiation exposure produced by X rays.

Score ● 20 units.

Sound, Speed of ● Usually placed at 1,088 feet per second at 32° F at sea level.

MISCELLANEOUS MEASUREMENTS

3 inches	=	1 palm
4 inches	=	1 hand
6 inches	=	1 span
18 inches	=	1 cubit
21.8 inches	=	1 Bible cubit
2-1/2 feet	=	1 military pace

Mathematics

This chapter is your guide to the language of mathematics. It lists and defines many of the common (and not so common) mathematical signs, symbols, shapes, and terms. The chapter also includes helpful math tables and easy-to-follow guidelines for solving word problems.

Common Math Symbols

+	plus (addition)	<	is less than	°	degree
−	minus (subtraction)	>	is greater than	′	minute (also foot)
×	multiplied by	±	plus or minus	″	second (also inch)
÷	divided by	%	percent	:	is to (ratio)
=	is equal to	$	dollars	π	pi
≠	is not equal to	¢	cents		

Advanced Math Symbols

√	square root	≅	is congruent to
∛	cube root	∠	angle
≥	is greater than or equal to	⊥	is perpendicular to
≤	is less than or equal to	∥	is parallel to
{ }	set	∴	therefore

A Chart of Prime Numbers Less Than 500

2	3	5	7	11	13	17	19	23	29
31	37	41	43	47	53	59	61	67	71
73	79	83	89	97	101	103	107	109	113
127	131	137	139	149	151	157	163	167	173
179	181	191	193	197	199	211	223	227	229
233	239	241	251	257	263	269	271	277	281
283	293	307	311	313	317	331	337	347	349
353	359	367	373	379	383	389	397	401	409
419	421	431	433	439	443	449	457	461	463
467	479	487	491	499					

Multiplication and Division Table

X	0	1	2	3	4	5	6	7	8	9	10
0	0	0	0	0	0	0	0	0	0	0	0
1	0	1	2	3	4	5	6	7	8	9	10
2	0	2	4	6	8	10	12	14	16	18	20
3	0	3	6	9	12	15	18	21	24	27	30
4	0	4	8	12	16	20	24	28	32	36	40
5	0	5	10	15	20	25	30	35	40	45	50
6	0	6	12	18	24	30	36	42	48	54	60
7	0	7	14	21	28	35	42	49	56	63	70
8	0	8	16	24	32	40	48	56	64	72	80
9	0	9	18	27	36	45	54	63	72	81	90
10	0	10	20	30	40	50	60	70	80	90	100

Decimal Equivalents of Common Fractions

1/2	.5000	1/32	.0313	3/11	.2727	6/11	.5455
1/3	.3333	1/64	.0156	4/5	.8000	7/8	.8750
1/4	.2500	2/3	.6667	4/7	.5714	7/9	.7778
1/5	.2000	2/5	.4000	4/9	.4444	7/10	.7000
1/6	.1667	2/7	.2857	4/11	.3636	7/11	.6364
1/7	.1429	2/9	.2222	5/6	.8333	7/12	.5833
1/8	.1250	2/11	.1818	5/7	.7143	8/9	.8889
1/9	.1111	3/4	.7500	5/8	.6250	8/11	.7273
1/10	.1000	3/5	.6000	5/9	.5556	9/10	.9000
1/11	.0909	3/7	.4286	5/11	.4545	9/11	.8182
1/12	.0833	3/8	.3750	5/12	.4167	10/11	.9091
1/16	.0625	3/10	.3000	6/7	.8571	11/12	.9167

Roman Numerals

I	1	VIII	8	LX	60	$\overline{V}$	5,000
II	2	IX	9	LXX	70	$\overline{X}$	10,000
III	3	X	10	LXXX	80	$\overline{L}$	50,000
IV	4	XX	20	XC	90	$\overline{C}$	100,000
V	5	XXX	30	C	100		
VI	6	XL	40	D	500	$\overline{D}$	500,000
VII	7	L	50	M	1,000	$\overline{M}$	1,000,000

Math Terms

Addition (+) is combining numbers to get a total, which is called a sum. The sum of 3 plus 5 is 8; 3 + 5 = 8.

An **angle** is made when two rays (lines) share a common endpoint. An angle is measured in degrees. The three most common angles are acute, obtuse, and right angles.

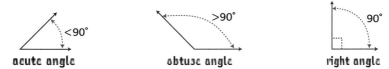

acutc anglc   obtusc angle   right anglc

Area is the total surface within a closed figure (circle, square, etc.). The area of a rectangle is figured by multiplying the length by the width. Area is measured in square units such as square inches or square feet.

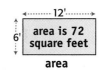

area

The **average** is found by adding a group of numbers together and then dividing that sum by the number of separate numbers (addends). The average of 7, 8, and 9 is 8, because 7 + 8 + 9 = 24, and 24 ÷ 3 (numbers) = 8. This is also called the mathematical *mean*.

A **circle** is a round, closed figure. All the points on its circumference (edge) are the same distance from the center of the figure.

circumference

Circumference is the measure of distance around the edge of a circle.

A **common denominator** is a multiple shared by the denominators of two or more fractions. For example, 6 is a common denominator of $\frac{1}{2}$ ($\frac{3}{6}$) and $\frac{1}{3}$ ($\frac{2}{6}$); 6 is a multiple of both 2 and 3. To add or subtract fractions, you must find a common denominator; $\frac{1}{2} + \frac{1}{3} = \frac{3}{6} + \frac{2}{6} = \frac{5}{6}$. The lowest common denominator is also called the least common multiple (LCM) of the denominators.

Congruent ($\cong$) is the term for two figures, angles, or line segments that are the same size and shape.

Data is a set of numbers collected to compare.

congruent triangles

A **decimal** is a fraction written in the decimal number system. (Decimal means "based on the number 10.") Decimals are written using a decimal point and place values—tenths, hundredths, thousandths, and so on. The fraction $\frac{1}{2}$ is .5, or $\frac{5}{10}$.

A **degree** is a unit of measurement for angles and arcs. It is written as a small circle [°]. You can write 90°, or 90 degrees. There are 360° in a circle.

The **denominator** is the bottom number of a fraction. In the fraction $\frac{1}{3}$, the denominator is 3. It indicates the number of parts needed to make a whole unit.

A **diagonal** is a line from one vertex (corner) of a quadrilateral to the opposite vertex.

The **diameter** is a length of a straight line through the center of a circle.

diameter

A **dividend** is a number to be divided. In the equation $12 \div 2 = 6$, 12 is the dividend.

Division (÷) is a basic math operation used to determine how many times one quantity is contained in another. Division also tells you how many times you have to subtract a number to reach zero. For example, $10 \div 5 = 2$ because you subtract 5 two times to reach zero ($10 - 5 = 5 - 5 = 0$).

The **divisor** is the number that divides the dividend. In the statement $12 \div 2 = 6$, 2 is the divisor.

An **equation** is a statement that says two numbers or mathematical expressions are equal to each other ($2 + 10 = 12$ or $x + 4 = 9$). Equations use the equal sign (=).

An **estimate** is a reasonable guess at an answer. If you add 6.24 and 5.19, you can estimate the answer will be around 11, because $6 + 5 = 11$.

An **even number** is a number that can be divided by 2 without having a remainder (2, 4, 6, and so on). For example, $4 \div 2 = 2$.

An **exponent** is the small, raised number to the right of the base number that shows how many times the base is to be multiplied by itself. In the expression 2^3, 3 is the exponent (2 is the base). So, 2^3 means you need to multiply 2 three times ($2 \times 2 \times 2 = 8$).

A **factor** is a number that is being multiplied. In $4 \times 3 = 12$, the factors are 4 and 3.

A **fraction** is a number that expresses a part of a whole. In the fraction $\frac{3}{4}$, 4 is the denominator—the number of equal parts that make up the whole. The number 3 is the numerator—the number of parts being talked about.

fraction

Geometry is the study of two-dimensional shapes (circles, triangles), three-dimensional solids (spheres, cubes), and positions in space (points).

A **horizontal** is a line parallel to the earth's surface, or horizon, going across rather than up and down. A vertical is a line that is straight up and down and perpendicular to the horizon.

A **hypotenuse** of a right triangle is the side opposite the right angle.

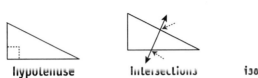

hypotenuse   Intersections   isosceles triangle

An **intersection** is the point where two figures in geometry cross each other. The points where they cross are called intersections.

An **isosceles triangle** is a triangle with two sides of equal length and two equal angles. (See *triangle.*)

Length is the distance along a line from one point to another.

A **line** is all points formed by extending a line segment both directions, without end.

line

Lowest common denominator (See *common denominator.*)

Mean is another word for average. (See *average.*)

The **median** is the middle number when a group of numbers is arranged in order from the least to the greatest, or greatest to least. In 1, 4, 6 the median (middle number) is 4. In 1, 4, 6, 8 the median is 5, halfway between 4 and 6.

A **multiple** is a quantity into which another quantity can be divided, with zero as the remainder (both 6 and 9 are multiples of 3).

Multiplication ($\times$) is like addition because you add the same number a certain number of times ($2 \times 4 = 4 + 4$). When you multiply numbers, the answer is called the product. The product of 2 times 4 is 8 because $2 \times 4 = 8$. (A raised dot also means multiplication. 2×3 is the same as $2 \cdot 3$.)

The **numerator** is the top number of a fraction. In the fraction $\frac{5}{6}$, the numerator is 5.

An **obtuse** angle is an angle greater than 90 degrees and less than 180 degrees. (See *angle.*)

An **odd number** is a number that cannot be divided evenly by 2. The numbers 1, 3, 5, 7, and so on, are odd numbers.

Opposite numbers are any two numbers whose sum is zero (−2 and +2 are opposite numbers).

Parallel refers to lines that never intersect.

parallel lines

Percent is a way of expressing a number as a fraction of 100. (Percent means "per hundred.") The percent symbol is %. So, 1/2 expressed as a percentage is $\frac{50}{100}$, which is 50%.

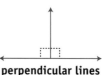
perimeter = 9'

The **perimeter** is the distance around the edge of a multi-sided figure. If a triangle has three sides, each 3 feet long, its perimeter is 9 feet (3 + 3 + 3 = 9).

Perpendicular refers to two lines that intersect forming right angles (90° angles.)

Pi (π) is the ratio of the circumference of a circle to its diameter. Pi is approximately 3.14.

perpendicular lines

Place value is the value of the place of a digit depending on where it is in the number.

3497 is 3—thousands, 4—hundreds, 9—tens, 7—ones
.3497 is 3—tenths, 4—hundredths, 9—thousandths, 7—ten-thousandths

A **point** is an exact location on a plane.

A **positive number** is a number greater than 0.

A **prime number** is a number that cannot be divided evenly by any number except itself and 1. The number 6 is not a prime number because it can be divided by 1, 2, 3, and 6. The number 5 is a prime number because it can only be divided evenly (without a remainder) by 1 and 5.

Product is the word used to indicate the result of multiplication. For example, 8 is the product of 2 times 4, because 2 × 4 = 8.

The **quotient** is the number you get when you divide one number by another number. If 8 is divided by 4, the quotient is 2, because 8 ÷ 4 = 2.

radius

The **radius** (r) is the distance from the center of a circle to its circumference. (The radius is half the diameter.)

A **ratio** is a way of comparing two numbers by dividing one by the other. The ratio of 3 to 4 is $\frac{3}{4}$. If there are 20 boys and 5 girls in your class, the ratio of boys to girls is $\frac{20}{5}$ ($\frac{4}{1}$ in lowest terms), or 4 : 1.

A **rectangle** is a four-sided closed figure with four right angles and with opposite sides parallel and congruent.

A **right angle** is an angle that measures 90 degrees. A right angle is formed when two perpendicular lines meet. (See *angle*.)

Rounding is a way to figure an approximate number if you don't need an exact number. If 2323 people attended a soccer game, you could say about 2000 people were there. If 2857 people attended, you could say 3000. Round up if the number is greater than half (2500 is halfway between 2000 and 3000). Round down if the number is less than half.

A **solid** is a three dimensional figure in geometry, like a cube, a cone, a prism, or a sphere.

solid

A **square** is a rectangle that has four sides of equal length and four right angles. Square also refers to the product of a number multiplied by itself. The square of 4 is 16 ($4^2 = 16$; $4 \times 4 = 16$). Square also refers to how area is measured.

square

The **square root** of a number is a number that, when multiplied by itself, gives the original number as the product. The symbol for square root is $\sqrt{}$. The square root of 4 is 2, because $2 \times 2 = 4$ ($\sqrt{4} = 2$).

Subtraction (−) is the inverse (opposite) of addition. Instead of adding one number to another, you take one number away from another. When you subtract two numbers, you find the difference between them. So, $11 - 6 = 5$.

The **sum** is the number you get when you add numbers. For example, 7 is the sum of 4 and 3, because $4 + 3 = 7$.

A **triangle** is a closed figure with three sides. The sum of the angles in every triangle is 180°. Triangles can be classified by *sides:* equilateral, isosceles, or scalene; or by *angles:* right, equiangular, acute, or obtuse.

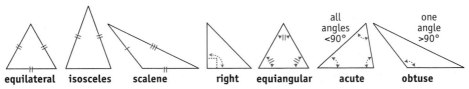

equilateral   isosceles   scalene   right   equiangular   acute   obtuse

A **vertex** is the point where two sides of a plane (flat) figure meet (corner). The plural of *vertex* is *vertices.*

Vertical (See *horizontal.*)

vertex

Word Problems

To solve word problems, you need strong reading and thinking skills, in addition to good math skills. It is important to solve word problems one step at a time, and to show steps as you work so that you can explain your solutions.

Steps for Solving Word Problems

1 **Read the problem carefully.**
You may need to read the problem several times to understand it completely. Some problems have two or more parts, and ask for more than one answer. Study any maps, charts, graphs, and tables that are part of the problem. To make sure you understand the problem, restate it in your own words, show the problem in a drawing, or even act out the problem.

2 **Gather the data.**
There are two kinds of data you may need: (1) data that is given in the problem, and (2) data that you need to know or look up. Write down the data from the problem that you will use in calculating the solution. Look up (and write down) any other data you need, such as formulas or information.

3 **Set up the equation(s) you will use to solve the problem.**
In this step, you decide how to use the data to solve the problem. This is a good time to look back at the problem, to make sure you understand what it asks you to do.

4 **Do the calculations to solve the equation(s).**
If the problem has more than one part, make sure you answer all parts of the problem.

5 **Check your answers.**
You can redo the problem, do it a different way, use a calculator, or start with the answer and work backward.

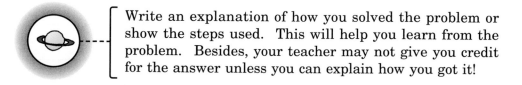

Write an explanation of how you solved the problem or show the steps used. This will help you learn from the problem. Besides, your teacher may not give you credit for the answer unless you can explain how you got it!

Exchanging Money

Word Problem: Imagine that your family is going to Canada. You have saved $35.00 to take with you. How many Canadian dollars will you get when you exchange your American money?

STEP 1   **Read and restate the problem.**
"How many Canadian dollars will I get for 35 U.S. dollars?"

STEP 2   **Gather the data.**
Data given in the problem. I have 35 U.S. dollars.
Data you need to know or look up: What is the U.S.-to-Canadian exchange rate?

You can find currency exchange rates on the Internet, in the newspaper, or by calling a bank. (Let's say that the U.S.-to-Canadian exchange rate is $1.00 U.S. = $1.46 Canadian.)

STEP 3   **Set up the equation you will use to solve the problem.**

$$\frac{\$1.00 \text{ U.S.}}{\$1.46 \text{ Canadian}} = \frac{\$35.00 \text{ U.S.}}{X \text{ Canadian}}$$

STEP 4   **Do the calculation to solve the equation.**

```
    $1.46
  x   35
    730
   438
  $51.10
```

I will get 51.10 Canadian dollars.

STEP 5   **Check your answer.**
Divide $51.10 by $1.46 to get the number of U.S. dollars you have (35).

```
            $35.
  $1.46. ) $51.10.
      ^        ^
           438
           730
           730
```

Mixed Numbers

Word Problem: A carpenter needs a total of 15 pieces of lumber to fix a fence. Each piece needs to be $2\frac{2}{3}$ feet long. How many eight-foot boards will she have to buy to get at least 15 pieces $2\frac{2}{3}$ feet long?

STEP 1
Read and restate the problem.
"How many eight-foot boards will the carpenter have to buy?"

STEP 2
Gather the data.
Data given in the problem: need 15 pieces $2\frac{2}{3}$ feet long from eight-foot boards.

STEP 3
Set up the problem.
To solve this problem, you first need to know how many $2\frac{2}{3}$-foot long pieces can be cut from each eight-foot board (call this number X). You then need to know how many eight-foot boards must be purchased to get 15 pieces (call this number Y).

$$8 \div 2\frac{2}{3} = X \quad \text{(number of } 2\frac{2}{3}\text{-foot pieces in one 8-foot board)}$$

$$15 \div X = Y \quad \text{(number of 8-foot boards needed)}$$

STEP 4
Solve the problem.
Next, you need to prepare your equation so that you can multiply rather than divide.

$$X = 8 \div 2\frac{2}{3} \ (2\frac{2}{3} = \frac{8}{3}) = 8 \div \frac{8}{3} = 8 \times \frac{3}{8} = \frac{24}{8} = 3$$

$X = 3$ ($2\frac{2}{3}$-foot pieces from each 8-foot board)

$Y = 15 \div X = 15 \div 3 = 5$

$Y = 5$ (8-foot boards)

STEP 5
Check your answer.
Check your answer with a picture and by addition or by multiplication.

$2\frac{2}{3} + 2\frac{2}{3} + 2\frac{2}{3} = 8$

3 pieces/board × 5 boards = 15 pieces

Computers

Throughout history, writers have used all kinds of writing tools—sharp metal to carve words into stone, pens made from feathers, and ink made from berries. And they have pounded away on typewriters.

Today's writers use computers. The computer may be the best tool writers have ever had. Just compare the computer to the ancient writing methods. Imagine revising a report carved in stone!

Computer Tips

A computer is a tool that can make many jobs easier, faster, and more fun. Whether you're a beginner or an experienced computer user, the following tips can help you.

LEARN ABOUT YOUR COMPUTER

Each computer is different. What a computer can do depends on the computer itself, and on the software that has been loaded into it. If your computer has a CD-ROM drive, you can use it to find information on CD-ROM's. If it has word-processing software, you can use it to write and edit your assignments. Learn about the computer you use. Here are some ways to find out what your computer can do:

- Ask computer "experts" to show you what they know.
- Use the "help" function on your program.
- Look at the computer and software manuals.
- Learn by doing. Practice writing, editing, and doing other jobs on the computer.

BECOME AN EXPERT KEYBOARDER

The keyboard is the way you "talk" to your computer. Practice until you can keyboard quickly and accurately. Use the diagram of a computer keyboard on the next page to help you remember where all the letters, numbers, and symbols are located. The blue row of keys is called the *home row*. All of your keyboarding should begin here with your fingertips slightly touching the keys.

Computer Keyboard

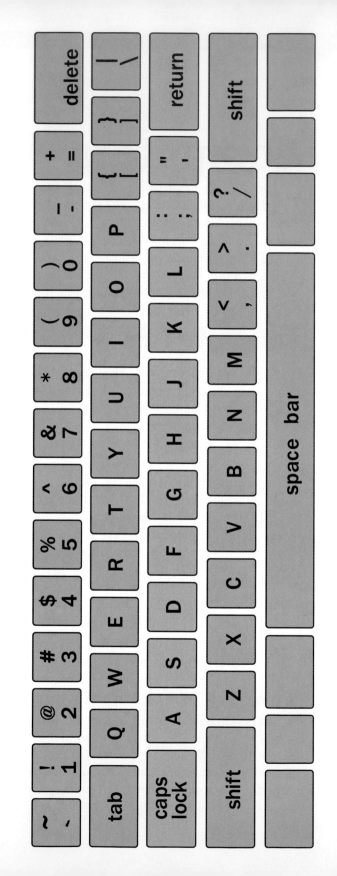

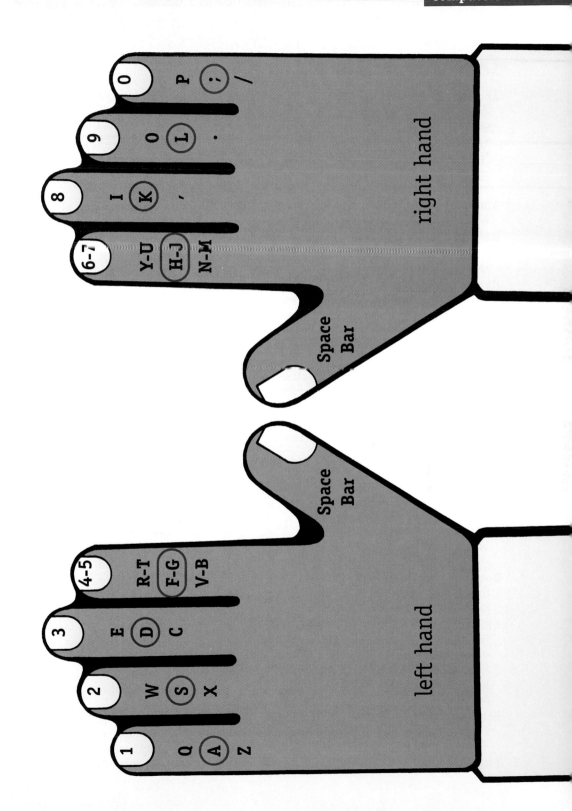

right hand

left hand

Computer Terms

Access: To open and use a computer file.

ASCII: (American Standard Code Information Interchange) A set of letters, numbers, and symbols that most computers use to store and work with data.

Audio file: A computer document that is made up of sounds *(audio)*.

Backup: A duplicate copy of a file or program, made in case the original is lost or destroyed.

Bandwidth: A measure of how fast data is transmitted from one computer to another. When more than one operation is transmitted at the same time, bandwidth is divided among them. (See *bps.*)

Binary system: The number system commonly used by computers because the values 0 and 1 can be represented electronically in the computer.

Bit: A unit of computer memory that can store either a 0 or a 1.

Bomb: A term describing what happens when a computer program stops working unexpectedly. Also called a *crash.*

Bookmark: A command to make a browser save an Internet address, so that the site can be visited again later.

Boot: To start up a computer system by loading a program into the memory. Also called *start up*.

BPS: (Bits Per Second) A measure of how fast data is transmitted over a network. (Sometimes called *baud rate*.) For example, a modem may have a speed of 56,600 bps. (See *bandwidth*.)

Browser: A type of program used to view and navigate the World Wide Web.

Bug: An error in a program.

Bulletin board: A service on the Internet where users can post messages for others to read.

Byte: Eight bits of information acting as a single piece of data. Computer memory is measured in bytes. (See *GB, K,* and *MB*. Also see *bit*.)

CD-ROM: A compact disc that can store large amounts of information, including audio, text, and video.

Character: A letter or number used to display information on a computer screen or printer.

Chat: A live conversation on the Internet.

Chip: A small piece of silicon containing thousands of electrical elements. Also known as an *integrated circuit*.

Circuit board: A flat board inside a computer, used to hold and connect computer chips and electrical parts.

Clear: To erase computer data.

Command: An instruction telling a computer to perform a certain task, such as "print."

Compress: To make a file smaller so that it can be easily stored or quickly sent to another computer. Special software is used to compress (and decompress) files.

Computer: A machine that can accept data, process it according to a stored set of instructions, and then output the results.

Computer program: A piece of software containing statements and commands that tell the computer to perform certain tasks.

Configuration: A computer and all devices connected to it.

CPU: (Central Processing Unit) The "brain" of the computer; the part that performs computations and controls other parts of the computer system.

CRT: (Cathode Ray Tube.) The electronic vacuum tube found in some computer monitors and TV screens.

Cursor: A pointer on the computer screen that shows where the next character typed on the keyboard will appear.

Cyberspace: The imaginary world perceived by humans when using a computer network or a virtual reality program. From William Gibson's novel *Neuromancer*. (See *network, Internet,* and *virtual reality*.)

Data: Information produced by or given to a computer.

Database: A program and a collection of information organized in such a way that a computer can access a certain item or group of items.

Desktop: The monitor screen as it appears when the computer is on but no programs are open.

Device: A piece of computer hardware that performs a certain task. Printers and hard drives are examples of devices.

Directory: The table of contents for all files on a disk.

Disk: A magnetic storage device used to record computer information. Each disk appears flat and square on the outside; inside, the disk is circular and rotates so information can be stored and accessed on its many tracks.

Disk drive: The device that writes and reads information from and to the disk.

Documentation: The printed book or program that explains how to use a piece of hardware or software.

Domain: In an Internet or e-mail address, the parts that name the server.

Download: To copy a program or file from another computer to your own.

Drag: To move items across the screen by holding down the mouse button while sliding the mouse.

E-mail: (Electronic mail) A system that uses telecommunications to send messages from one computer to another.

Emoticon: Often called a "smiley." A set of characters that, when viewed sideways, resembles a face. Used to add emotion to a message. :)

Error: A mistake in a program that causes the program to run either incorrectly or not at all.

Error message: A message, displayed by the computer, that tells you what type of error has occurred in a program.

Exit: To leave or quit a program. Also called *close*.

FAQ: (Frequently Asked Questions) A list of common questions and answers.

Fax modem: A type of modem that can send computer files to fax machines. Most can also receive fax transmissions.

File: A collection of information stored under a single title.

Flame: To post an insulting or an inflammatory message on the Internet.

Font: A typeface, or style of type, used by a printer. Most computer systems have several fonts.

Footprint: The space on a desk or table taken up by a computer.

Format: To prepare a blank disk for use. Also called *initialize*. Most disks are sold preformatted.

Freeware: Software in the public domain, which anyone can use free of charge.

FTP: (File Transfer Protocol) A system for transmitting files on parts of the Internet or on a network. Many military and university sites are FTP sites.

GB: (Gigabyte) A measure of computer memory; 1,000 megabytes (MB).

Graphics: Information displayed as pictures or images.

Hard copy: A printed copy.

Hard drive: A stack of disks mounted inside most computers. The hard drive is for long-term storage of important files and programs (such as the computer's operating system).

Hardware: The electronic and mechanical parts of a computer system. A hard drive is *hardware*; a program stored on it is *software.*

Home page: The Web page that gives basic information about a person or an organization. It contains links to other Web pages or sites.

Host: A computer whose programs serve another computer in a computer-to-computer link.

Hotlist: A list of bookmarks. (See *bookmark.*)

HTML: (HyperText Markup Language) The codes that tell a browser how to display text and graphics for a Web page.

Hypertext or hypermedia: A system of web-like links among pages on the Internet or within a program. A link from a "hot word" or "hot symbol" on one page opens directly to another page, which may have its own "hot links" to other pages.

Icon: A small picture or symbol used to identify computer folders, files, or functions.

Inkjet printer: A printer that uses tiny jets of ink for printing.

Input: Information placed into a computer from a disk drive, keyboard, mouse, or other device connected to a computer.

Interactive: A computer program in which the user and computer exchange information.

Interface: The hardware and software that is used to link one computer or computer device to another. Also the method by which a program communicates to a user.

Internet: A world-wide network of independent computer networks that communicate with one another.

ISP: (Internet Service Provider) A business providing its customers with access to the Internet.

K: (Kilobyte) A measure of computer memory; 1,024 bytes, or about 170 words.

Keyboard: An input device used to enter information on a computer by striking keys. (See page 484 for an illustration.)

Laser printer: A printer that uses a laser to produce high-quality printouts.

Link: A connection from one hypertext page to another.

List: A display or printout of a computer program or file.

Listserve: A program sending e-mail messages to a set of addresses. Each listserve is organized around a particular topic, allowing its subscribers to conduct a group discussion by e-mail. Also called a *mailing list* or a *mail server.*

Load: To move information from a storage device into a computer's memory.

Mainframe: A large computer, with many terminals, powerful enough to be used by many people at once. (See *terminal.*)

MB: (Megabyte) A measure of computer memory; 1,000 kilobytes (K).

Memory: The chips in the computer storing data and programs.

Menu: A list of choices from which a user can select. Many programs have menus.

Microcomputer: A small computer that uses a microprocessor as its CPU. The personal computers used in homes and schools are microcomputers.

Modem: (MOdulator DEModulator) A device that sends information or data over telephone lines.

Monitor: A video screen that displays information from a computer.

Mouse: A small manual input device that controls the pointer on the screen and sends information to the computer when it is clicked.

MUD: (Multi-User Domain) An imaginary world (usually text-based) made up of "rooms" where users can interact with the setting and other users. More recently called MOOs (multiuser domain, object oriented) or simply MUs.

Multimedia: A program capable of combining text, graphics, video, voice, music, and animation.

Multiuser: A computer system that allows several persons to use the same computer simultaneously.

Network: A series of computers (or other devices) connected together in order to share information and programs.

Newsgroup: An ongoing discussion in bulletin-board style on a timely or important topic. (See *Usenet.*)

On-line: To be connected to a computer network.

On-line service: A business that serves as a network for its users, providing e-mail, chat rooms, and so on. Most on-line services now also act as Internet providers.

Open: To load a program in order to use it.

Operating system: A software system that controls a computer. Some common operating systems for personal computers are Windows, Mac OS, and DOS.

Output: Information that a computer sends out to a monitor, printer, modem, or other device.

Peripheral: A device connected to a computer. (A printer or a monitor is a peripheral.)

Pixel: One dot on the screen. There are usually 72 pixels per inch.

Post: As a verb, to upload a message to a bulletin board, newsgroup, or listserve. As a noun, the message that is posted.

Printer: A device used to print out information from a computer.

Printout: A hard copy; a computer document printed on paper.

Program: A piece of software or set of instructions that tells a computer what to do.

Programmer: A person who helps write, edit, or produce a computer program.

Programming language: A special language used when writing a computer program. There are many programming languages. BASIC is one example.

Prompt: A question or an instruction on the screen that asks the user to make a choice or give information. Also called a *dialog box.*

Quit: To close a program, removing it from random access memory.

RAM: (Random Access Memory) The part of a computer's memory that stores programs and documents temporarily while you are using them.

Resolution: The number of dots per square inch (dpi) on a computer screen. Images on a screen are made up of tiny dots. The more dots there are, the higher the resolution and the clearer the picture.

Robot: On the Internet, a search engine.

ROM: (Read-Only Memory) The part of a computer's memory that has its permanent instructions. ROM cannot record new data.

Save: To transfer a document to a disk for permanent storage.

Scanner: A device used to read a printed image, picture, or text and save it as an electronic file.

Search engine: A program for locating sites on the Internet. Sometimes called a *robot, spider, rom,* or *webcrawler.*

Sector: A fraction of the recording surface on a disk; a sector is a fraction of a track.

Select: To identify part of a document to work on or change.

Server: The hosting computer of a network. (See *host.*)

Shareware: Programs intended as demos, to be used freely for a test period, then paid for.

Software: The program that tells a computer how to do a certain task.

Source document: A Web page viewed as text and HTML coding.

Spam: Bulk e-mails (often ads) that are sent to many people at once. Also called *electronic junk mail.*

Spreadsheet: A computer program that displays numbers and text in a worksheet form.

Surfing: Exploring the Net, going from link to link.

System: A collection of hardware and software that works together to form a working computer.

Telecommunications: The technology that allows computers to communicate with one another over phone lines, by satellite, etc.

Terminal: A keyboard and monitor sharing a mainframe (computer) with other terminals. A terminal is called a "dumb terminal" if it does not contain a CPU, or brain.

Text file: A computer document made up of ASCII characters only.

Track: A fraction of the recording surface on a disk. (A track can be compared to the space used by each song on an album.)

Upload: To send a file from your computer to another computer.

URL: (Universal Resource Locator) The letters that make up electronic addresses for a site on the Internet. The URL for The Write Source is http:// www.thewritesource.com/.

Usenet: The major collection of newsgroups on the Internet. (See *newsgroup.*)

User: A person using a computer.

Virtual reality: A technology that makes users feel that they are actually in the environment created by the computer.

Virus: A "bug" that is intentionally put into a computer system to cause problems.

Window: A box on a computer screen in which text or graphics is displayed.

Word processor: A program that allows a user to write, revise, edit, save, and print text documents.

Write-protect: To protect a floppy disk so that new information cannot be written onto the disk.

WWW: (World Wide Web) A major portion of the Internet, including graphic pages and hypertext links. (See *hypertext.*)

Geography

To study geography, you need maps, including political maps like the ones provided in this chapter. Political maps show how the world is divided into countries and states. The chapter also includes guidelines for using maps, a special time-zone map, and much more.

Using Maps

Mapmakers use special marks and symbols to show direction (north, south, east, and west). On most maps, north is at the top. But you should always check the *directional finder* (compass rose) to make sure you know where north is. If there is no symbol, you can assume that north is at the top of the page.

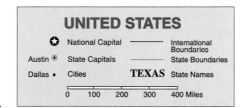

The Legend

Other important marks and symbols are explained in a box printed on each map. This box is called the *legend,* or *key.* It is included to help you understand and use the map. The sample map legend shown here includes keys for locating boundaries, cities, capitals, states, and so on.

The Map Scale

Legends also explain the map scale. The map scale shows you how far it really is between places. For example, a scale might show that one inch on the map equals 100 miles on the earth. If two cities are shown five inches apart, then they are really 500 miles apart. A ruler makes using a scale easy, but even an index card or a piece of paper will work.

Latitude and Longitude

Latitude and *longitude* lines are another part of many maps and are very useful. These are imaginary lines, placed on a map by map-makers, and used to locate any point on the earth.

LATITUDE

The imaginary lines that go from east to west around the earth are called lines of **latitude.** The line of latitude that goes around the earth exactly halfway between the North Pole and the South Pole is called the *equator.* Latitude is measured in degrees, with the equator being 0 degrees (0°).

Above the equator, the lines are called *north latitude* and measure from 0° to 90° north (the North Pole). Below the equator, the lines are called *south latitude* and measure from 0° to 90° south (the South Pole). On a map, latitude numbers are printed along the sides.

LONGITUDE

The lines on a map that run north and south from the North Pole to the South Pole are lines of **longitude.** Longitude is also measured in degrees, beginning with 0 degrees. The line of longitude located at 0° is called the *prime meridian* and passes through Greenwich, England.

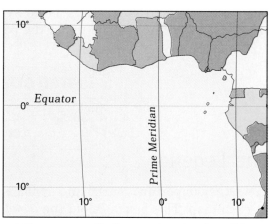

Lines east of the prime meridian are called east longitude. Lines west of the prime meridian are called west longitude. On a map, longitude numbers are printed at the top and bottom.

COORDINATES

The latitude and longitude numbers of a country or other place are called its **coordinates.** In each set of coordinates, latitude is given first, then longitude. To locate a place on a map using its coordinates, find the point where the two lines cross. (On the map above, Guinea is located at 10° N, 10° W. Can you find it? Check the map on page 493 to be sure.)

THE WORLD
MERCATOR PROJECTION

493

ARCTIC OCEAN

Bering Sea

A S I A

Bering Str.

Greenland Sea

Kuskokwim

Yukon

Nome

Seward Pen.

Arctic Circle

Bristol Bay

Beaufort Sea

Axel Heiberg I.

Lincoln Sea

ICELAND

Reykjavík

Str. of Denmark

G R E E N L A N D

(Denmark)

UNITED STATES
Alaska

Fairbanks
Anchorage
Alaska Pen.

Dawson

Aklavik • Inuvik

Prince Patrick I.

Sverdrup Is.

Prince of Wales I.

Queen Elizabeth Is.

Thule Air Base

Devon I.

Parry Channel

Lancaster Sd.

Baffin Bay

Ammassalik

Gulf of Alaska

Juneau

Ft. Simpson

Whitehorse

Norman Wells

Port Radium

Great Bear L.

Yukon

Mackenzie

Amundsen Gulf

Banks I.

Victoria I.

Somerset I.

G. of Boothia

Boothia Pen.

Melville Pen.

Baffin I.

Foxe Basin

Pangnirtung

Cumberland Sd.

Godthab

Davis Strait

Qaqortoq

Ketchikan

Prince Rupert

Dixon Entr.

Queen Charlotte Is.

Liard

Yellowknife

Fort Smith

Great Slave L.

Chesterfield Inlet

N o r t h w e s t T e r r i t o r i e s

Southampton I.

Hudson Str.

Ungava Bay

British Columbia

Vancouver Island

Victoria

Vancouver

Str. of Juan de Fuca

Alberta

Edmonton

Athabasca

Fort McMurray

L. Athabasca

Churchill

Churchill

Nelson

Saskatchewan

Saskatchewan

Prince Albert

Manitoba

L. Winnipeg

Hudson Bay

James Bay

La Grande-Rivière

Goose Bay

N e w f o u n d l a n d

Labrador

Battle Harbour

Str. of Belle Isle

Quebec

St. Lawrence

Olympia

Seattle

Portland

Columbia

Calgary

Medicine Hat

Regina

Winnipeg

Thunder Bay

Ontario

Albany

Nottaway

Moosonee

Timmins

Sault Ste. Marie

Quebec

Montreal

Ottawa

G. of St. Lawrence

Prince Edward Island

Charlottetown

Sydney

New Brunswick

Fredericton

Nova Scotia

Halifax

St. John

Spokane

Great Falls

Butte

Boise

Yellowstone

Snake

Pocatello

Fargo

Bismarck

Duluth

St. Paul

Minneapolis

L. Superior

L. Michigan

Huron

Milwaukee

L. Ontario

Toronto

Buffalo

Albany

Boston

Portland

Providence

Reno

Sacramento

San Francisco

Great Salt Lake

Salt Lake City

Casper

Cheyenne

Platte

Sioux City

Omaha

Des Moines

Chicago

Peoria

Indianapolis

Cleveland

L. Erie

Detroit

Columbus

Cincinnati

Pittsburgh

New York

Philadelphia

Washington

Richmond

Los Angeles

San Diego

Phoenix

Albuquerque

Amarillo

Denver

Pueblo

Colorado

U N I T E D S T A T E S

Kansas City

Wichita

St. Louis

Tulsa

Oklahoma City

Arkansas

Ohio

Louisville

Nashville

Memphis

Chattanooga

Charlotte

Winston-Salem

Norfolk

El Paso

Pecos

Fort Worth

Dallas

Austin

Red

Brazos

Little Rock

Birmingham

Atlanta

Mississippi

Jackson

Mobile

Charleston

Savannah

Jacksonville

Ciudad Juárez

Hermosillo

Chihuahua

Yaqui

Gulf of California

Baja California

New Orleans

Houston

San Antonio

Tampa

Miami

Gulf of Mexico

BAHAMAS

Strs. of Florida

Nassau

Havana

Bermuda (Br.)

ATLANTIC OCEAN

Monterrey

Torreon

Durango

C. San Lucas

Mazatlán

Aguascalientes

Guadalajara

San Luis Potosí

Tampico

M E X I C O

Santiago

Balsas

Mexico City

Veracruz

Bay of Campeche

Cancún

Mérida

Yucatan Pen.

Yucatan Chan.

W E S T

CUBA

Windward Pass.

DOMINICAN REP.

Virgin Is.

San Juan

HAITI

PUERTO RICO (U.S.)

Mona Pass.

JAMAICA

Kingston

Port-au-Prince

Santo Domingo

I N D I E S

Caribbean Sea

Acapulco

Oaxaca

Villahermosa

Belmopan

BELIZE

GUATEMALA

Guatemala City

HONDURAS

Tegucigalpa

San Salvador

EL SALVADOR

Managua

NICARAGUA

San José

COSTA RICA

Panamá

Panama Canal

PANAMA

G. of Panamá

VENEZUELA

COLOMBIA

C E N T R A L A M E R I C A

PACIFIC OCEAN

Tropic of Cancer

N

NORTH AMERICA

| 0 | 1000 Km |
| 0 | 1000 Mi. |

National Capitals ⊛
Provincial and Territorial Capitals ⊙
International Boundaries ——

60° 70° 80° 160° 140° 120° 90° 60° 40° 20° 80° 70°

120° 110° 100° Longitude West 90° of Greenwich 80° 70°

50° 40° 30° 20° 10°

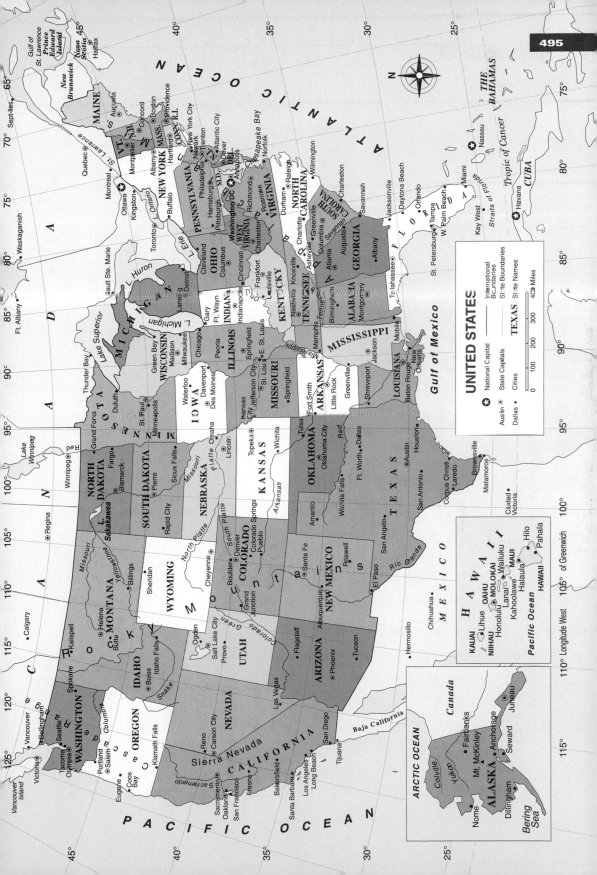

UNITED STATES

- ⚓ National Capital
- ⊛ State Capitals
  - Austin
- • Cities
  - Dallas
- International Boundaries
- State Boundaries
- State Names
  - **TEXAS**

Miles
0 100 200 300 400

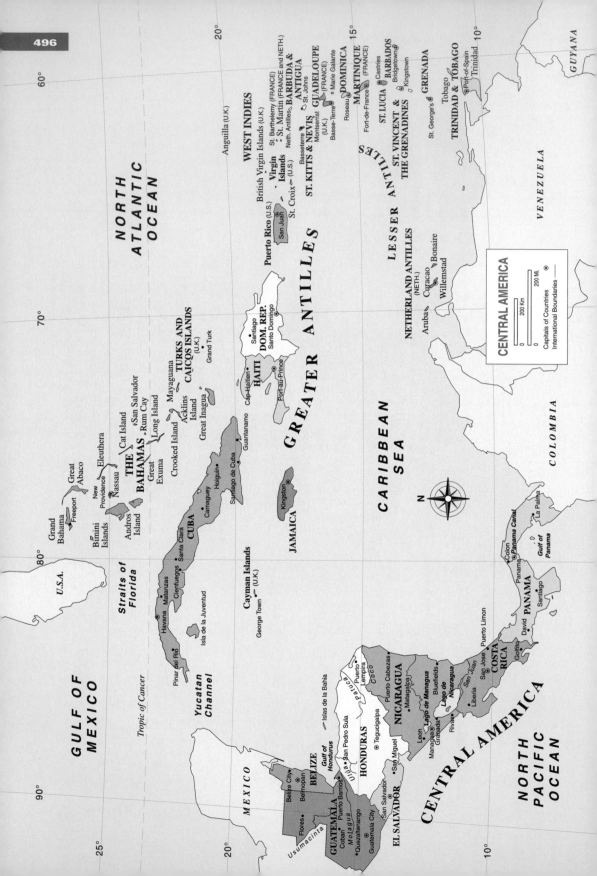

GULF OF MEXICO

NORTH ATLANTIC OCEAN

WEST INDIES

GREATER ANTILLES

LESSER ANTILLES

CARIBBEAN SEA

NORTH PACIFIC OCEAN

CENTRAL AMERICA

60°

70°

80°

90°

25°

20°

20°

15°

10°

10°

GUYANA

VENEZUELA

COLOMBIA

CENTRAL AMERICA
200 Km
200 Mi.
● Capitals of Countries
— International Boundaries

Anguilla (U.K.)

British Virgin Islands (U.K.)
Virgin Islands (U.S.)
St. Croix (U.S.)

Puerto Rico (U.S.)
San Juan

St. Barthelemy (FRANCE)
St. Martin (FRANCE and NETH.)
Neth. Antilles (Neth.)
ANTIGUA
BARBUDA &
ANTIGUA
St. Johns
GUADELOUPE (FRANCE)
Basse-Terre ● Marie Galante
DOMINICA
Roseau ●
MARTINIQUE (FRANCE)
Fort-de-France ●
ST. LUCIA
Castries
BARBADOS
Bridgetown ●
ST. VINCENT &
THE GRENADINES
Kingstown
GRENADA
St. George's ●
Tobago
TRINIDAD & TOBAGO
Trinidad Port-of-Spain ●

ST. KITTS & NEVIS
Basseterre ●
Montserrat
(U.K.)

NETHERLAND ANTILLES
(NETH.)
Aruba Curaçao Bonaire
Willemstad

Santiago ●
DOM. REP.
Santo Domingo ●
HAITI
Cap-Haïtien
Port-au-Prince ●

TURKS AND
CAICOS ISLANDS
(U.K.)
Grand Turk ●

Mayaguana

THE BAHAMAS
Grand Bahama
Freeport
Great Abaco
Bimini Islands
New Providence
Nassau ●
Eleuthera
Andros Island
Cat Island
San Salvador
Rum Cay
Long Island
Crooked Island
Acklins Island
Great Inagua
Great Exuma

U.S.A.

Straits of Florida

Yucatan Channel

Tropic of Cancer

CUBA
Pinar del Río
Havana ●
Matanzas
Cienfuegos
Santa Clara
Santiago de Cuba
Holguin
Camaguey
Guantanamo
Isla de la Juventud

Cayman Islands (U.K.)
George Town ●

JAMAICA
Kingston ●

N

MEXICO

BELIZE
Belize City
Belmopan ●
Gulf of Honduras
Islas de la Bahia

GUATEMALA
Puerto Barrios
Cobán
Quezaltenango
Guatemala City ●
Flores
Motagua
Usumacinta

EL SALVADOR
San Salvador ●
San Miguel

HONDURAS
Tegucigalpa ●
San Pedro Sula
Ulúa
Patuca
Coco
Puerto Cabezas
Puerto Lempira

NICARAGUA
Matagalpa
Managua ●
León
Lago de Managua
Granada
Lago de Nicaragua
Rivas
Bluefields
San Juan

COSTA RICA
Liberia
San José ●
Puerto Limón
Golfito

PANAMA
David
Santiago
Panama ●
Colón
Panama Canal
Gulf of Panama
La Palma

Caribbean Sea

West Indies

Pt. Gallinas

G. de Venezuela

Port of Spain

TRINIDAD & TOBAGO

Barranquilla
Maracaibo
Caracas
Cumana
Ciudad Guayana
Montería
Cucuta
San Cristobal
Orinoco
Georgetown
Paramaribo
Cayenne

PANAMA

G. of Panama

NORTH ATLANTIC OCEAN

Medellin
Buenaventura
Cali
Bogota
COLOMBIA
Pasto
Boa Vista

VENEZUELA

GUYANA

SURINAME

FR. GUIANA

Orinoco

Oyapock

Quito
ECUADOR
Guayaquil
Negro
Branco
Macapa
I. de Marajo
Equator

G. of Guayaquil

Iquitos
Benjamin Constant
Manaus
Amazon
Belém
Abaetetuba
Sao Luis

Suliana
Chiclayo
Trujillo

Maranon
Javari
Jurua
Purus
Amazon
Tapajos
Santarem
Xingu

Fortaleza
Teresina
Natal

Lima
Ica

PERU

Rio Branco
Porto Velho
Madeira
Roosevelt
Guapore

B R A Z I L

Juazeiro do Norte
Recife

Arequipa
Arica

Lake Titicaca
La Paz (de facto)
Cochabamba
Sucre (legal)
Santa Cruz

BOLIVIA
Trinidad

Cuiaba

Brasilia
Goiania

Sao Francisco

Porto Nacional

Aracaju
Salvador
Ilhéus

Belo Horizonte
Vitória

Tocopilla
Antofagasta

Mariscal Estigarribia
Pilcomayo

PARAGUAY

Campo Grande

Paraguay

Parana

Sao Paulo
Santos
Rio de Janeiro

Tropic of Capricorn

San Salvador de Jujuy
Asuncion
Encarnación
Curitiba
Paranaguá

Copiapó

San Miguel de Tucuman
Resistencia

Florianópolis

La Serena
Ovalle

Cordoba
Rosario

Salado

Parana

Uruguay

Santana do Livramento
Salto
Melo

L. dos Patos

Porto Alegre

Valparaiso
Santiago
Mendoza

CHILE

Concepcion

ARGENTINA

Buenos Aires
La Plata

URUGUAY
Montevideo

Rio de la Plata

C. San Antonio

Valdivia

Santa Rosa

Mar del Plata

Negro
Colorado

Bahia Blanca

Puerto Montt
Ancud

San Carlos de Bariloche
Pto. Madryn
Chubut

G. San Matias

I. Grande de Chiloé

ARCHIPIELAGO de los CHONOS

Comodoro Rivadavia

G. San Jorge

C. Tres Puntas

Puerto Aisén

San Julián

SOUTH AMERICA

0 ——— 600 Km

0 ——— 600 Mi.

⊙ Capitals of Countries
— International Boundaries

Bahia Grande
Rio Gallegos

FALKLAND ISLANDS
(Br. - claimed by Arg.)
Stanley

I. Santa Inés
Punta Arenas
I. de los Estados

Cape Horn

SOUTH GEORGIA ISLAND
(U.K.)

SOUTH PACIFIC OCEAN

SOUTH ATLANTIC OCEAN

N

80° 70° 60° 50° 40°
90° 80° 70° Longitude West of Greenwich 50° 40° 30° 20°

10° 10°
0° 0°
10° 10°
20° 20°
30° 30°
40° 40°
50° 50°

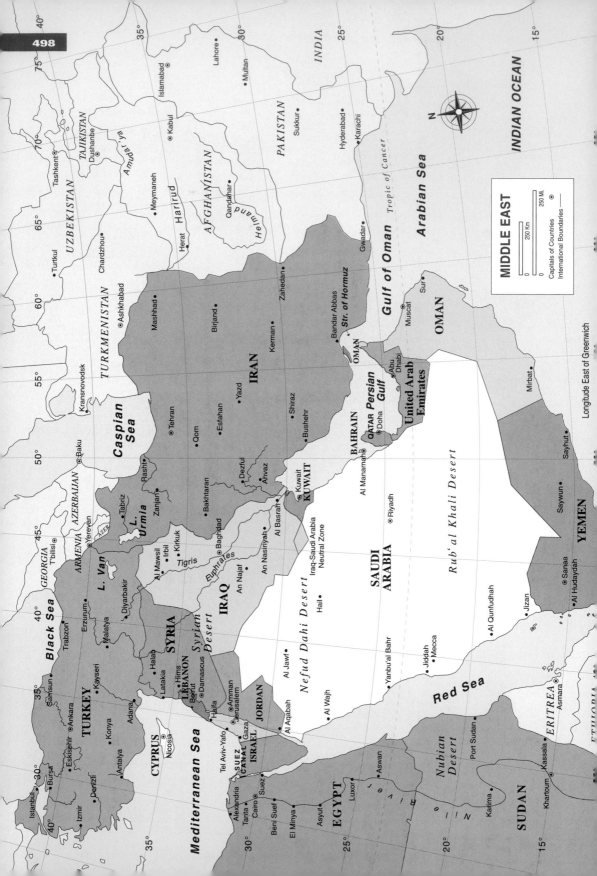

MIDDLE EAST

⊙ Capitals of Countries
── International Boundaries

0 ──── 250 Km
0 ──── 250 Mi.

INDIAN OCEAN

N

Arabian Sea

Tropic of Cancer

Longitude East of Greenwich

Gulf of Oman

Str. of Hormuz

OMAN

Muscat ⊙
Sur •

Mirbat •

Sayhut •

YEMEN

Saywun •

• Sanaa
⊙ Sanaa
Al Hudaydah •
• Jizan

• Al Qunfudhah

Red Sea

United Arab Emirates

Abu Dhabi ⊙

Persian Gulf

QATAR
Doha ⊙

BAHRAIN
Al Manamah ⊙

Kuwait ⊙
KUWAIT

Bandar Abbas •
Zahedan •

Gwadar •

PAKISTAN

Hyderabad •
Karachi •

Sukkur •

INDIA

Lahore •

Multan •

Islamabad ⊙

• Kabul

AFGHANISTAN

Qandahar •

Helmand

Meymaneh •

Herat •

Harirud

Mashhad •

IRAN

Birjand •

Kerman •

Yazd •
Esfahan •
Qom •
• Tehran
Shiraz •
Bushehr •

Ahvaz •
Dezful •
Bakhtaran •

Rasht •
Zanjan •
Tabriz •

TURKMENISTAN

Ashkhabad ⊙

Kransnovodsk •

Chardzhou •

Turtkul •

UZBEKISTAN

Tashkent ⊙

TAJIKISTAN
Dushanbe ⊙

Amu' dar'ya

Caspian Sea

AZERBAIJAN
Baku ⊙

ARMENIA
Yerevan ⊙
AZER.

GEORGIA
T'bilisi ⊙

L. Urmia

L. Van

Diyarbakir •

Erzurum •
Trabzon •

Black Sea

TURKEY

Samsun •
Ankara ⊙
Kayseri •

Malatya •

Adana •
Konya •

Antalya •

Denizli •

Izmir •
Bursa •
Istanbul •

Mediterranean Sea

CYPRUS
Nicosia ⊙

SYRIA

Halab •
Latakia •
Hims •

LEBANON
Beirut ⊙
Damascus ⊙

Syrian Desert

Amman ⊙
Jerusalem ⊙
JORDAN

ISRAEL
Tel Aviv-Yafo •
Haifa •
Gaza •

SUEZ CANAL

Al Aqabah •

Al Jawf •

Al Wajh •

Yanbu'al Bahr •

Jiddah •
• Mecca

SAUDI ARABIA

Riyadh ⊙

Rub' al Khali Desert

Nefud Dahi Desert

Hail •

Al Mawsil •
Kirkuk •
Irbil •

IRAQ

Baghdad ⊙

Tigris
Euphrates

An Najaf •
An Nasiriyah •
Al Basrah •

Iraq-Saudi Arabia Neutral Zone

EGYPT

Alexandria •
Cairo ⊙
Tanta •
Suez •
Beni Suef •
El Minya •
Asyut •
Luxor •
Aswan •

Nubian Desert

Port Sudan •

Kassala •

SUDAN

Khartoum ⊙

Karima •

ERITREA
Asmara ⊙

ETHIOPIA

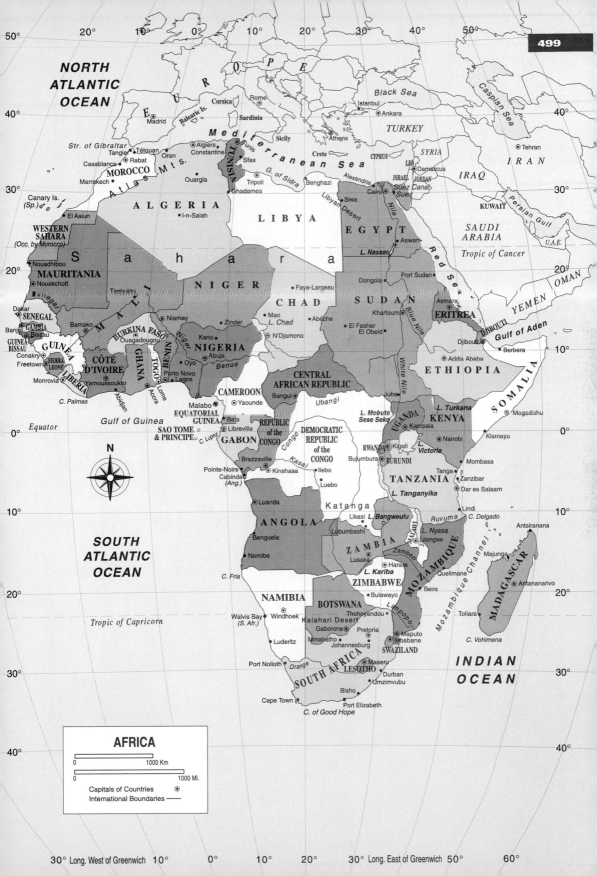

EUROPE

Capitals of Countries ⊙
International Boundaries ——

600 Km
600 Mi.

ATLANTIC OCEAN

ICELAND
Reykjavik

Arctic Circle

Faeroe Is.
(Den.)

Shetland Is.

Orkney Is.

HEBRIDES

GREAT
BRITAIN

Aberdeen
SCOTLAND
Edinburgh

Newcastle
UNITED
KINGDOM

Liverpool
ENGLAND
London

NORTHERN
IRELAND
Belfast

IRELAND
Dublin

Cork

WALES
Cardiff
Bristol

St. George's Channel

Land's End

English Channel

NORWEGIAN Sea

N O R W A Y

Tromsø
Narvik
Lofoten Is.
North Cape

Bodø

Trondheim

Bergen
Stavanger
Oslo

Skagerrak

North
Sea

S W E D E N

Luleå

Vaasa
F I N L A N D
Oulu

Tampere
Helsinki
Gulf of Finland
Gävle
Stockholm
Norrköping
Göteborg
Gotland
Baltic Sea

Kattegat
DENMARK
Copenhagen
Malmö

Gulf of Bothnia

ESTONIA
Tallinn
Riga
LATVIA
LITHUANIA
Vilnius

Kaliningrad
RUSSIA

Gdansk
(Danzig)
Poznan
P O L A N D
Warsaw
Krakow
Wisła

GERMANY
Hamburg
Berlin
Leipzig
Cologne
Bonn
Frankfurt
Elbe
Rhine
Munich

NETHERLANDS
Amsterdam
The Hague
BELGIUM
Brussels
LUX.
Strasbourg

FRANCE
Le Havre
Rouen
Paris
Seine
Loire
Nantes
Bordeaux
Toulouse
Marseille
Lyon
Rhône
Geneva
Nice

Pyrenees
ANDORRA
Barcelona
BALEARIC IS.
Minorca
Majorca

SPAIN
Bilbao
Ebro
Madrid
Valencia
Tagus
Sevilla
Malaga

PORTUGAL
Oporto
Lisbon
Tagus

C. Finisterre

C. St. Vincent

Str. of Gibraltar
GIBRALTAR
(U.K.)
Tangier

A F R I C A

Mediterranean Sea

Corsica
(French)
Ajaccio

Sardinia
(Italian)
Cagliari

I T A L Y
Rome
Naples
Florence
Milan
Venice
Tyrrhenian
Sea
Palermo
Sicily
Catania

VATICAN
CITY
MONACO
SAN
MARINO

SWITZERLAND
Bern
Geneva

LIECHT.
AUSTRIA
Vienna
Graz
Munich
Danube

SLOVENIA
Ljubljana
CROATIA
Zagreb

BOSNIA-
HERZEGOVINA
Sarajevo

YUGOSLAVIA
Belgrade
Serbia
Montenegro

Adriatic Sea

ALBANIA
Tirana

MACEDONIA
Skopje

Ionian
Sea

G R E E C E
Athens
Patrai
Larisa
Thessaloniki

Aegean Sea

CRETE
Iraklion

CZECH
REPUBLIC
Prague

SLOVAKIA
Bratislava

HUNGARY
Budapest

ROMANIA
Bucharest
Cluj-Napoca

BULGARIA
Sofia
Varna

Black Sea

Crimea
Sevastopol
Odessa

MOLDOVA
Chisinau

U K R A I N E
Kiev
Lviv
Dnipropetrovsk
Krivoy Rog
Dnieper
Donets'k
Kharkiv

Sea of
Azov

T U R K E Y
Istanbul
Sea of Marmara
Ankara
Izmir

CYPRUS

BELARUS
Minsk
Gomel'

Vitsyebsk

Smolensk
Kursk

R U S S I A
Moscow
Tver'
St. Petersburg
(Leningrad)
Andropov
Yaroslavl'
Nizhniy
Novgorod
Kirov
Izhevsk
Perm
Kama
Ufa
Orenburg
Samara
Kuybyshev Res.
Penza
Saratov
Volga
Voronezh
Don
Rostov
Volgograd
(Stalingrad)
Astrakhan

Rybinsk Res.

L. Ladoga
L. Onega
Petrozavodsk

White Sea
Arkhangel'sk
Northern Dvina
Murmansk
Kola Pen.

Barents
Sea
Nar'yan-Mar
Pechora
Kolguyev I.
Syktyvkar

U R A L   M O U N T A I N S

Yekaterinburg
Chelyabinsk
Magnitogorsk

Caspian Sea
Baku
AZERBAIJAN
ARMENIA
Yerevan
GEORGIA
Tbilisi
Caucasus Mts.
Grozny
Krasnodar

Longitude East of Greenwich
Longitude West of Greenwich

50°
40°
60°
50°
30°
20°
10°
0°
10°
20°
30°
40°
60°

ATLANTIC
OCEAN

GREENLAND

ARCTIC
North Pole
OCEAN

UNITED STATES
(Alaska)

ICELAND

BERING
SEA

EAST
SIBERIAN
SEA

Anadyr

BRITISH ISLES

Svalbard

BARENTS
SEA

NOVAYA ZEMLYA

SEVERNAYA
ZEMLYA

NEW
SIBERIAN IS.

Komandorskiye Is.

London

NORTH
SEA

KARA SEA

Nordvik

Srednekolymsk

Kolyma

Magadan

Petropavlovsk-
Kamchatskiy

Paris

Berlin

BALTIC
SEA

St. Petersburg

Dudinka

Arctic Circle

Lena

Yakutsk

Nikolayevsk

Sakhalin I.

SEA OF
OKHOTSK

Vienna

EUROPE

Warsaw

R

U

S

S

I

A

Salekhard

Tura

L.
Baykal

Kirensk

Komsomol'sk

Skovorodino

Khabarovsk

Kiev

Moscow

Perm'

Khanty-Mansiysk

Yekaterinburg

TOMSK

Krasnoyarsk

Chita

Qiqihar

Changchun

Hakodate

Vladivostok

Sendai

Honshu

Tokyo

Ural'sk

Magnitogorsk

Omsk

Novosibirsk

Irkutsk

Ulan-Ude

Shenyang

Dandong

N.
KOREA

SEA
OF
JAPAN

Gur'yev

Karaganda

Irtysh

Barnaul

Semipalatinsk

Hovd

Uliastay

Ulaanbaatar

Beijing

Pyongyang

Seoul

Hiroshima

Nagoya

KAZAKHSTAN

ARAL SEA

L. Balkhash

MONGOLIA

Gobi

Tianjin

S.
KOREA

YELLOW
SEA

Nagasaki

Shikoku

Kyushu

CASPIAN SEA

Krasnovodsk

Tashkent

Bishkek

Alma-Ata

Urumqi

SINKIANG

INNER MONGOLIA

Huang

Great Wall

Jinan

GRAND CANAL

Kaifeng

Shanghai

EAST
CHINA
SEA

RYUKYU IS.
(Jap.)

Tropic of Cancer

Izmir

TURKEY

Ankara

Erzurum

Tabriz

TURKMENISTAN

Ashkhabad

UZBEK.

Amu Darya

KYRGYZ.

Aksu

Kokand

TAJIK.

Shache

Yumen

Lanzhou

Xi'an

Wuhan

Nanjing

MED.
SEA

CYPRUS

Adana

Aleppo

SYRIA

Damascus

Tehran

Mashad

Herat

Hotan

C

H

I

N

A

Chongqing

Changsha

Fuzhou

Taipei

TAIWAN

LEBANON

Beirut

Jerusalem

ISRAEL

JORDAN

Amman

IRAQ

Baghdad

Basra

I

R

A

N

AFGHANISTAN

Kabul

Srinagar

Islamabad

TIBET

Lhasa

Chang (Yangtze)

Guangzhou

HONG KONG

PACIFIC
OCEAN

KUWAIT

BAHRAIN

QATAR

Shiraz

Bandar
Abbas

PAKISTAN

NEPAL

Thimphu

BHUTAN

Himalaya

Mandalay

Hanoi

Luzon

PHILIPPINES

Manila

Samar

Riyadh

UN. ARAB
EMIR.

Persian G.

G. of Oman

Gwadar

Muscat

Karachi

New Delhi

Kanpur

Kathmandu

Brahmaputra

Myitkyina

G. of Tonkin

SOUTH
CHINA
SEA

Hainan

Mindoro

Leyte

Mecca

SAUDI
ARABIA

RED
SEA

OMAN

Ahmadabad

I

N

D

I

A

Daman

Calcutta

Dhaka

BANGLA-
DESH

MYANMAR

LAOS

Rangoon

Vientiane

THAILAND

VIETNAM

Palawan

Negros

Davao

Mindanao

Sanaa

YEMEN

Aden

G. of Aden

Socotra

ARABIAN
SEA

Bombay

Hyderabad

Yanam

Bangalore

Madras

Karikal

BAY OF
BENGAL

Bangkok

CAMBODIA

Phnom Penh

Ho Chi Minh City
(Saigon)

G. of
Thailand

SABAH

Kota Kinabalu

BRUNEI

SARAWAK

CELEBES
SEA

Manado

AFRICA

Mahe

Madurai

SRI LANKA
(CEYLON)

Colombo

Kandy

MALDIVES

Male

George Town

Medan

Str. of Malacca

MALAYA

Kuala Lumpur

SINGAPORE

Kuching

Borneo

Banjarmasin

MALAYSIA

Celebes

Makassar Str.

Ujung Pandang

BANDA
SEA

SEYCHELLES

N

Sumatra

INDONESIA

Palembang

Jakarta

JAVA

Surabaya

JAVA SEA

Sumbawa

FLORES SEA

Flores

Timor

TIMOR
SEA

INDIAN OCEAN

SUNDA IS.

Broome

MADAGASCAR

Equator

Tropic of Capricorn

AUSTRALIA

Perth

ASIA

0   1200 Km

0   1200 Mi.

Capitals of Countries

International Boundaries

60°   Longitude East of Greenwich   80°   100°   120°

MEXICO

UNITED STATES

20°

CHINA

100°

120°

140°

160°

180°

160°

140°

120°

100°

Tropic of Cancer

Equator

Tropic of Capricorn

Longitude West of Greenwich

Easter Is.

French Polynesia

Society Is.
Tahiti

N

P A C I F I C   O C E A N

Hawaiian Islands
Maui
Hawaii

UNITED STATES
(*Hawaii*)

P   O   L   Y

International Date Line

K I R I B A T I

N

WESTERN
SAMOA
Apia

AMERICAN
SAMOA
Pago Pago

TONGA
Nuku'alofa
Tongatabu

TUVALU
Funafuti

FIJI
Suva
Viti Levu

Marshall Islands
Kwajalein
Majuro

Kosrae

Tarawa
Bairiki

NAURU

M I C R O N E S I A

C A R O L I N E   I S L A N D S
(*Fed. States of Micronesia*)

Chuck
Palikir
Pohnpei

Northern
Mariana
Islands
Saipan
Tinian
Rota

Guam
Agana

Yap

PALAU

M E L A N E S I A

SOLOMON ISLANDS
Santa Isabel
Guadalcanal
Honiara

VANUATU
Port Vila

New
Caledonia
Noumea
Loyalty Is.

Norfolk I.

Lord Howe I.

N.KOREA
S.KOREA
JAPAN

EAST
CHINA
SEA

TAIWAN

PHILIPPINES
Luzon
Laoag
Manila
Mindoro
Samar
Mindanao
Davao

SOUTH
CHINA
SEA

THAILAND
CAMBODIA
VIETNAM
LAOS

MALAYSIA
Brunei
Borneo

CELEBES
SEA

Celebes
Manado
Molucca Is.
Ceram

BANDA SEA

I N D O N E S I A

Java
Flores
Timor
Kupang

ARAFURA
SEA

TIMOR SEA

Melville I.

Darwin
Wyndham

Palawan

Makassar Str.

PAPUA
NEW
GUINEA
Port Moresby
Manokwari
Jayapura

NEW GUINEA

Gulf of
Carpentaria

CORAL SEA

Gt. Barrier Reef

Normanton
Townsville
Cloncurry
Mt. Isa
Longreach

Rockhampton
Bundaberg
Brisbane

Grafton

Newcastle
New South
Wales
Sydney
CANBERRA

Melbourne
Victoria
Geelong

Tasmania
Launceston
Hobart
Southeast Cape

Bass Str.

Queensland

A   U   S   T   R   A   L   I   A

Northern
Australia
Tennant Cr.
Alice Sprs.
Des.

South Australia
L. Eyre
L. Torrens
Port Augusta
Port Pirie
Port Lincoln
Adelaide

Gt.
Australian
Bight

Western
Australia
Gt. Victoria
Desert
Gibson Des.
Kalgoorlie
Wiluna
Perth
Fremantle
Albany
C. Leeuwin

Geraldton
Carnarvon
Onslow
Port Hedland
Hall's Cr.
Broome

Gt. Sandy Des.

Darling
Murray

Gulf

I N D I A N   O C E A N

20°

TASMAN
SEA

NEW
ZEALAND
North Island
East Cape
Napier
Wellington
Cook Str.
Nelson
South
Island
Christchurch
Invercargill
Stewart I.
Auckland
Hamilton
North Cape

Longitude East of Greenwich

Index to World Maps

Country	Latitude	Longitude	Country	Latitude	Longitude
Jordan	31° N	36° E	Pakistan	30° N	70° E
Kazakhstan	45° N	70° E	Palau	8° N	138° E
Kenya	1° N	38° E	Panama	9° N	80° W
Kiribati	0° N	175° E	Papua New Guinea	6° S	147° E
North Korea	40° N	127° E	Paraguay	23° S	58° W
South Korea	36° N	128° E	Peru	10° S	76° W
Kuwait	29° N	47° E	The Philippines	13° N	122° E
Kyrgyzstan	42° N	75° E	Poland	52° N	19° E
Laos	18° N	105° E	Portugal	39° N	8° W
Latvia	57° N	25° E	Qatar	25° N	51° E
Lebanon	34° N	36° E	Romania	46° N	25° E
Lesotho	29° S	28° E	Russia	60° N	80° E
Liberia	6° N	10° W	Rwanda	2° S	30° E
Libya	27° N	17° E	St. Kitts and Nevis	17° N	62° W
Liechtenstein	47° N	9° E	Saint Lucia	14° N	61° W
Lithuania	56° N	24° E	Saint Vincent and		
Luxembourg	49° N	6° E	the Grenadines	13° N	61° W
Macedonia	43° N	22° E	San Marino	44° N	12° E
Madagascar	19° S	46° E	São Tomé and		
Malawi	13° S	34° E	Príncipe	1° N	7° E
Malaysia	2° N	112° E	Saudi Arabia	25° N	45° E
Maldives	2° N	70° E	Scotland	57° N	5° W
Mali	17° N	4° W	Senegal	14° N	14° W
Malta	36° N	14° E	Serbia	45° N	21° E
Marshall Islands	7° N	172° E	Seychelles	5° S	55° E
Mauritania	20° N	12° W	Sierra Leone	8° N	11° W
Mauritius	20° S	57° E	Singapore	1° N	103° E
Mexico	23° N	102° W	Slovakia	49° N	19° E
Micronesia	5° N	150° E	Slovenia	46° N	15° E
Moldova	47° N	28° E	Solomon Islands	8° S	159° E
Monaco	43° N	7° E	Somalia	10° N	49° E
Mongolia	46° N	105° E	South Africa	30° S	26° E
Montenegro	43° N	19° E	Spain	40° N	4° W
Morocco	32° N	5° W	Sri Lanka	7° N	81° E
Mozambique	18° S	35° E	Sudan	15° N	30° E
Myanmar	25° N	95° E	Suriname	4° N	56° W
Namibia	22° S	17° E	Swaziland	26° S	31° E
Nauru	1° S	166° E	Sweden	62° N	15° E
Nepal	28° N	84° E	Switzerland	47° N	8° E
The Netherlands	52° N	5° E	Syria	35° N	38° E
New Zealand	41° S	174° E	Taiwan	23° N	121° E
Nicaragua	13° N	85° W	Tajikistan	39° N	71° E
Niger	16° N	8° E	Tanzania	6° S	35° E
Nigeria	10° N	8° E	Thailand	15° N	100° E
Northern Ireland	55° N	7° W	Togo	8° N	1° E
Norway	62° N	10° E	Tonga	20° S	173° W
Oman	22° N	58° E	Trinidad & Tobago	11° N	61° W

Country	Latitude	Longitude	Country	Latitude	Longitude
Tunisia	34° N	9° E	Uzbekistan	40° N	68° E
Turkey	39° N	35° E	Vanuatu	17° S	170° E
Turkmenistan	40° N	55° E	Venezuela	8° N	66° W
Tuvalu	8° S	179° E	Vietnam	17° N	106° E
Uganda	1° N	32° E	Wales	53° N	3° W
Ukraine	50° N	30° E	Western Samoa	10° S	173° W
United Arab			Yemen	15° N	44° E
Emirates	24° N	54° E	Yugoslavia	44° N	19° E
United Kingdom	54° N	2° W	Zambia	15° S	30° E
United States	38° N	97° W	Zimbabwe	20° S	30° E
Uruguay	33° S	56° W			

Geographic Facts

THE CONTINENTS

	Area (Sq Km)	Percent of Earth's Land
Asia	44,026,000	29.7
Africa	30,271,000	20.4
North America	24,258,000	16.3
South America	17,823,000	12.0
Antarctica	13,209,000	8.9
Europe	10,404,000	7.0
Australia	7,682,000	5.2

LONGEST RIVERS

	Length (Km)
Nile, *Africa*	6,671
Amazon, *South America*	6,437
Chang Jiang (Yangtze), *Asia*	6,380
Mississippi-Missouri, *North America*	5,971
Ob-Irtysk, *Asia*	5,410
Huang (Yellow), *Asia*	4,672
Congo, *Africa*	4,667
Amur, *Asia*	4,416
Lena, *Asia*	4,400
Mackenzie-Peace, *North America*	4,241

MAJOR ISLANDS

	Area (Sq Km)
Greenland	2,175,600
New Guinea	792,500
Borneo	725,500
Madagascar	587,000
Baffin	507,500
Sumatra	427,300
Honshu	227,400
Great Britain	218,100
Victoria	217,300
Ellesmere	196,200
Celebes	178,700
South (New Zealand)	151,000
Java	126,700

THE OCEANS

	Area (Sq Km)	Percent of Earth's Water Area
Pacific	166,241,000	46.0
Atlantic	86,557,000	23.9
Indian	73,427,000	20.3
Arctic	9,485,000	2.6

World Time Zones

The world's time zones start at the prime meridian and divide the world into 24 time zones. When going west, travelers must set their watches back one hour for each time zone they cross. Going east, they must set their watches forward one hour for each zone.

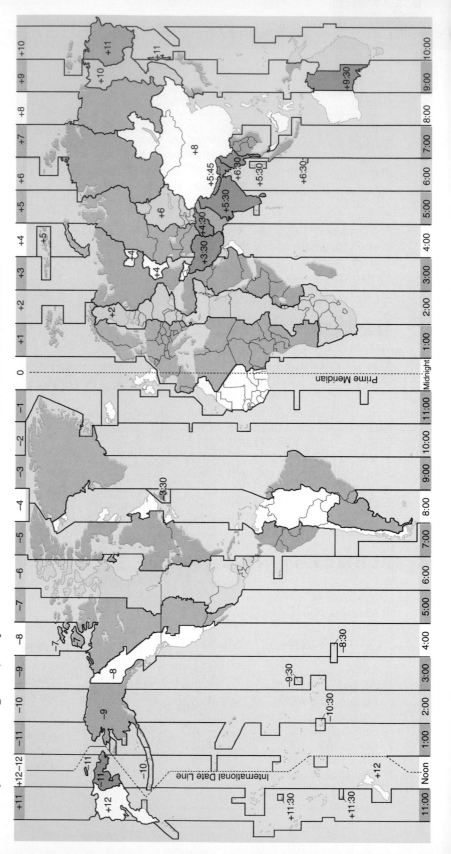

Government

Every country in the world has a government. The purpose of the government is to make and enforce laws and to protect the rights of its citizens. Every major country in the world also has a constitution, a basic set of laws by which the people are governed.

The U.S. Constitution establishes the form of the United States government and explains the rights and responsibilities of its citizens. This section of your handbook takes a closer look at those rights and responsibilities, and how the government is organized. We hope you find it interesting and useful.

Branches of the Government

Legislative Branch	Executive Branch	Judicial Branch
	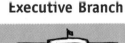	

Duties/Responsibilities

Makes Laws	Enforces Laws Makes Policy	Interprets Laws

Components

Congress	President	Supreme Court
Senate / House of Representatives	Vice President	Circuit Courts
President of the Senate / Speaker of the House	Cabinet	District and Special Courts

President's Cabinet

The Cabinet is a group of advisers appointed by the president to help set policies and make decisions. The Cabinet usually meets weekly with the president.

Department of State

Department of Education

Department of Health and Human Services

Department of Defense

Department of the Treasury

Department of Veterans Affairs

Department of Commerce

Department of the Interior

Department of Energy

Department of Housing and Urban Development

Attorney General

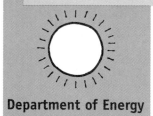

Department of Labor

Department of Agriculture

Department of Transportation

Individual Rights and Responsibilities

Individual Rights

Freedom of Assembly

Freedom to hold meetings. Meetings must be peaceful.

Freedom of Speech

Freedom to express ideas and opinions. No one may say untrue things about other citizens.

Freedom of Petition

Freedom to ask the government to pass laws.

Freedom of the Press

Freedom to print books, newspapers, and magazines. No one may print things that hurt American citizens.

Freedom of Religion

Freedom to practice the religion of your choice.

Freedom of Equal Justice

All persons accused of a crime must receive fair and equal treatment under law.

Freedom and Security of Citizens

No one may search someone's home. People have the right to bear arms to protect themselves.

American citizens must . . .

- serve as jury members when called upon.
- pay taxes to fund the government.
- attend school.
- testify in court.
- obey the law.
- help to defend the nation.

U.S. Presidents and Vice Presidents

1 George Washington........... April 30, 1789 – March 3, 1797 ....John Adams 1
2 John Adams .... March 4, 1797 – March 3, 1801.........Thomas Jefferson 2
3 Thomas Jefferson............. March 4, 1801 – March 3, 1805..................Aaron Burr 3
  Thomas Jefferson............. March 4, 1805 – March 3, 1809.............George Clinton 4
4 James Madison .... March 4, 1809 – March 3, 1813.............George Clinton
  James Madison .... March 4, 1813 – March 3, 1817 ....Elbridge Gerry 5
5 James Monroe.................. March 4, 1817 – March 3, 1821.....Daniel D. Tompkins 6
  James Monroe.................. March 4, 1821 – March 3, 1825
6 John Quincy Adams .... March 4, 1825 – March 3, 1829 ....John C. Calhoun 7
7 Andrew Jackson............... March 4, 1829 – March 3, 1833 ....John C. Calhoun
  Andrew Jackson............... March 4, 1833 – March 3, 1837 ....Martin Van Buren 8
8 Martin Van Buren .... March 4, 1837 – March 3, 1841 ....Richard M. Johnson 9
9 William Henry Harrison* March 4, 1841 – April 4, 1841 ....John Tyler 10
10 John Tyler .... April 6, 1841 – March 3, 1845
11 James K. Polk .... March 4, 1845 – March 3, 1849.........George M. Dallas 11
12 Zachary Taylor* .... March 5, 1849 – July 9, 1850 ....Millard Fillmore 12
13 Millard Fillmore .... July 10, 1850 – March 3, 1853
14 Franklin Pierce................ March 4, 1853 – March 3, 1857 ....William R. King 13
15 James Buchanan .... March 4, 1857 – March 3, 1861...John C. Breckinridge 14
16 Abraham Lincoln............. March 4, 1861 – March 3, 1865.........Hannibal Hamlin 15
  Abraham Lincoln* .... March 4, 1865 – April 15, 1865 ....Andrew Johnson 16
17 Andrew Johnson .... April 15, 1865 – March 3, 1869
18 Ulysses S. Grant.............. March 4, 1869 – March 3, 1873............Schuyler Colfax 17
  Ulysses S. Grant.............. March 4, 1873 – March 3, 1877 ....Henry Wilson 18
19 Rutherford B. Hayes .... March 4, 1877 – March 3, 1881 .....William A. Wheeler 19
20 James A. Garfield* .... March 4, 1881 – Sept. 19, 1881........Chester A. Arthur 20
21 Chester A. Arthur............. Sept. 20, 1881 – March 3, 1885
22 Grover Cleveland............. March 4, 1885 – March 3, 1889..Thomas A. Hendricks 21
23 Benjamin Harrison........... March 4, 1889 – March 3, 1893 ....Levi P. Morton 22
24 Grover Cleveland............. March 4, 1893 – March 3, 1897 ......Adlai E. Stevenson 23
25 William McKinley............. March 4, 1897 – March 3, 1901 ....Garret A. Hobart 24
  William McKinley* .... March 4, 1901 – Sept. 14, 1901 ......Theodore Roosevelt 25
26 Theodore Roosevelt.......... Sept. 14, 1901 – March 3, 1905
  Theodore Roosevelt.......... March 4, 1905 – March 3, 1909..Charles W. Fairbanks 26
27 William H. Taft................. March 4, 1909 – March 3, 1913.......James S. Sherman 27
28 Woodrow Wilson .... March 4, 1913 – March 3, 1917....Thomas R. Marshall 28
  Woodrow Wilson .... March 4, 1917 – March 3, 1921
29 Warren G. Harding* .... March 4, 1921 – Aug. 2, 1923...............Calvin Coolidge 29
30 Calvin Coolidge.................. Aug. 3, 1923 – March 3, 1925
  Calvin Coolidge................. March 4, 1925 – March 3, 1929 ....Charles G. Dawes 30
31 Herbert C. Hoover .... March 4, 1929 – March 3, 1933 ....Charles Curtis 31

32 Franklin D. Roosevelt ...... March 4, 1933 – Jan. 20, 1937..............John N. Garner 32

    Franklin D. Roosevelt .... Jan. 20, 1937 – Jan. 20, 1941..............John N. Garner

    Franklin D. Roosevelt .... Jan. 20, 1941 – Jan. 20, 1945 ....Henry A. Wallace 33

    Franklin D. Roosevelt* ...... Jan. 20, 1945 – April 12, 1945 ....Harry S. Truman 34

33 Harry S. Truman .... April 12, 1945 – Jan. 20, 1949

    Harry S. Truman............... Jan. 20, 1949 – Jan. 20, 1953 ....Alben W. Barkley 35

34 Dwight D. Eisenhower .... Jan. 20, 1953 – Jan. 20, 1957 ....Richard M. Nixon 36

    Dwight D. Eisenhower .... Jan. 20, 1957 – Jan. 20, 1961 ....Richard M. Nixon

35 John F. Kennedy* .... Jan. 20, 1961 – Nov. 22, 1963........Lyndon B. Johnson 37

36 Lyndon B. Johnson............. Nov. 22, 1963 – Jan. 20, 1965

    Lyndon B. Johnson............. Jan. 20, 1965 – Jan. 20, 1969 ...Hubert H. Humphrey 38

37 Richard M. Nixon .... Jan. 20, 1969 – Jan. 20, 1973 ....Spiro T. Agnew 39

    Richard M. Nixon* .... Jan. 20, 1973 – Aug. 9, 1974 ....Gerald R. Ford 40

38 Gerald R. Ford .... Aug. 9, 1974 – Jan. 20, 1977....Nelson A. Rockefeller 41

39 James E. Carter .... Jan. 20, 1977 – Jan. 20, 1981 ....Walter Mondale 42

40 Ronald W. Reagan .... Jan. 20, 1981 – Jan. 20, 1985........George H. W. Bush 43

    Ronald W. Reagan .... Jan. 20, 1985 – Jan. 20, 1989........George H. W. Bush

41 George H. W. Bush............. Jan. 20, 1989 – Jan. 20, 1993........J. Danforth Quayle 44

42 William J. Clinton .... Jan. 20, 1993 – Jan. 20, 1997..............Albert Gore, Jr. 45

    William J. Clinton .... Jan. 20, 1997 – ....Albert Gore, Jr. .....

(*Did not finish term)

ORDER OF PRESIDENTIAL SUCCESSION

1. Vice president
2. Speaker of the House
3. President pro tempore of the Senate
4. Secretary of state
5. Secretary of the treasury
6. Secretary of defense
7. Attorney general
8. Secretary of the interior
9. Secretary of agriculture
10. Secretary of commerce
11. Secretary of labor
12. Secretary of health and human services
13. Secretary of housing and urban development
14. Secretary of transportation
15. Secretary of energy
16. Secretary of education
17. Secretary of veterans affairs

The U.S. Constitution

The Constitution is made up of three main parts: a preamble, 7 **articles,** and 27 **amendments.** The *preamble* states the purpose of the Constitution, the *articles* explain how the government works, and the 10 original *amendments* list the basic rights guaranteed to all American citizens. Together, these parts contain the laws and guidelines necessary to set up and run a successful national government.

Besides giving power to the national government, the U.S. Constitution gives some power to the states and some to the people. Remember this when you study the Constitution.

The Preamble

We the people of the United States, in order to form a more perfect Union, establish justice, insure domestic tranquility, provide for the common defense, promote the general welfare, and secure the blessings of liberty to ourselves and our posterity, do ordain and establish this Constitution for the United States of America.

The Articles of the Constitution

The articles of the Constitution explain how each branch of government works and what each can and cannot do. The articles also explain how the federal and state governments must work together, and how the Constitution can be amended or changed.

ARTICLE 1 explains the legislative branch, how laws are made, and how Congress works.

ARTICLE 2 explains the executive branch, the offices of the President and Vice President, and the powers of the executive branch.

ARTICLE 3 explains the judicial branch, the Supreme Court and other courts, and warns people about trying to overthrow the government.

ARTICLE 4 describes how the United States federal government and the individual state governments work together.

ARTICLE 5 tells how the Constitution can be amended, or changed.

ARTICLE 6 states that the United States federal government and the Constitution are the law of the land.

ARTICLE 7 outlines how the Constitution must be adopted to become official.

The Bill of Rights

To get the necessary votes to approve the Constitution, a number of changes (amendments) had to be made. These 10 original amendments are called the Bill of Rights. They guarantee all Americans some very basic rights, including the right to worship and speak freely and the right to have a jury trial.

AMENDMENT 1 People have the right to worship, to speak freely, to gather together, and to question the government.

AMENDMENT 2 People have the right to bear arms.

AMENDMENT 3 The government cannot have soldiers stay in people's houses without their permission.

AMENDMENT 4 People and their property cannot be searched without the written permission of a judge.

AMENDMENT 5 People cannot be tried for a serious crime without a jury. They cannot be tried twice for the same crime or be forced to testify against themselves. Also, they cannot have property taken away while they are on trial. Any property taken for public use must receive a fair price.

AMENDMENT 6 In criminal cases, people have a right to a trial, to be told what they are accused of, to hear witnesses against them, to get witnesses in their favor, and to have a lawyer.

AMENDMENT 7 In cases involving more than $20, people have the right to a jury trial.

AMENDMENT 8 People have a right to fair bail (money given as a promise the person will return for trial) and to fair fines and punishments.

AMENDMENT 9 People have rights that are not listed in the Constitution.

AMENDMENT 10 Powers not given to the federal government are given to the states or to the people.

The Other Amendments

The Constitution and the Bill of Rights were ratified in 1791. Since that time, more than 7,000 amendments to the Constitution have been proposed. Because three-fourths of the states must approve an amendment before it becomes law, just 27 amendments have been passed. The first 10 are listed under the Bill of Rights; the other 17 are listed below. (The date each amendment became law is given in parentheses.)

AMENDMENT 11 A person cannot sue a state in federal court. (1795)

AMENDMENT 12 President and Vice President are elected separately. (1804)

AMENDMENT 13 Slavery is abolished, done away with. (1865)

AMENDMENT 14 All persons born in the United States or those who have become citizens enjoy full citizenship rights. (1868)

AMENDMENT 15 Voting rights are given to all (adult male) citizens regardless of race, creed, or color. (1870)

AMENDMENT 16 Congress has the power to collect income taxes. (1913)

AMENDMENT 17 United States Senators are elected directly by the people. (1913)

AMENDMENT 18 Making, buying, and selling alcoholic beverages is no longer allowed. (1919)

AMENDMENT 19 Women gain the right to vote. (1920)

AMENDMENT 20 The President's term begins January 20; Senators' and Representatives' terms begin January 3. (1933)

AMENDMENT 21 (Repeals Amendment 18) Alcoholic beverages can be made, bought, and sold again. (1933)

AMENDMENT 22 The President is limited to two elected terms. (1951)

AMENDMENT 23 District of Columbia residents gain the right to vote. (1961)

AMENDMENT 24 All voter poll taxes are forbidden. (1964)

AMENDMENT 25 If the Presidency is vacant, the Vice President takes over. If the Vice Presidency is vacant, the President names someone and the Congress votes on the choice. (1967)

AMENDMENT 26 Citizens 18 years old gain the right to vote. (1971)

AMENDMENT 27 No law changing the pay for members of Congress will take effect until after an election of Representatives. (1992)

History

A famous American author, Oliver Wendell Holmes, once said, "When I want to understand what is happening today or try to decide what will happen tomorrow, I look back." In other words, we can learn a lot about the world around us by looking at what has happened in the past—by studying history.

Historical Time Line

The historical time line included on the next 10 pages will help you look back. The time line covers the period from 1500 to the present. You'll notice that the time line is divided into three main parts: United States History, Science and Inventions, and Literature and Life. You'll discover many interesting things in the time line—when watches were invented (1509), when paper money was first used in America (1690), and who developed the first pair of blue jeans (Levi Strauss in 1850).

But even before the first European settlers arrived in the United States, there were many Native American tribes living here. As you'll see on the map below, each tribe lived in one of five major regions. American history really begins with the Native Americans.

Native American Regions

Coastal
Plains
Mountain
Desert
Woodland

1500   1520   1540   1560   1580

United States History

1492
Columbus reaches the West Indies.

1513
Ponce de León explores Florida.

1519
Magellan begins three-year voyage around the world.

1519
Aztec empire dominates Mexico.

1521
Cortez defeats Aztecs and claims Mexico for Spain.

1559
Spanish colony of Pensacola, Florida, lasts two years.

1565
Spain settles St. Augustine, Florida, first permanent European colony.

1570
League of the Iroquois Nations formed.

1588
England defeats the Spanish Armada and rules the seas.

1590
English colony of Roanoke vanishes.

Science and Inventions

1507
Book on surgery is developed.

1509
Watches are invented.

1530
Bottle corks are invented.

1531
Halley's Comet appears and causes panic.

1543
Copernicus challenges beliefs by claiming sun-centered universe.

1545
French printer Garamond sets first type.

1558
Magnetic compass invented by John Dee.

1585
Decimals introduced by Dutch mathematicians.

1590
First paper mill is used in England.

1596
Thermometer is invented.

Literature and Life

1500
Game of bingo developed.

1503
Pocket handkerchiefs are first used.

1507
Glass mirrors are greatly improved.

1536
First songbook used in Spain.

1538
Mercator draws map with America on it.

1541
Michelangelo completes largest painting, "The Last Judgement."

1564
First horse-drawn coach used in England.

1580
First water closet designed in Bath, England.

1582
Pope Gregory XIII introduces the calendar still in use today.

1599
First copper coins are made.

U.S. Population: (Native American)   (Spanish)

approximately 1,100,000   **1,021**

1600   **1620**   **1640**   **1660**   **1680**   **1700**

1619
House of Burgesses in Virginia
establishes first representative
government in colonies.

1664
The Dutch colony of
New Netherlands
becomes the English
colony of New York.

1690
Paper
money
first
used in
America.

1607
England
establishes
Jamestown,
Virginia,
first English
settlement.

1620
Pilgrims found Plymouth Colony.

1673
Marquette and Joliet
explore Mississippi
River for France.

1629
Massachusetts Bay Colony is established.

1609
Henry Hudson explores
the Hudson River.

1634
Colony of Maryland
is founded.

1682
William Penn
founds
Pennsylvania.

1608
Telescope is
invented.

1629
Human temperature measured
by physician in Italy.

1668
Reflecting
telescope
invented
by Sir
Isaac
Newton.

1641
First cotton
factories begin
operating in
England.

1682
Halley's Comet is
studied by Edmund
Halley and named
for him.

1609
Galileo makes
first observations
with telescope.

1643
Torricelli
invents the
barometer.

1671
First calculation
machine invented.

1600
William Shakespeare's
plays are performed at
Globe Theatre in London.

1630
Popcorn is
introduced to
Pilgrims by
Quadequina.

1685
First drinking
fountain used
in England.

1653
First postage stamps
used in Paris.

1622
January 1 accepted as
beginning of the year
(instead of March 25).

1697
*Tales of
Mother
Goose*
written by
Charles
Perrault.

1658
First illustrated book for
children, ***World of Visible
Objects in Pictures,*** written
by John Comenius.

1609
"Three Blind
Mice" is
written.

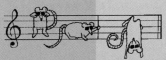

(English)

350   **2,302**   **26,634**   **75,058**   **151,507**

1700 **1710** **1720** **1730** **1740**

United States History

1700
France builds forts at Mackinac and Detroit and controls fur trade.

1705
Virginia Act establishes public education.

1707
England (English) and Scotland (Scots) unite and become Great Britain (British).

Scotland

England

1718
New Orleans founded by France.

1733
James Oglethorpe founds Georgia.

1733
British Molasses Act places taxes on sugar and molasses.

1735
Freedom of the press established during trial of John Peter Zenger.

1747
Ohio Company formed to settle Ohio River Valley.

Science and Inventions

1701
Seed drill that plants seeds in a row is invented by Jethro Tull.

1712
Thomas Newcomen develops first practical steam engine.

1709
The pianoforte (first piano) is invented by Christofori Bartolommeo.

1728
First dental drill is used by Pierre Fauchard.

1732
Sedatives for operations discovered by Thomas Dover.

1735
Rubber found in South America.

1738
First cuckoo clocks invented in Germany.

1742
Benjamin Franklin invents efficient Franklin stove.

Literature and Life

1700
The Selling of Joseph by Samuell Sewall is first protest of slavery.

1704
First successful newspaper in colonies, *Boston News-Letter,* is published.

1716
First hot-water home heating system developed.

1719
Robinson Crusoe written by Daniel Defoe.

1726
Gulliver's Travels written by Jonathan Swift.

1731
Ben Franklin begins first subscription library.

1736
First American cookbook is written by Mrs. E. Smith.

1744
John Newbery publishes children's book, *A Little Pretty Pocket-Book.*

U.S. Population: (English Colonies)

| 250,888 | 331,711 | 466,185 | 629,445 | 905,563 |

1750	1760	1770	1780	1790	1800

1750
The French and Indian War begins.

1750
Flatbed boats and Conestoga wagons begin moving settlers west.

1763
Britain defeats France in French and Indian War.

1765
Stamp Act tax imposed on colonies by Britain.

1775
First battles of the Revolutionary War are fought.

1776
Declaration of Independence signed at Second Continental Congress on July 4.

1781
British surrender at Yorktown Oct. 19.

1781
United colonies adopt Articles of Confederation as first government.

1787
The United States Constitution is signed.

1789
George Washington elected president of the United States.

1797
U.S.S. Constitution is launched.

1752
Benjamin Franklin discovers lightning is a form of electricity.

1758
Sextant for navigation is invented by John Bird.

1764
"Spinning jenny" for cotton is invented by James Hargreaves.

1770
First steam carriage is invented by French engineer Nicholas Cugnot.

1781
Uranus, first planet not known to ancient world, is discovered.

1783
First balloon is flown by Frenchmen Joseph and Jacques Montgolfier.

1793
Eli Whitney invents cotton gin that takes seeds out of cotton.

1798
Eli Whitney invents mass production.

1752
First general hospital is established in Philadelphia.

1757
Streetlights are installed in Philadelphia.

1764
Mozart writes first symphony.

1769
Venetian blinds are first used.

1780
The waltz becomes popular dance.

1782
The American bald eagle is first used as symbol of the United States.

1786
First ice-cream company in America begins production.

1790
Official U.S. census begins.

1795
Food canning is introduced.

1,170,760	1,593,625	2,148,076	2,780,369	3,929,157

1800   1810   1820   1830   1840

United States History

1800
Washington, D.C., becomes U.S. capital.

1803
Louisiana Purchase from France doubles U.S. size.

1803
Lewis & Clark explore Louisiana Territory & the Northwest.

1812-1814
War of 1812 fought between U.S. and Britain.

1819
U.S. acquires Florida from Spain.

1821
Sierre Leone established by U.S. for freed slaves.

1830
Indian Removal Act forces Native Americans west of Mississippi River.

1836
Texans defend the Alamo.

1838
Cherokee Nation forced west on "Trail of Tears."

1846
Mexican War gives U.S. Southwestern territories.

1846
Britain cedes Oregon Country to U.S.

1848
Gold discovered in California.

Science and Inventions

1800
The battery is invented by Count Volta.

1802
Steamboat is built by Robert Fulton.

1808
Chemical symbols are developed by Jöns Berzelius.

1816
Stethoscope invented by René Laënnec.

1817
The Erie Canal is begun.

1819
Electromagnetism discovered by Hans Christian Oestad.

1836
Samuel Morse invents telegraph.

1839
Bicycle is invented by Kirkpatrick Macmillan.

1841
Stapler is developed.

1844
Safety matches produced.

1846
Elias Howe invents sewing machine.

Literature and Life

1804
First book of children's poems is published.

1806
Gas lighting used in homes.

1812
Army meat inspector, "Uncle Sam" Wilson, becomes U.S. symbol.

1814
Francis Scott Key writes "The Star-Spangled Banner."

1816
J. Niepce takes first photograph.

1820
Rip Van Winkle is written by Washington Irving.

1827
Audubon's *Birds of America* is published.

1828
Webster's Dictionary is published.

1834
Louis Braille perfects a letter system for the blind.

1835
Hans Christian Anderson publishes *Tales Told to Children*.

1849
Elizabeth Blackwell becomes first woman doctor.

1849
Safety pin is invented.

U.S. Population:

| 5,308,080 | 7,240,102 | 9,638,453 | 12,860,702 | 17,063,353 |

1850   1860   1870   1880   1890   1900

1853
National Council of Colored People is founded.

1860
Abraham Lincoln elected 16th president of the U.S.

1861
Civil War begins when Confederates fire on Fort Sumter.

1862
Lincoln proclaims abolition of slavery in U.S.

1876
Custer defeated at Battle of Little Big Horn.

1876
U.S. Centennial celebrated.

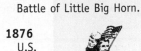

1869
Coast-to-coast railroad is finished in Utah.

1898
U.S. defeats Spain in Spanish-American War.

1889
Jane Addams founds Hull House in Chicago to help immigrants.

1851
Isaac Singer produces sewing machine.

1852
Elisha Otis invents first elevator with a safety brake.

1857
Atlantic cable is completed.

1860
Internal combustion engine built by Jean Lenoir.

1865
Antiseptic practices are introduced by Joseph Lister.

1874
Barbed wire introduced by Joseph Glidden.

1876
Alexander Graham Bell invents telephone.

1877
Thomas Edison invents phonograph.

1879
Edison makes incandescent lightbulb.

1887
Radio waves produced by Hertz.

1893
Charles and Frank Duryea build first successful U.S. gasoline automobile.

1896
Marconi invents wireless radio.

1850
Levi Strauss produces blue jeans.

1852
Uncle Tom's Cabin by Harriet Beecher Stowe strengthens antislavery movement.

1855
Alexander Parks produces first synthetic plastic.

1864
Red Cross is established.

1869
Chewing gum is patented.

1873
Zipper invented by Whitcomb Judson.

1876
National Baseball League established.

1882
Malted milk produced by William Horlick.

1883
Four U.S. time zones are established.

1886
Dr. Penberton invents Coca-Cola.

1889
Roll film produced by George Eastman.

1892
The first basketball game is played.

23,191,876   31,443,321   38,558,371   50,189,209   62,979,766

1900   1905   1910   1915   1920

United States History

1900
First Olympics involving women held in Paris.

1903
Orville and Wilbur Wright fly first successful airplane.

1909
National Association for the Advancement of Colored People (NAACP) is founded.

1913
Income Tax Amendment establishes a tax on wages people make.

1914
Panama Canal opens.

1914
World War I in Europe begins.

1917
United States enters World War I.

1918
World War I ends in Europe.

1920
Prohibition of alcoholic beverages begins.

1920
Women given right to vote.

Science and Inventions

1901
Walter Reed discovers yellow fever is carried by mosquitos.

1905
Albert Einstein announces theory of relativity $(E=mc^2)$ of time and space.

$E=mc^2$

1904
New York City opens its subway system.

1913
Henry Ford establishes assembly line for automobiles.

1915
Coast-to-coast telephone system established.

1921
Vaccine for tuberculosis is discovered.

1922
Philo T. Farnsworth develops electron scanner for television.

Literature and Life

1900
American Baseball League established.

1900
Hot-dog sausages created in New York City.

1903
First World Series played.

1903
Call of the Wild written by Jack London.

1905
First nickelodeon movie theater established in Pittsburgh.

1907
Artists Picasso and Braque create cubism.

1913
Boy's Life magazine published by Boy Scouts.

1917
Doughnuts created for the soldier "doughboys" fighting in World War I.

1917
American Girl magazine published by Girl Scouts.

1920
First radio station, KDKA, founded in Pittsburgh.

U.S. Population:

76,212,168   92,228,496   106,021,537

1925	1930	1935	1940	1945	1950

1927
Charles
Lindbergh
flies solo
across
the
Atlantic
Ocean.

1931
The 102-story Empire State
Building completed as
tallest in the world.

1939
Germany invades
Poland to begin
World War II.

1945
World War II ends.

1933
President Franklin
Roosevelt inaugurated
and begins New Deal to
end Great Depression.

1941
Japanese
bomb Pearl
Harbor
Dec. 7, and
U.S. enters
World
War II.

1929
Wall Street
Stock
Market
crashes.

1933
Prohibition of alcoholic
beverages repealed.

1945
United
States
becomes a
member of the
United Nations.

1926
John Baird
demonstrates his
television system.

1935
Radar is
invented.

1938
Modern-type
ballpoint pens
developed.

1947
Edwin Land
invents
Polaroid
camera.

1928
Alexander Fleming
develops penicillin.

1938
First photocopy
machine produced.

1947
Bell Lab
scientists
invent
transistor.

1929
Clarence Birdseye
introduces frozen foods.

1930
First analog computer
invented by Vannevar Bush.

1940
Enrico Fermi
develops
nuclear reactor.

1925
Potato chips are
produced in New
York City.

1931
"The Star-Spangled
Banner" becomes
U.S. national
anthem.

1937
First full-length animated film,
*Snow White and
the Seven Dwarfs,* is made.

1946
*Highlights
for Children*
magazine
published.

1925
First National Spelling
Bee is held.

1938
Superman
"Action
Comics"
created.

1947
Jackie Robinson
becomes the first
black major league
baseball player.

1927
First "talking movie,"
The Jazz Singer, is made.

1928
My Weekly Reader magazine is founded.

1939
Nestlés
chocolate chips
are produced.

1947
Anne Frank's
*Diary of a Young
Girl* is published.

123,202,624   132,164,569

| 1950 | 1955 | 1960 | 1965 | 1970 |

United States History

1950
United States enters Korean War.

1954
Korean War ends.

1955
Rosa Parks refuses to follow segregation rules on Montgomery bus.

1955
Martin Luther King, Jr., begins organizing protests against black discrimination.

1959
Alaska becomes 49th state.

1959
Hawaii becomes 50th state.

1961
Alan Shepard becomes first U.S. astronaut in space.

1963
President John F. Kennedy assassinated in Dallas, Tex.

1965
U.S. combat troops sent to Vietnam.

1968
Martin Luther King, Jr., is assassinated.

1969
Neil Armstrong and Buzz Aldrin are first men to walk on moon.

1974
President Richard Nixon resigns.

1971
Eighteen year olds are given right to vote.

Science and Inventions

1951
Fluoridated water discovered to prevent tooth decay.

1953
Watson and Crick map the DNA molecule.

1954
Jonas Salk discovers polio vaccine.

1957
Russia launches first satellite, *Sputnik 1,* beginning Space Age.

1958
Stereo long-playing records produced.

1960
First laser invented by Theodor Maiman.

1963
Cassette music tapes developed.

1967
Cholesterol discovered as cause of heart disease.

1968
First U.S. heart transplant is performed by surgeon Norman Shumway.

1971
Space probe *Mariner* maps surface of Mars.

1974
Sears Tower (110 stories) built in Chicago.

Literature and Life

1950
Peanuts comic strip produced by Charles Schulz.

1951
Fifteen million American homes have television.

1952
Charlotte's Web is published.

1955
Cat in the Hat is written by Theodor "Dr. Seuss" Geisel.

1957
Elvis Presley is the most popular rock 'n' roll musician in U.S.

1961
Peace Corps is established, helping others around the world.

1964
The Beatles appear on *The Ed Sullivan Show* and change American music.

1970
First Earth Day begins a focus on protecting the environment.

1970
Sounder by William Armstrong wins Newbery Award for children's literature.

1970
Sesame Street television show with Jim Henson's Muppets begins.

U.S. Population:

| 151,325,798 | 179,323,175 | 203,302,031 |

1975	1980	1985	1990	1995	2000

1975
Vietnam
War ends.

1981
Sandra Day
O'Connor
becomes first
woman on
Supreme Court.

1986
Challenger spacecraft
explodes, killing entire crew.

1994
NATO (North Atlantic
Treaty Organization)
expands to include
Eastern European nations.

1981
U.S. hostages returned
from Iran after 444 days.

1989
Berlin Wall
separating
East and West
Germany is
torn down.

1994
Earthquake rocks
Los Angeles,
California, killing
more than 50
people.

1979
Iran
seizes U.S.
hostages.

1983
Sally Ride
becomes first U.S.
woman in space.

1991
Persian Gulf War "Operation
Desert Storm" begins.

1976
Concorde
becomes world's
first supersonic
passenger jet.

1981
Scientists identify
AIDS (acquired
immune
deficiency
syndrome).

1988
NASA reports greenhouse effect on Earth's
atmosphere is caused by destruction of forests.

1977
Apple
Computers
produces
first personal
computer.

1983
Pioneer 10 space probe
passes Neptune and
leaves solar system.

1991
Environmental Protection
Agency cites growing danger
of hole in Earth's ozone layer.

1991
World Wide Web is launched.

1984
Compact disk (CDs) music
players developed.

1997
Scottish scientists clone
an adult sheep.

1976
Alex Haley's African-American
saga *Roots* published.

1986
Martin Luther King
Day proclaimed
national holiday.

1998
The Chicago Bulls win their
sixth NBA Championship.

1976
United States
celebrates Bicentennial.

1987
The Whipping Boy
by Sid Fleischman
wins Newbery Award.

1998
Titanic becomes the
top money-making
film in history.

1979
Yellow ribbons
displayed in
support of return
of U.S. hostages
in Iran.

1988
Thirty million U.S.
school children have
access to computers.

226,542,203   248,709,873

Credits

Index

This index is your personal guide to using the *Write Source 2000* handbook. For example, if your teacher asks you to review your writing with several of your classmates, you may not remember that the guidelines for reviewing are found in the "Group Advising" chapter. Fortunately, the index lists those same guidelines under several entries: **Advising** in groups; **Group** skills, Writing; **Guidelines,** Group advising; **Responding** to writing; and **Writing** group guidelines. If you don't find what you are looking for the first time you try, think of other "keywords" that may get you to the same information. Learning how to use an index will prove to be a valuable lifelong skill.